LOCKHEED SR-71 BLACKBIRD

Other titles in the Crowood Aviation Series

Aichi D3A1/2 Val	Peter C. Smith
Airco – The Aircraft Manufacturing Company	Mick Davis
Avro Lancaster	Ken Delve
Avro Shackleton	Barry Jones
BAC One-Eleven	Malcolm L. Hill
Boeing 737	Malcolm L. Hill
Boeing 747	Martin W. Bowman
Boeing B-17 Flying Fortress	Martin W. Bowman
Boeing B-29 Superfortress	Steve Pace
Bristol Beaufighter	Jerry Scutts
Bristol Britannia	Charles Woodley
British Experimental Turbojet Aircraft	Barry Jones
Concorde	Kev Darling
Consolidated B-24 Liberator	Martin W. Bowman
Curtiss SB2C Helldiver	Peter C. Smith
Douglas A-26 and B-26 Invader	Scott Thompson
Douglas Havoc and Boston	Scott Thompson
English Electric Canberra	Barry Jones
English Electric Lightning	Martin W. Bowman
Fairchild Republic A-10 Thunderbolt II	Peter C. Smith
Fairey Swordfish and Albacore	Bill Harrison
Hawker Hunter	Barry Jones
Hawker Typhoon, Tempest and Sea Fury	Kev Darling
Heinkel He 111	Ron Mackay
Ilyushin Il-2 and Il-10 Shturmovik	Yefim Gordon and Sergey Kommissarov
Lockheed F-104 Starfighter	Martin W. Bowman
McDonnell Douglas A-4 Skyhawk	Brad Elward
Messerschmitt Bf 110	Ron Mackay
Messerschmitt Me 262	David Baker
Nieuport Aircraft of World War One	Ray Sanger
North American B-25 Mitchell	Jerry Scutts
North American F-86 Sabre	Duncan Curtis
North American F-100 Super Sabre	Peter E. Davies
North American T-6	Peter C. Smith
Panavia Tornado	Andy Evans
Petlyakov Pe-2 *Peshka*	Peter C. Smith
V-Bombers	Barry Jones
Vickers VC10	Lance Cole
Vickers Viscount and Vanguard	Malcolm L. Hill
Vought F4U Corsair	Martin W. Bowman

LOCKHEED SR-71 BLACKBIRD

Steve Pace

First published in 2004 by
The Crowood Press Ltd
Ramsbury, Marlborough
Wiltshire SN8 2HR

www.crowood.com

© Steve Pace 2004

All rights reserved. No part of this publication may be reproduced or transmitted in any form or by any means, electronic or mechanical, including photocopy, recording, or any information storage and retrieval system, without permission in writing from the publishers.

British Library Cataloguing-in-Publication Data
A catalogue record for this book is available from the British Library.

ISBN 1 86126 697 9

Dedication

This reference is devoted to my wife and children, mother and father, sisters and brothers and to all of my relatives – past, present and future.

Acknowledgements

No reference of this magnitude could be presented without the many appreciated contributions of those with the vital resources that made this dissertation possible. This writer respectfully thanks these individuals as follows: Kent Burns, Executive Vice President, Lockheed Martin Leadership Association; Paul R. Kucher IV, SR-71 Online; An Online Aircraft Museum, sr-71.org; Tony R. Landis; Denny Lombard, Promotional Photography, Lockheed Martin Aeronautics Company – Palmdale; Mike Machat, publisher, Republic Press; Peter W. Merlin, archivist and historian, NASA Dryden Flight Research Center; Jay N. Miller, Aerofax, Inc; Dr Raymond L. Puffer, archivist and historian, USAF Flight Test Center History Office; Terry Panopalis; Major Brian Shul, USAF (Ret.), Gallery One; and John Stone, Blackbirds.net.

Typefaces used: Goudy (*text*),
Cheltenham (*headings*).

Typeset and designed by
D & N Publishing
Lambourn Woodlands, Hungerford, Berkshire.

Printed and bound in Great Britain by CPI Bath.

Contents

Foreword		6
Preface		7
1	FABULOUS TO FANTASTIC	8
2	BLACK MAGIC	25
3	AIR DEFENCE FIGHTER	45
4	PIGGYBACK PEEPERS: M-21 'MOTHER' AND D-21 'DAUGHTER'	55
5	SR-71: LEADER OF THE PACK	65
6	KEY PERSONALITIES IN THE BLACKBIRD PROGRAMME	83
7	STRUCTURES AND SYSTEMS	89
8	THE J58 ENGINE	99
9	BIRDS OF A FEATHER	106
10	NASA BLACKBIRDS	111
11	BLACKBIRD SURVIVORS	115
12	SUMMARIES	123
Appendix I	A-12, YF-12, M-21, SR-71 and D-21 Production	126
Appendix II	Significant Facts and Figures	129
Appendix III	Chronological Order of First Flights	131
Appendix IV	The *Oxcart* Story	133
Appendix V	World Records: SR-71 and YF-12	159
Appendix VI	Blackbird Flight Hours	160
Appendix VII	Blackbird Serial Numbers and Production Summaries	161
Appendix VIII	Blackbird Timeline, 1950s to the Early 2000s	163
Abbreviations, Acronyms and Codenames		171
Bibliography		172
Index		173

Foreword

In the first 100 years since the Wright Brothers first tamed manned flight, the crown jewel of aircraft design and performance was the SR-71. This opinion is held not only by those lucky enough to have flown this magnificent aircraft, but by anyone that has studied this plane's distinguished history.

Long cloaked in secrecy, the plane, now declassified, is a popular topic for aviation enthusiasts everywhere. In this highly researched volume, Steve Pace takes the reader deep behind the scenes of the development of the world's most famous, and most mysterious aircraft.

Less than 100 US Air Force pilots ever flew actual missions in the SR-71, and I am proud to say that I was one of the lucky few. While it was a very stable and honest airplane to fly, it routinely would let us know that it was not like other airplanes. Training was very intense, lasting nearly one year with many hours spent in the simulator. This training was vital to learning to fly this airplane well however, as there were no minor emergencies at Mach 3.

As phenomenal as the performance of the SR-71 was, the story of its development and construction is every bit as amazing. It is almost incomprehensible to envision that an aircraft such as this could be built in the early 1960s, prior to the advanced technological age of computers and composite materials. So well was the plane conceived and built by Kelly Johnson and his expert team of engineers, its basic design remained unchanged for the life of the aircraft. No one appreciated more the expertise with which this aircraft was constructed than those who flew it. There was no greater feeling of technological superiority than to be flying with impunity over hostile territory, being chased by the latest MiG fighters, designed decades after the SR-71, and leaving them in the dust, with several inches of throttle to spare.

The SR-71 represented all that was undefeated about our superior manufacturing capabilities. There was no greater aeronautical engineer in the twentieth Century than Kelly Johnson and our nation owes him a great debt of gratitude. His towering genius spanned three wars and his Blackbird helped win the Cold War. He often said the SR-71 was his proudest achievement.

Putting an aircraft together with titanium was no easy task. It had never been done before, or since. Kelly and his team literally had to invent technology in order to accomplish this seemingly impossible task. The result was the most successful and impressive reconnaissance aircraft of the century.

I never once felt like I was flying an 'old' airplane when in the SR-71. Built with such loving care and integrity, it always felt like the thoroughbred it was. Built for speed, the aircraft seemed to relish the higher Mach numbers and actually was more efficient at its higher speeds. Once I had flown the Blackbird for a year or two, all the other fighter jets I had flown seemed like mere 'mortal' planes. The plane continually impressed us with its performance and routinely humbled us. She truly seemed to have her own personality.

It was not an airplane that was mastered so much as understood. Flying this plane meant having an intimate relationship with the aircraft, and you could not do that for long without coming to love it. She would cruise with ease at 2,000mph and always seemed able to give you a little more speed if you wanted it. Sometimes we did, when people were shooting at us, and she never once hesitated to step it up.

The SR-71 has become a legend, mostly due to its incredible performance. But the story of how it all came to be is one that needs to be told, and Steve Pace does a remarkable job in this book of taking us behind the scenes, into the secret world of 'black projects', revealing piece by piece, the amazing Blackbird story. This aircraft helped shape our nation's foreign policy and affected world history. It represents the very best of what this nation can produce. I am proud to say I flew the SR-71, and now after reading this book, know a great deal more about its development.

The remaining SR-71s today sit proudly in twenty museums and air parks, its predecessors in numerous others. Though silent now, their presence speaks volumes about all that makes this nation proud and strong.

BRIAN SHUL
SR-71 Pilot
9SRW/1SRS

Having spent the earlier part of his career flying North American AT-28D Trojans, the Ling-Temco-Vought A-7D Corsair II and the Fairchild Republic A-10 Thunderbolt II, Major Brian Shul was assigned to the SR-71 Blackbird in 1984. He flew the SR-71 for four years, accumulating 478 flying hours, and he flew sixty-eight 'hot' missions. His book Sled Driver *is a Centennial of Flight commemorative celebrating the SR-71. It is a Limited Edition and available only through www.sleddriver.com.*

Preface

In the late 1950s four highly advanced aircraft were being designed in the USA, optimized for extreme flight envelopes where very high altitude and very high speed would be the norm. 'Very high altitude' meant 70,000ft (21,000m) or even higher; 'very high speed' meant 2,000mph (3,200km/h) or more. These advanced aircraft were: a strategic bomber, the North American B-70 Valkyrie; an all-missile-and-rocket-armed interceptor, the Republic F-103 'Thunderwarrior'; an all-missile-armed interceptor, the North American F-108 Rapier; and a reconnaissance aeroplane, the Lockheed A-12. At the time, however, only the B-70, F-103 and F-108 programmes were known to the world. The A-12 project, code-named *Oxcart*, was classified 'super-secret' and did not come to light until many years later – and then only in bits and pieces.

Unbeknownst to the world in the late 1950s and early 1960s, using US government funds from the Central Intelligence Agency (CIA), the Advanced Development Projects (ADP) group of the Lockheed company in Burbank, California, had been secretly designing the triplesonic A-12 as a replacement for the subsonic U-2 reconnaissance aircraft; the U-2 had become vulnerable to Soviet air defences, as proved on 1 May 1960 when Francis Gary Powers' U-2C was shot down over the USSR.

As the CIA *Oxcart* programme progressed into the early 1960s, under the direction of ADP group leader Clarence L. 'Kelly' Johnson, several versions of the A-12 were offered to the US Air Force (USAF) as potential substitutes for the B-70 and the by-now cancelled F-103 and F-108 aircraft; these included the AF-12 air-defence fighter and the RB-12 reconnaissance bomber. A third offering was the R-12, similar in a number of ways to the CIA A-12, but optimized for USAF reconnaissance missions. The AF-12 (the prefix 'AF' meaning air-defence fighter) ultimately became the YF-12A; the RB-12 (the B-70 substitute) was not proceeded with; and the R-12 eventually evolved into the aeroplane that is the subject of this book, the Lockheed SR-71 Blackbird.

The USAF SR-71 Blackbird became the definitive development of the A-12. From when it achieved Initial Operational Capability (IOC) in late 1966 until its retirement in early 1990, it was the best photographic aerial reconnaissance platform and the wonder of all spyplanes ever built. It remains the fastest and highest-flying aeroplane ever produced for daily operations.

Aerial reconnaissance has been ongoing in America since the US Civil War of 1861–65 during which manned lighter-than-air observation balloons were used to survey troop positions and movements. Both the Union and Confederate armies used balloons for reconnaissance during the conflict, and it was here that aerial reconnaissance was born.

Aerial reconnaissance did not become of critical necessity until World War One, when the combatants had to know exactly what their enemies were up to, as soon as possible. While it is true that observation balloons and a limited number of observation aircraft had performed this duty before 1914, there had never before been such a frantic need for observation, photographic reconnaissance and mapping from the air. But now, unlike the US Civil War, when observation balloons could not easily be shot down due to the limited range of black-powder rifles, observation aircraft and balloons could be shot down by anti-aircraft guns and fighter aircraft.

After World War One, the value of having dedicated observation, photographic reconnaissance and mapping aircraft having been proven, many air forces set about the creation of modern, high-performance aircraft for such duties. By the time World War Two ended on 2 September 1945, all the major powers involved, on both sides of the conflict, had a number of dedicated reconnaissance aircraft.

An untold number of these observation balloons and reconnaissance aircraft (most of which were unarmed) were lost to enemy fire in World War Two, however. Among the first post-war solutions to this problem was the development of aircraft that could fly so high that they would be out of range of existing and upcoming anti-aircraft defences.

At this very minute some air or space vehicle is performing its very important work of photographic reconnaissance. Whether they are surveying forest fires, or battlefield actions in the Middle East, these 'eyes in the sky' are vitally important. There are space vehicles capable of reading and digitally photographing the brand of cigarettes lying on somebody's outdoor patio table, in near and/or real time. Much closer to the ground there are growing fleets of unmanned aerial vehicles capable of doing the very same thing, but at a relatively low cost. It is for these systems that the USAF worked hard to retire the small but once very productive fleet of Lockheed SR-71 Blackbird aircraft.

Nonetheless, for nearly a quarter of a century the SR-71s performed their photographic reconnaissance, mapping and electronic intelligence-gathering duties with remarkable success. But they could not have had such a splendid career without the capable pilots that flew them, the dedicated officers who operated their reconnaissance systems and the hard-working groundcrews that kept them flying.

This, then, is the story of the Lockheed SR-71 Blackbird and the amazing flock of highly advanced triplesonic aircraft that preceded it.

STEVE PACE

CHAPTER ONE

Fabulous to Fantastic

The formal name of the informally named Skunk Works was Advanced Development Projects.
BEN RICH

All good airframe contractors continually strive to generate business in the military, civilian and space markets. To accomplish this, they set up special divisions to address the diverse needs of their different potential customers. Generally speaking, these divisions include commercial, military and aerospace. But some of the larger airframe contractors also deal in highly classified programmes for which the utmost secrecy is paramount. This usually requires a special group to be formed within a company, and in the Lockheed Martin Corporation this special group is the world-famous, yet top-secret, 'Skunk Works', which has been a bona fide success for more than sixty years.

The mission of the Skunk Works – properly, the Advanced Development Projects (ADP) group – is the quick, quiet and cost-effective development and production of limited numbers of specialized aircraft to meet any national need, using all the strengths of Lockheed Martin Corporation. The Skunk Works is headquartered in the vast USAF Plant 42 complex at Palmdale, California, and it is a prime part of the Lockheed Martin Aeronautics Company division of the Lockheed Martin Corporation. In mid-1943 it began working on Secret Project MX-409, which became the XP-80, and since then it has produced advanced aircraft, spacecraft and even marine craft without equal for aerial reconnaissance, combat and research. These include such extraordinary aircraft as: the F-80 Shooting Star, America's first operational jet fighter; the F-104 Starfighter, the world's first Mach 2 jet fighter; the U-2, the best manned high-altitude reconnaissance aeroplane in the world; the F-117 Nighthawk, the world's first dedicated stealth warplane; the F/A-22 Raptor, soon to become operational as the world's first multi-role stealth fighter; the F-35 'Shadow', a stealthy joint-service, multi-role strike fighter for the near future; and the subject of this book, the Lockheed SR-71 Blackbird strategic reconnaissance aircraft.

The company that would become the Lockheed Corporation was founded in 1913 by the Loughead brothers – Malcolm (1887–1958) and Allan (1889–1969). Malcolm and Allan's surname is pronounced 'Lock-heed', and since it was pronounced that way they changed the spelling to Lockheed to avoid confusion. The young company grew with ups and downs throughout the early to mid-twentieth century to produce a number of extremely successful aircraft, including the Lodestar, Electra, Super Electra, Constellation, P-2 Neptune, P-3 Orion, C-130 Hercules, C-141 Starlifter, C-5 Galaxy, S-3 Viking, P-38 Lightning, T-33 T-Bird, F-94 Starfire and F-104 Starfighter. Its continued successes into the late twentieth century spawned such notable ventures as the F/A-22 Raptor and F-35 'Shadow'. In the early 1990s the Lockheed Aircraft Corporation was one of the largest aerospace firms in the world, but after it merged with the Martin Marietta Corporation in 1995, to create the Lockheed Martin Corporation, it became the world's largest aerospace conglomerate.

In mid-1942 Lockheed was heavily involved in the production of military aircraft, rolling out thousands of P-38 Lightning fighters, F-4 and F-5 Lightning photographic reconnaissance aircraft, Hudson bombers, Ventura and Harpoon submarine

The Loughead brothers, Malcolm (left) and Allan, seated in their F-1 (Flying-boat 1), which made its first flight on 28 March 1918. Lockheed Martin

killers, and licence-built Boeing B-17F Flying Fortresses at its Burbank, California, production facilities. Simultaneously, its advanced aeronautical engineering department was proceeding with the preliminary design and even the manufacture of several new and interesting aircraft. These included two derivatives of the P-38 Lightning, the XP-49 and XP-58 Chain Lightning, neither of which entered production, but which showed the tremendous growth potential of the basic P-38 airframe.

But one of the most interesting of these pre-Skunk Works designs came about in 1940 when Lockheed offered the US Army Air Corps (USAAC) its first jet-powered aeroplane, the Model L-133. This was a twin-engined, single-seat turbojet-powered fighter design, and was extremely advanced for its day. It featured two Lockheed-designed axial-flow J37 turbojet engines, delivering some 5,000lb (2,300kg) thrust, a canard foreplane, 625mph (1,000km/h) top speed and stainless steel construction. Lockheed was the first airframe contractor in the USA to start work on a gas turbine- or turbojet-powered aircraft: the L-133 had originated in 1939 as a 'paper project' by chief engineer Hall L. Hibbard and his assistant, Clarence L. 'Kelly' Johnson. By 1940 preliminary work on the company-financed jet fighter had been started, which progressed to several different versions on the drawing board. In the meantime, Lockheed was also working on the aforementioned axial-flow turbojet engine of its own design, the Model L-1000 (later designated XJ37), which was intended to power the L-133.

The design was acknowledged by the USAAC, but at the time they showed no great interest in the idea of a turbojet-powered fighter and missed the opportunity of giving the USA an early start in this new technology. Without financial support from the USAAC, work on the L-133

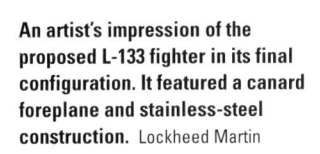

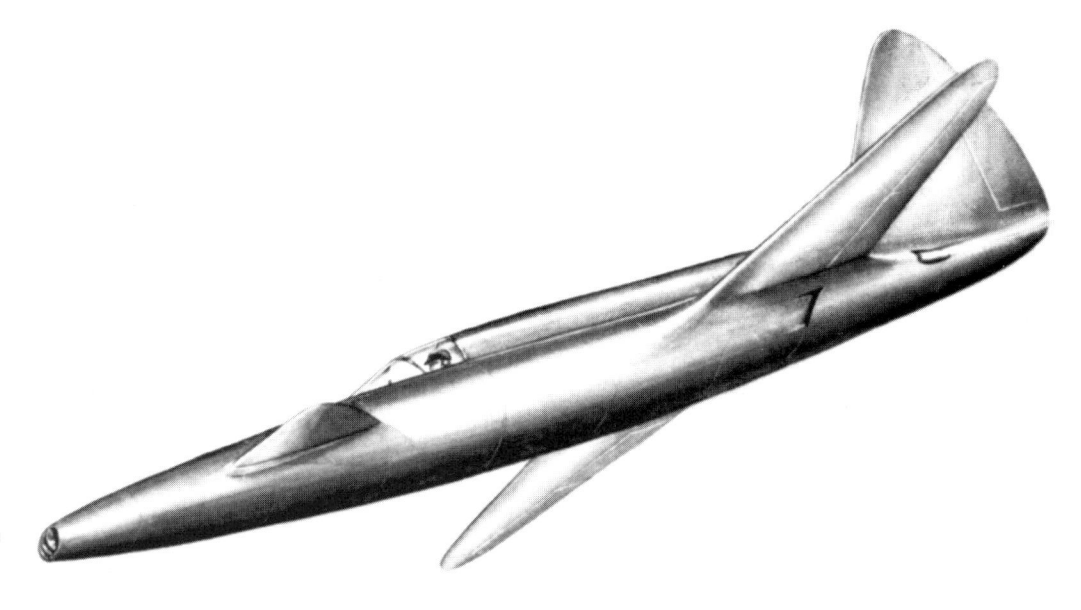

An artist's impression of the proposed L-133 fighter in its final configuration. It featured a canard foreplane and stainless-steel construction. Lockheed Martin

BELOW: **The L-1000 axial-flow turbojet engine, which was supposed to generate a whopping 5,500lb thrust to give the L-133 its projected 600mph speed. Later run tests, though promising, never produced such a thrust rating.** Lockheed Martin

fighter came to a halt. However, work on the then-unique axial-flow XJ37 turbojet engine went forward for a time. That is, until more advanced axial-flow designs surpassed it. (The USAAC had been established on 2 July 1926, becoming the US Army Air Forces, or USAAF, on 20 June 1941. The US Air Force was not established as a separate service of the US Armed Forces until 18 September 1947.)

However, when the USAAF suddenly began to show interest in the idea of an improved turbojet-powered fighter aircraft in 1942, spurred on by intelligence reports of the advances in jet propulsion by the Germans and British, and the lacklustre performance of the Bell P-59 Airacomet – America's first turbojet-powered aeroplane – it turned to Lockheed for what was to become the first operational turbojet-powered fighter in America, the Lockheed F-80 Shooting Star.

The design, development and manufacture of the F-80 began in close-guarded secrecy in mid-1943. Project head Kelly Johnson, assisted by Bill Ralston and Don Palmer, grabbed twenty-five other top-notch engineers and 105 assembly workers, and put them to work in a makeshift experimental aeroplane shop constructed out of empty aircraft engine crates and canvas.

One day, just after the permanent secret shop had been constructed, engineer Irving H. 'Irv' Culver was working near the phone desk. The phone rang. Culver was alone at the time and had not yet been briefed as to how to answer the phone. Being an avid fan of the *Lil' Abner* comic strips, familiar with *Hairless Joe's Dogpatch Kickapoo Joy Juice* brewery called the *Skonk Works*, where Joe made his brew out of old shoes, skunk and other foul-smelling goodies, Culver answered 'Skonk Works, Culver'. And, as it turned out, Lockheed's famed Skunk Works was born. (So as not to steal any part of the *Lil' Abner* franchise, which had been created by famed cartoonist Al Capp, the name *Skonk Works* was changed to Skunk Works.) Kelly Johnson, who had set up the Lockheed Advanced Development Projects (ADP) group, did not at first like the unofficial nickname of Skunk Works for his ADP group, though as the years went by he grew to become quite fond of it.

So for more than sixty years now, a large number of air and space vehicles have emerged from the Lockheed Advanced Development Projects group, or Skunk Works – too many, in fact, to discuss in this one book. But there follows a brief description of some of the most interesting and successful ones.

F-80 Shooting Star

On 17 June 1943, while they were watching the new dive flaps on a P-38J Lightning being evaluated at Eglin Army Air Field (AAF) in Florida, Kelly Johnson was approached by Colonel M.S. Roth of the USAAF Air Materiel Command based at Wright Field, Dayton, Ohio. Colonel Roth told Johnson of the disappointing XP/YP-59 Airacomet flight-test programme at Muroc AAF in California. Roth said that, with its General Electric Model I-A engine, the Airacomet was slower than the P-38 they were watching: Bell's aeroplane would be no match at all for German jet aircraft.

Roth asked 'Kelly, you wanted to build a jet for us once. Why don't you try your hand at putting a fighter airframe around the new de Havilland engine the English have promised us?'

The engine Roth was referring to was the Model H.1 Goblin, which had been designed by Major F.B. Halford. Johnson, filled with enthusiasm, replied 'Just give me the specifications on the engine.'

Johnson boarded an airliner and returned to Burbank. En route, he worked out some figures and preliminary design drawings on whatever paper he found available. After getting off the airliner on 18 June, he immediately reported to Lockheed president Robert E. Gross and chief engineer Hall L. Hibbard.

'Wright Field wants us to submit a proposal for building an airplane around a British jet engine', Johnson told them. 'I've worked out some figures. I think we can promise them a 180-day delivery. What do you think?'

'OK, Kelly, it's your baby. We'll give you all the help we can,' Gross said matter-of-factly.

And with this action, the saga of the P-80 (later F-80) Shooting Star began. Drawing boards and slide rules were attacked with vigour; top engineers suddenly found themselves up to their elbows in jet fighter-plane design. There was more to it than just a chance to build a new fighter, using a new type of engine for propulsion. It was more a matter of pride and the culmination of efforts dating back to 1939 when Lockheed had begun planning for what it thought would be the first jet fighter in America.

But 180 days was a very demanding time limit. Gross, Hibbard and Johnson knew that it was unheard of to design and build a prototype aeroplane in less than one year, let alone in only six months. Moreover, a jet-powered aircraft was a radical departure from contemporary piston-powered and propeller-driven machines.

One week after talking with Colonel Roth in Florida, on 24 June, Johnson was at Wright AAF showing the Air Materiel Command a sketch of the proposed single-engined, jet-powered pursuit interceptor and pages of detailed specifications. Johnson, with his bosses' blessing, promised the USAAF 'We'll build it in 180 days'!

'Just when would those 180 days start?' asked General Henry H. 'Hap' Arnold.

'Whenever you say. Just as soon as we get a letter of intent,' Johnson replied.

'Well you'd better get a move on then,' said Arnold. 'This is day number one. We'll have your letter of intent ready this afternoon.'

Thus, the letter of intent was dated 24 June 1943. The programme was classified and called Secret Project MX-409 (the prefix MX meaning 'Materiel, Experimental'). That fact in particular added difficulty to the 180-day time limit, as every phase of the aeroplane's creation would have to be closely guarded. With the letter of intent, the Air Materiel Command ordered three Lockheed Model L-140 aircraft, now officially designated XP-80.

The first XP-80 (the X in the designation denoting an experimental aircraft) was designed, engineered, built and readied for flight not in 180 days, but in 139! On day 139, having been secretly trucked to Muroc AAF, the British Goblin engine roared to life. On day 143, 15 November 1943, the aircraft, nicknamed *Lulu-Belle*, was accepted by the USAAF as ready for flight. Lockheed's chief engineering test pilot, Milo Burcham, would fly it the next morning. Everything had gone well – too well.

Late in the evening on the fifteenth, de Havilland jet-engine expert Guy Bristow gave the H.1 Goblin engine a final run-up prior to the scheduled first flight in the morning; as the engine roared at full power, both engine air-inlet ducts collapsed. Before Bristow could shut down the engine, pieces of ducting metal were sucked into the Goblin's mouth. A terrible grinding noise preceded engine stop. The damage to the rare engine was not repairable, so another engine would have to be delivered from England before *Lulu-Belle* would fly.

This took time, enough time to strengthen and fully repair the air-inlet ducting on the XP-80. A new Goblin engine was installed and tested, and the XP-80 was now scheduled to fly on the morning of 8 January 1944, fifty-four days later than had been originally planned. A successful first flight ensued, during which *Lulu-Belle* easily exceeded 500mph (800km/h) and the handful of USAAF officers in attendance were both delighted and surprised. They let it be known that they badly wanted production P-80s – and very soon.

The 2,450lb (1,100kg) thrust de Havilland H.1 Goblin engines, to be manufactured in America by Allis-Chalmers as the J36, would not be available in quantity anytime soon, however. This, of course, posed a serious problem for the USAAF and Lockheed. An answer was at hand, though. General Electric had speeded up production on its Model I-40 or J33 turbojet engine. This was a larger engine than the Goblin and had more thrust – 3,750lb (1,700kg), but it would require a larger airframe to accommodate it. The USAAF asked Lockheed, Kelly Johnson in particular, if the XP-80 design could be modified without a great deal of difficulty. 'Can do,' Johnson replied.

The sole XP-80, nicknamed *Lulu-Belle*, was the forerunner of the famed F-80 Shooting Star series, and the first aeroplane built in the 'Skonk Works' (later Skunk Works). Lockheed Martin

BELOW: **The first of two XP-80A aircraft (44-83021), named 'Gray Ghost' because of its paint scheme, is shown on its first flight with Tony LeVier at the controls. The second XP-80A (44-83022), in natural metal, was known as the 'Silver Ghost'.** Lockheed Martin

Thus the second and third XP-80s were built to accommodate J33-GE-11 engines. Due to their airframe redesign and their new power plant they were given a new Lockheed model number, L-141, and redesignated XP-80A; they were built on the same contract, amended.

Incredibly, Johnson's engineering and shop group finished the first XP-80A in a mere 132 days! And it was flown on day 139 – 10 March 1944. Both XP-80A aeroplanes performed even better than *Lulu-Belle* and on 4 April 1944, in addition to an order for thirteen service-test YP-80As, the USAAF ordered 1,000 production P-80A aircraft.

The P-80A was officially named Shooting Star and subsequent orders for P-80Bs and P-80Cs came through. Lockheed went on to build 1,731 Shooting Stars, of which 798 were produced as F-80Cs. (The P-80 became the F-80 after 10 June 1948 when the prefix 'P' for 'Pursuit' was changed to 'F' for 'Fighter'.)

When Lockheed completed its original XP-80 airframe in late 1943, it was totally unaware just how prolific that design would become. In all, more than 9,290 aircraft were moulded from the XP-80 matrix. As well as the various versions of the Shooting Star, it led to: the USAF's first jet-powered trainer, the T-33 T-Bird; the US Marine Corps' first jet-powered trainer, the TV-1; the US Navy's first jet-powered trainer, the T-1 SeaStar; and to the development of the F-94 Starfire series of fighters.

F-94 Starfire

In early 1948 the newly established USAF was in dire need of a two-seat night/all-weather fighter-interceptor to deal with hostile aircraft arriving from over the northern horizons of the US – and it wanted this aircraft in months rather than years. So it asked Lockheed, the ADP group in particular, if it could adapt the new Hughes E-1 radar and fire-control system to the airframe of the TF-80C (as the two-seat trainer version of the F-80, later to win fame as the T-33 T-Bird, was then known). Lockheed said 'yes', then 'yes' again when asked if it could provide the first production aeroplane by the end of 1949. Two TF-80Cs (USAF serial numbers 48-356 and 48-373) were taken from the back of the assembly line for modification. These were at first designated ETF-80C and, after 11 June 1948, ET-33A. But unofficially they were known as YF-94s.

On 16 April 1949 this relatively small service-test aircraft departed the Lockheed Plant B-9 Production Flight Test Center at San Fernando Valley Airport (now Van Nuys Airport) on its maiden flight. It was piloted by Tony LeVier with Glenn Fulkerson serving as flight-test engineer. It handled well but there were flame-out problems with the new afterburner installed on the thrust Allison J33-A-33 turbojet engine. These difficulties were corrected and the J33-A-33 was soon producing 6,000lb (2,700kg) thrust in afterburner, against 4,400lb (2,000kg) dry.

The type went into production as the F-94A Starfire and 109 F-94As were built. Next came the improved F-94B model, followed by the ultimate Starfire, the F-94C. In all, Lockheed produced some 850 Starfires in the three versions. The F-94C was very different from the earlier models, being all rocket-armed with forty-eight 2.75in Mighty Mouse air-to-air unguided rockets, as a result of which the prototype was temporarily designated YF-97A.

The world's first dedicated jet-powered pilot trainer and transition aeroplane was the T-33. The fifty-sixth production T-33A (formerly TF-80C) T-Bird is here. Lockheed Martin

FABULOUS TO FANTASTIC

ABOVE: **The first YF-94 Starfire prototype flies for the first time, with Tony LeVier at the controls and flight-test engineer Glenn Fulkerson in the back seat.** Lockheed Martin

BELOW: **The first YF-94C (formerly designated YF-97A) Starfire (50-955) heads skyward during its first flight at Edwards AFB on 19 January 1950. The F-94C became the ultimate Starfire.** Lockheed Martin

XF-90

Just after World War Two, as jet propulsion became more and more feasible for day-to-day use in combat aircraft, the USAAF put forth a requirement for what it called a Penetration Fighter. This was to be powered by two turbojet engines and to be armed with six 20mm cannon, with provision for two 1,000lb bombs or eight 5in rockets; it was also to have provision for external fuel tanks. It was to have a climb rate of 3,000ft/min (900m/min), a time-to-climb of ten minutes to 35,000ft (11,000m), a ceiling of 50,000ft (15,000m) and a combat range of 900 miles (1,500km).

The specific operational requirements for the Penetration Fighter were vague and flexible. Confusingly, the USAAF soon changed the combat range requirement to 1,500 miles (2,400km); it then reduced it to 600 miles (970km). It then cut the time-to-climb requirement in half, wanting a 7,000ft/min (2,000m/min) climb rate. The ever-changing requirements caused annoyance among the airframe and engine contractors: so much so that only two airframe contractors – Lockheed and McDonnell – chose to stay in the fray. In hope of obtaining 10,000lb (4,500kg) total thrust from two turbojet engines, both firms elected to propel their contenders with a pair of Model 24C Westinghouse J34 axial-flow turbojet engines. At the time, the J34 was projected to provide 5,000lb (2,300kg) thrust in developed form.

Lockheed offered its Model 090 design while McDonnell presented its Model 36C; both featured swept-back flying surfaces. These designs would be developed under USAAF Air Materiel Command project numbers MX-811 (McDonnell) and MX-812 (Lockheed). They were designated XP-88 and XP-90, respectively, and both types were ordered in mid-1946.

By the time the first XF-90 had been completed and trucked to Muroc AAF in early May 1949, both of McDonnell's XF-88 aircraft – named Voodoo – were flying. In fact, the first XF-88 had been flying for some seven months already. (Remember that the prefix 'P' for 'Pursuit' had been changed earlier to 'F' for 'Fighter' in June 1948.)

After the usual ground tests and evaluations, including low-, medium- and high-speed taxi runs to check nosewheel steering, braking and so on, XF-90 number one was ready for flight. On the morning of 3 June 1949, Tony LeVier flew the XF-90 up and away from the dry lake bed runway at Muroc. However, it was powered at this time by two interim J34-WE-11 engines, generating only 3,000lb (1,400kg) thrust each, instead of the afterburning 4,200lb (1,900kg) thrust J34-WE-15 engines that had been intended to be used. Predictably, performance was less than spectacular. The XF-90 did eventually get its -15 engines, with which the two XF-90s were re-designated XF-90A. In a series of dive tests the XF-90A hit a top speed of Mach 1.12, but could only manage 668mph (1,075km/h) in level flight.

In the meantime North American jumped into the fray with its late-coming YF-93A, first flown on 25 January 1950. This was powered by a single 8,000lb (3,600kg) thrust Pratt & Whitney J48-P-1 afterburning turbojet, which ultimately propelled it to a top speed of 708mph (1,140km/h). But it was not what the USAF wanted, and was quickly passed over.

The Penetration Fighter fly-off competition was held between 29 June and 7 July 1950 and on 11 September that year it was announced that the McDonnell XF-88A Voodoo had won. But by this time the Penetration Fighter requirement no longer existed, having been replaced by the Strategic Fighter programme for which the F-88's follow-on, the McDonnell F-101 Voodoo, went into production.

The first XF-90 (46-687) is shown here during its first flight, on 3 June 1949. After the two XF-90s received their J34 afterburning turbojet engines they were redesignated XF-90A. Even with these engines it took dangerous near-straight-down dives to exceed the speed of sound in this very heavy and woefully underpowered aeroplane. Lockheed Martin

F-104 Starfighter

When the swept-wing North American F-86 Sabre began to surpass the performance of the Lockheed F-80 Shooting Star in the late 1940s, and even the new Lockheed F-94 Starfire later in the Korean War, Kelly Johnson initiated an in-house programme to design and develop an air-superiority fighter with no equal.

He came up with a radical single-engine design with stubby wings and a T-tail known in-house as the Model 083, which promised speeds in excess of Mach 2. At the time the USAF was interested in very large, very heavy all-purpose fighter-bombers and fighter-interceptors, and the idea of fielding a lightweight air-superiority fighter had few supporters. However, after Johnson showed his design to the powers that be, a special priority Weapon System programme, WS-303A, was established by the USAF and US Defense Department, under which two prototypes were ordered on 12 March 1953. They were designated XF-104 and would be powered by interim Buick-built Wright YJ65-W-6 afterburning turbojet engines that gave 10,200lb (4,600kg) thrust, until the 14,800lb (6,700kg) General Electric J79-GE-3 became available. (The J65 was actually the British Armstrong-Siddeley Sapphire, produced in America by Buick under licence.)

The first XF-104, now named Starfighter, was trucked from Burbank to Edwards AFB (formerly Muroc AFB) in February 1953 where it was readied for flight-test. Immediately after its first take-off on 28 February 1954, with Tony LeVier at the controls, its landing gear would not retract, so LeVier quickly returned to the dry lake-bed. Its full first flight test was on 4 March, again flown by LeVier. LeVier continued to fly XF-104 number one while his fellow Lockheed test pilot Herman R. Salmon flew number two.

On 25 March 1955, powered by the interim J65 Sapphire engine, XF-104 number two reached a top speed of Mach 1.79 (1,327mph or 2,135km/h) in level flight. This was a remarkable accomplishment since it was powered by an engine giving some 4,600lb (2,100kg) less thrust than the airframe was designed for.

Seventeen service-test YF-104A Starfighters were ordered on 30 March 1955, to be powered by General Electric J79s. The first of these, piloted by LeVier, made a successful first flight on 17 February 1956. And on 27 April, now powered by a J79-GE-3 engine, the same YF-104A hit a maximum speed of Mach 2.13 (1,580mph or 2,540km/h) in level flight. The Starfighter had arrived!

I asked Tony LeVier in 1990 what he thought about the F-104. He answered:

The original XF-104 was a remarkable little plane. It was the first jet-powered plane to exceed 1,000mph [1,610km/h] and I did it! I had misgivings about the F-104 at first, but when I got acquainted with it, it was super! We had lots of development problems as one might expect, especially with the GE J79 series engines. Once all those things got fixed, the plane was very well accepted by all the pilots.

The success of the two XF-104s and seventeen YF-104As led to the production of 153 operational F-104A Starfighter aircraft for service with both USAF Aerospace Defense Command and Tactical Air Command, and ultimately to the manufacture in the USA and abroad of more than 2,575 Starfighters for the USAF and a number of foreign users.

XFV-1

In the late 1940s the US Navy initiated a convoy-fighter programme to find a turbojet-powered ship-borne interceptor for fleet defence. This was to be a vertical take-off and landing (VTOL) point-defence interceptor, which would take up far less deck space and would not need to use a catapult for launch and an arrestor cable for recovery. It was also intended to perform longer-range area-defence as convoy-escort fighter if necessary. A competition was held in early 1951 to find two airframe contractors to produce two prototypes each for a fly-off competition. This boiled down to Lockheed and Convair, and on 19 April 1951 Lockheed was given the go-ahead to build its Model 81 prototype entry, which was designated XFO-1. Convair was authorized to build two Model 5 prototypes with the designation XFY-1.

The XFO-1 was the Skunk Works' first US Navy fighter programme, and since there might be a need for as many as 500 such aircraft, it attacked it vigorously. Project engineer Art Flock, working with the assistance of Kelly Johnson, decided to use a single nose-mounted 5,850eshp Allison XT40-A-6 turbojet with two contra-rotating propellers.

The first Lockheed XFV-1, as the XFO-1 had by now been re-designated, was completed in early 1953 at Lockheed's Burbank facility. Herm Salmon had been appointed chief test pilot on the programme, and during a high-speed taxi test at Edwards AFB on 23 December 1953 the XFV-1 became airborne briefly. It was not until 16 June 1954, though, that Salmon officially flew the XFV-1 in conventional mode – in other words, using a temporary V-strut main landing-gear assembly, it took off and landed in the horizontal plane. In this conventional take-off and landing mode the XFV-1 made another twenty-one flights ending in March 1955 after 11½ hours' flying time. It was during this ten-month test phase that Herm Salmon took the aeroplane to vertical (nose straight up) flight in which the aeroplane hovered for a time on several occasions; mid-air returns to horizontal flight were easily accomplished.

In the end neither the Lockheed XFV-1 nor the Convair XFY-1 met the requirements put forth by the US Navy and the convoy fighter programme was cancelled on 16 June 1955. Moreover, neither firm fully completed nor flew their second prototypes. The empty airframes instead

Lockheed built two XF-104 Starfighters, each example powered by a single J65 afterburning turbojet engine, which eventually propelled XF-104 number one to a top speed of Mach 1.79. After the General Electric J79 was made available to the succeeding YF-104A service-test aeroplanes, Mach 2.3 was commonplace. In fact, the F-104 was the world's first Mach 2 fighter. XF-104 Starfighter prototype number two (53-7787) is shown here.
Lockheed Martin

became gate guards at naval installations; the two flying prototypes were sent to museums.

The proposed 600mph (1,000km/h) production version of the Lockheed entry was its Model 181, to be designated FV-2, which was to be powered by a projected 7,500eshp Allison T40 engine that was never built for the programme. It was to be armed with four 20mm cannon or forty-eight 2.75in folding-fin aerial rocket projectiles.

U-2

On 1 July 1953 three airframe contractors – Bell, Fairchild and Martin – were given study contracts for Secret Project MX-2147 under the classified code-name of *Bald Eagle*. By 31 December of that year these firms were to present their respective proposals to the USAF Air Research and Development Command (ARDC), the former Air Materiel Command. As projected, the subsonic *Bald Eagle* air vehicle was to be capable of unrefuelled flights at very high altitudes for very long distances. In part, the specifications called for a single-seat subsonic aircraft able to fly at 70,000ft (21,000m) or higher with a maximum range of at least 1,740 miles (2,800km) while carrying a reconnaissance payload weighing between 100–700lb (45–320kg).

When Lockheed – its Advanced Development Projects group in particular – found out about this project in early 1954 it immediately went into action to come up with a design of its own. However, it was an uninvited guest and would have to come up with something spectacular to unseat the other manufacturers with their mounting head-starts.

In the meantime Bell had come up with its Model 67, a twin-engine design; Fairchild its Model M-195, a single-engine design; and Martin its Model M-272D, a twin-engine design based upon its B-57 (which was itself based on the English Electric Canberra). Flight in the thin air at 70,000–100,000ft (21,000–30,000m) – the high stratosphere and low troposphere – would require a special power plant. Since the Pratt & Whitney J57 Turbowasp engine was considered to be the best at the time, with the more advanced J75 up and coming, each firm chose to power its design with a specially developed high-altitude derivative of the J57, designated J57-P-37 (formerly J57-P-19) and rated at 10,500lb (4,800kg) thrust.

The XFV-1 (formerly XFO-1) made its first flight on 16 June 1954 with Herm Salmon at the controls; he wound up being the only person to fly the type. The first of two XFV-1s (BuNo 138657) is shown. Lockheed Martin

The Bell and Martin designs were both favoured but Fairchild's was rejected. The Bell offering, which would have to be built from scratch, looked good for future operations while the Martin design, already 'flying' as the B-57, could provide an operational aircraft in the interim. Therefore, Martin was awarded a limited production contract for six aeroplanes, to be known as the RB-57D, and Bell was awarded a contract to build its Model 67, which for security reasons was given the fictitious research aircraft designation X-16.

Begun solely as a USAF project, the *Bald Eagle* programme had excited the interest of the US Central Intelligence Agency (CIA). With the growing threat of nuclear-armed Soviet long-range jet bombers and intercontinental ballistic missiles, the CIA was anxious to know what was on the ground throughout the USSR. For this, a high-flying reconnaissance platform was essential so in mid-1954 the CIA established a project code-named *Aquatone*, whereby it would field a secret fleet of aircraft to overfly the USSR with, it hoped, near impunity. At the time the USSR did not have surface-to-air missiles capable of reaching aircraft flying at the 70,000ft altitudes planned for *Bald Eagle*. In due course

Aquatone took precedence over the *Bald Eagle* programme. To help keep the former secret it was decided to use the latter purely as a cover and, as far as anyone knew, Bell was going to build its Model 67, now designated X-16, for high-altitude research.

The Lockheed ADP group had not stood still and on 5 March 1954 it offered its high-altitude aeroplane design, known in-house as Temporary Design Number CL-282. It was greeted with much interest at ARDC and Lockheed was asked to provide a detailed proposal. In early April 1954 the comprehensive CL-282 proposal was presented. As presented by Johnson, the proposal envisaged the manufacture of an initial batch of thirty aeroplanes whereby Lockheed, according to Johnson, 'would be responsible for the whole program, including servicing of the airplanes in the field'.

As proposed the CL-282 design would be closely associated with the XF-104 Starfighter, which had first taken flight a year earlier. While keeping the T-tailed XF-104 airframe for the most part, the CL-282 would have new, high-aspect-ratio long-span wings. As first offered, it would be powered by a single 9,300lb (4,200kg) thrust General Electric J73-GE-3 non-afterburning engine and have a fuel capacity of 925 US gallons (3,500ltr). To save weight, its F-104-style landing gear would be replaced by a jettisonable wheeled take-off dolly and an extendable skid for landing.

Eventually, at Kelly Johnson's own behest, the F-104 airframe and J73 engine were dropped from the *Bald Eagle/Aquatone* plans. Instead, an entirely new single-engine airframe with conventional tail surfaces was created, so that the fuselage could accommodate a larger camera bay and more fuel. The rather odd take-off dolly/landing skid arrangement was abandoned in favour of a single main landing gear with two wheels and a single tailwheel on the centreline. To keep the aircraft upright while it was on the ground, either outer wing would have small two-wheeled outrigger support gear. The J73 engine was replaced by the Pratt & Whitney J57-P-37, as used in the other *Bald Eagle* designs.

While work proceeded at Bell and Martin on their respective X-16 and RB-57D *Bald Eagle* aeroplanes for the USAF, Lockheed was awarded a contract to build an initial fleet of twenty *Aquatone* aeroplanes for the CIA. To hide its true nature as a dedicated spyplane, the Lockheed *Aquatone* aeroplane was designated U-2A (the U prefix standing for 'Utility'). The public was told it had been built for high-altitude research by the National Advisory Committee for Aeronautics (NACA, later to become NASA).

Since *Aquatone* was such a highly classified programme, the aircraft could not be flight-tested at any well-known flight-test facility like the Air Force Flight Test Center at Edwards Air Force Base, California. Therefore, in late March 1955 Kelly Johnson, after telling him of the top-secret programme, told his chief engineering test pilot, Anthony W. 'Tony' LeVier, to hop into the company-owned Beechcraft Bonanza and 'find us a place out on the desert somewhere where we can test this thing in secret. And don't tell anyone what you're up to.'

He also told LeVier that he would be the primary *Aquatone* test pilot. Afterward, LeVier and Dorsey Kamerer set out in the Bonanza on what was to be a two-week scouting trip. After a few days of searching at first around Death Valley, California and then eastward into Nevada, LeVier and Kamerer found what they called a 'ten plus' site, calling it Site I. LeVier drew up plans for a flight-test facility and determined construction costs. However, USAF Colonel Ozzie Ritland and CIA *Oxcart* programme manager Dick Bissell rejected the site because it was too close to populated areas.

Colonel Ritland then remembered an old USAAF airfield on the shore of Groom Lake, a dry lake bed about 3½ miles (5.6km) in diameter located at a desolate part of Nellis Air Force Base in southern Nevada, just north of Las Vegas. (Groom Lake and the nearby mountain range were named for a prospector who discovered lead and silver there around 1850, giving rise to the Groom Mining District that first saw precise metal production around 1871.) Ritland thought Groom Lake would be much more secure due to its proximity to the Nevada Nuclear Test Site. Kelly Johnson disliked the idea because it was so close to the nuclear facility and because it would nearly double construction costs. Nevertheless, Johnson, LeVier, Bissell and Ritland flew to Groom Lake on 12 April 1955. Upon their arrival they found the old airfield overgrown, but the dry lake bed itself was in perfect condition. They had found their site! Tony LeVier, with the approval of Kelly Johnson and CIA director Richard M. Bissell, Jr, named it 'Paradise Ranch'.

The Groom Lake site later became known as 'Area 51' in a land grab in June 1958, which encompassed a rectangle of land around the southern two-thirds of the dry lake bed that was then added to the Nevada Nuclear Test Site. It is now known as Restricted Area R-4808.

In early January 1955, while the general public waited to see the Bell X-16 materialize, U-2 number one, also known as CIA Article 341, began to take shape in Lockheed's super-secret Skunk Works building B-6 at Burbank, California. In-house, it was referred to as 'Kelly's Angel' and it was scheduled to fly before September. It was completed at Burbank on 15 July and on 23 July it was disassembled for aerial transport on board a Douglas C-124D to Groom Lake. Then, safely at the 'Ranch', she was moved into a partially completed hangar for reassembly.

Ground checks of its systems ensued and then on 1 August 1955 LeVier began what were to be preliminary low- and medium-speed taxi tests. However 'Angel', with her very long, high-lift, high-aspect-ratio wings was in reality a high-thrust, turbojet-powered glider, and was eager to become airborne. So, according to LeVier:

> ...at 70kt we were in the goddam air. The lake bed was so smooth I couldn't feel when the wheels were no longer touching. I almost crapped. Holy Christ, I jammed the goddam power in. I got into stall buffet and had no idea where the goddam ground was. I just had to keep the goddam airplane under control. I kept it straight and level and I hit the ground hard. Wham! I heard thump! thump! and thump! I blew both tyres and the damned brakes burst into flame right below the fuel lines. The fire crew came roaring up with extinguishers followed by Kelly in a jeep and boiling mad. 'Goddam it, LeVier, what in hell happened?' I said, 'Kelly, the son of a bitch took off and I didn't even know it.'

Without a full load of fuel and with no reconnaissance gear onboard, the U-2 was very light indeed. And since she was optimized for high-lift and more than adequately powered, she had leaped off the ground at what was a relatively low speed.

Article 341 made her official first flight on 4 August with Tony LeVier at the controls. LeVier flew another nineteen test-flights, during which he reached the design speed of Mach 0.85 and a maximum altitude

FABULOUS TO FANTASTIC

ABOVE: **The U-2A was the first operational version of the 'Dragon Lady'. An early production U-2A (56-6682) is shown here.** Lockheed Martin

A U-2S banks as it begins its landing approach into Beale AFB. Lockheed Martin

Project *Suntan*

After the demise of the hydrogen-fuelled Rex III-powered version of the proposed Lockheed Model CL-325 in January 1956, Lockheed's ADP offered up what it called its CL-400 programme to the USAF. In doing so it offered to build two CL-400 prototypes with the first flight just eighteen months after the date of contract. The USAF liked what it saw, and asked General Electric and Pratt & Whitney (P&W) for proposals on hydrogen-fuelled engines for the aircraft. In a relatively short time P&W was selected, and in April 1956 Lockheed was awarded a contract to build the two CL-400 prototypes with the first flight slated for October 1957. This was a highly classified programme and the project was given the code name *Suntan*.

The liquid-hydrogen-fuelled engine being offered by P&W was known as the Model 304, and P&W called it a 'hydrogen expander' engine. The Model 304 hydrogen expander engine was similar to the Rex III but it was much less complicated, in that only one heat exchanger was required. It was 79.92in (203cm) in diameter and it had a nacelle length of 35.15ft (10.7m); its dry

of 50,000ft (15,000m). Later test flights of 'Angel 1', as she had been nicknamed, allowed her to reach 74,500ft (22,700m) with a cadre of Lockheed ADP group test pilots – Bob Matye, Ray Goudey, Bob Schumacher and Bob Sieker. Flight endurances had exceeded ten hours and a maximum range of 5,060 miles (8,143km) had been achieved. The programme did nothing less than excel after these early test flights, and Lockheed received more orders. In October 1955 – just two months after the first flight of 'Angel 1', the Bell X-16 *Bald Eagle* programme was cancelled.

Later versions of the U-2 were powered by the 17,000lb (7,700kg) thrust Pratt & Whitney J75-P-13B non-afterburning turbojet. The last version of this still-operational spyplane is the U-2S, formerly known as the U-2R, which itself was previously designated TR-1A. This is powered by a 18,300lb (8,300kg) thrust General Electric F118-GE-101 non-afterburning turbofan.

The rest of the U-2 story, far too lengthy to cover within the space allotted here, is one of the most interesting in aviation history. Suffice it to say that more than 100 examples were built, culminating with the last U-2R/TR-1A in Fiscal Year 1980.

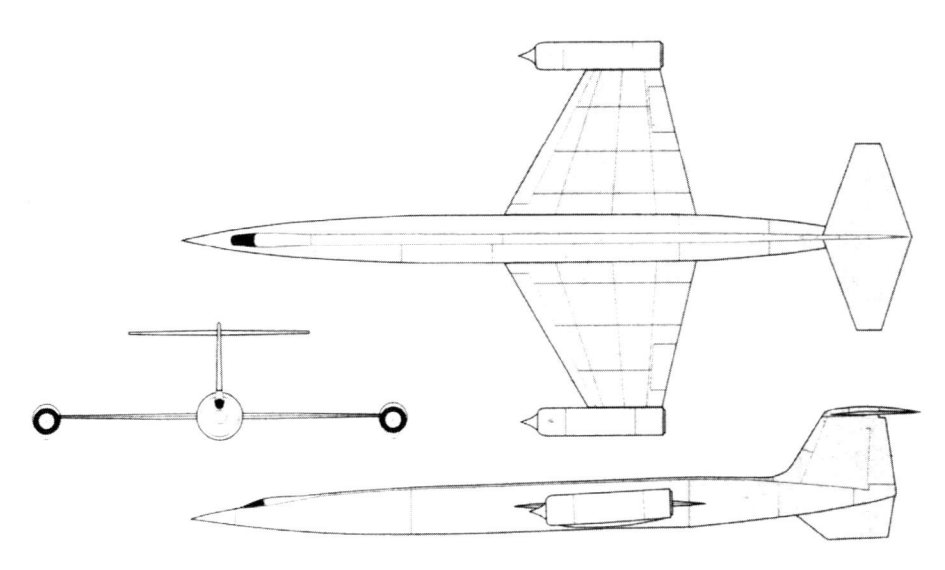

A fine line drawing of the CL-400-10 version of the proposed *Suntan* hydrogen-fuelled aircraft. Lockheed Martin

gross weight was 6,000lb (2,700kg). Its maximum thrust at the astonishing altitude of 116,470ft (35,500m) – where the CL-400 was intended to operate – was 4,800lb (2,200kg).

The proposed CL-400 aircraft themselves were gargantuan. In just one its many configurations, the CL-400-12, powered by four P&W 304-3 engines, it measured 272ft (82.90m) long and 50ft (15.25m) high with a wingspan of 110ft (33.5m); gross weight was 255,530lb (115,910kg). Its fuel capacity alone was to be 115,000lb (52,000kg).

In the end, as projected, the best range possible for a *Suntan* air vehicle was 2,500 miles (4,000km), far less than required. Since this could not be improved upon with existing technologies, Kelly Johnson himself recommended that the programme be terminated, and in February 1959 it was. But by this time there were something far more tasty brewing in the Skunk Works. That is, *Oxcart*, and the creation of the A-12.

Have Blue

In 1974 an arm of the US Department of Defense known as the Defense Advanced Research Projects Agency (DARPA) set out to achieve extremely low radar signatures to improve the survivability of new combat aircraft. DARPA created a government-funded anti-radar programme which it dubbed Project *Harvey*, the name 'Harvey' being borrowed from the well-known comedy movie of 1950 starring Jimmy Stewart and featuring a giant invisible rabbit of the same name.

Anti-radar measures for aircraft were not new, however. In the early 1960s they had been applied to modified Ryan Firebee target drones, which went on to serve in South-east Asia as the reconnaissance drones known as 'Fireflies' and 'Lightning Bugs'. Earlier, in late 1955, Lockheed began to apply anti-radar techniques to its U-2 aircraft in a programme called Project *Rainbow*. This programme was marginally successful and was accomplished for the most part with high-drag protuberances that led to the modified U-2s being given the nickname 'Dirty Bird'. And, of course, anti-radar was a big player in the design of the Blackbird series of aircraft, as described in Chapter 4.

From the outset, Project *Harvey* was intended to lead to a combat aircraft that could survive on its anti-radar characteristics alone. Such an aircraft would be designed as a 'pure-bred' for its anti-radar characteristics from the very start. In January 1975 DARPA awarded Project *Harvey* study contracts to McDonnell Douglas and Northrop. Lockheed, already well-versed in anti-radar techniques, was stunned not to be included in the programme. It opted to persuade DARPA to allow its entry into the programme using company funds. This was successful, and Lockheed and Northrop were each awarded contracts to build sub-scale models of their respective aircraft to be measured atop radar signature measuring poles in a 'pole fly-off'. (McDonnell Douglas, having not offered an adequate solution, had been eliminated.) In this case, sub-scale meant aircraft about two-thirds the size of the final product. DARPA named the anti-radar project *Have Blue* and named the aircraft the Experimental Survivable Testbed (XST).

The Lockheed entry, featuring a multi-faceted configuration, won the pole fly-off competition hands down, and in March 1976 Lockheed was contracted to build two XST demonstrator aeroplanes known as *Have Blue* 1 and *Have Blue* 2 (HB-1 and HB-2), with Lockheed build numbers 1001 and 1002. The former would be used for flight-test and some anti-radar evaluations, while the latter would be used for dedicated anti-radar measurements against all known ground- and air-based radar systems.

The *Have Blue* XST aeroplanes were powered by two 2,950lb (1,340kg) thrust General Electric J85-GE-4A non-afterburning turbojet engines which gave them a top speed of Mach 0.85 (630mph or 1,000km/h). They were 47ft 3in (14.42m) long and 7ft 6¼in (2.32m) high with a wingspan of 22ft 6in (6.89m); gross weight was 12,500lb (5,700kg). Their semi-delta wings were swept back at 72.5 degrees and had an area of 386sq ft (35.86sq m).

The first XST arrived at Groom Lake in a Lockheed C-5A Galaxy on 16 November 1977. After ground checks of its systems Lockheed test pilot Bill Park made a successful first flight on 1 December. In all, HB-1 made thirty-five successful flights, but at the end of the thirty-sixth, on 4 May 1978, the left main landing gear assembly was damaged as Park attempted to land. Since a good landing was out of the question, Park climbed to a safe altitude and ejected. Thus XST number one became a pile of rubble.

A C-5A delivered the second XST to Groom Lake in July 1978, and on 20 July it made its successful first flight, with USAF test pilot Lt Colonel Ken Dyson at the controls. While the number one XST had been used to prove that the radically shaped aircraft could indeed fly – being unstable about all three axes – the number two XST was used for dedicated very-low-observable (VLO) technology demonstrations in the air. It went on to fly until, during its fifty-second flight, on 11 July 1979, an onboard fire broke out and Dyson was forced to eject. And so the number two XST followed its predecessor.

All in all, however, the eighty-eight flights flown by the two *Have Blue* test-bed aircraft were deemed to have been more than successful. So successful, in fact, that on 16 November 1978, some eight months before the demise of XST number two, the USAF had ordered five aeroplanes, designated YF-117A, which were to become the world's first stealth fighters.

F-117A Nighthawk

Five full-scale development (FSD) YF-117A aeroplanes were ordered into production on 16 November 1978 under the USAF *Senior Trend* programme. They would be similar to the *Have Blue* aeroplanes with their multi-faceted anti-radar features, but would be much bigger and heavier aircraft, built as dedicated weapon systems.

Nicknamed Scorpion 1 to Scorpion 5, all five FSD YF-117A aeroplanes were built in ready-to-reassemble modules in Burbank and transported to Groom Lake in a C-5 for their final assemblies and flight-test/VLO technologies demonstrations. The first YF-117A – Scorpion 1 – arrived at Lockheed's Groom Lake facility in late May 1981 and made its maiden flight on 18 June with Skunk Works test pilot Harold C. 'Hal' Farley at the controls. By early 1982, the other four FSD aeroplanes had flown as well.

In late March 1982 what was to be the first production F-117A arrived at Groom Lake. Unfortunately on 20 April 1982, during its first take-off attempt, flown by Lockheed test pilot Bob Riedenauer, it crashed immediately after rotation. The cause was determined to be a faulty flight-computer program whereby pitch (nose-up/nose-down) commands were translated into yaw (nose-left/nose-right) movements, and vice versa. The aeroplane had crashed prior to USAF acceptance and therefore was not counted in the total procurement of fifty-nine production F-117As.

These fifty-nine F-117As were at first operated by the 4450th Tactical Group – later 37th Tactical Fighter Wing – from Tonopah Test Range Airfield, located far north within the boundaries of Nellis Air Force Base in southern Nevada. They are now operated from Holloman AFB in New Mexico by the 49th Fighter Wing of the USAF Air Combat Command.

The F-117A, now officially named Nighthawk, is a relatively large aeroplane roughly the same size as a Boeing F-15C Eagle and Lockheed Martin F/A-22 Raptor. It is 65ft 11in (19.85m) long and 12ft 5in (3.8m) high with a wingspan of 43ft 4in (13.2m); gross weight is 52,500lb (23,800kg). It is powered by two 10,800lb (4,900kg) thrust General Electric F404-GE-F1D2 non-afterburning turbofan engines, which give it a maximum speed of Mach 0.8 (594mph or 955km/h).

The F-117A Nighthawk, the world's first dedicated stealth aeroplane, has proved its worth in combat many times over during several campaigns, with only one loss due to enemy fire, on 26 March 1999 over Yugoslavia. But the Skunk Works, and the *Have Blue* XST/F-117A Nighthawk aircraft have proven that stealth technology really works and made it mandatory for use in all future combat aircraft.

One of the two *Have Blue* XST aircraft somewhere near Groom Lake, Nevada. The success of these two aircraft made the creation of the F-117A Nighthawk possible. Lockheed Martin

The first of five YF-117A Full-Scale Development aeroplanes, before the application of its black paint scheme, during a flight-test. Its nose boom, not found on production F-117As, is noteworthy. Lockheed Martin

A production F-117A Nighthawk of the 49th Fighter Wing, based at Holloman AFB, New Mexico.
Lockheed Martin

Advanced Tactical Fighter

In late 1983 the USAF began looking for an eventual replacement for its main air-superiority fighter, the McDonnell Douglas F-15 Eagle, and solicited design concepts from the industry for what it called the advanced tactical fighter (ATF). By mid-1984 seven airframe contractors – Boeing, General Dynamics, Grumman, Lockheed, McDonnell Douglas, Northrop and Rockwell – had all submitted proposals to the ATF Weapon System Program Office at Wright-Patterson AFB, Dayton, Ohio. Each firm then received a contract valued at about $1 million to further its studies.

Five of the competitors were eliminated from the competition early on and the two survivors, Lockheed and Northrop, teamed up with three of the ousted contenders: Northrop joined up with McDonnell Douglas while Lockheed teamed up with Boeing and General Dynamics. On 31 October 1986 each team received a demonstration and validation contract to build two ATF concept demonstrators each for an eventual winner-takes-all fly-off competition. The US Defense Department designated the Lockheed–Boeing–General Dynamics entry the YF-22A, and the Northrop–McDonnell Douglas contender the YF-23A.

There were two engine manufacturers vying for the production of the ATF power plant. Pratt & Whitney and General Electric were given contracts to build ATF demonstration engines, which were designated YF119 and YF120, respectively. This too was a winner-takes-all situation, but not before both engines were evaluated in flight. In other words, each pair of ATF prototypes would use the F119 in one airframe and the F120 in the other. In the end, it would be the best combination of airframe and power plant that would move forward.

The Lockheed YF-22A offering, known as Model 1132, was a company-wide design effort but with a great deal of input from Skunk Works engineers. It measured 64ft 2in (19.5m) in length and 17ft 8¾in (5.5m) in height with a wingspan of 43ft (13.1m); gross take-off weight was about 60,000lb (27,000kg). The first YF-22A was powered by two GE YF120 engines, the second by two P&W YF119 engines; each engine generated some 35,000lb (16,000kg) of thrust.

The number one YF-22A, unofficially dubbed 'Lighting II', made its first flight on 29 September 1990 piloted by Lockheed test pilot Dave Ferguson; it flew from Palmdale to Edwards AFB. On 30 October the number two YF-22A made its first flight, also from Palmdale to Edwards, but this time flown by Lockheed test pilot Tom Morgenfeld.

On 23 April 1991 Secretary of the Air Force Donald Rice announced that the

The General Electric YF120-GE-100-powered YF-22A 'Lightning II' (N22YF) flew first but was not the winning YF-22A. Instead the Pratt & Whitney YF119-PW-100-powered YF-22A (N22YX) won the airframe and power plant ATF competition. Lockheed Martin

Lockheed–Boeing–General Dynamics YF-22A powered by the Pratt & Whitney YF119-PW-100 turbofan engine had won the ATF fly-off competition, and that it would enter into the engineering, manufacturing and development (EMD) phase.

F/A-22 Raptor

The immediately following phase of the ATF programme called for the manufacture and flight-test of nine single-seat F-22As, two two-seat F-22Bs and two static-test fatigue and structural-test EMD aeroplanes. The F-22Bs were later cancelled and the first single-seat EMD F-22A, now officially named 'Raptor', made its first flight on 7 September 1997 with Lockheed test pilot Paul A. Metz at the controls. By this time the Lockheed Martin Corporation had bought the General Dynamics aircraft division at Fort Worth, Texas, and the Raptor production team became twofold – Lockheed Martin and Boeing. Moreover,

The first F/A-22 (formerly F-22A), known as Raptor 01, is shown on an early flight-test near Edwards AFB. Lockheed Martin

to better describe the multi-role mission of the Raptor, it was re-designated F/A-22 for 'fighter–attack'.

As this book goes to press in September 2004, the USAF plans to buy 224 F/A-22s by the year 2013. By mid-2004 the Lockheed Martin/Boeing team had built and flown eighteen of forty-three funded so far. And when it becomes operational in 2005 the F/A-22 Raptor will be the deadliest fighter, fighter-bomber, and fighter-interceptor in the world. It will be powered by two 40,000lb (18,000kg) thrust Pratt & Whitney F119-PW-100 afterburning turbofan engines, which will give the Raptor its unique 'supercruise' feature whereby speeds around Mach 1.5 will be possible without the use of afterburning; the aircraft's top speed is in excess of Mach 2. It is to initially supplement and ultimately replace the Boeing (formerly McDonnell Douglas) F-15C Eagle, arguably the world's best air-superiority fighter.

The Lockheed Martin/Boeing F/A-22A Raptor measures 62ft 1in (18.93m) in length and 16ft 5in (5.3m) in height with a wingspan of 44ft 6in (13.6m). For its role as an air-superiority fighter it will be armed with six Raytheon AIM-120C advanced radar-guided, medium-range air-to-air missiles, two Raytheon AIM-9X Sidewinder heat-seeking, short-range air-to-air missiles and one M61A2 six-barrelled 20mm rotary cannon.

Joint Strike Fighter

There were three versions of the Lockheed Martin X-35 Joint Strike Fighter (JSF) Concept Demonstrator Aircraft (CDA) built. These were: the X-35A, built to demonstrate conventional take-off and landing (CTOL) for the land-based version of the proposed JSF; the X-35B to evaluate short take-off and vertical landing (STOVL) characteristics for either land- or ship-based operations; and the X-35C, used to exhibit carrier variant (CV) handling operations. All three versions of the X-35 achieved their respective requirements, and in many cases, surpassed them. All three versions of the X-35 were powered by single afterburning 40,000lb (18,000kg) thrust Pratt & Whitney F119 turbofan engines.

The trio of X-35s outperformed the rival Boeing X-32 JSF CDA aeroplanes and on 26 October 2001 Lockheed Martin and its Joint Strike Fighter (JSF) partners – Northrop Grumman and BAE Systems – won a hard-fought JSF CDA competition. On that date, the designations F-35A, F-35B, and F-35C were issued, and the three engine variants became the Pratt & Whitney F135-PW-200, -400, and -600, respectively.

The System Development and Demonstration (SDD) phase of the F-35 JSF programme began when the SDD contract was awarded in October 2001; the first of the initial twenty-two SDD F-35s, an F-35A for the USAF, is scheduled to make its first flight in October 2005. These aeroplanes comprise fourteen flight-test aircraft and eight ground-test aircraft. Of the fourteen SDD flight-test aeroplanes there will be six USAF F-35As, four USMC F-35Bs and four USN F-35Cs. First delivery of a production F-35 is scheduled for the year 2008. A total of 3,002 F-35 aeroplanes will be needed by the armed forces of the USA and UK alone, and there are a number of other nations lining up to buy the aircraft as well.

The general specifications for the three versions of the F-35 vary. In the case of the conventional take-off F-35A for the USAF, its primary measurements are 50.75ft (15.5m) in length with a wingspan of 35.10ft (10.7m). Its maximum speed will be more than Mach 2 and it will be armed with a single 27mm cannon, air-to-air guided missiles and bombs housed internally and externally. It will be a multi-role fighter, fully capable of air-combat and/or ground-attack missions.

The X-35A demonstrated the conventional take-off and landing (CTOL) version of the Joint Strike Fighter for eventual use as the USAF F-35A. Lockheed Martin

TOP: **The X-35B confirmed the short take-off and vertical landing (STOVL) configuration of the JSF to be used by the US Marine Corps as the F-35B.** Lockheed Martin

ABOVE: **The X-35C showed the carrier-based (CV) option of the JSF for the US Navy, which became the F-35C.** Lockheed Martin

Postscript

Very few airframe contractors can boast of continued success since their founding in the early twentieth century. But Lockheed surely can. It has designed, engineered, developed and produced some of the world's most outstanding aircraft. The majority of the most exciting aircraft produced by Lockheed were created by the Advanced Development Projects group – the Skunk Works. And it was no different with the SR-71 Blackbird – the most fantastic aeroplane of them all.

CHAPTER TWO

Black Magic

'Keep it simple, stupid.'
KELLY JOHNSON

The creation of the A-12, F-12, M-21 and SR-71 Blackbird series of aircraft was little short of black magic: considering the technologies available to their creators at the time – technologies now more than forty-five years old – the design of these astonishing aircraft a remarkable achievement. To build this foursome of aircraft, a number of new materials and the methods in which to process them had to be invented, worked to perfection and then put into practice. Moreover, it was with these aircraft that the first generation of low-observability or 'stealth' technology was used: though common today, this was new science at the time.

The Lockheed SR-71 Blackbird is a delta-wing, two-place aeroplane powered by two axial-flow turbojet engines. It features titanium alloy and composite materials construction, and was designed to operate at high altitudes and high supersonic speeds. The aeroplane has very thin wings, twin inboard-canted, all-movable, vertical tails mounted on top of the engine nacelles, and a pronounced fuselage chine extending from the apex of the nose to the leading edges of the wings. The propulsion system used movable spikes to vary the engine air-inlet geometry. The flying controls are comprised of elevons and rudders, operated by irreversible hydraulic actuators with artificial pilot control feel. The aircraft could be refuelled either in flight or on the ground through separate receptacles that filled the fuel cells through a common refuelling line. A large drag parachute was provided to augment the stopping power of the six main landing-gear wheels' brakes. The aircraft were painted black to reduce internal temperatures when at high speed.

The SR-71 is the final result of what was begun as the twelfth and last version of the *Archangel* series of high-altitude, high-speed reconnaissance aircraft designs, the A-12, which also spawned the F-12 all-missile-armed interceptors and two high-speed reconnaissance drone-carrying M-21 aeroplanes. The technologies used to create these four machines were also employed to produce the D-21 reconnaissance drones that were initially carried by the M-21 aeroplanes. The Skunk Works team led by 'Kelly' Johnson, created these triplesonic, turbojet-powered aircraft at a time when the air-launched, rocket-powered North American X-15 was the only other aeroplane in the world that was capable of flying at 2,000mph (3,200km/h) on a regular basis.

Gusto-cum-*Oxcart*

In the autumn of 1957, with U-2 operations barely one year old, serious discussions, held in great secrecy, were begun between the Department of Defense (DOD), the CIA and the USAF to find a follow-on to the U-2. In late 1957 these three bodies created a U-2 follow-on programme calling for a 'High Speed Reconnaissance Aircraft' that would have previously unheard-of performance: a speed approaching and/or exceeding 2,000mph (3,200m/h) and a ceiling approaching and/or exceeding 100,000ft (30,000m).

The Gusto II concept from Lockheed ADP was basically a twin-engined, semi-flying-wing design with wingtip-mounted vertical stabilizers with rudders. It appears that it was to be manned by a pilot only, and as a semi-flying wing, it was to have had both long range and long loiter time. Lockheed Martin

ABOVE: **Bottom view of the short-lived Lockheed Arrow I configuration.**
Lockheed Martin

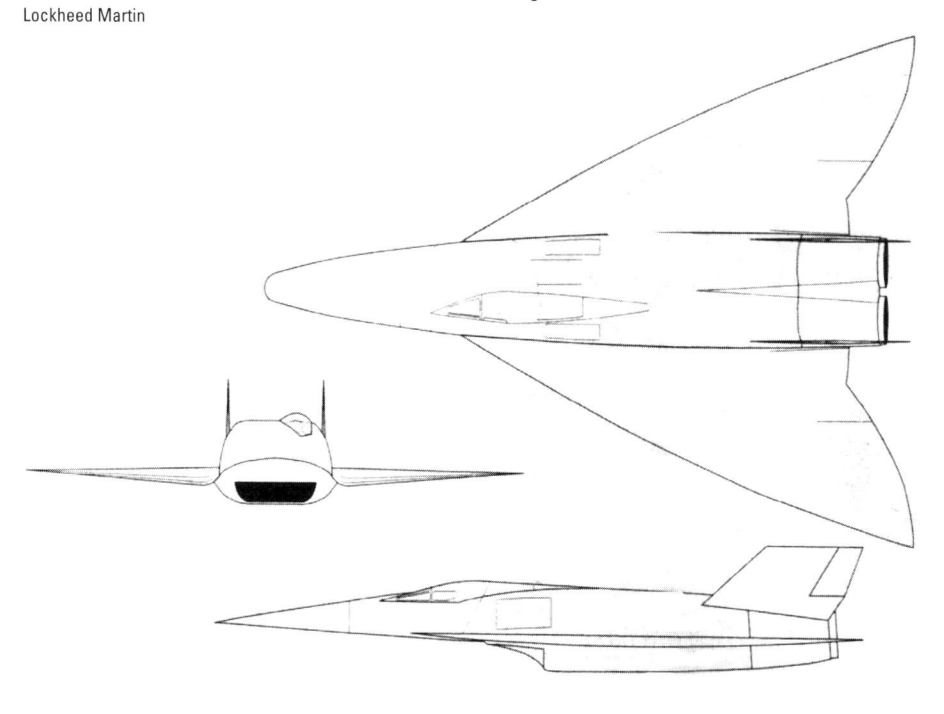

Designed for aerial launch from a B-58 Hustler, this is the final configuration for the Convair Fish Mach 4 parasite aircraft. artwork by Tony Landis

Moreover, it was to be built with a unique feature for aircraft design at the time, called anti-radar (AR), whereby its radar cross-section (RCS) would be very low.

Two airframe contractors, both well versed in the creation of high-speed aircraft, were given the basic requirements and a certain amount of time to carry out feasibility studies. Thus the Advanced Development Projects division of the Lockheed Aircraft Corporation and the Convair division of the General Dynamics Corporation began preliminary design studies into the creation of an aircraft that could not only fly 500–600mph (800–1,000km/h) faster than any other aircraft in the world, but could fly 40,000–50,000ft (12,000–15,000m) higher, while at the same time being nearly impossible to detect by radar.

By late November 1958 it began to look as if such a plane was indeed feasible. Further discussions were held, and in early 1959 President Dwight D. Eisenhower gave his approval. Lockheed and Convair were given the green light to submit definitive proposals and money was made available to them for the work. At this time the project was given the code name *Gusto*; early on, it was simply known as Project G.

Development of the U-2 had evolved under the CIA project name *Aquatone* and the Lockheed project name *Angel*. Early on, the 'High Speed Reconnaissance Aircraft' was known generically in house as the 'U-3', but this was quickly dropped so as not to confuse it with the U-2, and the project name *Archangel* was adopted. On 21 April 1958 Kelly Johnson came up with what he called 'Basic Approach to Design of U-3'. With the change of designation, this first *Archangel* offering became known as *Archangel* I or 'A-1'. By the end of Project *Gusto* in the autumn of 1959 the *Archangel* family had evolved through eleven subsequent submissions, which culminated in the A-12.

This is a very interesting evolution and on 26 April 1993, a paper called *A-12 Log (Abridged)*, written by Kelly Johnson himself, was publicly released. The paper's text is presented on pages 29–35.

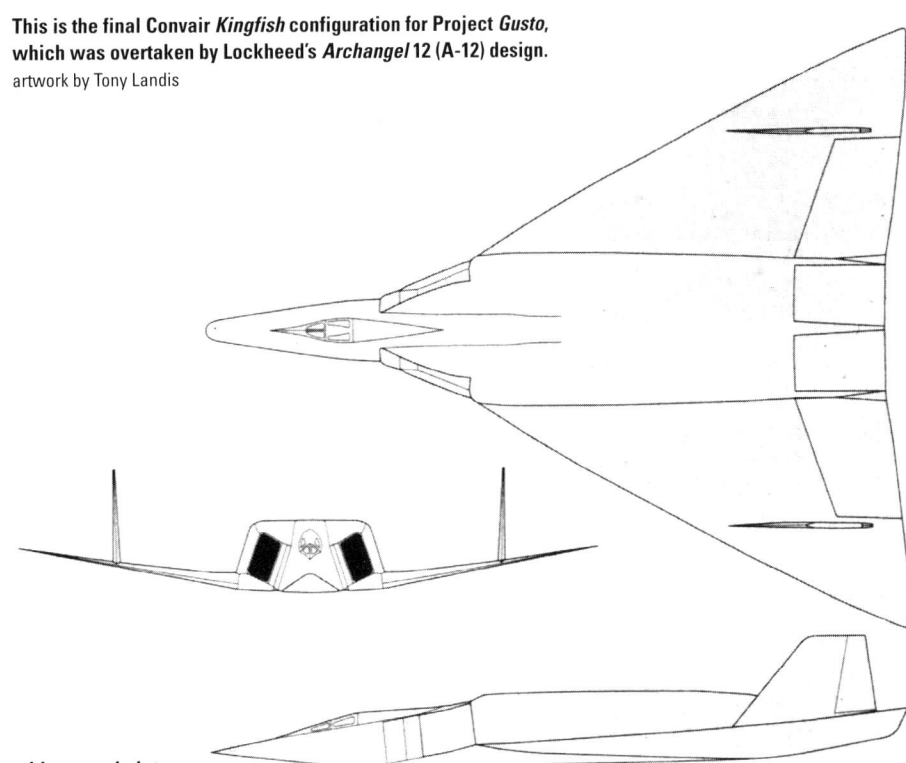

This is the final Convair *Kingfish* configuration for Project *Gusto*, which was overtaken by Lockheed's *Archangel* 12 (A-12) design. artwork by Tony Landis

BELOW: **The four-engine *Archangel* II (A-2) configuration with two turbojets and two ramjets (the latter on the wingtips) is shown alongside the starboard wing of *Gusto* II.** Lockheed Martin

BLACK MAGIC

Archangel 1 (A-1), shown here on 9 October 1957, was the first of twelve designs that eventually became *Archangel* 12 (A-12), the first of the Blackbird series of aircraft. Lockheed Martin

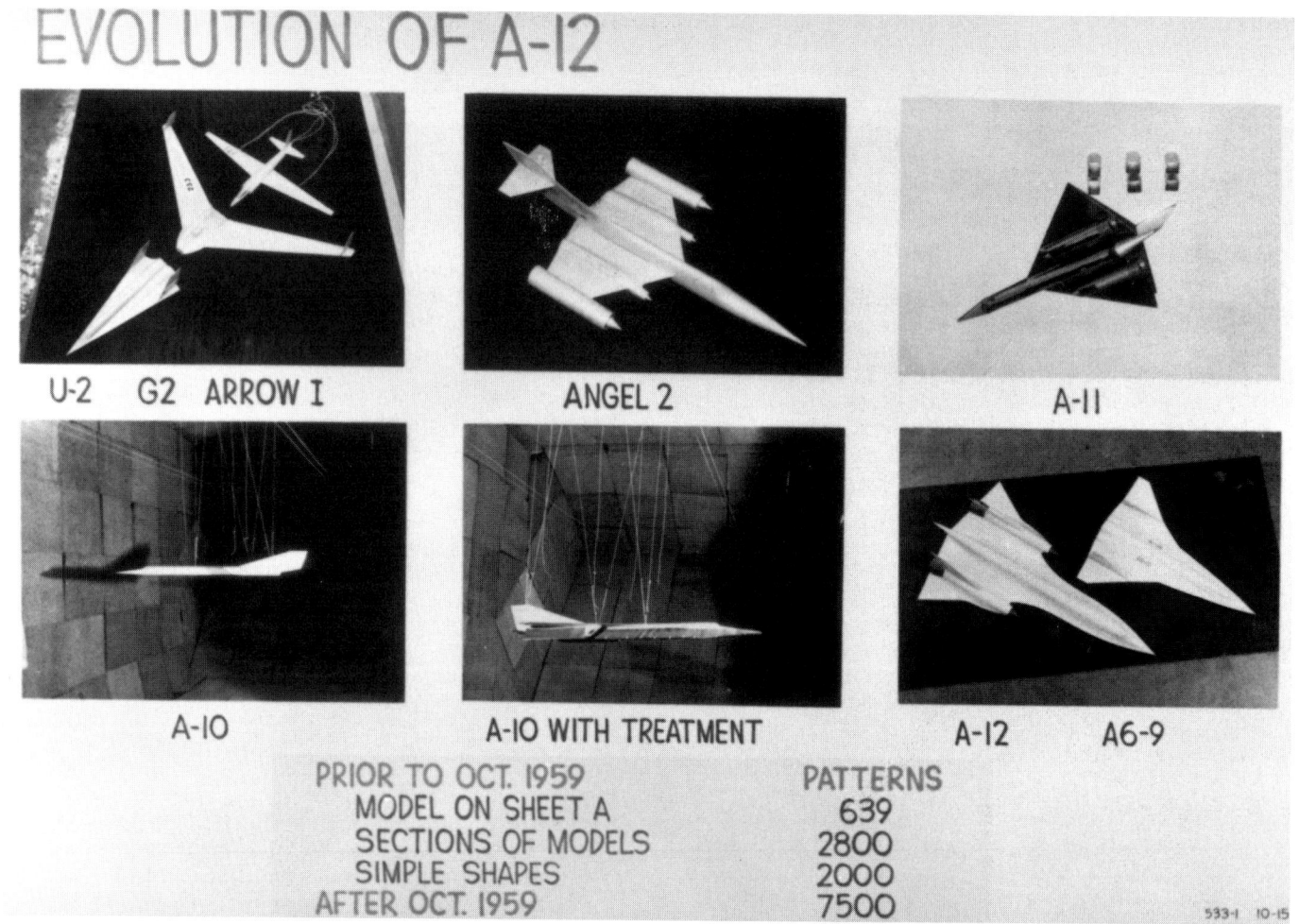

EVOLUTION OF A-12

U-2 G2 ARROW I   ANGEL 2   A-11

A-10   A-10 WITH TREATMENT   A-12   A6-9

PRIOR TO OCT. 1959   PATTERNS
  MODEL ON SHEET A   639
  SECTIONS OF MODELS   2800
  SIMPLE SHAPES   2000
AFTER OCT. 1959   7500

The evolution that led to the A-12 in various stages. Lockheed Martin

A-12 Log (Abridged) by Clarence L. Johnson

21 April 1958: I drew up the first Archangel proposal for a Mach 3 [2,224mph or 3,560km/h] cruise airplane having a 4,000nm [7,408km] range at 90,000 to 95,000ft [27,432 to 28,956m].

23 July 1958: I presented this airplane, along with the Gusto Model G-IIA, to the Program Office. It was well received. The [US] Navy mentioned a study they had been making on a slower, higher altitude airplane, on which the Program Office wanted my comments.

14 August 1958: [I] attended discussions with the Program Office. They gave me a description of an inflatable airplane which they stated to be capable of 150,000ft cruise altitude. It was ramjet-powered and carried to altitude by a balloon. I made some rapid notes and found the balloon would have to be over one mile in diameter.

25 August 1958: [I] have contacted Marquardt and P&W [Pratt & Whitney] and gotten some ramjet data. [I] have reconfigured the Archangel to include wing tip ramjets, as per our [earlier] proposal on the F-104 to the [US] Air Force in 1954. This appears to give us an airplane which would cruise at Mach 3.2 at 95,000 to 110,000ft for the full distance. As of today, it looks like the rubber blimp would have a radius of operation of 52mi.

17–24 September 1958: [I] spent considerable time in Washington [DC] and ended up in Boston [Massachusetts] on 22 and 23 September to review the Archangel project. I presented a report on evaluation of [US] Navy inflatable airplane design and also a revised version of the Archangel design for higher altitude performance.

The inflatable airplane concept appears to have been dropped for our particular mission.

Convair proposed a super-Hustler, which apparently was a piloted, Mach 4 ramjet-powered, with turbojet-assistance for landing, to be launched from the B-58 to do the mission.

I presented Gusto IIA, which was very well received and also Archangel II. This [latter] airplane was 135,000lb gross weight, powered by two J58 turbojets and two 75in ramjets. It could do 100,000ft mission and 4,000mi range. This airplane was not accepted because of its dependence on penta-borane [fuel] for the ramjet and the overall cost of the system.

We left Cambridge [near Boston, Massachusetts] rather discouraged with everything.

24 September 1958: On the way home [to Burbank], I thought it would be worth a try to break one existing [Skunk Works] ground rule – namely, that we should use engines in being. It was this factor which made the Archangel II so large, as we started out with some 15,000 to 18,000lb of installed power plant weight on the J58s alone. Because the JT-12A [should read JT11A; later JT11D-20B] is a low pressure ratio engine, it seemed to me to be well suited to high Mach number operation. I made a few numbers trying to scale down Archangel II to the 17,000 to 20,000lb gross weight, and it appears feasible.

December 1958–July 1959: During this period we studied [Archangel] models from A-3 to A-12. Gradually it became evident that we could not obtain radar invisibility and all other conditions desired for the airplane. In April 1959 I proposed the concept of a single base operation with air-to-air refuelling, operating out of Muroc [Air Force Base, now Edwards AFB]. The A-11 resulted, as an airplane on which we made no compromises for [anti-] radar but which had very good performance, and was a straight forward twin J58 Mach 3.2 airplane.

I gave the A-11 pitch and reported on about six months of radar studies which we had made, in which we proved, at least to ourselves, that improvements available to radars at the present time would enable detection of any conceivable airplane which would fly in the next three to five years. We specifically computed that the probability of detection of the A-11 was practically 100 percent.

I think I made some kind of an impression with the radar people, because the ground rules changed shortly after this and it was agreed that the A-11 would make such a strong [radar] target that it might be taken for a bomber.

Nevertheless, on 3 July, when the Director of the [Gusto] Program Office visited me again, just at about the same time when I thought we were ruled out, they extended our program and agreed to take lower cruising altitudes which we could obtain with a version of the A-11 adapted in [anti-radar] shape and treatment to reduce the [radar] cross section. I proposed the A-12 with the J58 engines in a mid-wing arrangement, the use of chines on the fuselage and serrations on the leading edge incorporating [anti-] radar treatment. This airplane weighs about 110,000 to 115,000lb and, by being optimistic on fuel consumptions and drag, can do a pretty good mission.

As of 8 July, it seems there is a good chance that, if an airplane will be built for the [high-speed reconnaissance aircraft] mission, it will be ours.

28 August 1959: [I] saw the Director of the [Gusto] Program Office alone. He told me that we had the project and that Convair is out of the picture. They accept our conditions (1) of the basic arrangement of the A-12 and (2) that our method of doing business will be identical to that of the U-2. He agreed very firmly to this latter condition and said that unless it was done this way he wanted nothing to do with the project either. The conditions he gave me were these:

1. We must exercise the greatest possible ingenuity and honest effort in the field of [anti-] radar.

2. The degree of security on this project is, if possible, tighter than on the U-2.

3. We should make no large material commitments, large meaning in terms of millions of dollars.

We talked throughout the morning on problems of security, location, manpower, and aircraft factors. At noon I took nine of the [Gusto] project people out for luncheon, in celebration of our new project.

29 August 1959: [We were] given a go-ahead for $4.5 million, to cover 1 September 1959 to 1 January 1960.

31 August 1959: Started immediate action in Building 82A to build a full-scale [engineering] mock-up and a ⅛th scale mock-up, an [anti-radar measurement test] elevation post, engineering reorganization and expansion, and plans for a complete re-arrangement of offices and shop. I reported results of the trip to Robert E. Gross, Courtlandt S. Gross, Cyril Chappellet, Charlie Barker, and Hall Hibbard.

1 September 1959: I consider this to be the first day on our new project, with a flight date set 20 months from today. The original 18-month program will be delayed to allow P&W [Pratt and Whitney] to make a by-pass version of the J58.

8–15 September 1959: We will go forward with greater confidence, having in 18 months completed the circle and come back to an airplane very similar to the A-1, which was our first proposal but considered to be too large, inadequate in the anti-radar concept, and to have too low performance. It was actually smaller than the A-12 and had better performance. All of this is now behind us and we have nothing to do but work.

15 September 1959: [I'm] very busy outlining the design requirements and the program for A-12, doing my best to get promotions for our top people and proper manpower from CALAC [California Aerospace Community]. At a time like this, I am always rather amazed at how many of my best people don't know how to start a program like this. They seem to be completely at sea in spite of the clearest directives you [I] can give them.

15 October 1959: Our full-scale [engineering] model [mock-up] is coming along well. Expect to send out for test during week of 9 November. I am having daily sessions on basic design features of the airplane. Low speed [wind] tunnel tests are underway [at our location] and I had [Dick] Fuller and Bert O'Laughlin go up to [NASA] Ames [at Moffett Field, California near San Jose] to make arrangements for high speed [wind] tunnel tests.

(continued overleaf)

A-12 Log (Abridged) continued

23 October 1959: [Wind] tunnel tests indicate the expected problems in regard to longitudinal stability [referring to stability around the lateral axis; also called pitch stability] with [the] chines. We are extending the wing after the afterburner and believe we have useable solutions coming up. The overall problem of weight, balance, and stability is extremely tough.

9 November 1959: Full-scale model complete.

16 November 1959: I think we have been fairly successful, in that a series of tests has now been instigated installing antennas in the afterburner to see whether we can ionize the gas and essentially provide a faired-over tail cone. [I'm] spending a great deal of time myself going over all aircraft systems, trying to add some simplicity and reliability. [Ernie] Joiner left our group 13 November.

20 November 1959: [I] talked to Larry Bohanan to see if he would become Joiner's replacement. He will give me an answer during the next month. [I] reviewed wheel, tire and brake situation with Goodyear people. It does not appear that water cooling of the brakes is in order for us.

7 December 1959: We are beginning to get the anti-radar return of the model down remarkably. [Engine] air inlets are the problem in the forward aspect and the [engine] exhaust [outlets] in the rear, as expected.

10 December 1959: [We're] reviewing revised P&W specification for the [J58 by-pass] engine, which now appears to be pretty good. [I'm] preparing quote on LAC [Lockheed Aircraft Corporation] construction of ejector. This [ejector] thing is fantastically hard to build, but we must take on the job because it involves so much of the airplane structure.

21 January 1960: We have no performance margins left; so this project, instead of being 10 times harder as anything we have done, is 12 times as hard. This matches the design number [A-12], and is obviously right.

26 January 1960: [We] talked to the Director of the [Oxcart] Program Office. He told us we had the project. We are not sure whether it is 10 airplanes plus a [structural loads] static test, or 12 airplanes plus a static test, but we are in!!

30 January 1960: [We] received notification of decision to procure 12 airplanes [plus a static test article].

4 February 1960: The [Director of the Oxcart] Program Office is proposing that we screen 60 pilots to get a total of 24, who can then be handled in the same way as the [NASA] Mercury [space capsule] Astronauts. He said they could help me design the airplane!! The last thing I need around this joint is an assemblage of pilots, and I told him strongly. It will be at least a year before we should have any [pilots] around except our own [test pilots]. I showed them the mock-up and had, in general, a disagreeable day.

24, 25 and 26 February 1960: We have an even year to complete the first airplane and this will be a fantastic job.

8 March 1960: The electrical and hydraulic systems have fallen out of bed [taken a turn for the worse], due to inability to provide power at approach idle rpm [revolutions per minute]. It seems that some of the boys didn't consider the fact we need maximum booster output on a power-off landing. We require a new gearbox from P&W and change in design approach on the boosters.

16–17 March 1960: [I] went to Washington [DC] to discuss the A-12 as an air defence fighter to replace the F-108. [The proposed all-missile-armed tri-sonic long-range interceptor known as the North American F-108 Rapier was cancelled on 23 September 1959.]

I was given information on the Hughes ASG-18 radar and the latest information on the Hughes GAR-9 [air-to-air] rocket. Before leaving, the USAF [Oxcart] Program Office clearly explained that they wanted to know whether we could make use of this equipment in the A-12 and that, if we could, they would propose it as a standby air defense fighter. They said there would not be any immediate order, but that they were interested in getting development aspects of the fighter system carried along. I told them we could get them an air defense airplane in a couple of years under our present commitments. This would be [production] A-12 number six or seven.

4 April 1960: We are deeply involved in all the design aspects of the [A-12] airplane. I have gotten Larry Bohanan aboard to replace Ernie Joiner. [I] have cleared [Louis A.] Lou Schalk to be the first pilot, but cannot yet use him here. We are all horrified at the extreme cost of [fabricating] the structure surrounding the [engine] nacelle[s]. We have asked CALAC, as well as Art Viereck, and two outside vendors, to bid on certain critical items. We will put in CALAC only such work as does not indicate the size or number of aircraft or anything about its type, and only things on which they are strictly competitive, on a cost and schedule basis. I am afraid this won't be much.

5 April 1960: [The] actual airplane parts are beginning to come [in from outside vendors]. The main jig frames are welded together and the fuel test rig should be in operation soon.

21 April 1960: [We] have stability problems with the airplane, which is stable at any given speed but does not have the proper control position over a wide range of speeds. [We] decided to incorporate air speed variation factor into the longitudinal stability augmenters.

19 July 1960: [I] wrote out a proposal for implementing a low risk, minimum cost approach to the AF-12 [the air defence fighter version of the A-12].

17 August 1960: The time has come when I have to announce officially, as well as unofficially, to the customer that we are late. Because of the extreme cost of [titanium alloy] machining, we are probably going to be over cost.

I spoke to our engineers yesterday, to be sure they are fully aware of our problem, and offered a $500 bonus to anyone who can find a dynamic seal for a high temperature hydraulic system. We have progressed well on other features in both the hydraulic and electrical systems.

30 August 1960: The stress and flutter boys presented a study on aeroelasticity which was woefully in error. If it had been correct, the airplane couldn't fly at all. It was easy to show where the errors of assumption had been made, so we will carry out a new study.

14 September 1960: [We] started design of a bomber version of the A-12.

30 September 1960: We are in desperate trouble trying to get [titanium alloy] extrusions for the wing beams. The material [on hand] is not acceptable.

3–24 October 1960: [We're] continuing to have shop problems. [We] can't get material, and it appears that the schedule is slipping some more. Weight problem is out of hand, so I got everyone together and gave them one of the attached forms [not shown]. This resulted in a weight saving of over 700lb in three weeks, but it was partly nullified by a 300lb increase for other reasons.

1 December 1960: [I'm] having almost daily shop meetings and always uncover problems. It's a fine way to push things along and keep things coordinated. [We] have Larry Billups and Jack Prosser from CALAC to learn the airplane and by next June [1961] work with us on a plan for putting the AF-12 [air defence fighter] into production.

20 December 1960: [I] have a very strong suspicion that [the] P&W [people] are not going to meet their schedule. They have run into trouble on the compressor with tip shrouds. Of course they didn't mention this as being a major problem.

13 February 1961: [We're] having a terrific time trying to get the wing built, due to lack of [titanium alloy] materials. It is apparent that we are going to be late, but I don't know how much we can make up with a three-shift [work schedule] on the wing. [We're] hoping to come out even with the [J58 bypass] engine, which I understand is going to be three to four months late.

A-12 Log (Abridged)

6 March 1961: [We were] having trouble with wing load distribution and have put [a] twist in [the] outboard leading edge [to correct the problem].

15 March –April 1961: [We have] just a great of work with the many problems we [continue to] have trying to get this [first A-12] airplane built. Everywhere you turn there are tremendous problems requiring invention, new systems, and [more] money.

12 April 1961: Some [unwanted] time is starting to build up on the [fabrication of the] wing. The fuselage looks [to be] in good shape. [We're] fighting a whole host of problems on [the J58 power plant, ejectors, plumbing, material shortages, lack of space. We are going to fly early in December [1961] on some basis, but it's going to be an extremely busy summer and fall. [We're] working three shifts in all critical areas.

27 April 1961: [I] reviewed instrumentation requirements and deleted many elements for measuring stresses in-flight which we have not yet invented and which are of questionable value at temperature. [But I] will stress the static test strain survey.

10 July 1961: [We're] having a horrible time building the first airplane and we are stopped on the second [airplane] by a change in [the] design of the [anti-] radar configuration of the chines. Have shop meetings often – about three times a week – but it's hard to drive a willing horse. Everyone [is] on edge [that is] connected with the production of the A-12 airplane and we have a long, long way to go.

I told Courtlandt Gross and Dan Haughton how tough our problems are, with no underestimation on my part of the extreme danger we will encounter in flying this revolutionary airplane. And [I] told them some of the steps we are taking to minimize these dangers.

11 September 1961: The day started with P&W coming in prior to the supplier's meeting and stating that the engines would be 1,000lb apiece overweight, considerably down in performance, and that it would be about March 1962 before we got the engines. I was in deep shock for the next week. We had mated the forward and aft [fuselage] sections on 9 September with very little difficulty. Our design and workmanship appeared to be superb, in that we can go from jig to jig with hundreds of mating points and hit every one the first time. [?] Hunter says that the fit of the forward fuselage to the aft end was so good that you could hardly tell there was a joint there. [It's very] fine tooling by Ed Mort and [his] group. We have at this time 500 people on tooling alone, and overall, about 2,400 people on the project.

Had a frightful meeting with P&W, the general [J58] engine status is terrible. I decided to get real good and mad and told off P&W very clearly.

28 September 1961: Pratt & Whitney told us the story on the engine, and said that the best delivery date we could get for the [first] two engines was March 1962. (They admitted this meant April, or 31 March.) The whole delivery schedule was slipped; so that we could not even meet the [US] Air Force [first] flight date in October 1962.

29 September 1961: After a sleepless night, I decided that we would have to try to fly with the [existing P&W 2.3 Mach-rated] J75 engine, doing everything possible to raise [its] take-off power, such as using water injection, and higher take-off rpm temperatures, and higher take-off rpm.

2 October 1961: [We] started an all-out drive to get J75 engines in the number one [A-12] airplane. I am greatly disappointed in the shop's progress, however.

3 October 1961: Norman Nelson brought in Lt Colonel Richmond L. Miller, Headquarters, Air Research and Development Command, who had been on the program two weeks. Miller said he was supposed to be their man 'in charge of the airframe', which neither he nor I understood. We know Miller from work on the U-2 at Edwards Air Force Base. He is competent in the flight-test area, but he follows the book religiously. He asked me for an A-12 flight manual, which I told him would be ready in about a year. I'll have trouble with him, but I had our boys do all they could to get him indoctrinated.

28 November 1961: [We're] spending lots of time in the shop trying to get the critical forward [engine] nacelles out [for installation]. For two days I went out there once an hour to see that we got enough people on it. It's moving, but late, and [it's] a very tough job.

1–31 December: [We're putting] extreme pressure on the airplane to get it completed. We were given credit for an acceptance [of the first air vehicle], on the basis that all [of the titanium alloy] sheet metal parts were either in place or have been [test] fitted and removed. Big problems are [fuel] tank sealing, fillets, and just time enough to do a thorough job. [We're] working three shifts and running engineering tests as we are able to get at [certain parts of] the airplane.

3–5 January 1962: [We] had a big meeting with P&W in Florida. I spent a day alone with them. Their troubles are desperate. It is almost unbelievable that they could have gotten this far with the engine without uncovering basic problems which have been normal in every jet engine I have ever worked with. This is the result of their putting a second team on the design, which is too far away from top management. [The] prospect of an early flight-rated engine is dismal, and I feel our program is greatly jeopardized. Hamilton Standard [supplier of J58 engine fuel controls] are not covering themselves with glory either.

It's a good thing we went to the [interim] J75, although these engines, too, have troubles and require new compressor discs.

24 January 1962: Bill Gwinn was here to discuss P&W problems. I am afraid the [J58] engine situation is quite desperate.

25 January 1962: [We're] working on completion of the number one A-12 around the clock and on a seven-day week basis. [We're] having the usual last minute problems.

February 1962: [We're] going all-out on finishing airplane number one. Everyone is putting in very long hours and meeting a tough schedule, outlined in one of my project memos. We are having trouble with high temperature greases, bearings, and [again, we're having] the usual host of last minute troubles.

15 February 1962: [We] got all the engineers together in the LERC [Lockheed Engineering and Research Centre] building and told them of our problems, our moves and [of] the new engineering building.

20 February 1962: [I] did the same thing with the shop people, but here [I] announced a new organizational setup for [Art] Viereck. It's very obvious that the project has gotten way beyond the old Skunk Works procedures and some of our best people have no grasp of [our former ways of aircraft] production. Hunter and Van [?] can no longer chase their own parts and we must organize better to get this brute into production. We are making 80,000 parts a month but have to reach 105,000 to get well schedule wise.

26 February 1962: The convoy [carrying the number one A-12 airplane] left [Burbank] at 2:30am to go to the area. Everything went smoothly and it arrived at 1:00pm on 28 February. Dorsey Kammerer did his usual splendid job on organizing the move.

1 March 1962: There is extreme pressure, actually from as high as the White House [President of the United States], to get this bird operational at the earliest possible date. [Representatives of the Kennedy Administration] asked us to put the [manufacture of] AF-12s at the end of production of the first ten A-12s, and said they could swing this deal with the USAF.

2 March 1962: I went to the area. [I] saw the bird, which was pretty well re-assembled, and worked with Larry Bohanon on flight test problems while they [CIA and USAF officials] toured the area.

(continued overleaf)

A-12 Log (Abridged) *continued*

6 March 1962: Fuel was put in the bird. It developed 68 leaks. [I] was [at first] told that the [fuel tank] sealing looked good, but later investigation showed that we had no adhesion to speak of between the [special Dupont] Viton [fluoroelastomer] compound and the titanium [alloy] metal, in spite of the fact that I had been told by several [who were] in the tank sealing game that airplane number two [had already] encountered this problem because of the use of different [cleaning] solvents.

This is apparently not the case. As of 8 March, we have to strip the [fuel] tanks completely and replace the sealant. This is a cruel blow, as it will delay us a month or more.

23 April 1962: [We're seeing] the usual last minute problem on possible flutter, arising from tests on the simulator. [We] shook the rudders again on the airplane and finally were able to compute that the simulator was different from the airplane. [I] went to the area to go over flight test status.

25 April 1962: [I] went to the area and stayed over night. [We] made our first flight under very difficult conditions. [Lou] flew about 1.5mi at altitudes of about 20ft. [The] airplane got off the ground with lots of right rudder on, and then required change of rudder angle to 24 degrees immediately. This set up lateral oscillations which were horrible to see. We were all concerned about the ability of Lou Schalk to stop, but he did this very nicely, without severe braking. The [dry] lake is soft enough so that we can roll onto it at fantastic speeds and stop readily. [The] actual [landing roll-out] trouble was later shown to be due to nosewheel steering problems.

26 April 1962: We decided to fly with the stability augmenter engaged on 26 April, which is obviously a day for the A-12, in that two times six equals 12. Everyone was awake just about through the night. We rolled out early, and at 7:05am [the airplane] took-off, making a beautiful take-off. However, due to failure of a forward fillet [mounting] bracket, we shed almost all of the left-hand fillets and one on the right side, starting before we left the runway. Fortunately, I had spent the previous day with [pilot] Lou Schalk, explaining that the fillets were non-structural and that we might have troubles [with them].

A beautiful landing was made, and in-flight we investigated the effect of the stability augmenters. We showed that the first flight troubles were not caused by basic aircraft stability.

30 April 1962: On the morning of the 30th, things were ready and in good shape. We flew for 59 minutes, with no particular difficulty. This was the official first flight. It was also the first one where we put the [landing] gear up. This worked well.

4 May 1962: [We] made a one hour and ten minute flight on the bird, going supersonic for the first time. The airplane handles well and we were going to make two more flights.

7 May 1962: I figured out what was wrong with nose [wheel] steering and have been able to correct it simply. [We] should fly again on 8 May. Reviewed [flight] test program with Larry Bohanon. I believe we will be able to fly quite often and I also predict that we will be seen within the next two weeks. [There is] trouble ahead.

7 to 31 May 1962: [We're] flying the aircraft. Testing is going well. Our main problems are [wheel] brake chatter with wing response, cracking of the vertical tail, and parachute failures. [The] airplane appears to be doing everything we can expect, with the exceptions noted.

22 June 1962: [The] static test [phase] on [the] basic bird has gone well to this point. We have had [structural] limit load on it 41 times, 130 percent of the limit load about 19 times, and ultimate load five times. [We're still] having dismal failures on [the vertical] fin, particularly our metal one, although the Narmco [made plastic vertical] fin is not sufficiently strong, either.

6 July 1962: [We] opened our new engineering building, number 311 [at Burbank]. This is the fifth Skunk Works building, and it is very nice. [We] built it for $14.20 per square foot, in less than five months. This will get our entire engineering group together again, except for the U-2 boys, who are moving into our old quarters in Building 82.

30 July 1962: [We] flew the [first] airplane on about its 28th flight. Flight testing [is] proceeding very well and [A-12] number two has gone on the [radar measurement] pole. [The] first results show it to be up five to 10 decibels, which is not unexpected to me.

1 August 1962: By this time we have completed our ultimate static tests on the basic airplane on all elements [of the structure] except the [vertical] fins. Both the Narmco plastic one and our [titanium alloy] metal one are breaking up above limit load.

16 August 1962: [We] hired [James D.] Jim Eastham, who is working for HAC [Hughes Aircraft Company] at the present time, to fly the A-12 and the AF-12 [air defence fighter].

5 October 1962: On this date we flew the bird [A-12 number one] taking the J58 engine into the air for the first time. The right engine was a J75. The flight was fairly successful.

We are having nose landing gear 'walk', probably due to [the still] chattering brakes [problem]. [We] have the main landing gear on the shimmy [test] tower. This is one of our biggest problems.

11 October 1962: [We] met with P&W people to discuss performance and [other J58] engine problems. We are having a terrible time trying to fly the prototype J58. It is down on thrust; fuel control is inconsistent; there are thrust jumps at different throttle positions; and we have continual trouble with the afterburner lighting system and plugged [nozzles on the fuel] spray bars.

2 November 1962: [We] finished testing full-scale [A-12] aircraft number 122 on the pole. [We're] taking it down after a series of over 15,000 [anti-radar] tests. We are having difficulty repeating the effect of small [anti-radar design] changes.

[We] reviewed [the] test results with Norm Nelson, and had concurrence from headquarters that tests on number 122 [A-12 number two] were complete except for the [radar measurements in the] flight phase. We do not intend, however, to rebuild the full-scale model and do further work on it.

14 November 1962: [We had a] meeting in Washington [DC] to discuss [J58] power plant problems with P&W. They presented data to show that their deliveries were practically stopped by lack of Hamilton Standard fuel controls; the thrust of the engine was down, specific fuel consumption [was] up. The initial [batch of] engines would not run well above 75,000ft. They showed their program for getting the performance back, but this could not be accomplished until engine number 19, due for delivery in April 1963.

6 December 1962–3 January 1963: [There is] much flying activity. We delivered [A-12] airplane number five to the Area on 19 December, meeting our schedule requirements for the year [1962]. However, it was delivered minus [J58] engines, due to lack of engines.

[We] made arrangements to hire [Robert J. 'Bob'] Gilliland as the fourth [should be third; Lockheed ADP test] pilot when he returns here about 15 January. [We're] having a hard time staffing the Area, to get the [A-12] airplanes flying. Number two and number four [A-12s] should be flying within a week, but [the] number one [A-12] has many changes [to it] required to make it suitable for hot [triplesonic] flight.

February 1963: Airplanes number 123 and 124 {A-12s number three and four], with J75 engines, are flying well, with number 124 [A-12 number four, the two-seat trainer, having] been delivered to the customer. [The future operational A-12] pilots are checking out well. [But] we have problems of pilot comfort, due to rudder pedal position, parachute straps, etc.

20 March 1963: We have been to 2.5 Mach number and as high as 70,000ft, but we are in trouble from Mach 2.0 [and] up.

A-12 Log (Abridged)

22 April 1963: [We] talked to the swing shift [workers], who object to our cutting back to a 56.5-hour work week. We certainly don't have the morale and type of people we had on the U-2 [program at the Area], but I must say they have a number of things to complain about. One of these is the deterioration of the food and housing conditions at the Area.

2 May 1963: I went to the Area to find out why we have not been able to get beyond Mach 2.0 during recent flights. It develops that Hamilton Standard had changed the gain on the [engine air inlet] spike control of the cam designed jointly by [Benjamin R. 'Ben'] Rich and Hamilton Standard, and the main control contributed to the instability. [I am] greatly displeased that [Ed] Martin, [Ben] Rich, [Larry] Bohanon and Hamilton Standard could not find this out on their own, and no one seemed to know which controls gave which performance, until I made a review of the [A-12 ships'] [flight log] records, and then it became perfectly clear.

A similar condition had developed in regard to engine damage due to foreign objects [entering the engine air inlets]. We have had 19 cases of engine damage [due to foreign object damage or FOD], almost always after high power ground run-up. [I] had Bohanon write up a summary [of this], which turned out to be wrong. He wrote up another, which also turned out to be wrong. [We] finally got it unscrambled, [and I'm] spending a couple of days at the Area between 6 and 8 May [1963].

24 May 1963: We lost airplane number 123 [A-12 number three]. [The] pilot was Ken Collins of [the] USAF [who ejected safely and was unhurt].

24 June 1963: During this month we have tried to pick [things] up in our airspeed/altitude profile. [We] have not gotten much [however], due to voluntary grounding during number 123 [crash] investigation and terrific problems with Hamilton Standard [engine air inlet] spike control.

As of this date we have five J58-powered airplanes flying or ready to fly. [We're] having the usual development difficulties matching the [air] inlet and engine.

15 July 1963: [We're] having difficulty getting aircraft to speed because of [engine air] inlet problems. [We] do not know whether it is an aircraft, engine, or inlet control problem.

22 July 1963: Am visiting Area often, trying to get instrumentation working to measure origin of trouble in propulsion system.

[It should be noted here that on 7 August 1963 the first YF-12A – formerly known as AF-12, made its first flight at the Area and it was piloted by Jim Eastham; not mentioned in Kelly's A-12 log.]

13 August 1963: Larry Bohanon went to the hospital [no reason given]. [Glen] Fulkerson took over. I have to spend a lot of time laying out flight test programs under this critical situation.

4 September 1963: [I] spent time with P&W showing them the results of our thrust measurements, which are not favorable.

12 September–10 October 1963: I am reviewing every test day by day. We are modifying the [air] bypass system of the [engine] nacelles. Having continual difficulties not associated with the propulsion [system] problem, as usual, on the [J58] engine and particularly the [air] inlet control.

We have been to 3.0 Mach number twice now, the first time being on 20 July 1963. On the second flight, we blew an engine at design speed [Mach 3.2]. It was very difficult to slow [the A-12] down and it rattled Lou Schalk around [in the cockpit] for three minutes. The aircraft SAS (stability augmentation system) did precisely as I asked it to do three years ago and no high structural loads were obtained.

8 November 1963: Today we flew the mice installation, to change the subsonic diffusion angles in the [air] duct. This change corrected the roughness encountered at 2.4 Mn up, and it is the first major improvement in the duct. [I] collected 25 cents from [Ben] Rich, [Dick] Fuller and [Dick] Boehme.

14 November 1963: Had a meeting with P&W on J58 problems, including low transonic thrust.

19 December 1963: Still having trouble with Hamilton Standard on [engine air] inlet controls.

6 January 1964: As of this date, when have flown 10 aircraft.

3 February 1964: Jim Eastham took number 121 [A-12 number one] to 3.3 Mn, with 15 minutes at 3.2 Mn or above. It [the flight] singed our old [fuel] tank sealing compound, but was a very good flight. I am building up a variable [geometry air] bypass area at the face of the [J58] engine and have refaired the upper outboard quadrant to get improved airflow distribution at high Mach number. At about this same time, we flew number 122 [A-12 number two] for 53 minutes at 2.65 Mn or above.

25 February 1964: Plans going forward for surfacing of the AF-12 [YF-12] program. I worked on the draft to be used by President [Lyndon B.] Johnson and proposed the terminology 'A-11', as it was the non-anti-radar version [of Gusto].

1 March 1964: President Johnson announced the AF-12 [as the 'A-11']. Twenty minutes after he did this, we flew the two [completed YF-12A] birds from the Area to Muroc [Edwards AFB]. Having rolled into the new hangar, it [they were] so hot that the fire extinguishing nozzles came on and gave us a free wash job.

March 1964: Still having terrific problem on getting proper transonic acceleration. Changing ejector configurations, but nothing seems to make any difference. Building fixed ejectors and ejectors with [a] larger throat.

29 April 1964: On this date, Jim Eastham flew 32 minutes at over 3.0 Mn. It happened to be in a continuous turn, so miles per [fuel] gallon did not look good.

28 May 1964: Today I talked to Henry Combs, Ed Martin, and briefly to Dick Boehme and Rus Daniell, to try to avoid having the Skunk Works develop into two distinct organizations. We are beset by military people and have now reached the point where we have half as many people writing manuals as we used to design the A-12. [I'm] still fighting the battle hard to prevent being forced into standard [operating] procedures.

9 July 1964: We lost airplane number 133 [A-12 number 13]. [William C.] Bill Park was flying it. He ejected laterally at 200ft] on approach. We readily determined the cause of the accident to be temperature gradients resulting in a stuck outboard elevon servo valve. Bill didn't get a scratch.

14 July 1964: Customer [CIA] personnel were here [Burbank]. We reviewed the A-12 problems of the time [at present]. Our major problems are transonic acceleration, [engine air] inlet controls, and [maximum] engine thrust [output].

17 August 1964: Last week there was an all-out drive to set the world speed record and altitude record with the AF-12 [YF-12A]. This meant pulling people and parts from the Area and equipping airplanes number 1001 and 1003 [YF-12A airplanes one and three] with the latest [engine air] inlet controls, [J58] engines, etc.

We are going forward with maximum energy to provide four operational [A-12] airplanes with the limited capability to fly over Cuba on 5 November [1964]. We have been told by the Soviets that immediately after the [presidential] election they intend to shoot down every U-2 [over Cuba], which we are [currently] operating at a rate of 18 sorties per month. Should this be done, we would be unable to find out whether they put [ballistic] missiles back in [Cuba]; so the A-12 is vital for this purpose.

(continued overleaf)

A-12 Log (Abridged) continued

November 1964: We are getting widely varied data on the performance of the [A-12] airplane with different [J58] engines on different days. Sometimes we just about get design performance – other times we are 15 to 20 percent off. I am going to instrument number 129 [A-12 number nine] for the most detailed duct pressure surveys and am instigating anew (for the fourth time) wind tunnel tests on the [engine air] inlet – this in spite of the fact, with the proper control settings, there are many flights out of which we get excellent agreement between our expected performance and the actual performance.

December 1964: By using 450 knots versus 400 knots EAS [estimated air speed] in climb, we have overcome transonic problems. We are trying to get number 129 [A-12 number nine] in shape for a long flight, but are having continual engine problems on compressor discs, blade cracking, etc.; so are not flying much.

[It should be noted here that SR-71A number one made its first flight out of Palmdale, California on 22 December 1964 with Robert J. 'Bob' Gilliland at the controls. In addition, the first M-21 'Mother' and D-21 'Daughter' flight was accomplished on the same day at the Area; the M-21 was piloted by Bill Park. These first flights were not mentioned in Johnson's A-12 Log.]

4 January 1965: It appears that our duct problems at high speed are stemming from excess [air] leakage at the engine face and various bypass doors. [We've] concluded 10,764 wind tunnel tests on the [engine air] inlet alone, and every one of them confirms our present design. The addition of mice not only solved the roughness problem by gained us two percent in ram [jet thrust action]. We will gradually work up to our basic performance, as close as we can expect to get it, considering the [J58] engine overweight and added equipment in the [A-12] airplane.

18 March 1965: [We] just completed the fourth series of wind tunnel tests on the [engine air] inlet duct. [We're] still unable to find a reason for duct roughness and lack of ram [jet thrust action] at high speeds. We have now run well over 10,000 wind tunnel tests on this subject and have taken over 1,250,000 readings, but we keep getting the same answers.

On this date I sent Hamilton Standard a letter saying we could not continue trying to develop the AIC-10 [engine air] inlet control. We have spent $17,000,000 on this thing to this point, but it [air inlet control system] just will not do the job and is totally unpredictable.

April 1965: Half of our [flight] aborts at this time are due to false fire warning indications, inability to measure oil pressure and exhaust gas temperatures. It is an extremely frustrating period, because it would seem that our above problems were very straightforward, which they are not.

14 May 1965: Hamilton Standard [is] withdrawing a number of their people. Our long battle with them is coming to a sorry end. [Hamilton Standard is now Hamilton Sundstrand, a subsidiary of United Technologies Corporation.]

21 June 1965: [Airplane number] 121 [A-12 number one] is back in the factory to be brought up to date after a long hard test career.

5 August–30 September 1965: The situation regarding our operational capability is critical. I had long discussions with the [CIA Oxcart] Program Office. They proposed that I spend full time at the Area to get the program moving. During August and September [1965] I put in about six weeks of flying up [to the Area from Burbank] and down [from the Area to Burbank] every day.

I uncovered many items of managerial, materiel, and design nature. [I] went intensively into the delivery scheduling of the airplanes, rewired much of the aircraft, threw out questionable [electrical] plugs, designed and improved terminal blocks, tied down the wiring in the airstream and got P&W, after two flights, to fix the [J58] engine wiring. I had meetings with vendors to improve their operation, got five times as many AirResearch people on the scene and improved their quality control. [I] changed supervision and had daily talks with them, going over in detail all problems on the aircraft. [I] got [Larry] Bohanon and [?] Bertelli to talk to each other. [I] increased the supervision in the electrical group by 500 percent. [I] had Ab Baker, Ron Harris' assistant, full time at the Area with me. We tightened up our inspection procedures a great deal and made inspection stick.

It appears the problems are one-third due to bum engineering. Workmanship is poor, but much of this is due to having to work in inaccessible [aircraft interior] areas and with components that are almost childish in their design concept. The addition of so many [newly added] systems to the A-12 has greatly complicated the problems, but we did solve the overall problem.

In September [1965], we sent an [A-12] aircraft to Florida [Eglin AFB] to run tests in rain and high humidity. These tests were very successful.

4–21 October 1965: Starting 4 October, I gave up my daily Area trips, but on 21 October I was requested to resume them.

[We're] still having basic problems of obtaining [design] range on all aircraft. [I] do not know whether it is [airframe] drag or [engine] thrust. We have a desperate shortage of [J58] engines and many new engine problems have cropped up as a result of our increased flying. [Fuel] tank sealing is a major problem.

30 November 1965: As of this date, we consider we have three [A-12] aircraft that are operational. We are instructed to maintain a degree of readiness so the aircraft could be deployed in [as little as] two weeks.

28 December 1965: Airplane 126 (A-12 number six) crashed on takeoff [at the Area]. It was flown by Mel Vojvodich, Jr. The airplane took off and immediately upon lift-off it went into a yaw. The yaw was corrected, [then] the airplane pitched up. In correcting the motions, the pilot yawed and pitched a second time. He ejected at about 100ft safely. The airplane, of course, crashed and burned.

Coming down [to Burbank] in the [company] airplane with Bill Park and Bert McMaster, we analyzed the situation within a half hour. The SAS [Stability Augmentation System] gyros were hooked up backwards. This is the first thing I told the accident [investigation] board to look at. Prior to leaving the Area [for Burbank], Ed Martin cut the gyros out, keeping the wires connected to them. Low and behold – the pitch and yaw gyro connections were interchanged in the rigging, which explained the accident completely.

I have just about given up on speeches to engineers to design things so that they cannot possibly be hooked up wrong. I just don't seem to get a response from either my supervision or men on the board.

12 May 1966: As of this date, there is still no go-ahead for the deployment, although it seems fairly optimistic. The [A-12] airplanes are ready to go. We do not yet have the range up to design value, but two-thirds of the [range] loss has been due to weight changes [increases] due to added equipment. One-third of it is due to loss in range cruising. We [Lockheed pilots] can do about 3,000nm, but they [CIA pilots], of course, do not get the range that we can.

15 August 1966: We do not yet have permission to deploy, although this looks a little more favourable now. Our morale is poor, as there seems to be no direction to the program.

[We've] completed tests on [engine] nacelle leakage at [our] Rye Canyon [California] facility and it seems to be the last place to look for the range deficiency. We apparently leak six to eight percent of the air taken aboard, and this factor, together with engine deficiencies and the higher [airframe] weights, makes up the range deficiency.

10 October 1966: Still no [A-12] deployment.

We are making 40 flights a month. The airplane is working quite well. It has not yet obtained its [design] range. We are down to working on [engine air inlet] duct leakage and basic engine performance.

3 January 1967: The [CIA Oxcart] Program Office called in reference to terminating the program. A committee, recommended storing the A-12 airplanes by the end of the calendar [year] 1967, and keeping the SR-71s as the basic manned aircraft reconnaissance unit for the US.

A-12 Log (Abridged)

5 January 1967: We lost Walter Ray and A-12 number 125 [A-12 number five] on a training mission. Our seat belt, a standard USAF type, did not release and Ray was killed [on impact with the ground while still] in the seat, this being the first failure of the [A-12 emergency] ejection system.

26 January 1967: We are still not clear on going about storing the airplanes. I spent some time yesterday with [Larry] Bohanon going over the personnel problems in our flight test crew. It is inevitable that we lose half of our good people this year. And there is no flight test activity in CALAC [California Aerospace Community] to use them.

In spite of the plans to store the airplanes, [CIA] headquarters are going ahead putting changes in the airplanes, because the word hasn't gotten around. I'm trying to get some direction to this program, to prevent further waste of money.

I think back to 1959, before we started this airplane, to discussions with the [CIA Gusto] Program Office where we seriously considered the problem of whether there would be one more round of aircraft before the satellites took over. We jointly agreed there would be just one round, and not two. That seems to have been a very accurate evaluation, as it seems that 30 SR-71s give us enough over-flight reconnaissance capability and we don't need the additional ten A-12 aircraft [previously ordered].

14 March 1967: In Washington [DC], where we had a dinner at the Statler [Hotel], we discussed the conclusion of the A-12 program and a sad evening was had by all.

21 March 1967: The [US] Air Force and the [CIA Oxcart] Program Office are having quite a time about storing the A-12s. It appears that half of them will be stored by the middle of this year and all of them by February 1968. In the meantime, five airplanes will be kept on alert status for deployment.

18 April 1967: The [A-12] aircraft at the Area are operating well.

31 May 1967: Three [A-12] airplanes were deployed very successfully. The planning on deployment was excellent. They flew non-stop from Area 51 across the Pacific [to Kadena AB], refuelling to get a full load off the coast of Hawaii and then off Midway. [They flew] across the ocean in something like six hours.

18 July 1967: The [photographic reconnaissance] results of the deployment appear to have been very successful. In six flights, more data was obtained than had been gathered the prior year by all other reconnaissance methods. In spite of this favourable performance, I am shocked and amazed to find that the airplane will be returned in December [1967] and be stored at Palmdale. At that time, SAC [Strategic Air Command] will be deployed with the SR-71.

9 August 1967: In spite of the success of the A-12 airplanes, we are still under instructions to prepare for their storage at Palmdale, probably three months later than originally proposed. I doubt if they will ever be stored. [They were, however.]

14 February 1968: The A-12 airplanes are doing well.

The SR-71s are scheduled for deployment shortly to the same base in Kadena. They will, however, have about three times as many people to run the same number of airplanes!!

April 1968: The A-12 aircraft are operating with a 30-day overlap with three SR-71s deployed from Beale [AFB, California]. The photographic take of the A-12 is considerably better than that of the SR-71s', because the Hycon camera in the latter airplane isn't doing its job.

There are rumblings that after the 30-day period, the A-12s will be returned to the [United] states.

24 May 1968: The decision was taken to phase out the A-12 by about mid-June [1968].

29 May 1968: Plans were put into effect for storing the A-12 aircraft at Palmdale [California].

4 June 1968: [A-12] aircraft numbers 130 and 132 [A-12 numbers ten and 12] were flown to Palmdale and stored, as per our previous plans. Aircraft 129 [A-12 number nine], on a shakedown flight out of Kadena, flown by Jack Weeks, was lost over the Pacific.

17 June 1968: We are rapidly phasing down all A-12 activity.

24 June 1968: While the intelligence community in Washington [DC] wanted very much to keep the A-12 program going, the present financial situation cannot stand the strain. It's a bleak end for a program that has been overall as successful as this.

In this paper the reader will notice that the A-12 aeroplanes are factory-numbered 121–133. The factory numbers 134 and 135 (not mentioned in the paper) were the two M-21 'Mother' aeroplanes that carried the D-21 'Daughter' reconnaissance air vehicles. The three YF-12A aeroplanes, built in the production run of A-12s, received their own factory numbers of 1001, 1002 and 1003.

The paper illustrates the difficulties in creating these highly advanced Mach 3 aircraft at a time when operational USAF Mach 2 aircraft – such as Lockheed's own F-104 Starfighter – were 'the best of the best'. A great deal of credit must go to the unique cadre of individuals mentioned in Johnson's *A-12 Log*, for without them, the *Gusto*-cum-*Oxcart* programmes would have gone for nothing.

A proposed but short-lived configuration of the A-12 with canard foreplanes. Lockheed Martin

A-12 wind tunnel model. Lockheed Martin

The first A-12 is shown in various stages of its assembly processes at Burbank. Lockheed Martin

The manufacturing processes to complete these unique aircraft were cutting edge. Then, packaged in major sub-assemblies, they had to be secretly transported to Groom Lake on specially built oversized trailers pulled by eighteen-wheel tractor trucks. They then entered final assembly and ground tests before they could fly.

After the A-12s and subsequent Blackbirds came out of final assembly at Area 51, they underwent numerous ground-test procedures which included avionics checkouts, cockpit instrumentation calibrations, engine run-tests, flight-control actuation evaluations and fuel-system checks, to name but a few. Only after these tests were conducted could flight testing begin.

The flight-test evaluations of these early J75-powered A-12s proved that these aircraft were indeed airworthy – that their structures were sound and that their systems worked. The J75, optimized for much lighter, fighter-type aircraft, powered the A-12 to a maximum speed of Mach 1.6 (1,186mph or 1,909km/h) at 50,000ft (15,000m). This was far short of maximum speed and altitude of the J58-powered Blackbirds, but sufficient to evaluate the aeroplane in flight.

The number two A-12 (60-6925) under early construction. When it was completed it served as the radar cross-section test vehicle. Lockheed Martin

BELOW: **A-12 number three (60-6926) under construction.** Lockheed Martin

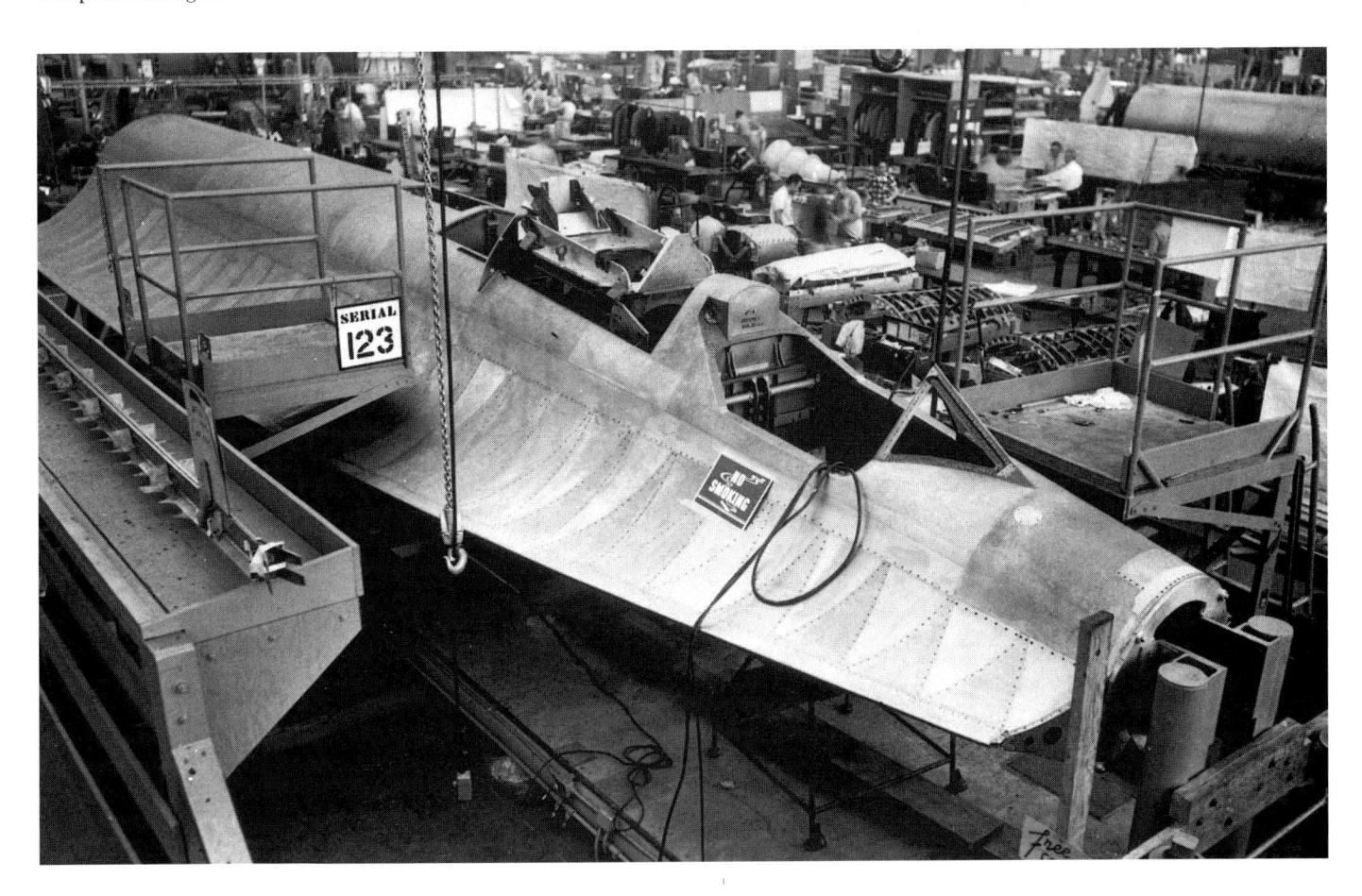

BLACK MAGIC

A-12 number twelve (60-6939) under construction. Lockheed Martin

A-12 number two (60-6925) sits atop the radar cross-section test pylon. Lockheed Martin

Another view of A-12 number two on the radar pole, but without the boat-tail drag-measurement extensions. Lockheed Martin

The first A-12 (60-6924) being prepared for engine-run tests. The upside-down external fuel tanks mounted atop the wings, inboard of the engine nacelles, replenished the fuel that had leaked out. Lockheed Martin

38

INSET: **A-12 number one (60-6924) lifts off for its official first flight on 30 April 1962.** Lockheed Martin

ABOVE: **Engine run-up test of A-12 number one, in early 1964 after it was painted black.** Lockheed Martin

RIGHT: **The dashboard of A-12 number one.** Lockheed Martin

THIS PAGE:

RIGHT: **The third A-12 (60-6926) banks left during its first flight, showing details of its underside.** Lockheed Martin

BELOW: **The two-seat TA-12 (60-6927) was never retrofitted with J58 engines and kept its J75s throughout its 614-flight flying career.** Lockheed Martin

BOTTOM: **The TA-12 lifts-off from the Groom Lake runway, early 1963.** Lockheed Martin

OPPOSITE PAGE:

TOP: **A-12 number four (60-6928) taxiing out for take-off.** Lockheed Martin

MIDDLE: **A number of A-12s and YF-12s, and the sole TA-12 on the Groom Lake flight line.** Lockheed Martin

BOTTOM: **A fine study of A-12 number eight (60-6932) in flight.** Lockheed Martin

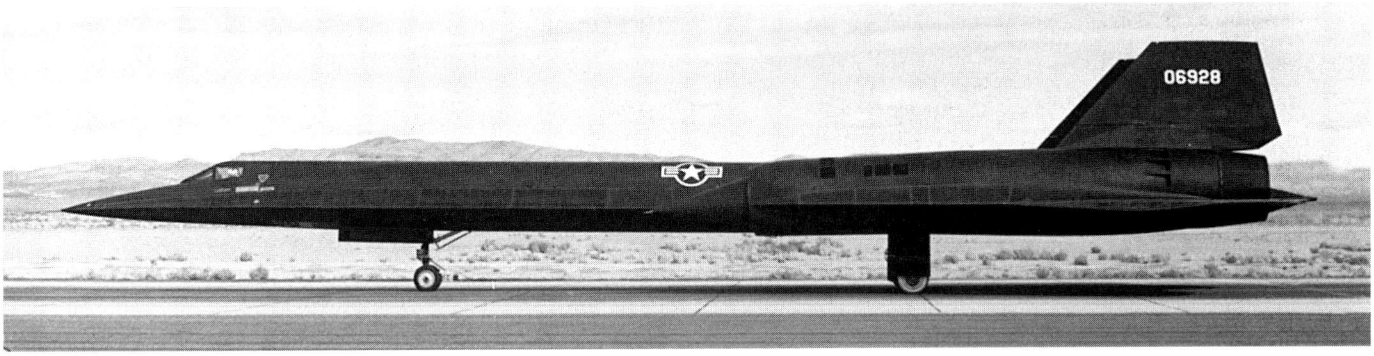
06928

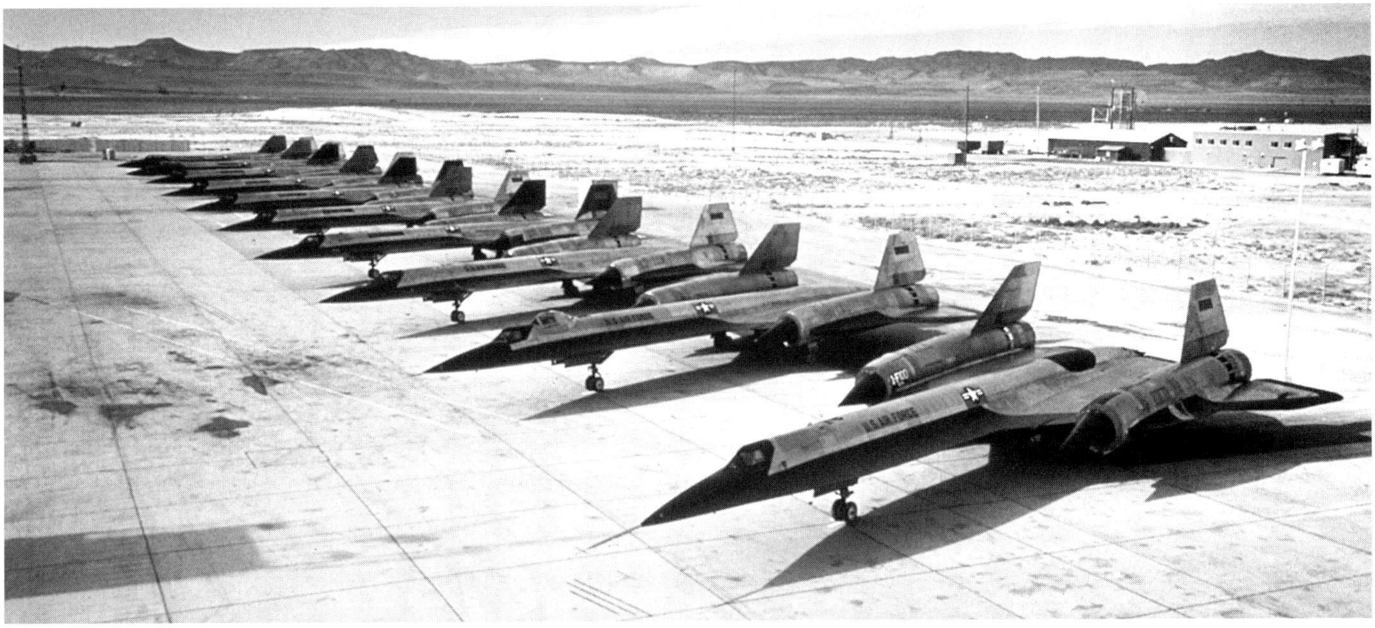

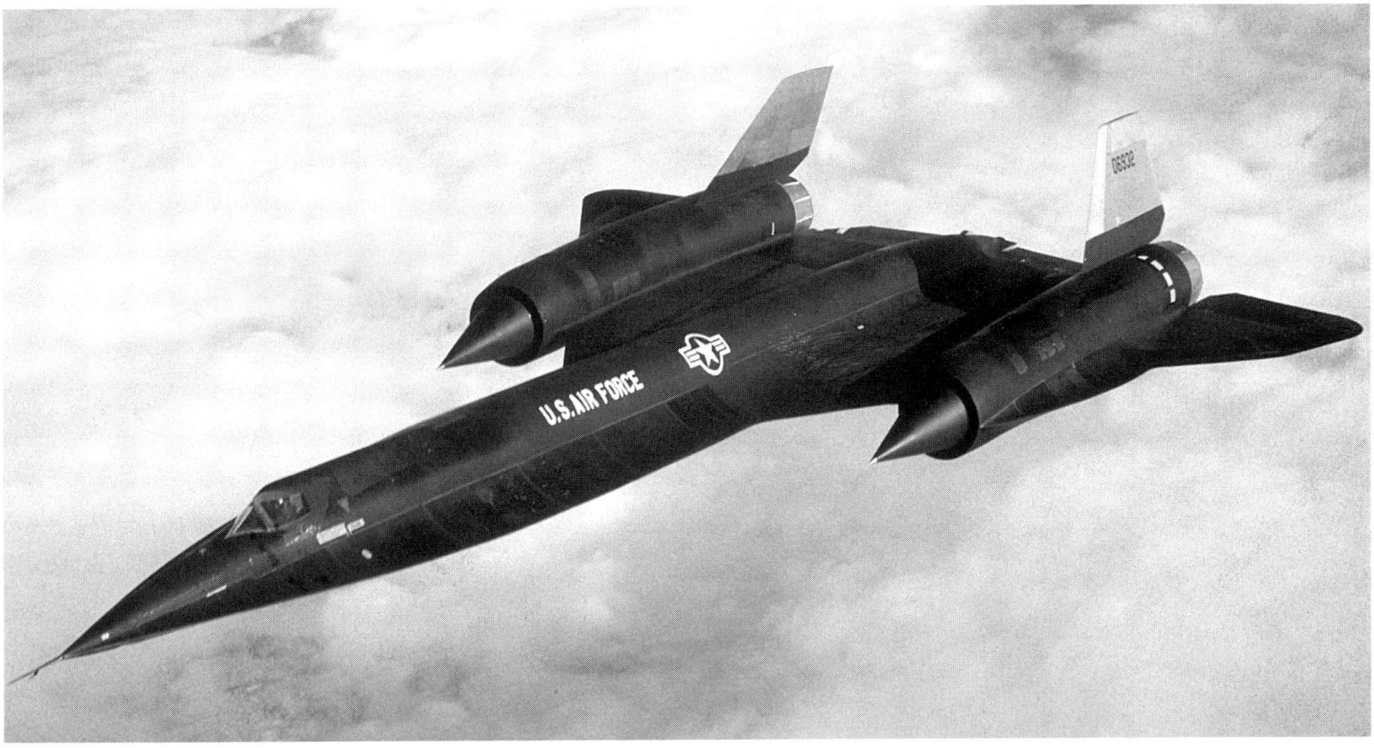
U.S. AIR FORCE
06932

ABOVE: **A-12 number 11 (60-6938) taxis out for take-off from Groom Lake in spring 1963.** Lockheed Martin

There were many successes and some failures in the A-12 flight-test programme. Once they began flying with the J58 engines for which they had been designed, their performance envelopes – altitude, range and speed – were fully opened. The first flight of an all-J58-powered A-12 was on 15 January 1963, some nine months after Lou Schalk had successfully completed the first official flight on A-12 number one.

Oxcart Flight-Test Operations

It was a given that zero public knowledge of the *Oxcart* programme was the chief prerequisite of the upcoming super-secret flight-test operation. The flight-test site had to be far away from populated areas, away from civilian and military air corridors, easily reached by air, with good weather conditions, able to accommodate large numbers of personnel, near an air force base, and have a runway with a minimum length of 8,000ft (2,400m) and be able to support aircraft weighing up to 200,000lb (90,000kg). No such place existed, however. It was soon agreed that, with modest modifications, the former U-2 flight-test site at Groom Lake would be used.

Construction of the *Oxcart* aircraft final assembly, flight-test and operations site at Groom Lake began in September 1960. Work crews were flown from Burbank to Groom Lake, via Las Vegas, in C-47 transports. The modest construction programme included housing for USAF, CIA and Lockheed personnel, underground storage tanks

Lou Schalk (facing the camera) is congratulated by CIA and Lockheed officials following the first official flight of A-12 number one, on 30 April 1962. Lockheed Martin

for JP-4 and JP-7 fuels, and runway modifications. The new 8,500ft (2,600m) runway was completed on 15 November 1960.

The projected delivery date of the first A-12 was 1 August 1961. Since it and subsequent *Oxcart* aeroplanes would have to be delivered by truck and trailer, and to accommodate heavy fuel trucks, 18 miles (30km) of road leading to the site had to be repaved. The US Navy supplied three surplus aircraft hangars – which had to be dismantled, moved and reassembled – and more than 100 surplus housing units to the north side of Groom Lake. Everything was ready in time for the arrival of the first A-12, but this did not happen on 1 August 1961 as had been forecast.

The acquisition and fabrication of titanium alloy had become difficult, which slowed the programme; and the J58 engine was not yet ready. Moreover, since it had been decided to proceed with flight-testing using, as an interim power plant, the Pratt & Whitney J75-P-19W, the A-12's engine nacelles had to be modified to accommodate it. With the J75 engines installed a maximum speed of only Mach 1.6 (1,1200mph or 1,900km/h) at 50,000ft

(15,000m) was contemplated. And these numbers were never exceeded. (Giving some 26,500lb/12,000kg of thrust, the J75-P-19W engine was among the most powerful of the day and was perfect for the aircraft it normally powered, the Republic F-105 Thunderchief and Convair F-106 Delta Dart.)

These delays increased programme costs, and to help alleviate this the CIA reduced its original twelve-plane order to ten. This financial loss to Lockheed was later offset when the USAF ordered three service-test AF-12 aeroplanes and, later, when the CIA ultimately ordered thirty-eight D-21 reconnaissance drones, which required the modification of two A-12s to carry and launch them (see Chapter Four).

The first A-12 – called Article 121 – was finally completed and tested at Burbank during January and February 1962. It was then partially disassembled for transportation to Groom Lake on a specially built trailer. The fuselage alone required the building of a covered crate 105ft (32m) long and 35ft (10.7m) wide. Transportation of this outsized crate for hundreds of miles required that roadside signs and obstacles had to be levelled, trimmed and/or removed. Article 121 departed Burbank after midnight on 26 February 1962 and arrived at the flight-test site two days later.

After the fuselage arrived, its wings and vertical tails were attached and its J75 engines were installed. Numerous and persistent fuel leaks and ways to stop them delayed the first flight of A-12 number one. While some fuel leaks were eliminated many more were not. At speed and altitude the airframe was to tighten up due to metal expansion, which would eliminate all leaks. Therefore it was decided to put only just enough fuel into the A-12 to get it airborne and up to a rendezvous with a Boeing KC-135Q Stratotanker, which would top up its tanks for its continued flight to higher altitudes and faster speeds. This became the standard operating procedure for the lifetime of the *Oxcart* programme.

In the 1940s, 1950s and into the 1960s, the Skunk Works management liked to make sure its aircraft would fly right before dignitaries were on hand: so it was with A-12 number one. On 25 April 1962, Lou Schalk flew Article 121 on an unofficial and unannounced first flight. But he only flew it at about 20ft (6m) above the ground for a distance less than 2 miles (3km). The reason for this relatively strange test 'hop' was that several flying-surface control devices were improperly attached and the aeroplane was literally all over the place, winding up in a cloud of dust on the dry-lake bed. Schalk had done a marvellous job getting it down safely with negligible damage. The devices were properly attached overnight and Article 121 was to fly on the morning of the 26th – on what was to be the unofficial official first flight.

Lou Schalk took off, did not retract the landing gear and began what turned out to be a challenging 40-minute test hop. A number of the triangular-shaped fillets attached to the chines shed off while the aeroplane was in flight. The lost fillets were replaced over the next four days, which meant recovering the chine fillets and reattaching them to the airframe using epoxy resins.

Finally, on 30 April 1962 with various dignitaries on hand to watch, the official first flight was successfully accomplished. The aeroplane took-off after rotating at 170kt (196mph or 315km/h), retracted its landing gear and headed skyward to what became a maximum altitude of 30,000ft (9,000m); Lou Schalk flew it for fifty-nine minutes. It achieved supersonic speed during its second test flight on 2 May 1962, hitting Mach 1.1 (815.6mph or 1,312.6km/h).

By the end of 1962 four more A-12s had arrived at the site including a two-seat trainer, which was designated TA-12 (the prefix 'T' meaning 'Trainer'). By January 1963 Pratt & Whitney had delivered ten J58 engines to the site. The first flight of an A-12 with two J58s installed finally came about on 15 January 1963; Lou Schalk was the pilot, naturally!

As J58-powered A-12s increased their flight-test speeds to between Mach 2.4 and 2.8 (1,780–2,076mph, or 2,864–3,341km/h) the supersonic shockwaves generated by the aircraft began to interfere with airflow patterns into the engines: the resulting unruly airflow could actually blow out the fire in the combustion chamber. To cure this problem, a flat-translating air-inlet spike was employed, which would move as much as 3ft (0.9m) fore-and-aft to control the airflow into the engine properly: extended all the way forward for minimum air; retracted all the way rearward for maximum air. Another serious problem for the J58 engine was the powerful, vacuum cleaner-like suction that it generated while it was running on the ground. Foreign object damage (FOD) became critical and all available FOD-policing measures

> **A-12 Losses**
>
> The first loss of an A-12 occurred on 24 May 1963 when the cockpit airspeed indicator on Article 123 (60-6926) – the third A-12 built and second to fly – became unreliable and seriously incorrect, to the extent that CIA pilot Ken Collins opted to bale out; he ejected safely. The A-12 crashed near Wendover AFB, Utah and, to cover the event up, the press release said that an F-105 jet from Wendover had crashed.
>
> On 9 July 1964 Article 133 (60-6939) crashed while making a landing at Groom Lake. A pitch-control servo device had frozen up, which rolled the A-12 into a wing-down position. This forced Lockheed test pilot Bill Park to eject horizontally at an altitude of only 129ft (39.3m). He hit the ground immediately after the first swing of his parachute, but was not injured.
>
> The third crash of an OXCART aircraft, A-12 number six (Article 126, 60-6929) occurred on 28 December 1965 immediately after it had taken off. This was due to improper wiring of the stability augmentation system, and CIA pilot Mel Vojvodich was forced to eject. He did so safely and was unhurt.
>
> The first pilot to lose his life while flying an A-12 was CIA pilot Walter L. Ray, on 5 January 1967 while performing a training flight on A-12 number five (Article 125, 60-6928); he ejected but did not separate from his seat.

were implemented to stop, or at least, minimize, engine damage during ground manoeuvres. Ramps, taxiways and the runway were constantly policed by workers, and these personnel even had to sweep and vacuum the runway before take-offs.

The first long-range, high-speed flight of an A-12 was on 27 January 1965. The time of the flight was 100 minutes, of which seventy-five were spent at Mach 3.1 (2,300mph or 3,700km/h) or higher. The distance flown was 2,850 miles (4,600km) at altitudes between 75,600–80,000ft (23,000–24,400m).

By this time in the A-12 flight-test programme the aeroplanes were performing well. The J58 engine air inlet, camera, hydraulic, navigation and flight-control systems were all demonstrating reliable operation. But there were still a number of problems. These included ongoing engine air inlet malfunctions, overheating of the electrical wiring, communications equipment problems and difficulties with the electronic countermeasure (ECM) gear. Eventually all of these gremlins were addressed and for the most part cured.

By 20 November 1965 the final validation flights for *Oxcart* deployment were finished. During one of these test flights a blistering maximum speed of Mach 3.29

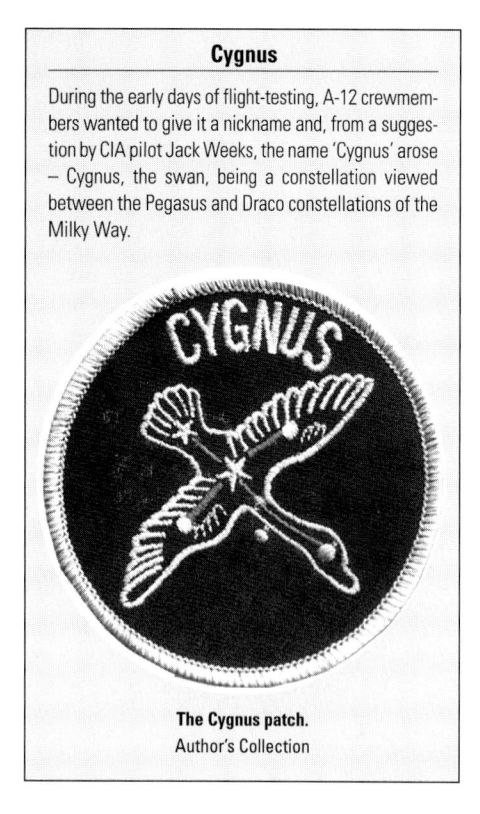

> **Cygnus**
>
> During the early days of flight-testing, A-12 crewmembers wanted to give it a nickname and, from a suggestion by CIA pilot Jack Weeks, the name 'Cygnus' arose – Cygnus, the swan, being a constellation viewed between the Pegasus and Draco constellations of the Milky Way.
>
> **The Cygnus patch.**
> Author's Collection

(2,439mph or 3,926km/h) and a lofty maximum altitude of 90,000ft (27,400m) had been attained with sustained flight time above Mach 3.2 (2,372.5mph or 3,818.5km/h) on the same flight of seventy-four minutes. This was indeed incredible performance: no other manned aeroplane on the planet, except the North American X-15, could surpass them. And the A-12 was turbojet-powered and took off under its own power, whereas the X-15 was rocket-powered and had to be air-launched!

By the end of 1965 the A-12 fleet had completed 1,160 test flights in 1,616 hours; nine hours of this being above Mach 3. In November 1965 the A-12 was ready for operational use, and on the 22nd Kelly Johnson told the head of the US Office of Special Activities (OSA) 'The time has come when the bird should leave its nest.' Thus, three years and seven months after the A-12 had made its first flight, the *Oxcart* was ready for operational use.

A-12 Operations

The first operational A-12 mission was flown some sixty-one months after its first flight, on 31 May 1967, and the last one exactly ten months later, on 31 March 1968. By the end of June 1968, all surviving A-12s, the lone surviving M-21 and the sole TA-12 had been placed into extended storage. It may seem odd that just as A-12 operations had begun in earnest, the *Oxcart* fleet was retired. But this was due in large part to the engine-development problems discussed elsewhere: by the time these were cured, the A-12's follow-on, the SR-71, had reached its Initial Operational Capability. Nonetheless, in just ten short months of A-12 operations and twenty-nine missions flown, the *Oxcart* aircraft performed splendidly, gathering a treasure trove of intelligence over Southeast Asia. And the only serious mishap that occurred came after the last mission had been flown.

The relatively small fleet of A-12 aeroplanes were initially based at the Area 51, and they were operated by the 1129th Special Activities Squadron (SAS), the 'Road Runners'. Their first and only operational deployment, called Operation *Black Shield*, was to Kadena Air Base, Okinawa, which is located between the East China and Philippine Seas south of Japan and came under the operational command of Detachment 1 (Det. 1) of the 1129th SAS. The first *Oxcart* support components were airlifted to Okinawa on 17 May 1967. President Lyndon B. Johnson had formally authorized the joint USAF/CIA Operation *Black Shield* programme and awaited early results.

The first A-12 (Article 131, 60-6937) left Groom Lake on 22 May flown by CIA pilot Mel Vojovodich and arrived at Kadena after a 6hr 6min flight. A second A-12 (Article 127, 60-6930), flown by CIA pilot Jack Layton, arrived on 24 May, followed by a third (Article 129, 60-6932), flown by CIA pilot Jack Weeks, on 27 May 1967. En route, due to a problem with its Inertial Navigation System, Article 129 was forced to make a stopover on Midway Island.

Under the command of Colonel Hugh Slater, Det. 1 was declared operationally ready on 29 May 1967. Operation *Black Shield* began two days later on 31 May with *Oxcart* mission number one: Mel Vojovodich flew a 3hr 39min flight out of Kadena in Article 131 during which he attained Mach 3.1 at 80,000ft (24,000m). On this, the type's first operational mission, his A-12 photographed seventy of the 190 known Surface-to-Air Missile (SAM) sites while he flew over North Vietnam and the Demilitarized Zone (DMZ).

Seven more *Black Shield* missions were flown over North Vietnam between 31 May and 15 August 1967, followed by fifteen more between 15 August and 31 December. Six more missions were flown between 1 January and 31 March 1968, bringing the total to twenty-nine missions. After each *Black Shield* mission the film from the aircraft's cameras was processed at a USAF facility in Japan and the photographs were delivered to Vietnam War commanders within twenty-four hours of the flight.

On 30 October 1967, during an A-12 mission over North Vietnam with CIA pilot Dennis Sullivan at the controls, six SAMs were fired at him, three of which detonated nearby. After the flight, a small piece of metal from one of the SAMs was found protruding from the bottom part of a wing fillet.

On 23 January 1968 North Korean naval vessels and MiG fighters attacked the USS *Pueblo* while it was on an intelligence-gathering mission off the coast of North Korea. One crewman was killed and eleven others were wounded. The ship was boarded and the remaining crew of eighty-two were captured and eventually held prisoner for eleven months. On 26 January, during the early days of what became known as the Pueblo Crisis, the first A-12 mission over North Korea was flown, by CIA pilot Frank Murray.

On 8 March 1968, following its flight from Beale AFB, California the first SR-71A (61-7978) arrived at Kadena AB, which was designated Operating Location 8 or OL-8. It was piloted by USAF Major Buddy L. Brown, with Captain David Jensen as the RSO. By 15 March 1968, three SR-71As had been declared as operational at Kadena, and on 8 May Jack Layton flew the last A-12 *Black Shield* mission, over North Korea.

After the twenty-ninth *Black Shield*, during a post-maintenance functional check flight out of Kadena on 4 June 1968, Jack Weeks and A-12 number eight (60-6932) were lost somewhere in the Philippine Sea. Neither the body nor the aeroplane were ever found; he had been scheduled to return to Groom Lake on the following day. By this time the A-12s were being flown back to Area 51. The last of these, on 9 June 1968, was 60-6930 flown by Denny Sullivan. Det. 1 of the 1129th SAS was also deactivated in June 1968. The last A-12 flight (Article 131, 60-6937), Groom Lake to Palmdale, was flown by Frank Murray. All surviving A-12s were then placed into storage in a large hangar at US Air Force Plant 42, Palmdale. These A-12s were parked nose-to-tail, tail-to-nose, next to the sole TA-12 and the lone surviving M-21.

CHAPTER THREE

Air Defence Fighter

The United States has developed an advanced experimental jet aircraft, the A-11, which has been tested in sustained flight at more than 2,000mph and at altitudes in excess of 70,000ft.

PRESIDENT LYNDON B. JOHNSON

In the early 1960s the best interceptor in service with the USAF was the single-seat F-106A Delta Dart, built by the Convair Division of the General Dynamics Corporation in San Diego, California. First flown on 26 December 1956 – it hit Mach 1.9 at 57,000ft (17,000m) on its very first flight! – the F-106A, also known as Weapon System 201B, or WS-201B, began to enter service in the summer of 1959. This highly sophisticated aeroplane was an all-missile/rocket-armed, all-weather, high-altitude interceptor capable of Mach 2.3 and featuring the advanced Hughes MA-1 radar and missile/rocket fire-control system. It was an advanced version of the Convair F-102 Delta Dagger (WS-201A), powered by a single Pratt & Whitney J75 afterburning turbojet engine. The J75 was an outgrowth of the P&W J57 that powered the F-102, but had more than double its power.

As good as the F-106 was, the USAF was looking for its replacement even during the late 1950s. After a competition between a number of US airframe contractors, it selected the 'Long Range Interceptor, Experimental' (LRI,X) proposal from North American Aviation, which was soon designated the F-108 Rapier, or WS-202A. To be powered by two General Electric J93-GE-3 afterburning turbojet engines producing 30,000lb (14,000kg) thrust, the F-108 was intended to fly long distances at a cruise speed of Mach 3 (2,000mph or 3,200km/h) above 70,000ft (21,000m), to intercept and destroy enemy bomber aircraft. It was to be an all-weather interceptor, incorporating the Hughes pulse-Doppler AN/ASG-18 radar and missile fire-control

A Convair F-106A Delta Dart near Edwards AFB. NASA photo by Tony Landis

AIR DEFENCE FIGHTER

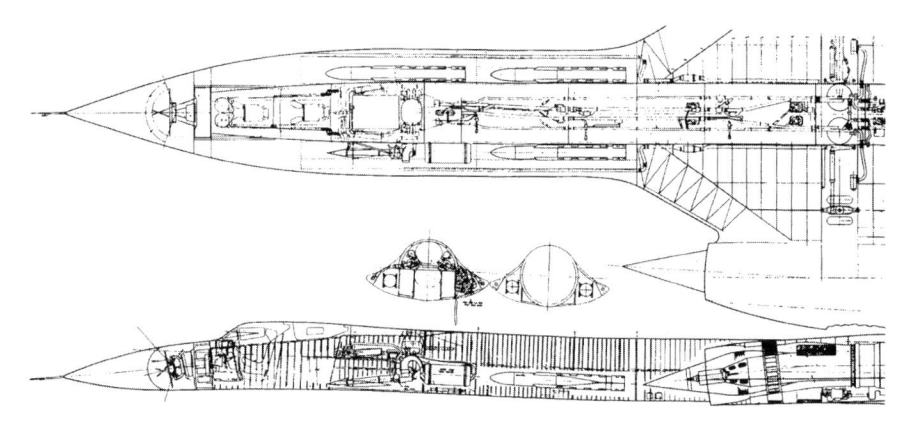

Inboard profile of early AF-12 configuration with three air-to-air missiles and a rotary-action, six-barrel M61 20mm Vulcan cannon. Lockheed Martin

system, and armed with three Hughes AIM-47 (formerly GAR-9) Falcon infra-red-guided (heat-seeking) air-to-air missiles. The first F-108 was expected to fly by mid-1961.

In the meantime another Mach 3 all-missile/rocket-armed interceptor was taking shape, at the Republic Aviation Corporation. This was known as the Republic Model AP-57 and it was to be built under Weapon System 204A as the XF-103. It was to have a unique, highly advanced power plant being developed under Project MX-1787, which incorporated a Wright J67-W-1 turbojet engine coupled to a combined afterburner/ramjet unit, also built by Wright, which was designated RJ55-W-1. In the event, the XF-103 programme was deemed to be a bit too complex and was cancelled on 31 August 1957, just as parts of XF-103 number one were going into their jigs. Moreover, the USAF felt that production F-108s could be available much sooner than production F-103s.

However, on 23 September 1959 the USAF told North American Aviation and its employees that it had cancelled the F-108 Rapier. At this point only a full-scale engineering mock-up had been completed; no production F-108 was under construction. This unexpected and abrupt cancellation was attributed by the USAF to a shortage of funds and other priorities in USAF programming. No technical difficulties were involved with the F-108 and all programme objectives had been met. The USAF said it would continue 'at a reduced level' the development of the Hughes AN/ASG-18 pulse-Doppler radar and fire-control system and the Hughes AIM-47 Falcon AAM which, as far as anyone out-of-the-know knew, had been under development solely for the proposed F-108. Only later did it become clear why this surprising cancellation came about.

The AF-12

As development of the A-12 under the CIA *Oxcart* programme proceeded into 1959, Kelly Johnson was busy creating numerous derivatives from the basic A-12 airframe and power-plant combination, which Lockheed hoped to sell to the USAF Air Defense and Strategic Air Commands. One of these was a highly advanced, long-range, high-altitude, Mach 3-cruise all-weather interceptor known as the AF-12 (the 'AF' prefix meaning Air Defense Fighter), which was to outperform the F-108. After its design was frozen and a full-scale engineering mock-up was built, Lockheed offered the AF-12 to the USAF as a dedicated air-defence fighter. The term 'fighter' for the AF-12 was, strictly speaking, a misnomer, as in its final configuration the aeroplane was instead a dedicated interceptor. In USAF phraseology, a fighter is capable of air-to-air dog-fighting combat with other fighters, whereas an interceptor is specifically deployed to pursue and destroy incoming bombers and is not at all a dog-fighter. Still, in this case, the 'F' for Fighter prefix was used.

The AF-12 version of the A-12 was discussed with Brigadier General Howell M. Estes Jr of the USAF (who would later get a VIP piloting flight in an SR-71B on 5 November 1987) in Washington, DC, on 16 and 17 March 1959. General Estes and Dr Courtlandt Perkins, USAF secretary for research and development, were impressed with the AF-12 proposal and Johnson was directed to have further discussions with General Marvin Demler at Wright-Patterson AFB, Dayton, Ohio. With his engineering and performance data, Johnson convinced the USAF that the AF-12 would be considerably better than the F-108 while carrying the same

The North American F-108 Rapier in its full-scale engineering mock-up stage in mid-1959. North American Aviation via Gene Boswell

46

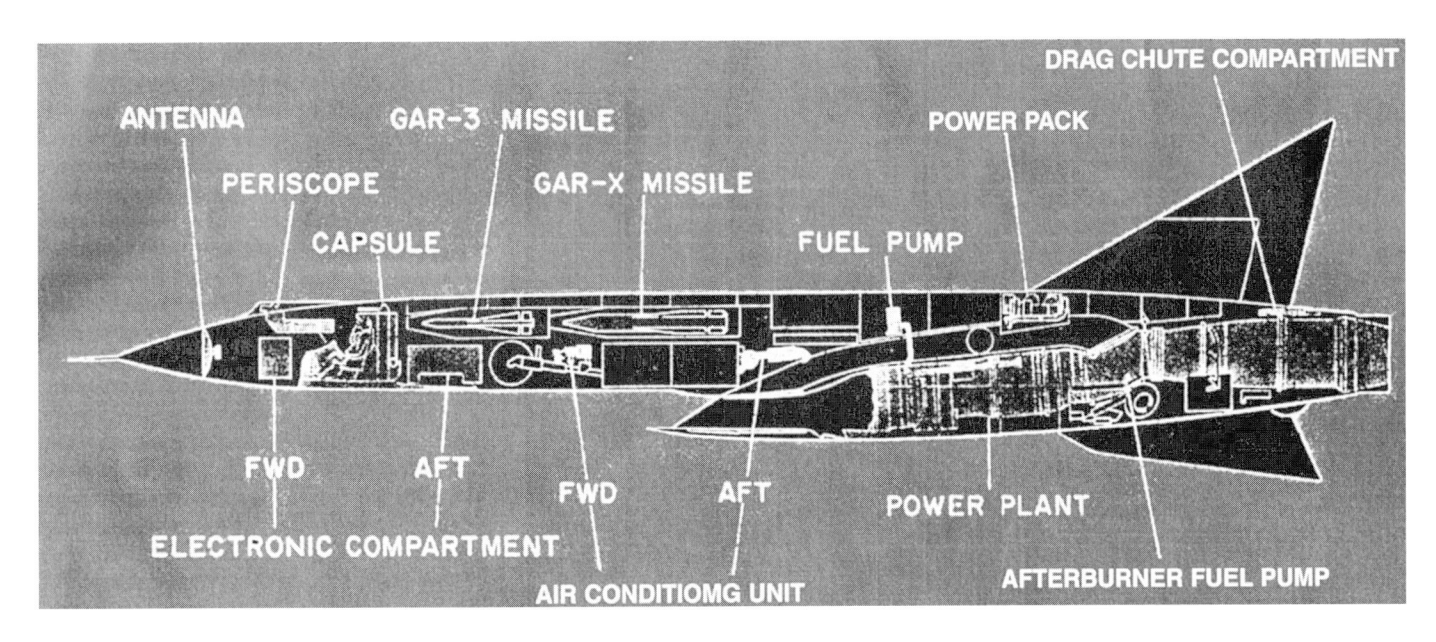

ABOVE: **Inboard profile of Republic XF-103 'Thunderwarrior'.** Cradle of Aviation Museum

The Hughes AIM-47 Falcon (left) eventually evolved into the Hughes AIM-54 Phoenix. Their respective sizes are aptly illustrated by the man standing between them. Hughes Aircraft

complement of three AIM-47 missiles. The USAF immediately created the improved manned interceptor (IMI) programme for the AF-12, right after it cancelled the F-108.

In mid-1960, the USAF secretly ordered three service-test AF-12 aeroplanes from Lockheed ADP under what it called Project *Kedlock*. While the first A-12s were being built it was decided that the seventh, eighth and ninth A-12 airframes would be assembled as the three AF-12s, at first only known as Lockheed factory serial numbers 1001, 1002, and 1003. They later received USAF serial numbers 60-6934, 60-6935 and 60-6936.

The Falcon Missile

The ADP was directed to incorporate the Hughes AN/ASG-18 pulse-Doppler radar and missile fire-control system (including the infra-red sensor package) and Hughes AIM-47 Falcon AAM on the aircraft. The AN/ASG-18 had been in development since late 1957 for use on the F-108. The F-108 was to carry three Hughes GAR-9 Falcon air-to-air radar-guided missiles internally on a rotary launcher (GAR standing for 'Guided Aerial Rocket'). The GAR-9 missile was originally designed to carry a small-yield nuclear warhead, allowing it to destroy a box-type formation of six to nine bombers with one shot. It was at first dubbed the Super Falcon, but when it was decided to use a conventional high-explosive warhead instead, the name Super was dropped and the GAR-9 Falcon was born.

The GAR-9 was to have a range of about 160 miles (260km) with a maximum speed of approximately Mach 7 (5,200mph or 8,400km/h). It measured 10ft 6in (3.2m) in length with a body diameter of 13.2in (33.5cm); gross weight was 800lb (360kg). It was to use a solid-propellant rocket motor built by Lockheed.

To test the AN/ASG-18 and GAR-9 radar and missile systems, Hughes Aircraft, Lockheed ADP and the USAF engaged in a thorough evaluation programme using a modified Convair B-58A Hustler (55-0665, the sixth Hustler built) nicknamed 'Snoopy'. Authorized for modification on 17 October 1958 with a contract from Hughes Aircraft, it was given the AN/ASG-18 radar nose with its 40in-diameter (1m) dish, which in turn called for a long-nose configuration making this B-58 about 7ft (2m) longer than a standard Hustler. Further modifications called for the creation of missile pods with infra-red seekers which were carried ventrally on the belly of 'Snoopy'. These pods (two were built) each housed a single GAR-9 with associated equipment.

Flight testing of the sophisticated radar system came first, beginning in early 1960 over ranges near Edwards AFB, California. But it was not until 25 May 1962 that the first GAR-9 was test-fired. Subsequent test firings were accomplished and by early 1964 the radar and missile systems were deemed suitable for use by the Lockheed interceptor, which by then had been flying for about six months. 'Snoopy' was used for radar/missile tests until February 1964, after which all of its modifications except for its lengthened radome were removed. This particular B-58A, now stripped of its engines and other parts, remains at Edwards where it is parked on the photographic range.

After the tri-service action on 18 September 1962 to re-designate military aircraft and missiles, the GAR prefix was dropped and the prefix AIM ('Air Intercept Missile') put into place. Thus the GAR-9, also now given a new number, became the AIM-47.

AIR DEFENCE FIGHTER

ABOVE: **This is the B-58A (55-665), nicknamed 'Snoopy', that was used to evaluate the Hughes ASG-18 pulse-Doppler radar and missile fire-control system as well as the AIM-47 Falcon.** AFFTC/HO

The number one YF-12A under construction with the F-12B mock-up shown to left. Lockheed Martin

The YF-12A

In September 1962, while the three AF-12s were being manufactured, the Department of Defense decided it wanted to eliminate high-digit numbers and inter-service confusion with the then-current military aircraft designation system. As far as fighters went, designations began anew with F-1. The last fighter in development under the old system was the General Dynamics F-111, so there would be no F-112. By the time the AF-12 was to receive its USAF designation, the new system had reached F-11A for the Grumman F11F-1F Tiger, so the AF-12 received the designation YF-12A (Y for service test, F for fighter, 12 for model, A for version). Thus the Lockheed YF-12A was born.

Working in concert with Hughes Aircraft, Johnson's team of ADP engineers and assembly workers modelled, produced and flew the first AF-12/YF-12A in just under three years. To do this, in part, a successful full-scale engineering mock-up review had been held and completed on 31 May 1963; Lockheed ADP's assigned chief test pilot James D. 'Jim' Eastham had begun writing the YF-12A Flight Manual two months earlier. Then in July 1963 the first YF-12A was trucked from Burbank to Groom Lake

48

AIR DEFENCE FIGHTER

The first YF-12A lands after its first flight on 7 August 1963. Lockheed Martin

BELOW: **The first YF-12A (60-6934) on an early test flight prior to being painted in its later all-black colour scheme.** Lockheed Martin

RIGHT: **YF-12A number two (60-6935) during a functional check flight in mid-1965.** Lockheed Martin

where it underwent final assembly, numerous ground checks – including low-, medium- and high-speed taxi tests – prior to its first flight. Then on 7 August 1963, with Jim Eastham at the controls, the first YF-12A (60-6934) made a successful first flight.

The second YF-12A made its maiden flight on 26 November 1963 and YF-12A number three followed on 13 March 1964; they were flown by, respectively, Lockheed ADP test pilots Lou Schalk and Bob Gilliland. Suddenly, without fanfare, the USAF had a new interceptor that was far superior to any other on earth. And almost no one was aware of its existence! Knowing full well of the matchless capabilities of the YF-12A, USAF officials requested its procurement and production to one day replace the so-called 'ultimate interceptor', the F-106 Delta Dart.

The YF-12A programme was highly classified and its true role could not be put into the public domain. On 29 February 1964 President Lyndon B. Johnson announced the existence not of the YF-12A but of the 'A-11'. This designation was a ploy engineered by Kelly Johnson himself, since the A-11 was not the anti-radar version of *Oxcart*, which became the A-12. So at Johnson's request, President Johnson complied with the designation A-11.

49

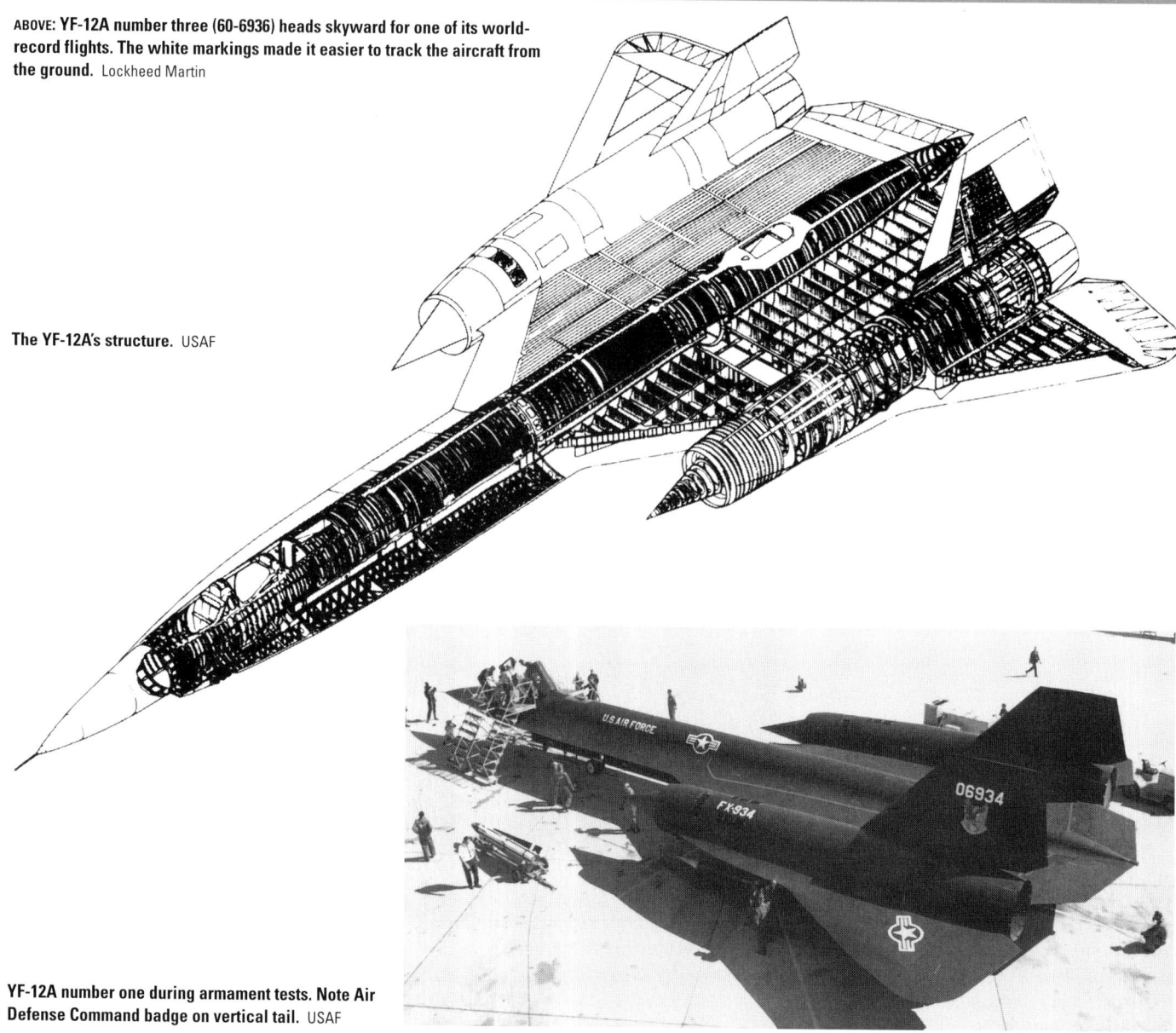

ABOVE: **YF-12A number three (60-6936) heads skyward for one of its world-record flights. The white markings made it easier to track the aircraft from the ground.** Lockheed Martin

The YF-12A's structure. USAF

YF-12A number one during armament tests. Note Air Defense Command badge on vertical tail. USAF

A YF-12A poses (MAIN PIC), having just been equipped with the AIM-47 missile (INSET). USAF

Although very similar in appearance to the A-12, the YF-12A was quite a different aeroplane. It still had the A-12's chines but they were bobbed at the nose for installation of the infra-red eyeballs. Moreover, it was a two-seater, with separate cockpits in tandem. It also had slightly different dimensions, with a length of 101ft (30.78m) and height of 18ft 6in (5.64m), though the same wingspan of 55ft 7in (16.91m); gross weight was 127,000lb (58,000kg).

The YF-12A aircraft was proposed as a weapon system for the USAF Air Defense Command, and weapon system evaluations began on 16 April 1964 when the first AIM-47 ejection test was performed successfully; Jim Eastman was pilot and Ray Scalise served as the Fire Control Officer (FCO). However, it took several years to actually track and launch a radar-guided AIM-47 missile at an airborne target. The missiles were stored in internal missile bays from which they were ejected downward; what proved difficult was firing the missile so that it would fly straight and true, rather than penetrating the launch aircraft between the pilot's and fire control officer's cockpits. Even at low speeds serious problems plagued missile launches. To keep the Falcons away from the YF-12As, Kelly Johnson and his engineers had to develop onboard thruster units, one above each end of the missile, to push the missile downward with adequate and equal force. After the missile had been ejected downward some 40ft (12m) below the aircraft, its rocket motor would then ignite.

The design speed of the YF-12A was achieved on 9 January 1965 when Eastman

AIR DEFENCE FIGHTER

ABOVE: The number one YF-12A lifts off at Edwards AFB. AFFTC/HO

A fine study of YF-12A-1 on the ground. AFFTC/HO

BELOW: The third YF-12A (60-6936) on a test flight near Edwards AFB in mid-1965. Lockheed Martin

AIR DEFENCE FIGHTER

A live AIM-47 Falcon has been uploaded into the forward left-hand missile bay on YF-12A number one. Lockheed Martin

Specification – Lockheed YF-12A	
Crew:	Two: pilot and fire control officer
Power plant:	Two Pratt & Whitney J58 (Model JT11D-20A) bleed bypass turbojet engines; 34,000lb (15,000kg) thrust each
Weights:	Empty 70,000lb (32,000kg); gross 124,000lb (56,000kg)
Dimensions:	Length 101ft 8in (31m); wingspan 55ft 7in (16.98m); wing area 1,795sq ft (166.75sq m); height 18ft 6in (5.67m)
Performance:	Maximum speed in excess of Mach 3.2; maximum range (unrefuelled) 3,000 miles (4,800km); maximum ceiling in excess of 80,000ft (24,000m)
Armament:	Three Hughes AIM-47A Falcon air-to-air radar-guided missiles

flew one of the aircraft to Mach 3.2 for five minutes. Then on 18 March 1965 the first live firing of an AIM-47 from an YF-12A was successfully accomplished; Eastman was again the pilot, with FCO John Archer. Four Hughes Aircraft engineers, working as FCOs, fired service-test AIM-47s at a number of Ryan Q-2C target drones at altitudes ranging from sea level to more than 35,000ft (11,000m), and hit targets more than 140 miles (230km) distant over ocean or over land. On 28 September 1965 an AIM-47 was fired from one of the YF-12As while it flew at Mach 3.2 at an altitude of 75,000ft (23,000m). The target was 36 miles (58km) distant and the missile missed the target by 6 feet (1.8m). But this event proved that an AAM could be successfully launched at more than 2,000mph (3,200km/h). Fired from an YF-12A flying at Mach 3-plus, and accelerating on its own, an AIM-47 sped hypersonically at Mach 7 (5,000mph or 8,400km/h) at the peak of its flight profile.

With the launch problem eliminated, the AN/ASG-18 Doppler radar system and AIM-47A missile performed very well, achieving a success rate of over 90 per cent. Development of this weapon system for the YF-12A led to the successful development of the Hughes/Raytheon AN/AWG-9 radar, fire-control system and AIM-54 Phoenix missile used in the Grumman F-14 Tomcat of today.

The three YF-12As were intended to lead to a production air-defence fighter for the USAF, the F-12B, as related in the next section. The first YF-12A (60-6934) was placed in storage. Then, after the loss of one of the two SR-71B dual-control trainers on 11 January 1969, the aft half of YF-12A number one was mated to the static structural loads test SR-71A to become a flyable aeroplane. This creation became the unique SR-71C (61-7981). The SR-71C, nicknamed 'The Bastard', was fitted with a second, raised, cockpit to serve as a pilot trainer and transition aeroplane to replace the lost SR-71B. It made its first flight on 14 March 1969.

On 24 June 1971, YF-12A number three (60-6936) was lost in a crash east of Edwards AFB. The crash was caused by a fuel line that had ruptured because of metal fatigue, starting a fire in the right engine nacelle. The pilot, Lt Colonel Ronald 'Jack' Layton, and his FCO, Major Billy Curtis, ejected safely without injuries.

F-12B

The F-12B was to be the operational version of the service-test YF-12A, which had passed all of its test phases and proved it would have been an effective weapon system. The USAF Aerospace Defense Command requested an initial production run of ninety-three F-12Bs to serve as dedicated all-weather, all-missile-armed interceptor aircraft with very high speed and high-altitude capabilities. The US Congress allocated $90 million for the programme and the ninety-three F-12Bs for the USAF Aerospace Defense Command (formerly Air Defense Command) were ordered into production on 14 May 1965.

To be armed with four AIM-47 missiles, operated by the AN/ASG-18 radar/fire-control system, the production F-12B was to be capable of intercepting and destroying incoming bombers (at any speed, any altitude) while they were still more than 100 miles (160km) away. As projected, the F-12Bs would have been powered by two 34,000lb (15,000kg) thrust J58 bleed bypass turbojet engines like its sibling, the SR-71. And with this combined thrust rating of 68,000lb (31,000kg), the F-12B was anticipated to top out at Mach 3.5 (2,600mph or 4,200km/h) and 90,000–100,000ft (27,000–30,000m).

Due to the rising costs of what would soon become known as the Vietnam War, however, the new Secretary of Defense Robert S. McNamara and his 'whizz kids' saw it another way. Even though Congress voted three times in three years to appropriate the $90 million to start production of the F-12B, McNamara froze this funding each time, opting instead to fund the less expensive – he said – but also less capable F-106X proposal from the Convair division of the General Dynamics Corporation. On 5 January 1968 the Skunk Works received official USAF notification to terminate all

Specifications – Lockheed F-12B (projected)

Crew:	Two: pilot and fire control officer
Power plant:	Two Pratt & Whitney J58 (Model JT11D-20A) bleed bypass turbojet engines; 34,000lb (15,000kg) thrust each
Weights:	Empty 70,000lb (32,000kg); gross 125,000lb (57,000kg)
Dimensions:	Length 101ft 8in (31m); wingspan 55ft 7in (16.98m); wing area 1,795sq ft (166.75sq m); height 18ft 6in (5.67m)
Performance:	Maximum speed in excess of Mach 3.3 (2,250mph/3,620km/h); maximum range (unrefuelled) 3,000 miles (4,800km); maximum ceiling 100,000ft (30,000m)
Armament:	Three Hughes AIM-47B Falcon air-to-air radar-guided missiles and one six-barrel 20mm M61 Vulcan rotary-action cannon, or four AIM-47B AAMs with no cannon

Missile Ejection Tests and Live Firings

Date	Aeroplane	Comment
16/4/64	YF-12A-1 (60-6935)	First ejection test from forward left-hand missile bay of XAIM-47 Super Falcon AAM
18/3/65	YF-12A-2 (60-6935)	Fired YAIM-47A at Ryan Q-2C drone flying at 40,000ft (12,000m) while flying at Mach 2.2 and 65,000ft (20,000m); target destroyed
19/5/65	YF-12A-2 (60-6935)	Fired YAIM-47A at Ryan Q-2C drone flying at 20,000ft (6,000m) while flying at Mach 2.3 and 65,000ft (20,000m)
28/9/65	YF-12A-1 (60-6934)	Fired YAIM-47A at Ryan Q-2C drone flying at 20,000ft (6,000m) while flying at Mach 3.2 and 75,000ft (23,000m); target destroyed
22/3/66	YF-12A-3 (60-6936)	Fired YAIM-47A at Ryan Q-2C drone flying at 1,500ft (500m) while flying at Mach 3.15 and 74,500ft (23,000m); target destroyed
25/4/66	YF-12A-1 (60-6934)	Fired YAIM-47A at Boeing QB-47 Stratojet flying at 1,500ft (500m) while flying at Mach 3.2 and 75,000ft (23,000m); target destroyed
13/5/66	YF-12A-3 (60-6936)	Fired YAIM-47A at Ryan Q-2C drone flying at 20,000ft (6,000m) while flying at Mach 3.17 and 74,000ft (22,500m); target destroyed
21/9/66	YF-12A-3 (60-6936)	Fired YAIM-47A at Boeing QB-47 Stratojet flying at a very low altitude near sea level while flying at Mach 3.2 and 75,000ft (23,000m); target destroyed

YF-12A Record Flights (All flown on 1 May 1965 in YF-12A-3 60-6936)

Record Flight	Crewmembers
Group III Sustained Altitude (absolute): 80,258ft (24,462.6m)	USAF Colonel Robert Stephens, pilot; USAF Lt Colonel Daniel Andre, FCO
15/25km (9.3/15.5-mile) closed circuit course: 2,070.102mph (3,331.5km/h)	USAF Robert Stephens, pilot; USAF Lt Colonel Daniel Andre, FCO
500km (310.7-mile) closed circuit course: 1,643.042mph (2,644.2km/h)	USAF Major Walter Daniel, pilot; USAF Major Noel Warner, FCO
1,000km (621.4-mile) closed circuit course: 1,688.89mph (2,718km/h)	USAF Major Walter Daniel, pilot; USAF Capt James Cooney, FCO

of its YF-12A/F-12B operations. This was followed by the order to destroy all tooling for the YF-12A.

The Convair Division of the General Dynamics Corporation, based in San Diego, California had earlier proposed this advanced version of its already highly respected F-106A Delta Dart, which was arguably the best all-weather, all-missile/rocket-armed interceptor of its day. The proposed single-seat F-106C, as the F-106X was ultimately designated, was to be powered by a single 32,500lb (14,700kg) thrust Pratt & Whitney JT4B-22, a highly advanced version of the J75, giving the 'C' model its projected Mach 3 dash speeds. Additional high-speed aerodynamic stability and control was to be achieved by the use of canard foreplanes.

What was really going on, however, was that McNamara had been favouring the Tactical Fighter, Experimental (TFX) programme whereby the General Dynamics F-111A and F-111B was to suit both the USAF and US Navy. These aircraft had made their first flights on 21 December 1964 and 18 May 1965, respectively. Aerospace Defense Command wanted to buy 350 F-106Cs but, to its dismay, on 23 September 1968 this programme was also cancelled. Thus, there would be no F-12Bs and no F-106Cs, but plenty of F-111s.

One capability of the proposed F-12B was that of intercepting incoming nuclear warheads from Intercontinental Ballistic Missiles. This little-known concept was actually tested, and the YF-12A's AN/ASG-18 radar did in fact lock on to Boeing LGM-30 Minuteman ICBMs launched from Vandenberg AFB, California on several occasions. No missiles were actually fired at these friendly targets, however.

F-12B Operations (Projected)

It is now 15 May 1970 and the 318th Fighter Interceptor Squadron (FIS) of the USAF Aerospace Defense Command 325th Fighter Wing (FW) based at McChord AFB near Tacoma, Washington, has just scrambled four of its twenty-four Lockheed F-12B aircraft to intercept eight large and unknown radar contacts approaching from the northeast, over northern Canada.

Each one of these four all-weather interceptors is armed with a single M61 Vulcan 20mm cannon while carrying three Hughes AIM-47B Super Falcon radar-guided air-to-air missiles. In association with the Semi-Automatic Ground Environment (SAGE) system of the North American Aerospace Defense (NORAD) Command and their onboard Hughes AN/ASG-18 pulse-Doppler radar and missile fire-control systems, they will soon acquire these targets with their own radar systems. Then, once identified as friend or foe, they will either be directed to fire upon the targets or to break off and to return to base.

The foregoing is of course fictitious, but it pretty much explains how an operational F-12B air-defence scenario might have gone. As a dedicated weapon system the F-12B was to be the fastest-flying, highest-flying and longest-ranged interceptor ever built. But this was not to be for its production was not proceeded with. But, as one high-ranking USAF Aerospace Defense Command officer said, 'It was the best interceptor that we *never* built.'

CHAPTER FOUR

Piggyback Peepers: M-21 'Mother' and D-21 'Daughter'

The most sensitive project during my years at the Skunk Works [was the Tagboard project] fewer than one hundred people were involved or knew about it.

BEN RICH

Some two years and five months after Francis Gary Powers had been shot down while overflying the Soviet Union in a Lockheed U-2C on 1 May 1960, and some four years, seven months before the first A-12 mission of Operation *Black Shield* was flown on 31 May 1967, the CIA went to Lockheed ADP with its plan to field an unmanned strategic reconnaissance drone. The drone was to be carried piggyback and air-launched from a centreline pylon mounted atop the aft section of an A-12, fly its mission over enemy territory, then return to have its reconnaissance payload recovered in friendly territory after parachute descent. The drone was then to self-destruct. The projected speed and altitude performance of the drone was to be at least equal to that of the A-12. The reason for having such a drone was that if it was shot down there would be no pilot to interrogate or to hang out to dry in front of God and the World, as had happened to Powers.

On 10 October 1962 Lockheed ADP received authorization from the CIA and USAF to study the drone idea: two modified A-12 aircraft would be used as carrier aircraft. Since the prefix Q denotes 'Drone', the reconnaissance drone was given what became an interim designation of Q-12 under Project *Tagboard*. Lockheed intended to power the drone with a ramjet engine, and at first, to save development time and money, the ADP studied and proposed the use of a ramjet-powered QF-104: this, however, was not favoured by the CIA and was soon rejected. At the time, the Marquardt RJ43 ramjet was the best such engine available. Lockheed ADP had previous knowledge of the Marquardt engines as a number of them had previously been thoroughly tested on the Lockheed X-7 and other unpiloted aircraft. Moreover, the RJ43 was the primary engine in the Boeing IM-99 BOMARC surface-to-air missile. Therefore, the ADP selected the type as the Q-12's intended power plant.

Eventually Lockheed ADP came up with a completely new design for its Q-12, based in part upon its existing A-12 airframe and radar cross-section technologies; on 20 March 1963 Lockheed received a CIA letter contract for the manufacture of the Q-12. Two A-12 aeroplanes, manufacturer numbers 134 (60-6940) and 135 (60-6941), were modified for the Q-12 mission requirement. To do this, a second cockpit was added for the launch control officer (LCO) and carry/launch pylons were fitted, with the launch controls (electrical wiring, fuel supply, pneumatics, and so on) being built into the pylons.

The D-21 mock-up.
Lockheed Martin

THIS PAGE:
LEFT: **The Marquardt RJ43 ramjet engine as first installed in the first D-21.** Lockheed Martin

BELOW: **D-21 test fit to M-21 number one.** Lockheed Martin

OPPOSITE PAGE:
TOP: **The first D-21.** Lockheed Martin

BOTTOM: **The first M-21 with a mounted D-21 at Groom Lake in late 1964.** Lockheed Martin

PIGGYBACK PEEPERS: M-21 'MOTHER' AND D-21 'DAUGHTER'

ABOVE: **Close-up view of D-21 mounted to its pylon atop an M-21.** Lockheed Martin

BELOW: **A rare view of the second M-21 number two (60-6941) with a D-21, just prior to its loss.** Lockheed Martin

PIGGYBACK PEEPERS: M-21 'MOTHER' AND D-21 'DAUGHTER'

To avoid confusion with the A-12, AF-12 (later YF-12) and upcoming R-12/RB-12 (later RS-71/SR-71) designations the drones and the carrier aeroplanes were given their own designations. To get away from the number 12, it was reversed to 21, and to further emphasize the differences, the carrier aircraft was designated M-21 ('M' meaning 'Mother') and the Q-12 drone was redesignated D-21 (the prefix 'D' meaning 'Daughter', not 'Drone').

Project *Tagboard*

There were no dedicated operations *per se* for the M-21 and D-21, but these unique aircraft did complete a series of flight-test sorties. The first of these, a functional check flight (FCF) of the first M-21 with a D-21 mounted for the first time, was flown on 22 December 1964 at Groom Lake. Lockheed ADP's test pilot and chief test pilot on the M-21/D-21 programme, William M. 'Bill' Park, flew the mission with Ray Torick serving as the LCO, in this case just to monitor the D-21's systems, as there would be no launch. This test of the M-21/D-21 combination went very well indeed, and moved the *Tagboard* programme closer to reality. Ironically, on that very same day, the first SR-71A made its first flight at Palmdale. Moving to and fro, Kelly Johnson attended both events.

TOP: **The first M-21 (60-6940) on its first flight with a D-21 attached.** Lockheed Martin

ABOVE: **The gross take-off weight of an M-21 with a D-21 attached was about 125,000lb (56,700kg).** Lockheed Martin

59

ABOVE: **The D-21 mission profile called for a maximum speed of at least Mach 3.5 (2,595mph or 4,176.5km/h) above 90,000ft (27,000m).** Lockheed Martin

Close-up view of a D-21 mounted on an M-21. Lockheed Martin

Air-launching a relatively large aircraft from the back of another while they were travelling at a very high speed was 'risky business' in the truest sense of that phrase. In fact, it had never been done before. Several more M-21/D-21 FCF tests were flown before the go-ahead for the first aerial launch of a D-21 was given, but on 4 March 1966 it was. On the morning of 5 March, M-21 number one (60-6940) lifted off with D-21 number three (503) attached to her back. Bill Park was pilot and the LCO was Keith Beswick.

Park and Beswick rode their rather strange machines to a US Navy missile test range over the Pacific Ocean. The ensuing launch was a success and the D-21 flew some 120 miles (190km) before its telemetry was lost. The second successful test launch came about on 27 April 1966. This time Ray Torick was the LCO for pilot Bill Park and the D-21 (number 506) flew

ABOVE: **The M-21 was powered by two 34,000lb thrust J58 engines while the D-21 was driven by a single 1,500lb thrust ramjet engine.** Lockheed Martin

An F-104 chase plane with the M-21 and D-21 on their first flight together. Lockheed Martin

1,200nm (2,200km) and hit a top speed of Mach 3.3. The third successful test launch was held on 16 June 1966 with Park as pilot and Beswick as LCO. This D-21 (number 505) flew 1,600nm (2,960km) and made eight pre-programmed course corrections. A fourth test launch was scheduled for 30 July 1966, but this time the second M-21 (60-6941) would be used with D-21 number four (504).

As before, the M-21 lifted off from Groom Lake and headed westward out over the Pacific Ocean. Bill Park was again the pilot and Ray Torick was LCO for the second time. Once on station at altitude and while flying at Mach 3.25 (2,400mph or 3,900km/h) – the highest launch speed yet attempted – the D-21 was released by Torick. As soon as the D-21 began to lift away from its pylon, according to the crew of M-21 number one, which was flying 'chase', it immediately made contact with the M-21. After contact the M-21 was seen to pitch up and then its nose section broke away. Park and Torick both ejected and landed in the ocean, some 150 miles (240km) off the coast of California. However, by the time the rescue helicopter reached them about an hour later, Torick was dead: he had prematurely opened his helmet, and then drowned as water rushed in and filled his flight suit. Park was safely rescued.

This unfortunate loss of a loyal flight-test engineer caused an agonizing reappraisal of the *Tagboard* programme, and put the M-21/D-21 in a most unwanted spotlight.

PIGGYBACK PEEPERS: M-21 'MOTHER' AND D-21 'DAUGHTER'

Senior Bowl

After the tragic loss of long-time Lockheed employee Ray Torick and M-21 number two, it was decided that D-21 launches from M-21s were too dangerous to continue. The M-21/D-21 programme was cancelled and the sole surviving M-21 was removed from flight status – there would be no further piggyback missions.

But the CIA wanted to continue D-21 operations, and to do this two specially modified Boeing B-52H Stratofortress bombers were secretly obtained from the USAF Strategic Air Command. These were modified to carry two D-21Bs, one under either wing mounted on pylons between the inboard engine nacelles and the fuselage. This B-52H/D-21B operation became known as *Senior Bowl*. The B-52H was the final version of the Stratofortress built and was powered by eight 17,000lb (7,700kg) thrust Pratt & Whitney TF33-P-3 (or P-103) turbofan engines.

The sixth and subsequent production D-21s would be built as the D-21B model and the earlier D-21s were brought up to D-21B standard. The two *Senior Bowl* B-52Hs were assigned to 'A' Flight of the 4200th Test Wing's 4200th Test Squadron (TS) at Beale AFB, which was established on 1 January 1967. The 4200th TS, although this is undocumented, may have been the 4200th Air/Support Squadron (A/SS).

There were several B-52H/D-21B FCF missions before any operational launches were authorized. Then, from 9 November 1969 to 20 March 1971, four operational D-21B launches were made from the B-52Hs. The D-21 programme officially ended on 8 July 1971 when the *Senior Bowl* programme was terminated.

The seventh D-21 reconnaissance drone being test-fitted to a pylon used by the B-52H in the *Senior Bowl* programme. Lockheed Martin

The first D-21, with a booster rocket, mounted to a B-52H. Lockheed Martin

62

PIGGYBACK PEEPERS: M-21 'MOTHER' AND D-21 'DAUGHTER'

ABOVE: **A B-52H carrying two D-21s.** Lockheed Martin

The view from above of a D-21 immediately after being dropped from a B-52H. Lockheed Martin

BELOW: **Booster ignition.** Lockheed Martin

Specification – D-21B	
Power plant:	One 1,500lb (680kg) thrust Marquardt RJ43-MA-11 ramjet engine
Dimensions:	Length 42ft 10in (12.83m); height 7ft ¼in (2.14m); wingspan 19ft ¼in (5.79m); wing area n/k
Weights:	Empty n/k; gross 11,000lb (5,000kg)
Performance:	Maximum speed Mach 3.35; cruise speed Mach 3.25 at 80,000–95,000ft (24,000–29,000m); ceiling 95,000ft (29,000m); maximum range 3,000nm (4,800km); 2,969nm (4,778km) was the maximum actually flown

Specification – M-21	
Power plant:	Two afterburning 34,000lb (15,400kg) thrust Pratt & Whitney J58 bleed bypass turbojet engines
Weights:	Empty n/k; gross 125,000lb (57,000kg)
Dimensions:	Length 102ft 3in (31.18m); height 18ft 6in (5.67m); wingspan 55ft 7in (16.98m); wing area 1,795sq ft (166.75sq m)
Performance:	Maximum speed Mach 3.2+; ceiling 95,000ft (29,000m); maximum range 3,000 miles (4,800km)

D-21 Production

A/C	Lockheed Build Number	Comment
D-21	501	Updated to D-21B; erroneously ejected from port pylon on B-52H on 28/9/67
D-21	502	Updated to D-21B; stored at DM AFB ARMARC
D-21	503	Test launched 5/3/66 by LCO Keith Beswick; flew 120m (190km); Bill Park was pilot; first *Tagboard* launch mission
D-21	504	Launched 30/7/66 from M-21 number two (60-6941) by LCO Ray Torick over the Pacific Ocean; it collided with M-21 which caused the M-21 to crash; pilot Bill Park and LCO Ray Torick ejected safely but Torick drowned when he removed his helmet too soon; last *Tagboard* mission; M-21/D-21 programme cancelled due to Torick's death
D-21	505	Launched 16/6/66 from M-21 number one (60-6940) by LCO Keith Beswick; flew 1,600nm (2,960km); pilot was Bill Park
D-21	506	Launched 27/4/66 by LCO Ray Torick; flew 1,200nm (1,900km); pilot was Bill Park
D-21B	507	Launched 6/11/67 from B-52H; flew 134nm (248km); first *Senior Bowl* mission
D-21B	508	Launched 19/1/68 from B-52H; flew 260nm (480km)
D-21B	509	Launched 2/12/67 from B-52H; flew 1,430nm (2,650km)
D-21B	510	Stored at DM AFB AMARC; now mounted atop sole surviving M-21 (60-6940) at the Museum of Flight in Seattle, Washington
D-21B	511	Launched 30/4/68 from B-52H; flew 150nm (280km)
D-21B	512	Launched 16/6/68 from B-52H; flew 2,850nm (5,300km)
D-21B	513	Stored by NASA-Dryden FRC at Edwards AFB, California
D-21B	514	Launched 1/7/68 from B-52H; flew 80nm (150km)
D-21B	515	Launched 15/12/68 from B-52H; flew 2,953nm (5,469km)
D-21B	516	Launched 28/8/68 from B-52H; flew 78nm (145km)
D-21B	517	Launched 9/11/69 from B-52H; first operational mission
D-21B	518	Launched 11/2/69 from B-52H; flew 161nm (298km)
D-21B	519	Launched 10/5/69 from B-52H; flew 2,972nm (5,504km)
D-21B	520	Launched 10/7/69 from B-52H; flew 2,937nm (5,439km)
D-21B	521	Launched 20/2/70 from B-52H; flew 2,969nm (5,499km)
D-21B	522	Stored at DM AFB AMARC
D-21B	523	Launched 16/12/70 from B-52H; second operational mission
D-21B	524	US Air Force Museum, Dayton, Ohio
D-21B	525	Blackbird Air Park, Palmdale, California
D-21B	526	Launched 4/3/71 from B-52H; third operational mission
D-21B	527	Launched 20/3/71 from B-52H – fourth and last operational mission
D-21B	528	Stored at US Air Force Museum, Dayton, Ohio
D-21B	529	Stored by NASA-Dryden FRC, Edwards AFB, California
D-21B	530	Displayed at DM AFB, Arizona
D-21B	531	Stored at DM AFB AMARC
D-21B	532	Stored at DM AFB AMARC
D-21B	533	Pima Air Museum, Arizona
D-21B	534	Stored at DM AFB AMARC
D-21B	535	No data
D-21B	536	Stored at DM AFB AMARC
D-21B	537	Stored by NASA-Dryden FRC, Edwards AFB, California
D-21B	538	Museum of Aviation – Robins AFB, Georgia

NB: DM AFB AMARC – Davis-Monthan Air Force Base Aerospace Maintenance and Regeneration Center

ABOVE: **The first M-21 'Mother' (60-6940) is shown carrying a D-21 'Daughter' on its back for the first time on 22 December 1964. This M-21 made eighty flights before it was placed into storage. There it remained until it was donated to the Museum of Flight in Seattle, Washington, where it can be seen today – complete with a D-21 mounted on its back.** Lockheed Martin

Another view of M-21 number one with a D-21, showing its size relative to the Blackbird. The number two M-21 (60-6941) was lost in a crash on 30 July 1966, during its ninety-fifth flight, which killed LCO Ray Torick. Lockheed Martin

BELOW: **A Boeing B-52H Stratofortress (61-0021) carrying a pair of D-21Bs on its two inboard wing pylons during the** *Senior Bowl* **programme in mid-1965. The B-52 was no stranger in the carriage of heavy loads under its wings (witness the NASA B-52A that carried the 56,000lb X-15A-2 under its right-hand wing).** Lockheed Martin

ABOVE LEFT: **The YF-12A instrument panel was not as complex as one might expect of such a sophisticated aircraft.** Lockheed Martin

ABOVE: **A good view of an YF-12A on the ground. The position of the infra-red 'eye balls' is noteworthy.** (LMSW)

LEFT: **An SR-71A (61-7966) approaches Beale AFB in central California.** Lockheed Martin

BELOW: **Looking like something from another world even today, some forty years after its debut in December 1964, this sleek SR-71A strikes a beautiful pose while parked on the ramp at the DFRC facility at Edwards AFB.** NASA

ABOVE: A-12 number one (60-6924) during its pre-flight J58 engine run-up at Groom dry lake. Subsequent to this, some nine months after it had first flown, the first A-12 finally flew with its design engine, a P&W J58 housed in the left-hand nacelle only, on 31 January 1963. *Lockheed Martin*

The sole A-12 pilot trainer and transition aeroplane (60-6927), nicknamed the 'Titanium Goose', prepares for take-off in late 1963. On this occasion, instead of a student pilot being seated in the front cockpit, it was none other than Kelly Johnson himself. *Lockheed Martin*

ABOVE: The fifth production A-12 (60-6928) taxis back to the flight line. During its 202nd flight on 5 January 1967 things went wrong and pilot Walter J. Ray was forced to eject. He did not separate from his ejection seat, however, and was killed. *Lockheed Martin*

A-12 number 10 (60-6933) sits outside its hanger. Between 27 November 1963 and August 1965 it successfully completed 217 flights; it now resides at the San Diego Aerospace Museum in California. *Lockheed Martin*

ABOVE: The flight line at Groom Lake was crowded during this photo opportunity with ten of the fifteen A-12s built. The 'Titanium Goose' is parked in the second position. Lockheed Martin

BELOW: A poor-quality but rare photograph of the first YF-12A (60-6934) during its first flight on 7 August 1963. Its aft section and wings were later mated with the forward section of the SR-71A static test airframe to create the unique SR-71C. Lockheed Martin

RIGHT: The Lockheed Skunk Works holds the distinction of creating the world's first double- and triplesonic turbojet-powered aeroplanes: the F-104 Starfighter and the Blackbird. Here a NASA F-104N (811) and YF-12A number two (60-6935) fly together near Edwards AFB in 1966. NASA

ABOVE: Here the YF-12C/SR-71C banks west toward the setting sun during its first flight on 14 March 1969. The YF-12 aft end, with ventral fins, and the SR-71 forward end, with chines running to the apex of it nose, are clearly visible. NASA

LEFT: This is the fictitious 'YF-12C' with a phoney USAF serial number (60-6937). It was in fact the sole SR-71C (61-7981), which had been created by mating the aft section and wings of the number one YF-12A with the forward section of the SR-71A static test airframe. Due to the unusual nature of its creation it was nicknamed 'The Bastard'. NASA

ABOVE: An SR-71A (61-7955) flies in formation with its subsonic sibling, the U-2-based TR-1A. The TR-1A, the first example of which made its first flight on 1 August 1981, piloted by Ken Weir, was redesignated U-2R in 1992. Today, powered by a lighter 17,000lb thrust General Electric F118-GE-101 turbofan engine, and with other modifications, the U-2R is now the U-2S. The last U-2R was converted to U-2S standard in 1999. *Lockheed Martin*

ABOVE RIGHT: With Skunk Works test pilot Bill Weaver at the controls and Daniel Andre serving as RSO, the sixth production SR-71A lifts off from Palmdale for its first flight on 17 August 1965. It last flew on 24 January 1985. *Lockheed Martin*

BELOW: Afterburners lit, shock diamonds visible, an SR-71A heads for its operating altitude of about 90,000ft in 1980. In its final form the P&W J58 engine produced almost 40,000lb thrust, which gave the 170,000lb SR-71 about 80,000lb total thrust and a maximum speed approaching Mach 3.3. *Lockheed Martin*

Blackbird number six (61-7955), retained by Lockheed to serve as company flight-test aircraft, flew a total of 1,993.7 flying hours before it was retired. It now resides at the AFFTC Museum at Edwards AFB. *Lockheed Martin*

A Pratt & Whitney J58 engine on display next to SR-71A (61-7976) at Blackbird Air Park, Palmdale, California. Paul R. Kucher IV Collection

BELOW: One of the two NASA-operated SR-71A Blackbirds taxis toward the camera at DFRC in 1992. If we did not know these aircraft existed when they were flying, just how many UFO sightings would they have generated when seen from this angle? NASA

RIGHT: A fine in-flight study of an SR-71A astern a KC-135Q tanker. Lockheed Martin

BELOW: The twenty-fifth production SR-71A (61-7976) is freeze-framed during its first flight in May 1967 with Bob Gilliland at the helm and Steve Belgau serving as RSO. It was this SR-71A that flew the first Blackbird mission on 9 March 1968 out of Kadena AB, Okinawa. The pilot on that occasion was Major Jerome F. O'Malley and the RSO was Captain Edward D. Payne. Lockheed Martin

ABOVE: **The SR-71A Blackbird looks ominous from any angle. For nearly twenty-five years it did its job, and did it well. And though it was fired upon hundreds of times it was never hit by enemy fire.** Lockheed Martin

A Blackbird at Beale AFB with nine pilot/RSO crewmember pairs all suited up for a public relations photograph. One has to wonder how these men could stand being confined within their cumbersome 'space suits' for the long-duration missions, of which so many were flown. Lockheed Martin

BELOW: **Ten SR-71As and the lone surviving SR-71B (61-7956) are shown here at Beale AFB in mid-1968. The other SR-71B (61-7957) crashed to destruction on 11 January 1968.**
Lockheed Martin

ABOVE: **The sixth production SR-71A (61-7955) returns to Palmdale after its first flight on 17 August 1965. This was a dedicated SR-71 test aircraft operated primarily by Air Force Logistics Command out of Palmdale. The Skunk Works logo on its tail is noteworthy.** Lockheed Martin

RIGHT: **Another PR photo showing a pair of Blackbirds and their respective crew members.** Lockheed Martin

If the Blackbird did not already look sinister enough, this shot of two SR-71s at Beale AFB in the early morning fog of central California's San Joaquin Valley really makes them look spooky, giving credence to their venomous 'Habu' nickname. Lockheed Martin

BELOW: **This close-up view of the seventeenth production SR-71A (61-7968) clearly shows the exotic lines of the famed Blackbird. Even now, some forty years after the flight of an SR-71, no other turbojet-powered aeroplane in the world has flown faster or higher.** Lockheed Martin

CHAPTER FIVE

SR-71: Leader of the Pack

I would like to announce the successful development of a new strategic manned aircraft system, which will be employed by the Strategic Air Command. This system employs the new SR-71 aircraft, and provides a long- range advanced strategic reconnaissance plane for military use, capable of worldwide reconnaissance for military operations. The Joint Chiefs of Staff, when reviewing the [North American] RS-70, emphasized the importance of the strategic reconnaissance mission. The SR-71 aircraft reconnaissance system is the most advanced in the world. The aircraft will fly at more than three times the speed of sound. It will operate at altitudes in excess of 80,000ft.

PRESIDENT LYNDON B. JOHNSON
24 July 1964

SR-71 production at Burbank. Lockheed Martin

When President Johnson announced the existence of the Lockheed SR-71 some five months before it flew, the US Department of Defense, Lockheed and the USAF were more than just a little dismayed. Not because of its early revealing to the public, but because of its name: when the aeroplane was ordered into production, it had been called the RS-71, which remained its official designation until the time of President Johnson's announcement. But he had called it the SR-71 and something had to be done, immediately, so as not to lay ridicule upon the mispronunciation error by the President of the United States. So, before the aircraft had even flown, the Department of Defense, Lockheed and the

SR-71: LEADER OF THE PACK

LEFT: **The premier SR-71A (61-7950) being trucked to Palmdale in early December 1964.** Lockheed Martin

ABOVE: **The first SR-71A is shown here prior to its first flight on 22 December 1964.** Lockheed Martin

Looking more like something from outer space than from planet earth, an SR-71A is silhouetted in this worm's eye view. Lockheed Martin

SR-71: LEADER OF THE PACK

TOP: Two SR-71As pose in the customary morning San Jacquin Valley fog at Beale AFB. Lockheed Martin

ABOVE: An SR-71A banks away from a tanker immediately after being refuelled. Note the fuel streaks atop the inner wings. Lockheed Martin

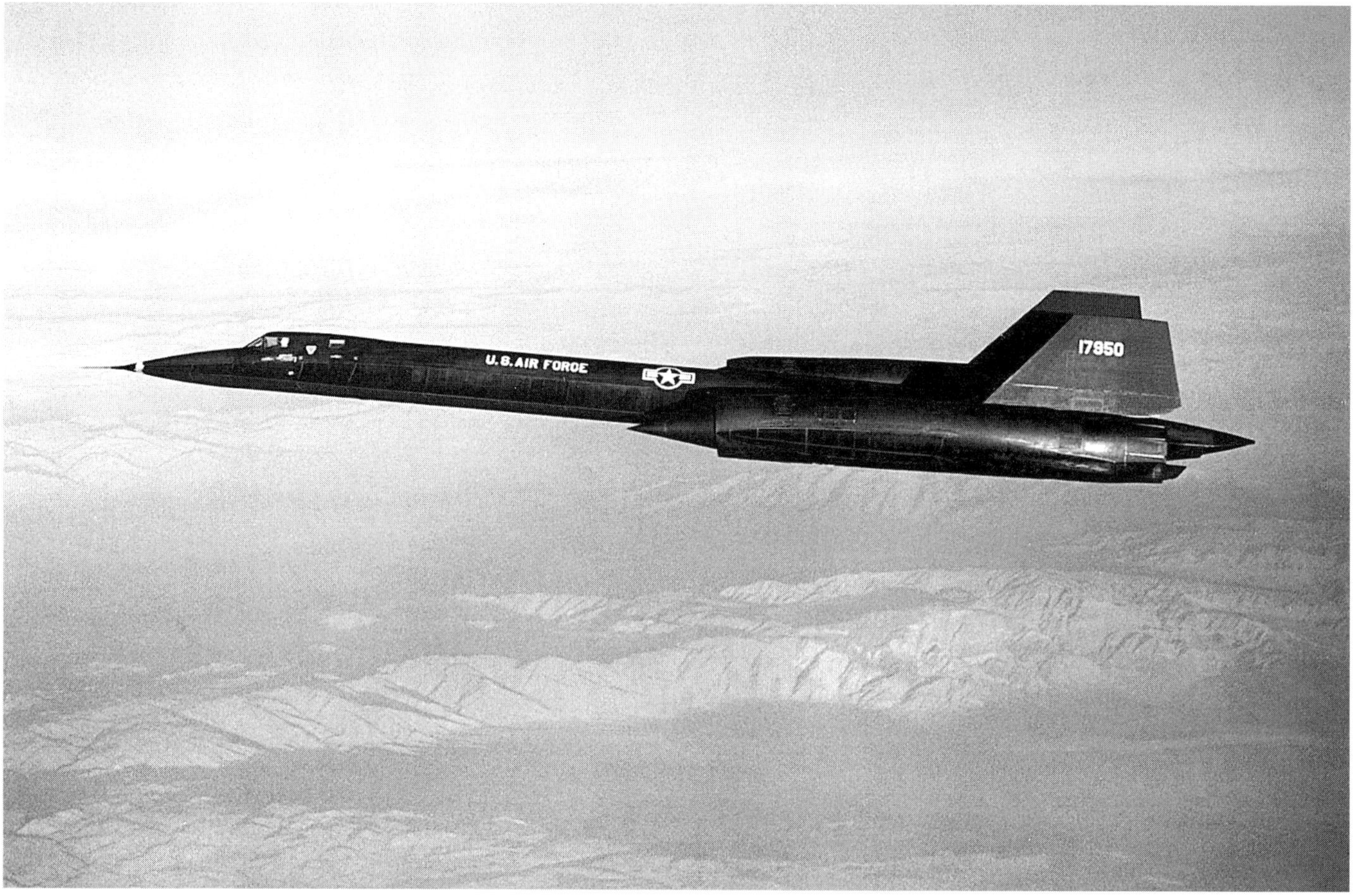
U.S. AIR FORCE
17950

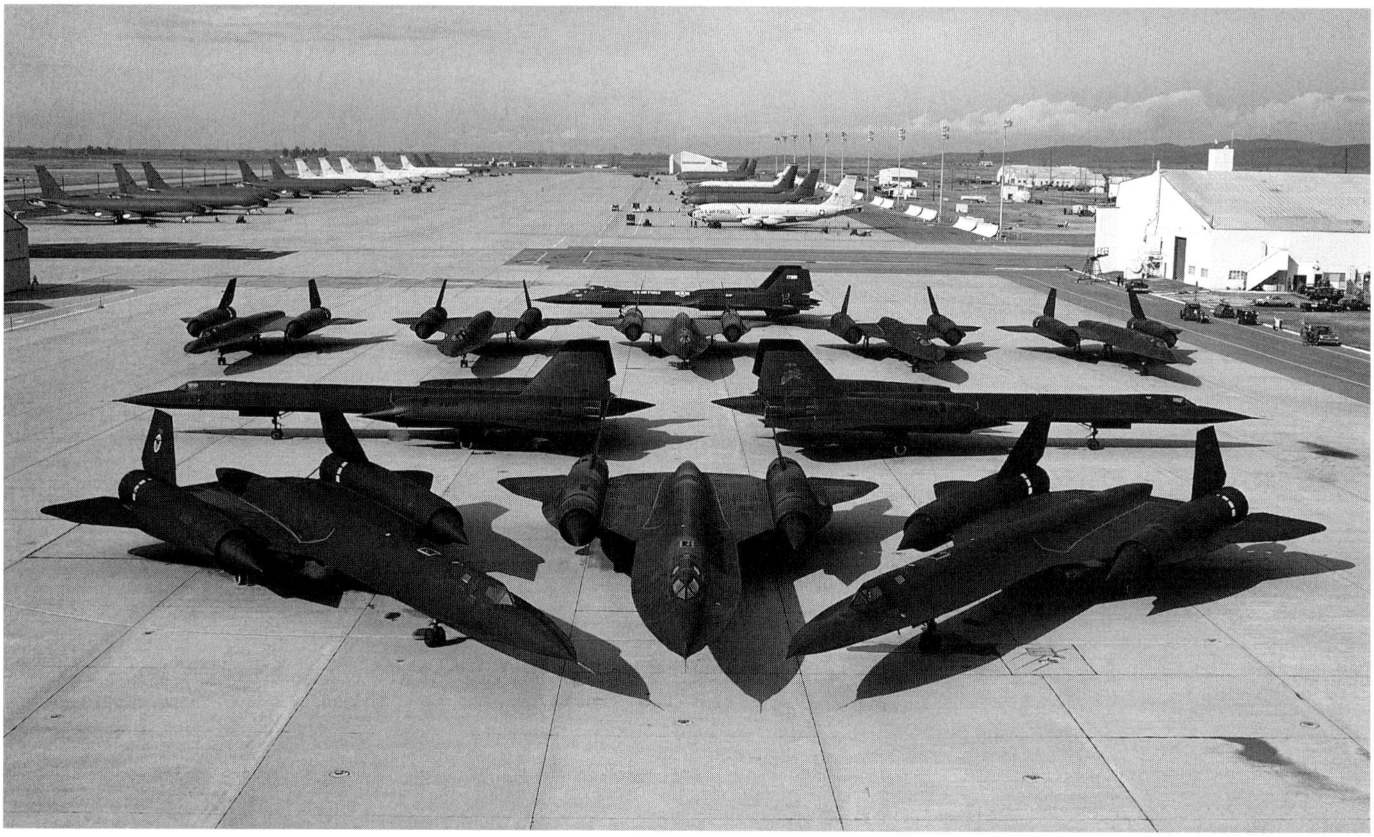

OPPOSITE PAGE:
TOP: **The first SR-71A (61-7950) on an early test flight; this aircraft would be lost at Edwards AFB on 10 January 1967.** AFFTC/HO

BOTTOM: **Ten SR-71As and the sole surviving SR-71B (far background) at Beale AFB in December 1983.** Lockheed Martin

THIS PAGE:
A fine in-flight study of an SR-71A (61-7976). Lockheed Martin

USAF opted to change the official designation from RS-71 to SR-71. (The prefix 'RS' means Reconnaissance Strike whereas 'SR' means Strategic Reconnaissance.) This involved literally tons of paperwork, as everything from contractual agreements to technical manuals had to be altered to read properly.

Since the SR-71 was originally ordered into production as the RS-71, would it be capable of delivering strike weapons such as the then-upcoming Short-Range Attack Missile (SRAM)? Assuming it would, with a high degree of speculation, there might have been a plan for two different aircraft configurations forward of the wings: a pure reconnaissance platform with a camera-nose; and a reconnaissance and strike platform with a combined camera-/weapon-nose. This assumption is undocumented and remains to be proven. But given the fact that the RS-71/SR-71 had killed off the proposed North American RS-70 Valkyrie, the assumption is well founded.

The RS-70

In March 1961 the Kennedy Administration's Defense Secretary, Robert S. McNamara, cancelled the proposed North American B-70 Valkyrie Mach 3 strategic bomber. The USAF then attempted to resuscitate the programme in March 1962 by requesting a fleet of RS-70 aeroplanes to be built instead. The proposed RS-70 was configured to carry up to twenty air-launched SRAMs, armed with nuclear warheads, mounted on two rotary launchers in its two in-line weapon bays. (This missile ultimately became the air-to-ground AGM-69 built by Boeing.) As a reconnaissance/strike weapon system, the RS-70 was to strike ten or more strategic targets, return for detailed bomb damage assessment (BDA) and then, if necessary, re-strike some of the very same targets. The US Congress voted funds for the RS-70 programme but McNamara refused to release them. So, like the B-70, the RS-70 died on the vine.

What most did not know, because of its highly classified nature, was that the RS-70 had faced serious competition in the form of the Lockheed RS-71. This was the reconnaissance-bomber version of the A-12 airframe, previously designated RB-12. Although the RS-71 carried far less ordnance (four SRAMs rather than twenty), it was preferred over the RS-70 because its development was further advanced and its

SR-71: LEADER OF THE PACK

projected initial operational capability was to be considerably sooner than that of the RS-70. In the end, however, neither the North American RS-70 nor the Lockheed RS-71 would be built as dedicated reconnaissance strike aircraft.

Birth of the SR-71

On 13 June 1962 the USAF reviewed the full-scale SR-71 (then RS-71) engineering mock-up at Burbank. The RS-71 was essentially a two-seater development of the A-12, manned by a pilot and a weapon/reconnaissance system operator (WRSO), with a different forward fuselage section designed to carry four SRAMs with nuclear warheads.

On 28 December 1962 the USAF ordered an initial production batch of six aeroplanes. The first example (61-7950), which would serve as the prototype, was completed in major subassemblies in late October 1964 and delivered to Palmdale for final assembly on 29 October. By now the USAF had assigned its fleet of SR-71s to the Strategic Air Command, and on 7 December 1964 announced that their official stateside base of operations would be Beale AFB, California, assigned to the 9th Strategic Reconnaissance Wing (SRW). The 9th SRW was established on 25 June 1966. It replaced the 4200th SRW which was disestablished on the same date.

After the first SR-71 completed final assembly at Palmdale it underwent a series of ground tests including avionics tests, engine runs, and so on. It then performed a number of low-, medium- and high-speed taxi tests to make sure its flight-control system, wheel brakes and nosewheel steering all worked properly. It was time to fly.

Assigned earlier as chief test pilot on the SR-71 programme, Skunk Works engineering test pilot Robert J. 'Bob' Gilliland made a very successful first flight on 22 December 1964. Gilliland flew the aeroplane just shy of one hour and hit a maximum speed of just over Mach 1.5 (1,112mph/1,790km/h) at 50,000ft (15,000m). Such performance was a tremendous accomplishment for the

This view of an SR-71A clearly shows the aeroplane's characteristic chines. Lockheed Martin

TOP: SR-71A 955 touches down with its brake parachute deployed. *Lockheed Martin*   **ABOVE:** SR-71A 955 in flight with the Skunk Works logo on its tail. *Lockheed Martin*

An SR-71A departs Beale AFB to the south as the sun sets in the west. Lockheed Martin

maiden flight of a previously untried airframe configuration. Gilliland, in fact, had planned higher speeds, but at Mach 1.2 the 'Canopy Unsafe' caution light on the instrument panel warned that the canopy locks might be loose. Therefore, as a precaution, immediately after hitting Mach 1.5 he slowed down for the return to Palmdale. Of course, these historic events had already been preceded by some five years of highly classified work to develop the other aircraft of the A-12 family. But without the hard-earned successes that were achieved by these earlier models the SR-71 would never have been able to join the unique Blackbird series.

Production and deliveries of flight-test SR-71s to Edwards AFB began in earnest in

An SR-71A taxis in after a mission. Lockheed Martin

ABOVE: **The same SR-71A after engine shut-down. Note that the brake parachute doors are still open.** Lockheed Martin

BELOW: **An SR-71A touching down at Palmdale.** Lockheed Martin

ABOVE: **An SR-71A in its hangar being prepared for a flight at Beale AFB.**
Lockheed Martin

SR-71A 955 flies alongside a TR-1A near Beale AFB during the mid-1980s. The TR-1A was later redesignated U-2R, but is now the U-2S.
Lockheed Martin

SR-71: LEADER OF THE PACK

ABOVE: **Another view of SR-71A 955.** Lockheed Martin

The SR-71A and (profile only) SR-71B. artwork by Tony Landis

Lockheed SR-71 Blackbird

SR-71B Pilot Trainer

T. Landis 1/03

1965. The first six SR-71As assigned to flight-test joined the three YF-12As already there. Thus by the end of 1965 nine Blackbirds were under the wing of the YF-12/SR-71 Combined Test Force (CTF). Stability and control were investigated using the first three SR-71As (61-7950/-7952); SR-71A number four (61-7953) served as the performance test aeroplane; and numbers five and six (61-7954 and 61-7955) were used for systems evaluations.

The first Blackbird to be delivered to the 9th SRW was the first of two SR-71B two-seater pilot training and transition aeroplanes. This SR-71B (61-7956) made its first flight on 18 November 1965 and was delivered to Beale AFB by the commander of the 9th SRW, Colonel (later Major General) Douglas 'Doug' Nelson on 7 January 1966.

Getting the opportunity to fly the SR-71 was no easy task. Any potential Blackbird pilot had to have thousands of unblemished and well-documented flying hours before he could even be considered

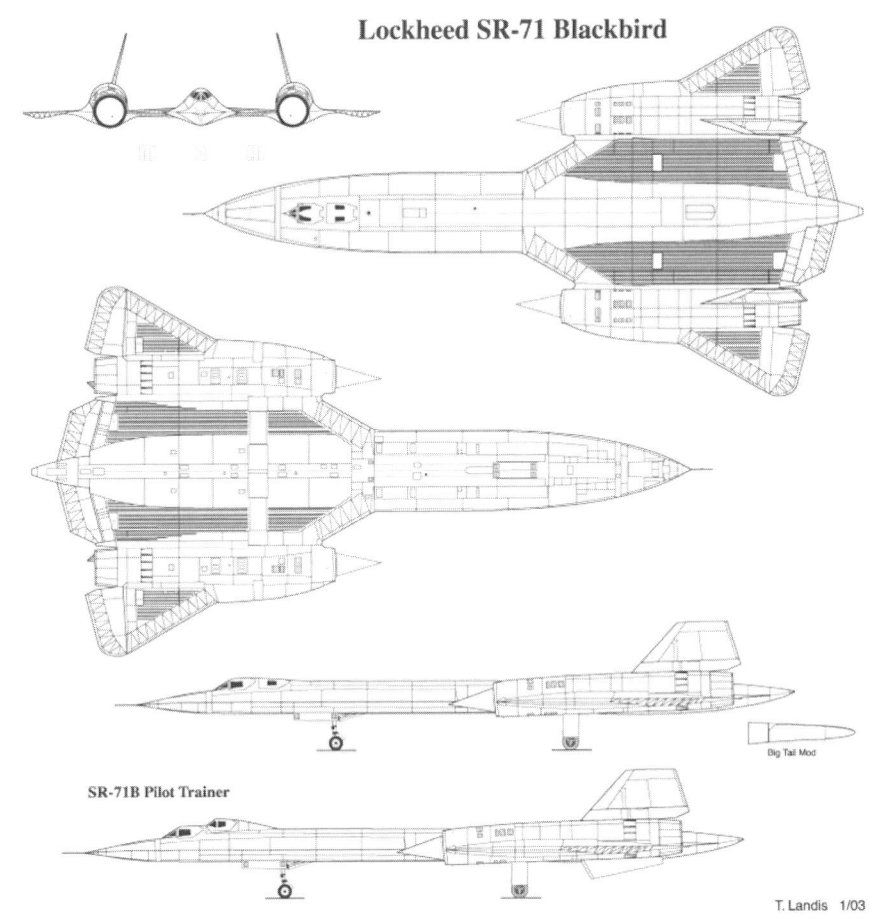

75

TOP: **The J58 engine nacelles on the SR-71A are nearly half the length of the entire aircraft.** Lockheed Martin

ABOVE: **This SR-71A (61-7968) logged 2,279 flight hours before it was placed into flyable storage.** Lockheed Martin

SR-71A at sunset. Lockheed Martin

for the job. When one considers that fewer than 100 USAF pilots actually got to fly the SR-71, it becomes apparent just how special the *Senior Crown* programme was.

After a highly experienced pilot was selected for the SR-71 an astronaut-type physical followed. Once the physical was passed there were hundreds of hours spent in the classroom and SR-71 cockpit simulator. After all of this education it became time for a check flight in which the student would be evaluated in flight by an instructor. These check flights were always flown in the dual-control SR-71B, not an SR-71A.

The SR-71 check flights were assigned numbers beginning with 101, since check flight numbers 001 through 100 were allocated to the *Oxcart* programme (only numbers 001 to 034 actually having been used). The SR-71 check flight numbering sequence ultimately ended at 466. But it was not only trainee SR-71 pilots that took check flights. In the check flight numbering sequence of 101–466 were included pilots, Reconnaissance Systems Operators (RSO), high-ranking USAF staff members and VIPs.

For example, check flight number 405 was for a 'special' VIP: none other than Charles E. 'Chuck' Yeager, who on 14 October 1947 had become the first man on earth to pilot an aeroplane faster than the speed of sound when he hit Mach 1.06 (786mph/ 1,265km/h) at 42,000ft (13,000m). During his VIP check flight in the SR-71B, Yeager hit Mach 3.23 (2,395mph/3,854km/h) at 78,000ft (24,000m). Not higher, but quite a bit faster than he had ever flown.

One of the flight-test SR-71As operating out of Edwards – SR-71A number three (61-7952) – was lost on 25 January 1966 near Tucumcari, New Mexico. It was being flown by Lockheed test pilot Bill Weaver with RSO Jim Zwayer. At a speed of Mach 3 or more, and at about 80,000ft, the aeroplane began to disintegrate because of numerous malfunctions during the high-Mach drag-characteristics tests it was performing. The aeroplane broke up so fast that the crew had no time to make their emergency ejections. They instead were literally thrown out of the aircraft while travelling at more than 2,000mph (3,200km/h), some 15 miles (24km) above the earth. Somehow Weaver survived that horrifying ordeal with only minor injuries; Zwayer did not.

Kelly Johnson retired as senior vice president of the Lockheed Corporation in January 1975 and from the board of directors in May 1980. But he continued to serve as senior advisor to corporate management and the firm's Advanced Development Projects group – the Skunk Works – until his death in 1990. In 1981 he wrote a revealing paper on the development of the SR-71, published in the winter 1981–2 issue of *Lockheed Horizons*, which is reproduced on pages 78–80.

On 10 January 1967 Lockheed test pilot Art Peterson was performing braking tests on SR-71A number one (61-7950) at Edwards AFB. The magnesium wheels caught fire and the entire plane burned out. Peterson escaped the horrendous fire with minor injuries but the first SR-71 was gone. The last production SR-71A (61-7980) was delivered to Beale AFB on 10 October 1967.

The sole SR-71C (61-7981) made its first flight on 14 March 1969. This last manufactured Blackbird was a hybrid in that it was purpose-built as a pilot trainer and transition aeroplane to replace the second SR-71B (61-7957), which had crashed in a landing accident at Beale on 11 January 1968. The SR-71C, also known as 'The Bastard', was created from the aft section of YF-12A number one (60-6934) and the forward section of the SR-71A static structural test article. After only 556.4 hours of flying time, mostly at Edwards AFB, the SR-71C went into storage at Beale to be used for spare parts.

SR-71 Operations

There is no one Mach number that the plane would do, it was a temperature limit, not a Mach limit on the speed, so that is why we normally don't have one number that stands out. Anything over Mach 3.3 was risky due to temperature limits and unstart [engine air inlet stall] considerations.

Brian Shul

Even before VJ-Day on 2 September 1945, when World War Two officially ended, relations between the USA and its allies on the one hand and the USSR on the other had begun to deteriorate. It was a time of ever-increasing suspicions and rising tension, and since there was no actual fighting between the two sides, it was not long before someone coined the term 'Cold War' to describe the new world situation. Over time this Cold War heated up, cooled down and re-heated with numerous disagreements and more serious crises.

One such 'heating up' occurred on 3 August 1947, during the Aviation Day display of aircraft at Moscow's Tushino Airport, when what appeared to be three US-built B-29 Superfortress bombers took part. Three USAF B-29s had accidentally landed in the USSR and been interned by the Soviets during World War Two, but western observers soon realized that these were not the same aircraft: they were instead Tupolev Tu-4 'Bulls', near-identical copies of the B-29, which the USSR had put into full-scale production. With the advent of the Tu-4, the Soviets could now threaten the USA and its allies with strategic bombing. Moreover, as the USSR developed a nuclear capability, attack with atomic weapons was not out of the question.

One of the first real crises began in 1948, when the USSR mounted a road and railway blockade of West Berlin (which, though occupied by the British, French and Americans, was entirely surrounded by the Soviet-occupied zone of Germany). In other words, the people of West Berlin would no longer receive the life-support (clothing, food, medicine and so on) that they had been receiving from the west. To deal with this crisis the western allies mounted the 'Berlin Airlift', in which thousands of tons of supplies were flown into West Berlin. This was a highly successful operation and in mid-1949 the crisis ended.

The USSR successfully detonated its first atomic bomb, code-named 'Joe 1' on 29 August 1949. Its radiation was detected over the Kamchatka peninsula, on the USSR's Pacific coast, by an RB-29 reconnaissance plane. With the Tu-4 already in squadron service, the USA and its allies suddenly faced a serious threat. The Cold War was heating up and it was time for agonizing reappraisal: this meant there was a need for improved aerial reconnaissance over the USSR itself to monitor its military activities.

At the time, there were not too many dedicated aerial reconnaissance aircraft available, especially those with the altitude, photographic quality, range and speed required for such a dangerous operation as overflights of Soviet territory. The most suitable photographic reconnaissance aircraft of the day included Convair RB-36s, North American RB-45s, and Boeing RB-47s and RB-50s; it would still be some seven years before the Lockheed U-2 came on line. So it was clear that there was a need for better photographic reconnaissance aircraft.

Development of the Lockheed SR-71 Blackbird

CLARENCE L. JOHNSON
Senior Advisor, Lockheed Corporation

This paper has been prepared by the writer to record the development history of the Lockheed SR-71 reconnaissance aeroplane. In my capacity as manager of the Lockheed Advanced Development Division (more commonly known as the 'Skunk Works') I supervised the design, testing, and construction of the aircraft referred to until my partial retirement five years ago. Because of the very tight security on all phases of the program, there are very few people who were ever aware of all aspects of the so-called 'Blackbird' program. Fortunately, I kept as complete a log on the subject as one individual could on a program that involved thousands of people, over three hundred subcontractors and partners, plus a very select group of US Air Force and Central Intelligence Agency personnel. There are still many classified aspects of the design and operation of the Blackbirds but by avoiding these, I have been informed that I can still publish many interesting things about the program.

In order to tell the SR-71 story, I must draw heavily on the data derived on two prior Skunk Works programs – the first Mach 3-plus reconnaissance type, known by our design number as the A-12, and the YF-12A interceptor, which President Lyndon B. Johnson announced publicly on 29 February 1964. He announced the SR-71 on 24 July of the same year.

Background for Development
The Lockheed U-2 subsonic, high-altitude reconnaissance plane first flew in 1955. It went operational a year later and continued to make overflights of the Soviet Union until 1 May 1960. In this five-year period, it became obvious to those of us who were involved in the U-2 program that Russian developments in the radar and missile fields would shortly make the U-Bird too vulnerable to continue overflights of Soviet territory, as indeed happened when Francis Gary Powers was shot down on May Day of 1960.

Starting in 1956, we made many studies and tests to improve the survivability of the U-2 by attempting to fly higher and faster as well as reducing its radar cross-section and providing both infra-red and radar jamming gear. Very little gains were forthcoming except in cruise altitude so we took up studies of other designs. We studied the use of new fuels such as boron slurries and liquid hydrogen. The latter was carried into the early manufacturing phase because it was possible to produce an aircraft with cruising altitudes well over 100,000ft and a Mach number of 2.5. The design [CL-400] was scrapped, however, because of the terrible logistic problems of providing [hydrogen] fuel in the field.

Continuing concern for having a balanced reconnaissance force made it apparent that we still would need a manned reconnaissance aircraft that could be dispatched on worldwide missions when required. From vulnerability studies, we derived certain design requirements for this craft. These were a cruising speed well over Mach 3, cruising altitude over 80,000ft, and a very low radar cross-section over a wide band of frequencies. Electronic countermeasures and advanced communications gear were mandatory. The craft should have at least two engines for safety reasons.

Getting a Grasp on the Problem
Our analysis of these requirements rapidly showed the very formidable problems, which had to be solved to get an acceptable design.

The first of these was the effect of operating at ram-air temperatures of over 800°F. This immediately ruled out aluminium as a basic structural material, leaving only various alloys of stainless steel and titanium to build the aircraft. It meant the development of high-temperature plastics for radomes and other structures, as well as a new hydraulic fluid, greases, electrical wiring and connectors, and a whole host of other equipment. The fuel to be used by the engine had to be stable under temperatures as low as minus 90°F in subsonic cruising flight to over 350°F at high cruising speeds when it would be fed into the engine fuel system. There it would be first used as hydraulic fluid at 600°F to control the afterburner exit flap before being fed into the burner cans of the power plant and the afterburner itself.

Cooling the cockpit and crew turned out to be seven times as difficult as on the X-15 research aeroplane which flew as much as twice as fast as the SR-71 but only for a few minutes per flight. The wheels and tires of the landing gear had to be protected from the heat by burying them in the fuselage fuel tanks for radiation cooling to save the rubber and other systems attached thereto.

Special attention had to be given to the crew escape system to allow safe ejection from the aircraft over a speed range and altitude range of zero miles per hour at sea level to Mach numbers up to 4.0 at over 100,000ft. New pilot's pressure suits, gloves, dual oxygen systems, high-temperature ejection seat catapults, and parachutes would have to be developed and tested.

The problems of taking pictures through windows subjected to a hot turbulent airflow on the fuselage also had to be solved.

How the Blackbird Program Got Started
In the time period of 21 April 1958 through 1 September 1959 I made a series of proposals for Mach 3-plus reconnaissance aircraft to Mr. Richard Bissell of the CIA and to the US Air Force. These aeroplanes were designated in the Skunk Works by design numbers of A-1 through A-12 [the prefix 'A' meaning Archangel; Archangel 1 through Archangel 12].

We were evaluated against some very interesting designs by the [Convair Division of the] General Dynamics Corporation and a US Navy in-house design. The latter concept was proposed as a ramjet-powered rubber inflatable machine, initially carried to altitude by a balloon and then rocket boosted to a speed where the ramjets could produce thrust. Our studies on this aircraft rapidly proved it to be totally unfeasible. The carrying balloon had to be a mile in diameter to lift the unit, which had a proposed wing area of 1/7th of an acre!

Convair's proposals were much more serious, starting out with a ramjet-powered Mach 4 aircraft to be carried aloft by a B-58 and launched at supersonic speeds. Unfortunately, the B-58 couldn't go supersonic with the bird [named Fish by Convair] in place, and even if it could, the survivability of the piloted vehicle would be very questionable due to the probability of ramjet blow-out maneuvers. At the time of this proposal the total flight operating time for the Marquardt ramjet was not over seven hours, and this time was obtained mainly on a ramjet test vehicle for the Boeing Bomarc [surface-to-air interceptor] missile. Known as the X-7, this test vehicle was built and operated by the Lockheed Skunk Works!

The final Convair proposal, known as the Kingfisher [typo: this should read Kingfish], was eliminated by US Air Force and Department of Defense technical experts, who were given the job of evaluating all designs.

On 29 August 1959 our A-12 design was declared the winner and Mr. Bissell gave us a limited go-ahead for a four-month period to conduct tests on certain models and to build a full-scale [engineering] mock-up. On 30 January 1960 we were given a full go-ahead on the design, manufacturing, and testing of 12 [A-12] aircraft. The first one flew 26 April 1962.

The next version of the aircraft, an air defense long-range fighter, was discussed with General Hal Estes in Washington, D.C. on 16 and 17 March 1960. He and Air Force Secretary for Research and Development, Dr. Courtlandt Perkins, were very pleased with our proposal so they passed me on for further discussions with General Marvin Demler at Wright Field. He directed us to use the Hughes AN/ASG-18 radar and GAR-9 air-to-air missile which were in the early development stages for the [cancelled] North American F-108 interceptor. This we did, and when [since] the F-108 was eventually [had already been] cancelled Lockheed worked with Hughes in the development and flight testing of that armament system. The first YF-12A flew 7 August 1963. [The F-108 program was cancelled on 23 September 1959.]

In early January 1961 I made the first proposal for a strategic reconnaissance bomber to Dr. Joseph Charyk, Secretary of the Air Force; Colonel [later General] Leo Geary, our Pentagon project officer on the YF-12A; and Mr. Lew Meyer, a high financial officer in the US Air Force. We were encouraged to continue our company-funded studies on the aircraft [known in-house as the RB-12]. As we progressed in the development, we encountered very strong opposition in certain USAF quarters on the part of those trying to save the North American B-70 program, which was in considerable trouble. Life became very interesting in that we were competing the SR-71 [read RS-71; as it was designated at the time] with an aeroplane five times its weight and size. On 4 June 1962 the USAF evaluation team reviewed our [RB-12] design and the mock-up – and we were given good grades.

Our discussions continued with the Department of Defense and also, in this period, with General Curtis E. LeMay and his Strategic Air Command [SAC] officers. It was on 27 and 28 December 1962 that we were finally put on contract to build the first group of six SR-71 [RS-71] aircraft.

Development of the Lockheed SR-71 Blackbird

One of our major problems during the next few years was in updating our Skunk Works operating methods to provide SAC with proper support, training, spare parts, and data required for their special operational needs. I have always believed that our SAC is the most sophisticated and demanding customer for aircraft in the world. The fact that we have been able to support them so well for many years is one of the most satisfying aspects of my career.

Without the total support of such people as General Leo Geary in the Pentagon and a long series of extremely competent and helpful commanding officers at Beale Air Force Base, we could never have jointly put the Blackbirds into service successfully.

Basic Design Features
Having chosen the required performance in speed, altitude, and range, it was immediately evident that a thin delta-wing planform was required with a very moderate wing loading to allow flight at very high altitude. A long, slender fuselage was necessary to contain most of the fuel as well as the landing gear and payloads. To reduce the wing trim drag, the fuselage was fitted with lateral surfaces called chines, which actually converted the forward fuselage into a fixed canard [forward-mounted horizontal stabilizer] which developed [additional] lift.

The hardest design problem on the aeroplane was making the engine air inlet and ejector [exhaust outlet] work properly. The [air] inlet cone [spike] moves almost three feet to keep the shockwave where we want it. A hydraulic actuator, computer controlled, has to provide operating forces of up to 31,000lb under certain flow conditions in the nacelles. To account for the effect of the fuselage chine airflow, the inlets [spikes] are pointed down and in toward the fuselage.

The use of dual vertical tails canted inward on the engine nacelles took advantage of the chine vortex in such a way that the directional stability improves as the angle of attack of the aircraft increases.

Aerodynamic Testing
All the usual low-speed and high-speed wind tunnel tests were run on the various configurations of the A-12, YF-12A, and continued on the SR-71. Substantial efforts went into optimizing chine design and conical camber of the wing leading edge. No useful lift increase effect was found from the use of wing flaps of any type so we depend entirely on our low wing-loading and powerful ground effect to get satisfactory take-off and landing characteristics.

Correlation of wind tunnel data on fuselage trim effects was found to be of marginal value because of two factors: structural deflection due to fuselage weight distribution; and the effect of fuel quantity and temperature. The latter was caused by fuel on the bottom of the tanks, keeping that section of the fuselage cool, while the top of the fuselage became increasingly hotter as fuel was burned, tending to push the chines downward due to differential expansion of the top and bottom of the fuselage. A full-scale fuel system test rig was used to test fuel feed capability for various flight attitudes.

By far the most [wind] tunnel time was spent optimizing the nacelle inlets, bleed designs, and the ejector. A quarter-scale model was built on which over 250,000 pressure readings were taken. We knew nacelle air leakage would cause high drag so an actual full-size nacelle was fitted with end plugs and air leakage was carefully measured [to over 50 pounds per square inch]. Proper sealing paid off well in flight testing.

With the engines located half way out on the wingspan, we were concerned with the very heavy yawing moment that would develop should an inlet stall. We therefore installed accelerometers in the fuselage that immediately sensed the yaw rate and commanded rudder booster to apply nine degrees of correction within a time period of 0.15sec. This device worked so well that our test pilots very often couldn't tell whether the right or left engine blew out. They knew they had a blowout, of course, by the bad buffeting that occurred with a 'popped shock'. Subsequently, an automatic restart device was developed which keeps this engine-out time to a very short period.

We learned that it often required over 600 horsepower to get the engine up to starting RPM on the ground. So we devised an interesting approach to the problem of ground starting the J58. To obtain this power, we took two Buick racing car engines and developed a gear box to connect them both to the J58 starter drive. We operated for several years with this setup until more sophisticated air starting systems were developed and installed in the hangars.

Structural Problems
The decision to use various alloys of titanium for the basic structure of the Blackbirds was based on the following considerations:

1. Only titanium and steel had the ability to withstand the operating temperatures encountered.
2. Aged B-120 titanium weighs one half as much as stainless steel per cubic inch but its ultimate strength is almost up to stainless.
3. Conventional construction could be used with fewer parts involved than with steel.
4. High strength composites were not available in the early 1960s. We did develop a good plastic which has been remarkably serviceable but it was not used for primary structure.

Having made the basic material choice, we decided to build two test units to see if we could reduce our research to practice. The first unit was to study thermal effects on our large titanium wing panels. We heated up the element with the computed heat flux that we would encounter in flight. The sample warped into a totally unacceptable shape. To solve this problem we put chordwise [leading edge to trailing edge] corrugations in the outer skins and reran the tests very satisfactorily. At the design heating rate, the corrugations merely deepened by a few thousandths of an inch and on cooling returned to the basic shape. I was accused of trying to make a 1932 Ford Trimotor go Mach 3 but the concept worked fine. [The Ford Trimotor used corrugated aluminium alloy for part of its exterior skin.]

The second test unit was the forward fuselage and cockpit, which had over 6,000 parts in it of high curvature, thin gages, and the canopy with its complexity. This element was tested in an oven where we could determine thermal effects and develop cockpit cooling systems.

We encountered major problems in manufacturing this test unit because the first batch of heat-treated titanium parts was extremely brittle. In fact, you could push a piece of structure off your desk and it would shatter on the floor. It was thought that we were encountering hydrogen [gas] embrittlement in our heat treat processes. Working with our supplier, Titanium Metals Corporation of America [TMCA, now Titanium Metals Corporation or TIMET], we could not prove that the problem was in fact hydrogen. It was finally resolved by throwing out our whole acid pickling setup and replacing it with an identical reproduction of what TMCA had in their mills.

We developed a complex quality control program. For every batch of ten parts or more we processed three test coupons which were subjected to the identical heat treatment of the parts in the batch. One coupon was tensile tested to failure to derive the stress/strain data. A quarter-of-an-inch cut was made in the edge of the second coupon by a sharp scissor-like cutter and it was then bent around a mandrel at the cut. If the coupon could not be bent 180deg at a radius of X times the sheet thickness without breaking it, it was considered to be too brittle. (The value of X is a function of the alloy used and the stress/strain value of the piece.) The third coupon was held in reserve if any reprocessing was required.

For an outfit that hates paperwork, we really deluged ourselves with it. Having made over 13 million titanium parts to date we can trace the history of all but the first few parts back to the mill pour and for about the last 10 million of them even the direction of the grain in the sheet from which the part was cut has been recorded. On large forgings, such as landing gears, we trepanned out 12 sample coupons for test before machining each part. We found out the hard way that most commercial cutting fluids accelerated stress corrosion on hit titanium so we developed our own.

Titanium is totally incompatible with chlorine, fluorine, cadmium, and similar elements. For instance, we were baffled when we found out that wing panels which we spot welded in the summer, failed early in life, but those made in the winter lasted indefinitely. We finally traced this problem to the Burbank water system which had heavily chlorinated water in the summer to prevent algae growth but not in the winter. Changing to distilled water to wash the parts solved this problem.

Our experience with cadmium came about by mechanics using cadmium-plated wrenches working on the engine installation primarily. Enough cadmium was left in contact with bolt heads which had been tightened so that when the bolts became hot the bolt heads just dropped off! We had to clean out hundreds of tool boxes to remove cadmium-plated tools.

(continued overleaf)

Development of the Lockheed SR-71 Blackbird *continued*

Drilling and machining high strength titanium alloys, such as B-120, required a complete research program to determine best tool cutter designs, cutting fluids, and speeds and feeds for best metal removal rates. We had particular trouble with wing extrusions, which were used by the thousands of feet [metres]. Initially, the cost of machining a foot out of the rolled mill part was $19.00 which was reduced to $11.00 after much research. At one time we were approaching the ability at our vendor's plants to roll parts to net dimensions, but the final achievement of this required a $30,000,000 new facility which was not built.

Wyman Gordon was given $1,000,000 for a research program to learn how to forge the main nacelle rings [J58 engine mounts] on a 50,000-ton press which was successful. Combining their advances with our research on numerical controls of machining and special tools and fluids, we were able to save $19,000,000 on the production program.

To prevent parts from going under-gage while in the acid bath, we set up a new series of metal gages two thousandths of an inch thicker than the standard gages and solved the problem. When we built the first Blackbird, a high-speed drill could drill 17 holes before it was ruined. By the end of the program we had developed drills that could drill 100 holes and then be resharpened successfully.

Our overall research on titanium usage was summarized in reports which we furnished not only to the US Air Force but to our vendors who machined over half of our machined parts for the program. To use titanium efficiently required an ongoing training program for thousands of people – both ours in manufacturing and in the US Air Force in service.

Throughout this and other programs, it has been crystal clear to me that our country needs a 250,000-ton metal forming press – five times as large as our biggest one available today. When we have to machine away 90 percent of our rough forgings today both in titanium (SR-71 nacelle rings and landing gears) and aluminium (C-5 fuselage side rings) it seems that we are nationally stupid! My best and continuing efforts to solve this problem have been defeated for many years. Incidentally, the USSR has been much smarter in this field in that they have more and larger forging presses than we do.

Fluid Systems

Very difficult problems were encountered with the use of fuel tanks sealants and hydraulic oil. We worked for years developing both of these, drawing as much on other industrial and chemical companies as they were willing to devote to a very limited market. We were finally able to produce a sealant which does a reasonable job over a temperature range of minus 90°F to over 600°F. Our experience with hydraulic oil started out on a comical situation. I saw ads in technical journals for a 'material to be used to operate up to 900°F in service'. I contacted the producer who agreed to send me some for testing. Imagine my surprise when the material arrived in a large canvas bag. It was a white powder at room temperature that you certainly wouldn't put in a hydraulic system. If you did, one would have to thaw out all the lines and other elements with a blow torch! We did finally get a petroleum-based oil developed at Penn State University to which we had to add several other chemicals to maintain its lubricity at high temperatures. It originally cost $130 per gallon so absolutely no leaks could be tolerated.

Rubber O-rings could not be used at high temperatures so a complete line of steel rings was provided which have worked very well. Titanium pistons working in titanium cylinders tended to gall and seize until chemical coatings were invented which solved the problem.

The Flight Test Phase

The first flight of the A-12 took place 26 April 1962 or thirty months after we were given a limited go-ahead on 1 September 1959. We had to fly with Pratt & Whitney J75 engines until the J58 engine became available in January 1963. Then our problems really began!

The first one was concerned with foreign object damage (FOD) to the engines – a particular problem with the powerful J58 and the tortuous flow path through the complicated nacelle structure. Small nuts, bolts, and metal scraps not removed from the nacelles during construction could be sucked into the engines on starting with devastating results. [In one instance] damage to the first-stage compressor blades from an inspector's flashlight used to search for such foreign objects [caused $250,000 engine damage!] Besides objects of the above type, the engine would suck in rocks, asphalt pieces, etc. from the taxi-ways and runways. An extensive campaign to control FOD at all stages of construction and operation – involving a shake test of the forward nacelle at the factory, the use of screens, and runway sweeping with double inspections prior to any engine running – brought FOD under reasonable control.

The hardest problem encountered in flight was the development of the nacelle air inlet control. It was necessary to throw out the initial pneumatic design after millions of dollars had been spent on it and go to a design using electronic controls instead. This was very hard to do because several elements of the system were exposed to ram-air temperatures over 800°F and terrific vibration during an inlet duct stall. This problem and one dealing with aircraft acceleration between Mach numbers 0.95 to 2.0 are too complex to deal with in this paper.

Initially, air temperature variations along a given true altitude would cause the Blackbird to wander up and down over several thousand feet in its flight path. Improved autopilots and engine controls have eliminated this problem.

There are no other aeroplanes flying at our cruising altitude except for an occasional U-2 but we were very scared by encountering weather balloons sent up by the Federal Aviation Authority. If we were to hit the instrument package while cruising at over 3,000ft/sec, the impact could be deadly!

Flight planning had to be done very carefully because of sonic boom problems. We received complaints from many sources. One such stated that his mules on a pack-train wanted to jump off the cliff trail when they were 'boomed'. Another complained that fishing stopped in the lakes in Yellowstone Park if a boom occurred because the fish went down for hours. I had my own complaint when one of my military friends boomed my ranch and broke a $450 plate glass window. I got no sympathy on this, however.

Operational Comments

The SR-71 first flew 22 December 1964. It was in service with the Strategic Air Command a year later.

In-flight refuelling from KC-135s turned out to be very routine. Over 18,000 such refuellings have been made to date by all versions of the Blackbirds and they have exceeded Mach 3 over 11,000 times.

The SR-71 has flown from New York to London in 1 hour 55 minutes then returned non-stop to Beale Air Force Base, including a London-to-Los Angeles time of 3 hours 48 minutes.

It has flown over 15,000mi with refuelling to demonstrate its truly global range. It is by far the world's fastest, highest flying aeroplane in service. I expect it to be so for a long time to come.

This need became apparent between mid-1950 and mid-1953 when the Korean War was fought. During this war, to the surprise of the West, the USSR deployed a very capable jet-powered fighter, the Mikoyan-Gurevich MiG-15 'Fagot', which gave America's best fighter – the North American F-86 Sabre – all it could handle. If adequate aerial reconnaissance had been in place beforehand, the USA would have been forewarned about the MiG-15, and so more ready to meet it head-on.

Since the Korean War there have been many more dangerous periods in the relations between East and West, such as the Cuban Missile Crisis. Many of these crises have been documented by an uncounted number of photographs taken by photographic reconnaissance aircraft such as the A-12, which was discussed in the previous chapter. After the retirement of the A-12 it was the SR-71 that added enormously to this vast collection of high-resolution imagery.

Home Bases in the USA

Beale Air Force Base, California

Beale AFB, California was the home base of the Blackbird in the USA. The 4200th Strategic Reconnaissance Wing (SRW) was formed for upcoming Blackbird operations on 1 January 1965. But on 25 June 1966 the 4200th was re-designated as the 9th SRW. Eventually the 9th SRW had two SR-71 Strategic Reconnaissance

Squadrons (SRS): the 1st SRS and the 99th SRS. When the Strategic Air Command was absorbed by the Air Combat Command on 1 June 1992 the 9th SRW was re-designated 9th Wing.

Edwards Air Force Base, California

On 1 September 1995 the Air Combat Command (ACC) assigned three reactivated Blackbirds of the 9th Wing – headquartered at Beale AFB – to Det 2 at Edwards AFB. These three Blackbirds, two SR-71As (61-7967 and 61-7971) and an SR-71B (61-7956), did not fly a great many sorties before they were once again deactivated when President Clinton vetoed further expenditure on USAF Blackbird operations. The last USAF flight of a Blackbird – the lone surviving SR-71B assigned to Det 2 – was on 19 October 1997 at Edwards AFB.

Eilson Air Force Base, Alaska

In 1979 and 1980 a number of random operational missions, as needed, were flown by SR-71As of Det 5 out of Eilson AFB. Moreover, it was here that the Blackbird was evaluated on its cold-weather performance capabilities.

Palmdale, California

The SR-71s were assembled and flight tested at USAF Plant 42, Lockheed Plant 10 (formerly known as Site 2) from 1964 until the type's final retirement in 1999. Under Det 51, a number of SR-71s of the USAF 2762nd Logistics Squadron (LS) of Air Force Logistics Command (AFLC) flew sporadic sorties of an unknown nature from Palmdale during these years. Det 51 became Det 6 in August 1977.

Norton Air Force Base, California

Norton AFB is where the Blackbird supply depot was located. This was an auxiliary part of the aforementioned 2762nd LS, AFLC, headquartered at Palmdale. It was part of Det 6 (formerly Det 51).

Griffiss Air Force Base, New York

Griffiss AFB, Rome, New York was known as OL-KB which was established for Black-

ABOVE: Close-up view of SR-71A touching down at Edwards AFB. Lockheed Martin

BELOW: SR-71A 959 lands after first test flight with its 'Big Tail' configuration. USAF via Peter W. Merlin

bird reconnaissance flights – Operation *Black Knight* – during the 1973–74 Yom Kippur War. However, because of the bad weather conditions at Griffiss, these SR-71s were moved to OL-SB at Seymour Johnson AFB in North Carolina.

Seymour Johnson Air Force Base, North Carolina

OL-SB was established on 11 October 1973 and the first mission in Operation *Giant Reach* was flown from here on 13 October 1973. The SR-71s of OL-SB flew numerous non-stop reconnaissance missions over Egypt, Israel and Syria during the Yom Kippur War.

Warner-Robins Air Force Base, Georgia

Warner-Robins AFB, Georgia was not a base of SR-71 operations but it was used as the Senior Year Programs Office (SYPO). There are no further details on SYPO.

Overseas Deployments

Kadena Air Base, Okinawa

The former base of operations for the A-12s was Kadena Air Base, Okinawa, Japan. But beginning on 9 March 1968, Kadena became the first overseas home of the Blackbird. On this date, after a 6.6-hour ferry flight from Beale AFB the first SR-71A (61-7978) – piloted by Buddy Brown with RSO Dave Jensen – arrived at Kadena, which was known as operating location number eight or OL-8. The first SR-71As to arrive were assigned to the 1st Strategic Reconnaissance Squadron (SRS) of the 9th Strategic Reconnaissance Wing (SRW), and while at OL-8 operated as Detachment 1 or Det 1.

The second and third SR-71As (61-7976 and 61-7974) arrived on 11 and 13 March 1968, respectively. They were crewed by pilots Jerome 'Jerry' O'Malley and Bob Spencer, and RSOs Edward 'Ed' Payne and Keith Branham. These aircraft were refuelled by Boeing KC-135Qs off the California coast and again northwest of the Hawaiian Islands by other Stratotankers based at Hickam AFB, Hawaii; a third and final refuelling took place west of Wake Island. In these early days of SR-71A deployments to OL-8, the refuelling missions were called Operation *Glowing Heat*.

It was at Kadena that the Blackbird earned one of its most ensuring nicknames. The local people near Kadena thought the A-12s – and later SR-71s – looked a lot like the Habu, a poisonous pit viper found in south-east Asia, and referred to them as such. Thus, the nickname 'Habu' was adopted by SR-71 crewmen.

The actual date for the Initial Operational Capability (IOC) milestone for the 9th SRW and its growing fleet of mission-capable SR-71A aeroplanes remains unclear – suffice it to say that when the first operational mission was flown on 21 March 1968 – *Habu* one or mission number one – IOC had been met. This first *Habu* mission, flown by Jerry O'Malley and Ed Payne lasted 5.1 hours. They flew the second *Habu* mission on 10 April 1968. Buddy Brown and Dave Jensen flew *Habu* mission number three on 18 April 1968.

One must remember that at this time in history the USA was heavily embroiled in the Vietnam War and these *Habu* missions were dedicated combat missions in which North Vietnamese air defences – comprised of ever-improving Soviet-supplied air-defence radar and missiles – was a major concern. However, with the tremendous operating speeds and extreme altitudes of the Blackbirds during the thousands of enemy airspace penetrations that were eventually flown, the SR-71As proved to be untouchable, even though many were tracked by radar and actually fired upon. Eventually, out of some 2,700 *Habu* missions planned, 2,410 missions were successfully flown by Det 1 at OL-8.

Royal Air Force Mildenhall, United Kingdom

The second overseas base of operations for the Blackbird was in England at Royal Air Force Mildenhall in Suffolk. These 99th SRS, 9th SRW SR-71s were assigned to Det 4, which was established on 31 March 1979. Slower and lower-flying U-2s were also based at RAF Mildenhall at the time, but from 1980 to 1991 only SR-71s flew out of this United States Air Force Europe (USAFE) air base. It remains unclear as to what sort of operations these SR-71As flew but, most likely, they were super-clandestine flights very near the borders of the former USSR.

Bodo Air Base, Norway

This Norwegian air base, referred to as OL-Bodo, was used a couple of times for emergency Blackbird landings, though only two SR-71s landed here, both with equipment malfunctions.

Diego Garcia

Diego Garcia has an air base used in part by USAF aircraft. It is an island of the British Indian Ocean Territory in the Chagos Archipelago. For a relatively short time – 1978 and 1979 – Det 8 Blackbirds conducted operations from there, but what those operations were is a mystery.

End of the Road

On 26 January 1990 the SR-71 was ceremoniously decommissioned at Beale AFB. Then on 6 March 1990, after some twenty-two years of operations without a single loss to enemy action, despite having been fired upon hundreds of times, the fleet of SR-71s was officially retired from further operational duties. In that 22-year period they had flown a total of 3,551 missions.

Specification – SR-71A, SR-71B and SR-71C

Crew:	*SR-71A*: pilot and reconnaissance systems operator; *SR-71B* and *SR-71C*: pilot and instructor pilot
Power plant:	Two Pratt & Whitney J58 (Model JT11D-20A) bleed bypass turbojet engines; 34,000lb (15,400kg) thrust each
Dimensions:	Length 107ft 5in (32.75m) normally, 121ft 4in (37m) for 'Big Tail'; wingspan 55ft 7in (16.98m); wing area 1,795sq ft (166.75sq m); height 18ft 6in (5.67m)
Weights:	Empty 59,000lb (27,000kg); gross 170,000lb (77,000kg)
Performance:	Maximum speed 2,250mph (3,620km/h); Mach 3.3+ (limit CIT of 427°C/800°F); maximum range (unrefuelled) 3,000 miles (4,800km) at design speed of Mach 3.2; ceiling 100,000ft (30,000m)

CHAPTER SIX

Key Personalities in the Blackbird Programme

Clarence L. Johnson

The achievements of Clarence L. 'Kelly' Johnson, the aeronautical engineering wizard who created Lockheed's super-secret Skunk Works and designed the world's fastest and highest-flying air-breathing aircraft, made him an aerospace legend in his own time.

Johnson's numerous achievements go back to the 1930s, but he may be best remembered for organizing the Lockheed Skunk Works in mid-1943. It started as a small unit of engineering and production specialists to hurriedly create, build and fly the World War Two XP-80 jet fighter prototype for the US Army Air Forces. Johnson at first did not especially care for the name 'Skunk Works' for his advanced aircraft shop but eventually grew to accept it.

Born in Ishpeming, Michigan, on 27 February 1910, Clarence Johnson received his nickname of Kelly in elementary school from a popular song of the day, 'Kelly from the Emerald Isle'. His classmates figured that someone who licked the school bully should be known by a somewhat more

Johnson in cockpit of the TA-12. Lockheed Martin

Kelly Johnson poses with the third of three service-test YF-12A air defence fighters. Lockheed Martin

pugilistic name than Clarence. The nickname stayed with him from that point on, and he never backed away from controversy on aircraft design, materials and production techniques.

Johnson joined Lockheed in Burbank, California, in 1933 as an $83-per-month tool designer after receiving a master's degree in aeronautical engineering from the University of Michigan, working his way through college with the aid of some grants. Johnson had earlier impressed Lockheed management as a graduate student when he tested examples of the proposed Lockheed Model 10 Electra transport in the university's wind tunnel and suggested significant design changes.

Five years after joining Lockheed, Johnson was named the company's chief research engineer. He became chief engineer in 1952 and corporate vice-president for research and development in 1956. Even as he advanced in management, Johnson continued as a creator of innovative aircraft. He designed the twin-boom P-38 Lightning – the 'Fork-tailed Devil', as Germany dubbed it in World War Two – and was instrumental in converting the commercial Lockheed Model 14 Super Electra into the celebrated Hudson bomber.

Johnson played a leading role in the design of more than forty other aircraft, including the triple-tailed Constellation transport, the P-2 Neptune anti-submarine patrol plane, the record-setting F-104 Starfighter, the U-2 reconnaissance aircraft and, of course, the Blackbird series.

Johnson became known for his strict adherence to principles. On several occasions he turned back development contracts to the US Department of Defense after initial work indicated the proposed aircraft would not be effective, no matter how much money it was willing to provide. He also returned to the US government approximately $2 million on a $20 million U-2 contract after building twenty-six aircraft for the same money intended to cover twenty aircraft.

He won every major aircraft design award in the industry, some for the second and third time. Included were two Theodore von Karmen Awards, the Wright Brothers Memorial Trophy, two Sylvanus Albert Reed Awards, and the Daniel Guggenheim Medal.

In 1964, President Lyndon B. Johnson presented him the nation's highest civilian honour, the Medal of Freedom. President Ronald W. Reagan honoured him with the National Security Medal in 1983 and the National Medal of Technology in 1988. Johnson was enshrined in the National Aviation Hall of Fame in 1983, which is an honour usually reserved for the deceased.

Kelly Johnson retired from Lockheed in 1975 as a corporate senior vice-president. He resigned from the corporation's board of directors in 1980 but continued to serve as senior advisor until his death. Johnson died on 21 December 1990 at the age of eighty and is honoured by America and by the aerospace community for his outstanding and innovative contributions in advancing aviation and safeguarding the free world.

Anthony W. LeVier

Anthony W. 'Tony' LeVier joined Lockheed in 1941 as an engineering test pilot. Famed for his air-racing ventures, he became chief test pilot and head of flight-

LeVier in the cockpit of the XF-90. Lockheed Martin

test operations before his retirement in 1974 after thirty-three years with Lockheed. He accumulated some 10,000 flying hours during as many as 24,000 flights before hanging up his helmet.

Tony LeVier was a test pilot's test pilot as well as Kelly Johnson's most trusted. He flew everything Lockheed had to offer from its P-38 Lightning onward until his retirement from flight-test activities, having last been chief test pilot on the U-2 programme. He then became head of flight test within the Skunk Works organization. Tony LeVier also played an important part in the 'finding' of Area 51 in 1955 where the U-2s, A-12s, YF-12s and M-21s were secretly assembled and flight tested from early 1962 until mid-1968. He passed away on 6 February 1998 at the age of eighty-four.

Benjamin R. Rich

When the new Lockheed Advanced Development Company was formed in May 1990 from the former Advanced Development Projects group – the Skunk Works – Benjamin R. 'Ben' Rich was named the first president of the Skunk Works and was dubbed 'Chief Skunk'.

Ben Rich, the son of British subjects, was born on 18 June 1925 in Manila, the Philippine Islands. He had planned to become a medical doctor, but a career detour took him to Lockheed in 1950 as an aeronautical engineer and then, in 1954, to the Skunk Works where he cured complications in the design of advanced aircraft.

Rich participated in the thermodynamics, propulsion and preliminary design aspects of the F-104, the U-2 and the Blackbirds. He joined the Blackbird programme

Benjamin R. 'Ben' Rich poses with a Blackbird. Lockheed Martin

in its initial A-1 to A-12 phases in 1958 as an aerothermodynamics engineer. At his suggestion, the Blackbird aircraft were eventually painted black to reduce the searing temperatures upon them.

In 1963, Rich was senior engineer for advanced programmes. Nine years later, he had advanced to vice-president for fighter programmes and preliminary design. In 1975, Ben Rich succeeded Kelly Johnson as a company vice-president and general manager of the Skunk Works, a job he held until 1990 – except for a 1984–86 interim assignment as president of the Lockheed Advanced Aeronautics Company.

Rich became a Lockheed corporate vice-president in 1977.

After retiring in December 1990 following a forty-year Lockheed career, Rich continued to be of service to Lockheed Advanced Development Company and the corporation as a consultant. Leading the development of the F-117A stealth fighter, Rich won the 1989 Collier Trophy in association with the entire Lockheed/USAF team responsible for the success of programme – coincidentally, the first F-117A made its first flight on 18 June 1981, exactly fifty-six years after Rich's birth.

On 5 January 1995 Ben Rich died from cancer at the age of sixty-nine. At his request, his ashes were scattered from an aeroplane near his beachfront house on the California coast in Oxnard. At the moment his ashes were released, a lone F-117A appeared out of the clouds and rocked its wings, waving goodbye, in a final salute to its creator.

Louis W. Schalk Jr

Lou Schalk was born on 29 May 1926 in Alden, Iowa. In 1954 he became a USAF test pilot at Edwards AFB where he performed testing on then-current USAF jet fighters including the F-104 Starfighter. He tested fighters from 1954 to 1957 and then decided to leave the USAF.

Schalk joined Lockheed as an experimental test pilot in July 1957, and the Lockheed ADP group as a test pilot in 1959. He was appointed chief test pilot on the A-12 programme shortly thereafter and was first to fly the type, unofficially on 26 April 1962 and officially on 30 April. He played a major role in the design of the A-12 cockpit and flew the first thirteen test flights on the first A-12. He also made the first four A-12 flights over Mach 3, hitting Mach 3.287 (2,287mph or 3,922.25km/h) at altitudes well over 85,000ft (26,000m).

He co-received the 1964 Society of Experimental Test Pilots Iven C. Kincheloe Award, and retired from flight-test that year. In April 2002 he was inducted into the Blackbird Laurels fraternity, an elite society founded by the Flight Test Historical Foundation.

Lou Shalk died of leukaemia on 16 August 2002, aged seventy-six.

James D. Eastham

James D. 'Jim' Eastham was chief test pilot on the YF-12A programme. He was first to fly the YF-12A on 7 August 1963, second pilot to fly the SR-71A and third pilot to fly the A-12. He joined Lockheed Skunk Works in 1962 as a civilian test pilot and was soon appointed YF-12A chief test pilot.

Jim Eastham was born on 19 June 1924 in El Dorado, Kansas. He flew P-51 Mustangs of the 31st and 55th Fighter Groups in World War Two. He also flew A-26s, F-6s and B-17s of the 45th Reconnaissance Squadron. He flew C-47s of the 60th Troop Carrier Group in the Berlin Airlift.

LEFT: **Louis W. 'Lou' Schalk by an F-104.** Lockheed Martin

ABOVE: **James D. 'Jim' Eastham and a YF-12A.**
Lockheed Martin

He flew F-84s of the 31st Strategic Fighter Wing in the Korean War.

After his post-war employment as an engineer and production test pilot with McDonnell Aircraft he joined the experimental flight-test department of Hughes Aircraft in 1956. He was then project test pilot on the Falcon air-to-air missile programme for four years. During this time, he flew about 800 test missions in the F-102, F-106 and B-58. He fired about 350 missiles, which is a record for the number of missiles fired by one person. He also did development testing on various fire-control systems, infra-red systems and automatic flight-control systems for the F-101, F-102 and F-106 aircraft.

After attending the Strategic Air Command's B-58 Combat Crew Training School in 1961 – graduating number one in his class – he became Hughes Project Test Pilot on a modified B-58, which was used as a test vehicle for developing the AN/ASG pulse-Doppler radar system and the AIM-47 missile. He flew the B-58 until the conclusion of that programme in 1964.

He flew the B-58, A-12 and YF-12A programmes while working simultaneously for both Hughes and Lockheed. He was instrumental in the world speed records established by the YF-12A on 1 May 1965 because he was first to fly the speed courses to perfect the required manoeuvring techniques that the USAF pilots used to officially set the records. He is the author of the YF-12A Flight Manual.

He is a holder of the 1964 Kincheloe award as top test pilot by the Society of Experimental Test Pilots and Aerospace Walk of Honour nominee.

Robert J. Gilliland

Robert J. 'Bob' Gilliland was born in Memphis, Tennessee, and joined Lockheed in 1960 as a civilian test pilot. He was first assigned to the F-104 Starfighter programme, flying all models. He had previously served in the US Navy and US Air Force, having flown numerous combat missions in the Korean War. He flew F-84s in Korea and, later, F-86s in Germany.

In 1962 he joined the Skunk Works and, at Groom Lake, flew the A-12 and

ABOVE: William M. 'Bill' Park. Lockheed Martin

LEFT: Robert J. 'Bob' Gilliland and an SR-71A. Lockheed Martin

YF-12A. He was later appointed chief test pilot on the SR-71 programme and made the first flight of SR-71A number one on 22 December 1964. He made the first flight on SR-71B number one on 18 November 1965. He had earlier made the first flight of YF-12A number three on 13 March 1964.

Bob Gilliland is now retired from Lockheed, but during his flight-test days in the Blackbird programme he accumulated more time above Mach 3 than any other test pilot. He holds the Kincheloe award as top test pilot by the Society of Experimental Test Pilots and became a trustee of the Association of Naval Aviation. And he is credited with full performance envelope expansion on both the SR-71A and SR-71B aeroplanes.

William M. Park

William M. 'Bill' Park was chief test pilot on the M-21 programme, and made the first captive-carry D-21 test flight on 22 December 1964. He was second to pilot the A-12 in May 1962 and later became heavily involved in the *Have Blue* XST and F-117 programmes.

Bill Park was born 8 March 1926 in Columbia, South Carolina. Serving as a USAF combat pilot flying the Lockheed F-80 Shooting Star, he flew 112 combat missions in the Korean War and earned the Distinguished Flying Cross. He joined Lockheed in 1957 as an engineering test pilot and at first flight-tested F-104 Starfighters.

He was assigned to the A-12 programme in late 1961 and, on 21 December 1966, Park flew 10,198 miles (16,409km) in six hours. That long-endurance flight set a record unapproachable by any other aircraft at the time.

He later became chief test pilot on the Lockheed *Have Blue* XST programme, making the first flight of the type on 1 December 1977. He was injured during his emergency ejection in May 1978 when *Have Blue* XST number one had to be abandoned in flight and, due to injuries incurred, he was forced to retire from flying.

He was awarded two Kincheloe Awards for outstanding achievement in flight-test, and was one of five pilots inducted into the Aerospace Walk of Honour.

CHAPTER SEVEN

Structures and Systems

The CIA code-named the project Oxcart, a misnomer to end all: at Mach 3, our spyplane would zip across the skies faster than a high-velocity rifle bullet.

BEN RICH

SR-71A 955 just before touch-down at Beale AFB. Lockheed Martin

The Blackbirds – the A-12, YF-12, M-21 and SR-71 – were large delta-wing, single- and two-seater aeroplanes powered by two axial-flow J58 bleed-bypass turbojet engines. Built of titanium alloy construction, they were designed to operate at very high altitudes and very high supersonic speeds. They had very thin wings, twin inward-canted vertical stabilizer/rudder assemblies mounted on top of the engine nacelles, and a pronounced fuselage 'chine' extending from the leading edge of the wings to the nose. While each and every one of the Blackbirds' large number of structures and systems cannot be covered in detail in the confines of this one book, what follows is an overview of the most important ones.

Camera Systems The A-12 employed two different types of cameras: a 48in (121.9cm) focal length Itek KA-102A and a 60in (152.5cm) focal length Actron Type H. Both types offered negatives in 4.5 × 4.5in (11.43 × 11.43cm) format which provided very large, high-resolution photographs. In fact, from an altitude of 80,000ft (24,000m) on a clear day, an A-12 photograph could show the brand name on a pack of cigarettes lying flat on a picnic table.

The SR-71 first used an Itek camera with a focal length of 36in (91.4cm), but later one with a focal length of 48in (121.9cm) was used. In one hour the SR-71 could photograph 100,000sq miles (260,000sq km) from the pilot's left horizon to his right horizon.

STRUCTURES AND SYSTEMS

ABOVE: **A KC-135Q pumps JP-7 into SR-71A 968.** Lockheed Martin

BELOW: **A fine study of SR-71A 955 with the Skunk Works logo.** Lockheed Martin

STRUCTURES AND SYSTEMS

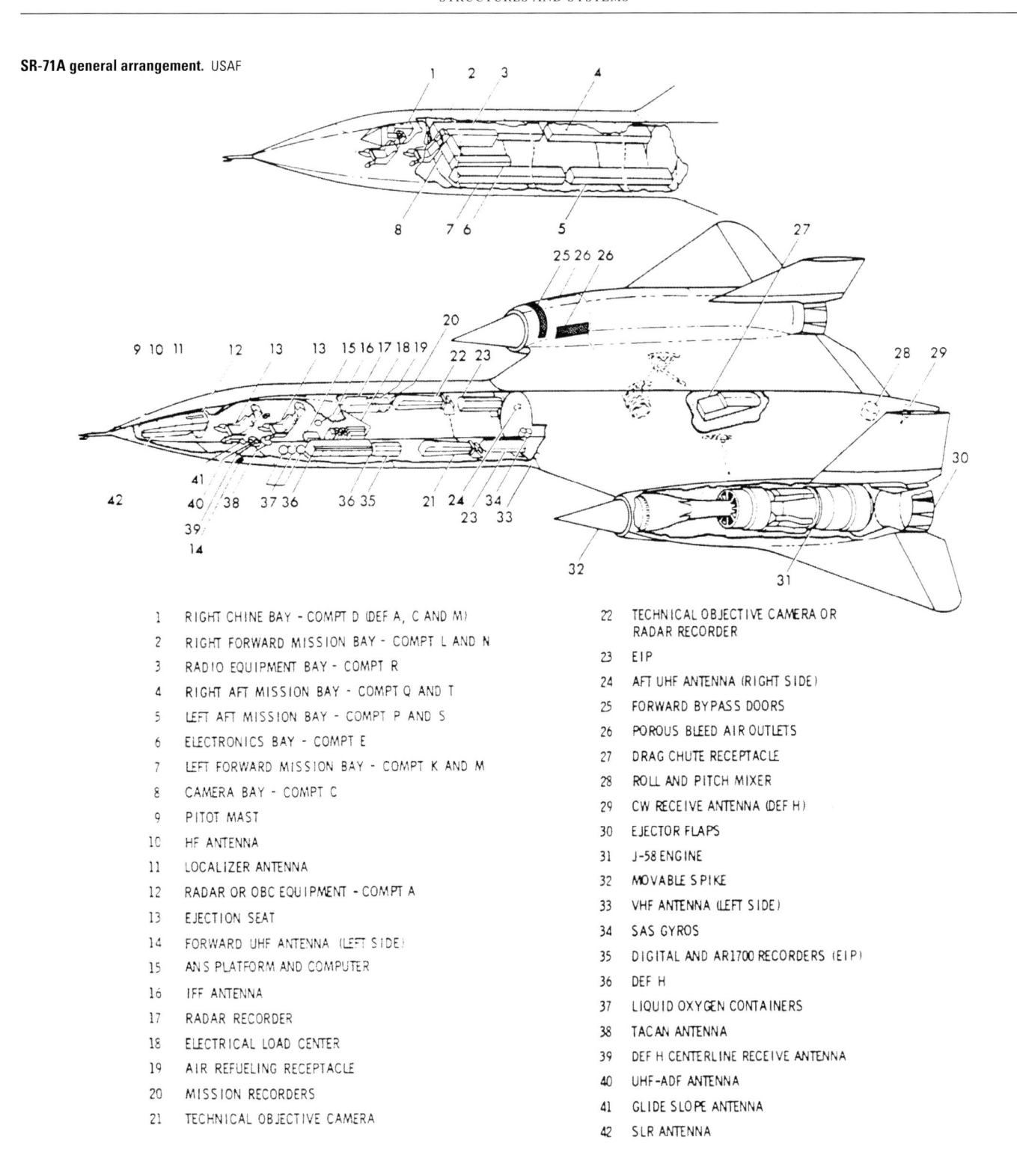

SR-71A general arrangement. USAF

1	RIGHT CHINE BAY - COMPT D (DEF A, C AND M)
2	RIGHT FORWARD MISSION BAY - COMPT L AND N
3	RADIO EQUIPMENT BAY - COMPT R
4	RIGHT AFT MISSION BAY - COMPT Q AND T
5	LEFT AFT MISSION BAY - COMPT P AND S
6	ELECTRONICS BAY - COMPT E
7	LEFT FORWARD MISSION BAY - COMPT K AND M
8	CAMERA BAY - COMPT C
9	PITOT MAST
10	HF ANTENNA
11	LOCALIZER ANTENNA
12	RADAR OR OBC EQUIPMENT - COMPT A
13	EJECTION SEAT
14	FORWARD UHF ANTENNA (LEFT SIDE)
15	ANS PLATFORM AND COMPUTER
16	IFF ANTENNA
17	RADAR RECORDER
18	ELECTRICAL LOAD CENTER
19	AIR REFUELING RECEPTACLE
20	MISSION RECORDERS
21	TECHNICAL OBJECTIVE CAMERA
22	TECHNICAL OBJECTIVE CAMERA OR RADAR RECORDER
23	EIP
24	AFT UHF ANTENNA (RIGHT SIDE)
25	FORWARD BYPASS DOORS
26	POROUS BLEED AIR OUTLETS
27	DRAG CHUTE RECEPTACLE
28	ROLL AND PITCH MIXER
29	CW RECEIVE ANTENNA (DEF H)
30	EJECTOR FLAPS
31	J-58 ENGINE
32	MOVABLE SPIKE
33	VHF ANTENNA (LEFT SIDE)
34	SAS GYROS
35	DIGITAL AND AR1700 RECORDERS (EIP)
36	DEF H
37	LIQUID OXYGEN CONTAINERS
38	TACAN ANTENNA
39	DEF H CENTERLINE RECEIVE ANTENNA
40	UHF-ADF ANTENNA
41	GLIDE SLOPE ANTENNA
42	SLR ANTENNA

Cockpit Several different cockpit configurations were featured in the Blackbird aircraft. The A-12 had a cockpit for a pilot only. The other variants had two cockpits: one for the pilot and one for (YF-21) a Fire Control Officer (FCO); (M-21) a Launch Control Officer (LCO); (SR-71A) a Reconnaissance Systems Officer (RSO). The TA-12, SR-71B and SR-71C had cockpits for two pilots, student and instructor; the rear cockpits of these subtypes were raised so the pilots could see forward and the visibility was more than adequate for the instructors.

Equipment Bays The SR-71 had eight equipment bays to house its camera, sensors and other specialized equipment. These were located in the fuselage chines and carried up to 2,770lb (1,260kg) of electronic sensors and photographic reconnaissance equipment. These sensors

91

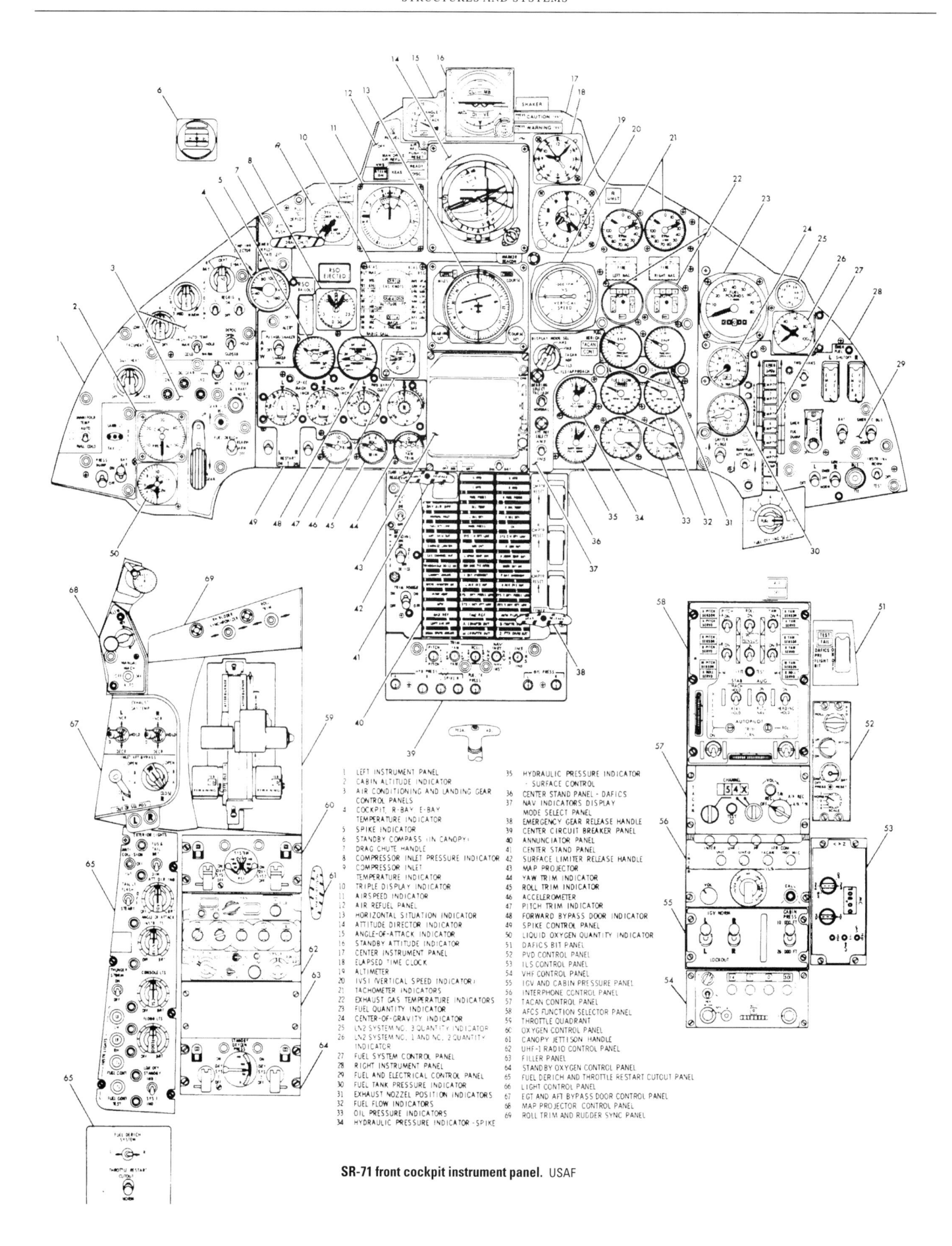

STRUCTURES AND SYSTEMS

1. LEFT INSTRUMENT PANEL
2. CABIN ALTITUDE INDICATOR
3. AIR CONDITIONING AND LANDING GEAR CONTROL PANELS
4. COCKPIT, R-BAY E-BAY TEMPERATURE INDICATOR
5. SPIKE INDICATOR
6. STANDBY COMPASS (IN CANOPY)
7. DRAG CHUTE HANDLE
8. COMPRESSOR INLET PRESSURE INDICATOR
9. COMPRESSOR INLET TEMPERATURE INDICATOR
10. TRIPLE DISPLAY INDICATOR
11. AIRSPEED INDICATOR
12. AIR REFUEL PANEL
13. HORIZONTAL SITUATION INDICATOR
14. ATTITUDE DIRECTOR INDICATOR
15. ANGLE-OF-ATTACK INDICATOR
16. STANDBY ATTITUDE INDICATOR
17. CENTER INSTRUMENT PANEL
18. ELAPSED TIME CLOCK
19. ALTIMETER
20. IVSI (VERTICAL SPEED INDICATOR)
21. TACHOMETER INDICATORS
22. EXHAUST GAS TEMPERATURE INDICATORS
23. FUEL QUANTITY INDICATOR
24. CENTER-OF-GRAVITY INDICATOR
25. LN2 SYSTEM NO. 3 QUANTITY INDICATOR
26. LN2 SYSTEM NO. 1 AND NO. 2 QUANTITY INDICATOR
27. FUEL SYSTEM CONTROL PANEL
28. RIGHT INSTRUMENT PANEL
29. FUEL AND ELECTRICAL CONTROL PANEL
30. FUEL TANK PRESSURE INDICATOR
31. EXHAUST NOZZEL POSITION INDICATORS
32. FUEL FLOW INDICATORS
33. OIL PRESSURE INDICATORS
34. HYDRAULIC PRESSURE INDICATOR - SPIKE
35. HYDRAULIC PRESSURE INDICATOR - SURFACE CONTROL
36. CENTER STAND PANEL - DAFICS
37. NAV INDICATORS DISPLAY MODE SELECT PANEL
38. EMERGENCY GEAR RELEASE HANDLE
39. CENTER CIRCUIT BREAKER PANEL
40. ANNUNCIATOR PANEL
41. CENTER STAND PANEL
42. SURFACE LIMITER RELEASE HANDLE
43. MAP PROJECTOR
44. YAW TRIM INDICATOR
45. ROLL TRIM INDICATOR
46. ACCELEROMETER
47. PITCH TRIM INDICATOR
48. FORWARD BYPASS DOOR INDICATOR
49. SPIKE CONTROL PANEL
50. LIQUID OXYGEN QUANTITY INDICATOR
51. DAFICS BIT PANEL
52. PVD CONTROL PANEL
53. ILS CONTROL PANEL
54. VHF CONTROL PANEL
55. IGV AND CABIN PRESSURE PANEL
56. INTERPHONE CONTROL PANEL
57. TACAN CONTROL PANEL
58. AFCS FUNCTION SELECTOR PANEL
59. THROTTLE QUADRANT
60. OXYGEN CONTROL PANEL
61. CANOPY JETTISON HANDLE
62. UHF-1 RADIO CONTROL PANEL
63. FILLER PANEL
64. STANDBY OXYGEN CONTROL PANEL
65. FUEL DERICH AND THROTTLE RESTART CUTOUT PANEL
66. LIGHT CONTROL PANEL
67. EGT AND AFT BYPASS DOOR CONTROL PANEL
68. MAP PROJECTOR CONTROL PANEL
69. ROLL TRIM AND RUDDER SYNC PANEL

SR-71 front cockpit instrument panel. USAF

92

STRUCTURES AND SYSTEMS

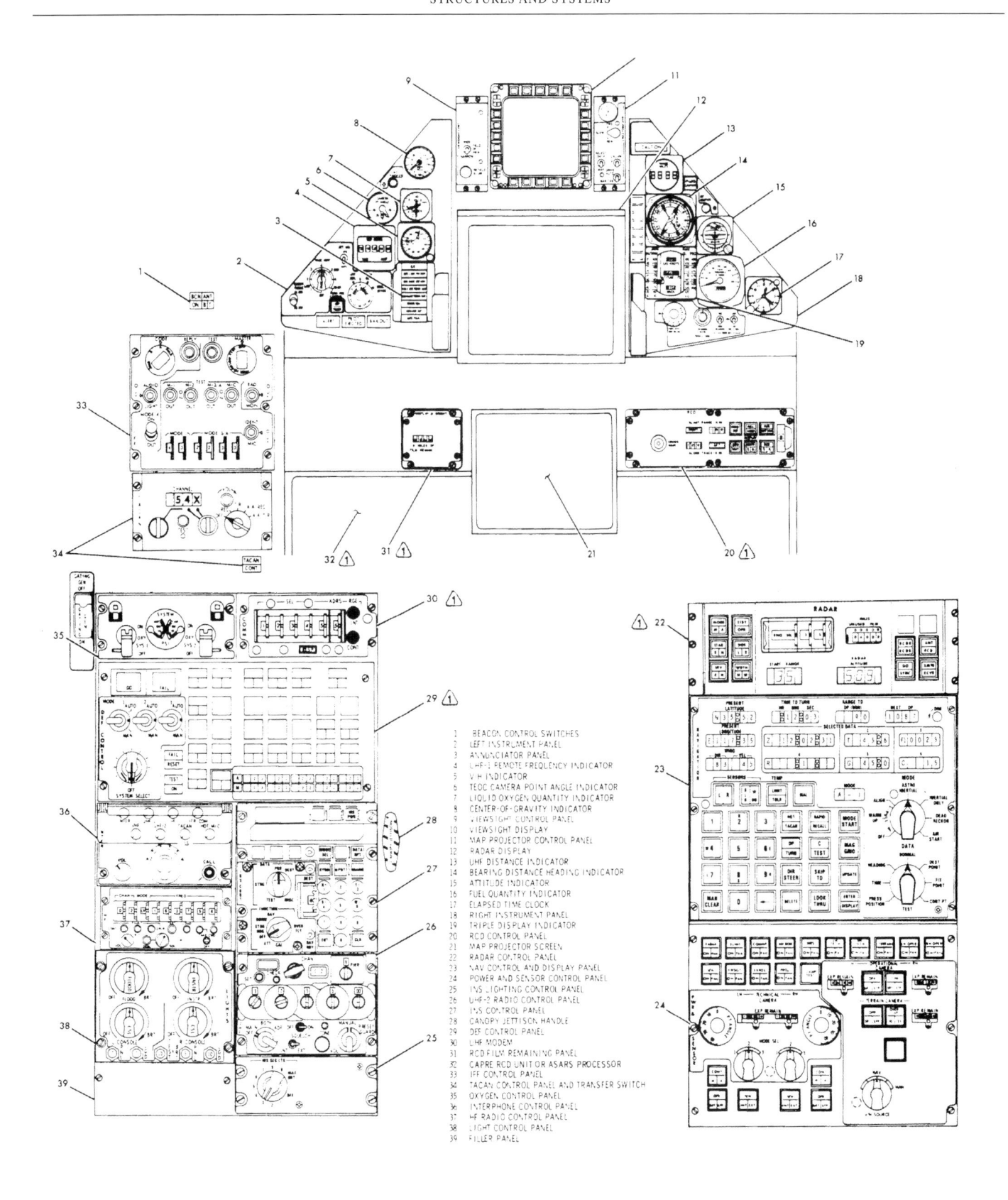

1. BEACON CONTROL SWITCHES
2. LEFT INSTRUMENT PANEL
3. ANNUNCIATOR PANEL
4. UHF-1 REMOTE FREQUENCY INDICATOR
5. V/H INDICATOR
6. TEOC CAMERA POINT ANGLE INDICATOR
7. LIQUID OXYGEN QUANTITY INDICATOR
8. CENTER-OF-GRAVITY INDICATOR
9. VIEWSIGHT CONTROL PANEL
10. VIEWSIGHT DISPLAY
11. MAP PROJECTOR CONTROL PANEL
12. RADAR DISPLAY
13. UHF DISTANCE INDICATOR
14. BEARING DISTANCE HEADING INDICATOR
15. ATTITUDE INDICATOR
16. FUEL QUANTITY INDICATOR
17. ELAPSED TIME CLOCK
18. RIGHT INSTRUMENT PANEL
19. TRIPLE DISPLAY INDICATOR
20. RCD CONTROL PANEL
21. MAP PROJECTOR SCREEN
22. RADAR CONTROL PANEL
23. NAV CONTROL AND DISPLAY PANEL
24. POWER AND SENSOR CONTROL PANEL
25. INS LIGHTING CONTROL PANEL
26. UHF-2 RADIO CONTROL PANEL
27. INS CONTROL PANEL
28. CANOPY JETTISON HANDLE
29. DEF CONTROL PANEL
30. UHF MODEM
31. RCD FILM REMAINING PANEL
32. CAPRE RCD UNIT OR ASARS PROCESSOR
33. IFF CONTROL PANEL
34. TACAN CONTROL PANEL AND TRANSFER SWITCH
35. OXYGEN CONTROL PANEL
36. INTERPHONE CONTROL PANEL
37. HF RADIO CONTROL PANEL
38. LIGHT CONTROL PANEL
39. FILLER PANEL

SR-71 rear cockpit instrument panel. The triangle icons denote non-viewable areas of this schematic. USAF

Afterburners ablaze, an SR-71A heads out on a mission. Lockheed Martin

were optimized to gather electronic intelligence (ELINT) and signal intelligence (SIGINT). Some of these bays had several compartments for varied equipment. They are as follows: right chine bay, compartment D; right forward mission bay, compartments L and N; radio equipment bay, compartment R; right aft mission bay, compartments Q and T; left aft mission bay, compartments P and S; electronics bay, compartment E; left forward mission bay, compartments K and M; and camera bay, compartment C. Compartment A in the nose bay housed the radar system. The A-12 had a similar arrangement of equipment bays but came with a special type of Q-bay for a larger and heavier camera.

Flight Control Characteristics The SR-71 and its predecessor aeroplanes, operated in a large Mach number and altitude envelope. Typical SR-71 take-off and landing airspeeds were 210 and 155kt (240 and 180mph, or 390 and 290km/h), respectively; climbs were at 400–450kt estimated airspeed or KEAS, and normal supersonic cruise was from 310 to 400 KEAS, depending on altitude, temperature and aircraft weight. These aircraft obtained maximum cruise performance near Mach 3.2 at altitudes from 74,000–85,000ft (22,000–26,000m). The external configuration (aerodynamics), engine air inlet system, J58 engine, and fuel sequencing were optimized for Mach 3.2. True airspeeds attained were near 2,130mph (1,850kt or 3,400km/h). The aircraft was fitted with a Digital Automatic Flight and Inlet Control System (DAFICS), which consisted of five major subsystems: Stability Augmentation System (SAS); autopilot/Mach trim system; automatic pitch warning and high angle-of-attack system; automatic/manual engine air-inlet control system; and air-data system. The three-axis SAS was an integral part of the aircraft-control system and was normally used for all flight conditions.

Stability Augmentation System The Blackbirds all employed a Stability Augmentation System (SAS) to aid their pilots with aircraft controllability. The SAS was a combination of electronic and hydraulic equipment and was an integral part of the Blackbird's flight-control system. It was normally engaged during all phases of flight, but could be disengaged manually. Each axis of SAS (pitch, roll and yaw) was provided with two SAS channels. The SAS detected

STRUCTURES AND SYSTEMS

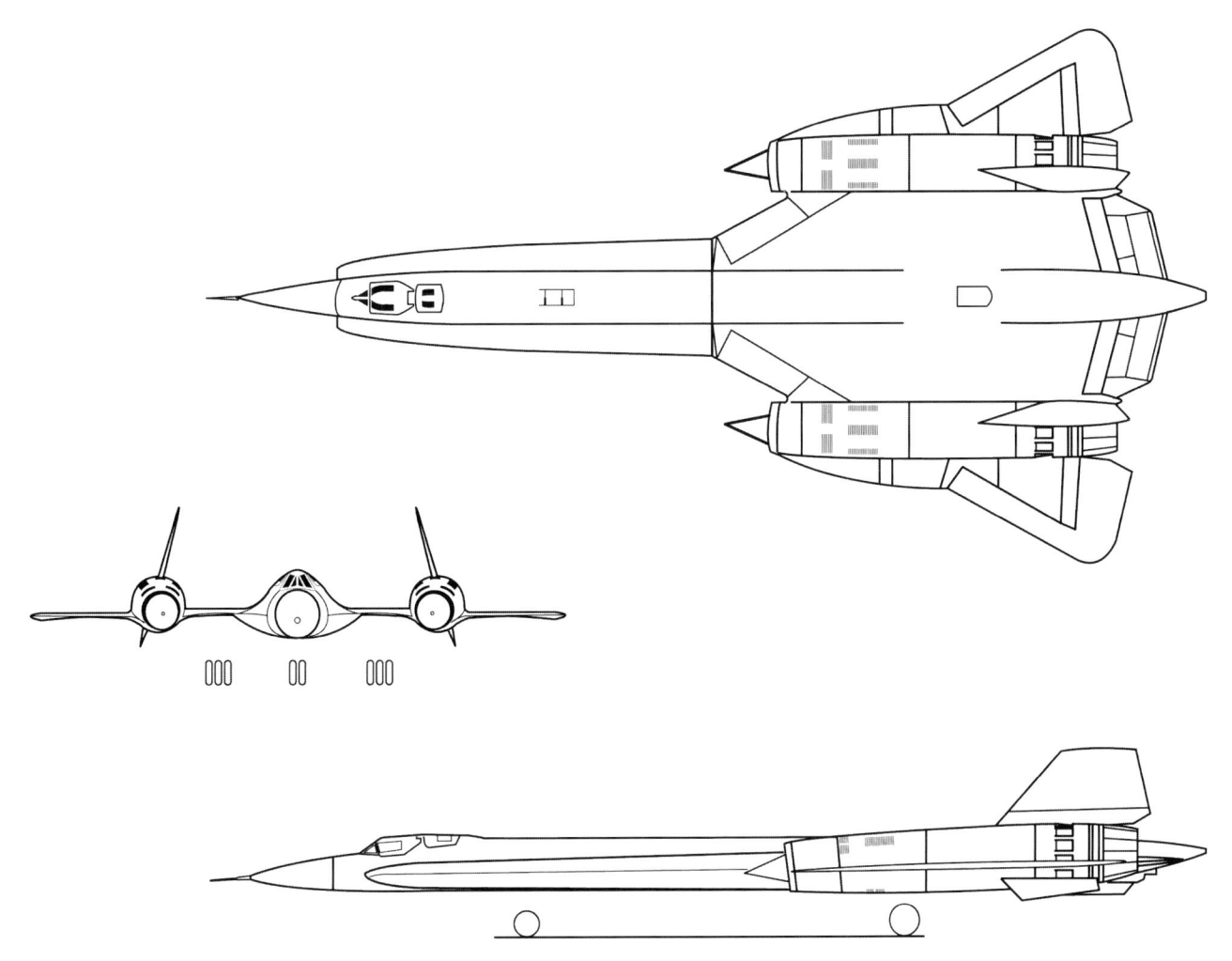

YF-12A general arrangement. NASA

aircraft attitude changes and initiated control-surface deflections to counteract the changes. Normally, the Digital Automatic Flight Inlet Control System A or DAFICS A computer ran the A channel in pitch and yaw, and the DAFICS B channel ran the B channel in pitch and yaw. The DAFICS M computer could take over for A computer or B computer, or both, in the pitch and yaw axis should A and/or B computer fail. The M computer could drive through servo amplifiers in the A and B computer to provide surface control. The roll SAS was configured so that either A or B computer was capable of driving both roll servo channels. Sensor and servo monitors provided detection and automatic disengaging capability for faults.

During normal flight conditions the aircraft experienced many small changes in attitude due to air loads or control inputs. These attitude changes were sensed by pitch, yaw and roll sensors in each axis (three rate gyros in the pitch axis, three rate gyros plus three lateral accelerometers in the yaw axis, and two rate gyros in the roll axis). Analytical redundancy derived from the DAFICS computers from attitude displacements provided added redundancy for pitch, yaw and roll rate gyros, but not for the lateral accelerometers. The attitude changes detected by the sensors were sent to the DAFICS computers which electronically commanded the transfer-valve positions of the SAS servos. The transfer valve converted the electrical signal(s) into a proportional hydraulic flow into the SAS servo actuators. The SAS servos positioned the flight-control surfaces to compensate for the original sensed rate of attitude change. In the SR-71 the three pitch and the three yaw gyros are mounted in the number two fuel tank; the two roll gyros in the R bay; and the lateral accelerometers are in the nose-gear wheel well. The SAS controlled the autopilot as well as Mach number hold while in the autopilot mode and every single flight function of the aircraft.

Delta Wing The large delta wings were made of corrugated titanium alloy and had elevons (combined elevators and ailerons) attached to the trailing-edge, two inboard and two outboard, for pitch and roll control. The 6,000lb (2,700kg) engines were housed in very large-diameter engine nacelles at mid-span. The outboard portion of the wing's leading edge had negative conical camber. This moved the centre of lift inboard to relieve loading on the engine nacelle carry-through structure. It also improved the maximum lift characteristics of the outboard wing at high angles of attack, and enhanced crosswind landing capability.

The SR-71's wing had normal delta-wing characteristics. There was a large

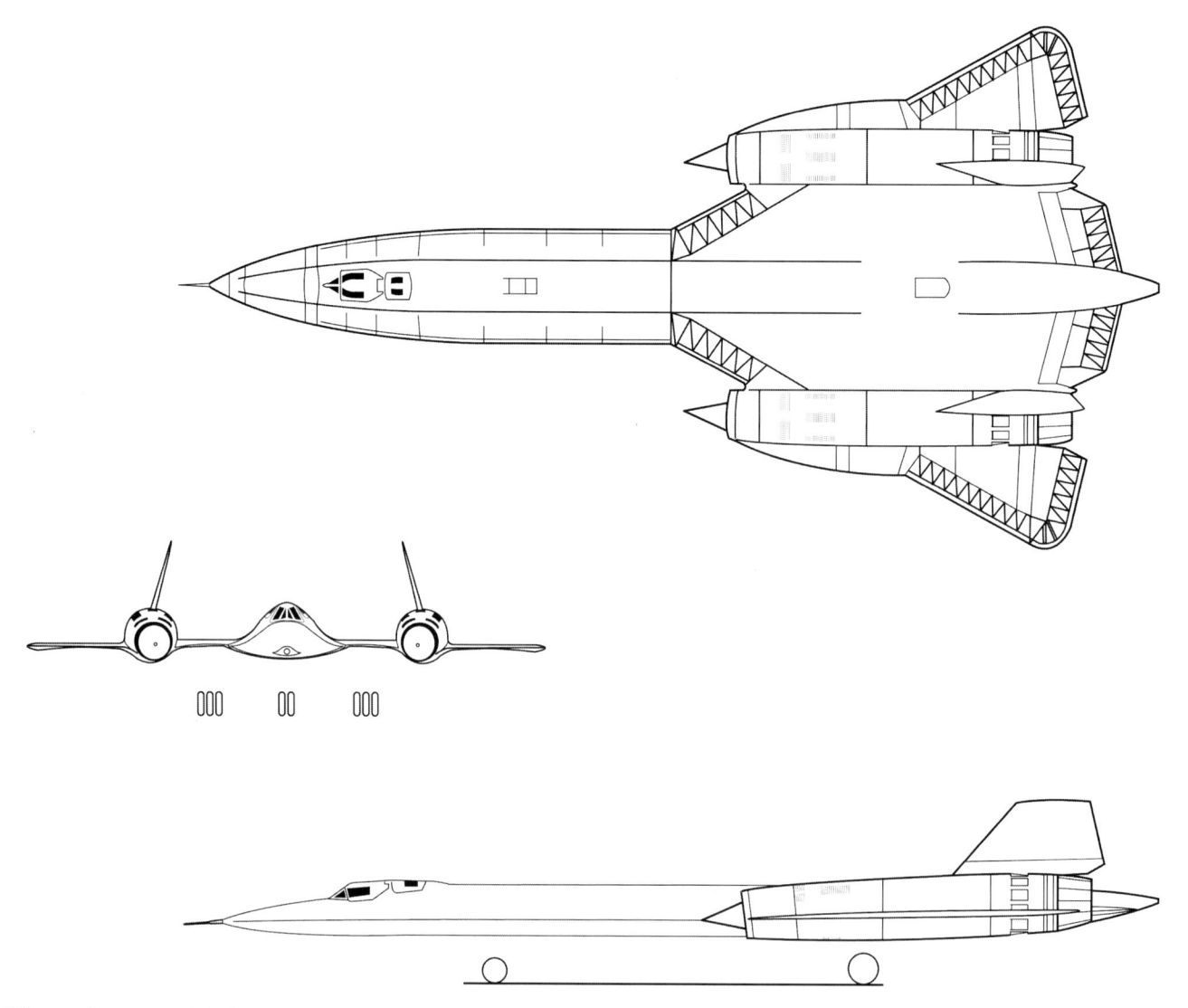

SR-71A general arrangement. NASA

increase in drag as the limiting angle of attack was approached. This could cause very high rates of sink to develop if the aircraft was flown too slow. Dihedral effect was positive, but diminished at higher Mach numbers. Roll damping was relatively low over the entire speed range and lateral-directional qualities were poor with SAS off.

Chines The SR-71 had a blended forward wing (chine) extending from the nose to the wing leading edge. This chined forebody represented approximately 40 per cent of the aircraft length. The chines improved directional stability with increasing angle of attack at all speeds. However, their primary purpose was to provide a substantial portion of the total lift at high supersonic speeds and eliminate a need for canard foreplane-type flying surfaces or special nose-up trimming devices.

Rudders The Blackbirds had two full-moving vertical tails mounted on stubs to fixed bases for yaw (directional) control and stability. They were canted inward 15 degrees and served double duty as the aircraft's vertical stabilizers and rudders.

At first the vertical stabilizers/rudders were made of titanium alloy but they were soon replaced by plastic-like structures that could resist the very high-temperature environment in which the Blackbirds flew. This plastic-like composite honeycomb sandwich panel structure is known as Narmco plastic, and was made of asbestos and fibreglass laminates.

Fuel System The fuel system for all the Blackbird variants was similar, but it is the SR-71A and SR-71B fuel system that is now discussed. These aircraft had five individual fuselage fuel tanks – tanks 1A, 1, 2, 4 and 5 – and two wing/fuselage fuel tank groups – tanks 3 and 6. Tank 6 is further divided into 6A and 6B.

Tank 1A was a small tank located immediately forward of tank 1, which it fed into. Tanks 3 and 6 consisted of three and five tank groups, respectively. The number 3 tank group consisted of the forward section of each wing and a fuselage tank. The number 6 tank group was located in the wings on either side of tanks 4 and 5, and included a small sump tank (about 12 US gallons or 10 Imperial gallons) at the extreme aft end of the fuselage, which contained the boost

STRUCTURES AND SYSTEMS

SR-71B general arrangement. NASA

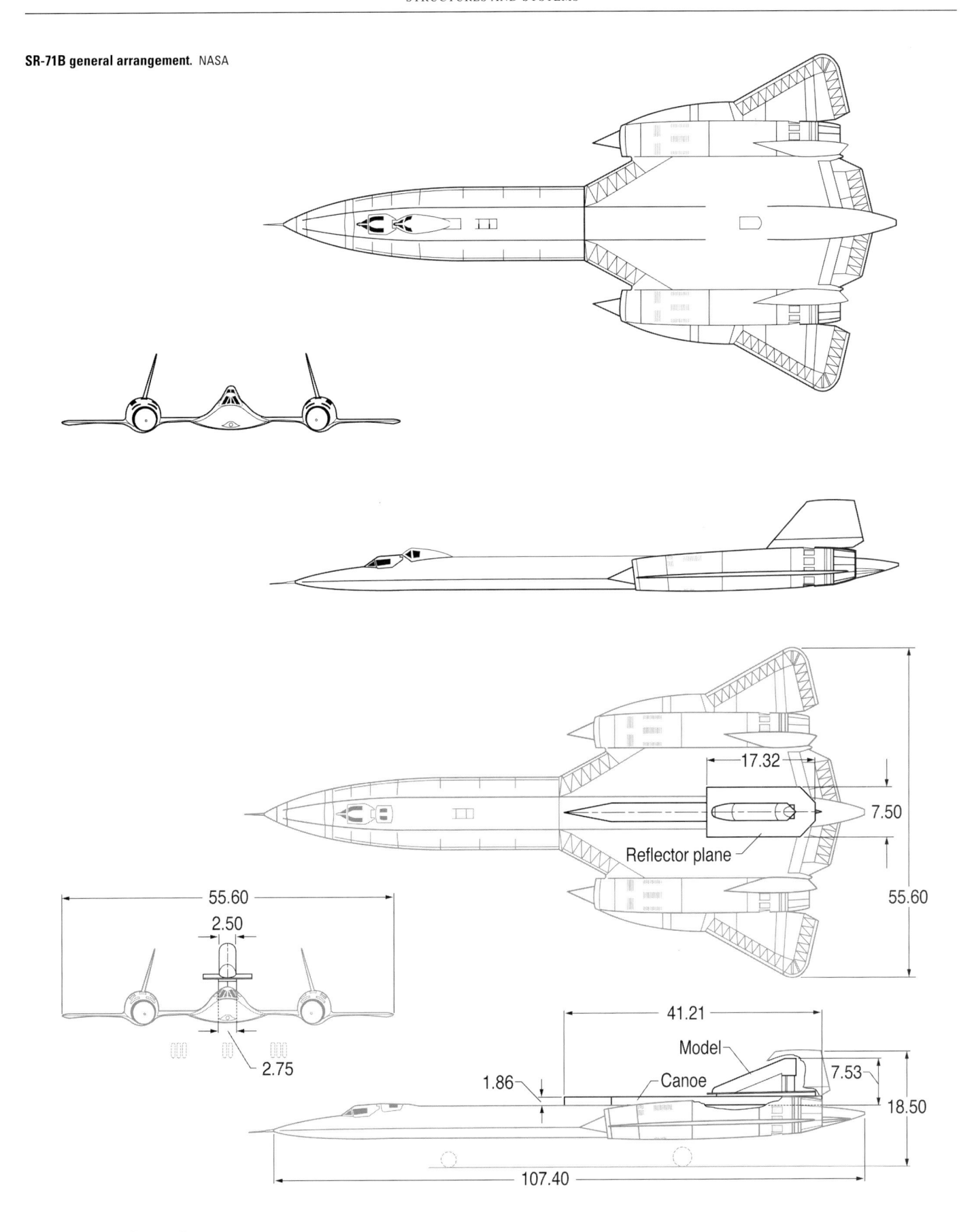

SR-71A with LASRE general arrangement. NASA

97

STRUCTURES AND SYSTEMS

Fuel tank arrangement. USAF

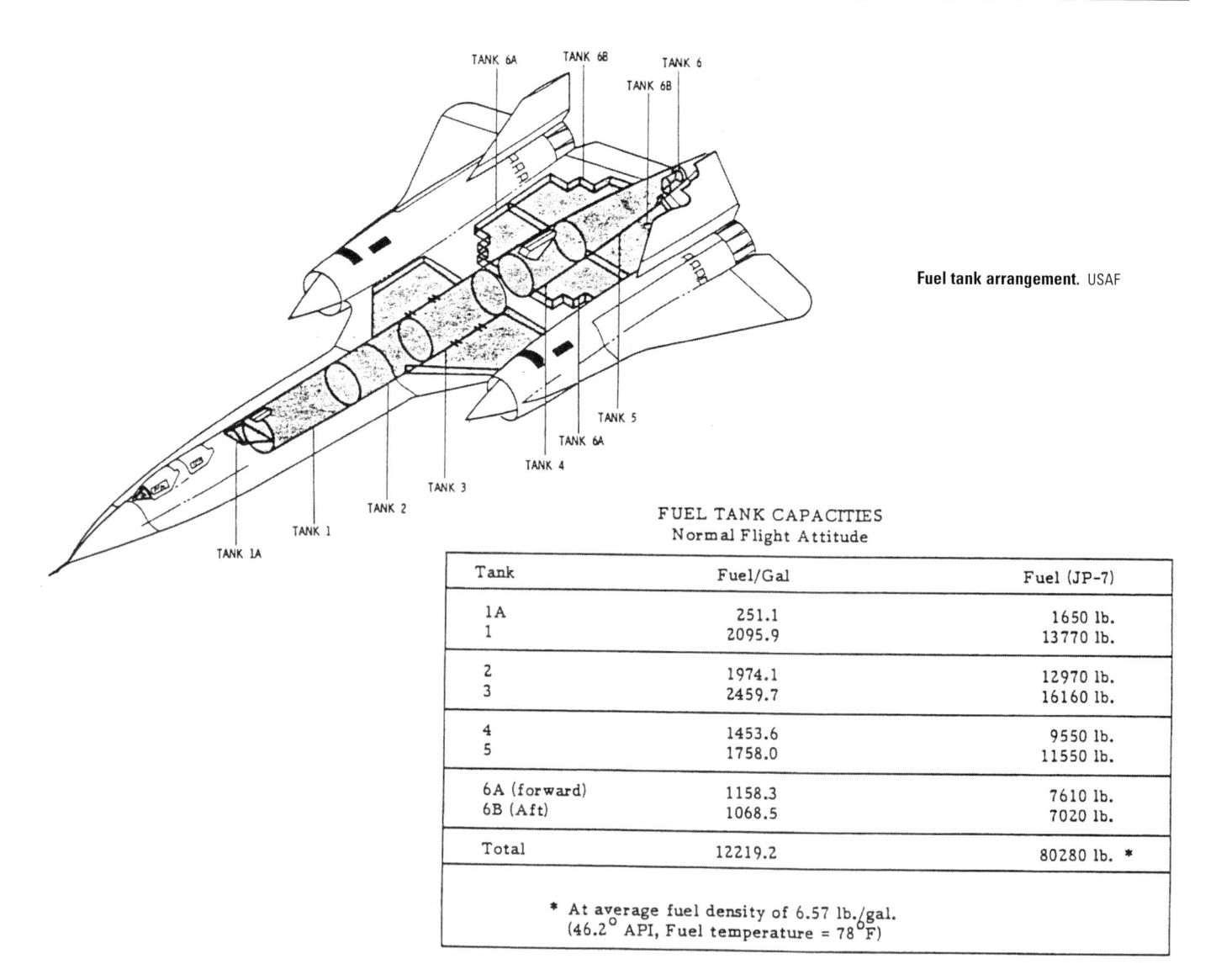

FUEL TANK CAPACITIES
Normal Flight Attitude

Tank	Fuel/Gal	Fuel (JP-7)
1A	251.1	1650 lb.
1	2095.9	13770 lb.
2	1974.1	12970 lb.
3	2459.7	16160 lb.
4	1453.6	9550 lb.
5	1758.0	11550 lb.
6A (forward)	1158.3	7610 lb.
6B (Aft)	1068.5	7020 lb.
Total	12219.2	80280 lb. *

* At average fuel density of 6.57 lb./gal.
(46.2° API, Fuel temperature = 78°F)

pumps for the group. The left engine was supplied from the left fuel manifold which was normally fed from tanks 1, 2, 3 and 4. The right engine was supplied from the right fuel manifold, which was normally fed from tanks 1, 4, 5 and 6. However, a crossfeed feature allowed either engine to be fed from any tank. A maximum of 12,219.2 US gallons (10,175 Imperial gallons) of the specially blended JP-7 fuel, which weighed 80,280lb (36,415kg), was carried by the SR-71.

Fuselage The titanium alloy and composite honeycomb fuselages of the A-12, YF-12 and SR-71 appeared similar at first glance but are quite different in their respective configurations. The A-12 featured a single-place configuration with a Q-bay aft of the cockpit for its special camera. It also had less-pronounced chines, which curved slightly inward before meeting the apex of the nose. The YF-12 had abbreviated chines to accommodate the infra-red 'eyeballs' associated with the missile radar and fire-control system. The SR-71 chines were of a broader chord than those of its predecessors and had an unbroken sweep angle all the way to the apex of the nose. The SR-71s also had the greatest fuselage length of the series.

Landing Gear System and Drag Chute
The landing gear arrangement was for the most part identical on all three versions of the Blackbird. It was a standard tricycle arrangement, each nose landing-gear assembly having two wheels and tyres, while each main landing-gear assembly had three wheels and tyres, for a total of eight wheels and tyres per aeroplane. The nose-gear retracted forward while the main landing-gear retracted inward toward the centreline. The landing gear was electrically controlled and hydraulically actuated.

The drag chute reduced landing roll and aborted take-off roll-out distance. The drag chute assembly – comprised of a 42in (107cm) diameter vane-type pilot parachute, a 10ft (3m) diameter ribbon-type extraction parachute and a 40ft (12m) diameter ribbon-type main parachute, was stowed in an aft fuselage compartment above fuel tank number 4. It was normally deployed electrically, but could be deployed manually if needed.

Q-bay The A-12 was the only version of the Blackbird that featured a special Q-bay. The large-capacity Q-bay, located just aft of the cockpit and on centreline, housed the special 60in (153cm) focal length Actron Type H or 48in (122cm) focal length Itek KA-102A cameras exclusively employed by the A-12 aeroplanes. (The SR-71 has a Q-bay but it was for electronic sensors, not a camera, and is quite different than that employed by the A-12.)

CHAPTER EIGHT

The J58 Engine

The centreline of the basic J58 engine was laid down in late 1956. It was to be an afterburning turbojet rated at 26,000lb maximum take-off thrust and was to power a US Navy attack aircraft, which would have a dash capability of up to Mach 3 for several seconds.

WILLIAM H. BROWN

It is often said that an airframe is only as good as its power plant. No powered aeroplane, whether it is the Wright Flyer of 1903 or the Blackbird of the early 1960s can be successful without an efficient engine. In the case of the 1903 Wright Flyer it was a homebuilt four-cylinder, 12bhp engine weighing about 200lb (90kg), which was perfect for its purpose. But in the case of the Blackbird it was an axial-flow 32,500–34,000lb (14,700–15,400kg) thrust behemoth, the Pratt & Whitney (P&W) Model JT11D-20 or J58 bleed bypass turbojet engine, weighing approximately 6,000lb (2,700kg). It was these high bypass ratio engines that gave the A-12, YF-12, M-21 and SR-71 aircraft their unparalleled high-speed, high-altitude performance.

So special was the P&W J58 engine it required a special fuel, called JP-7. This was exclusively delivered to the Blackbirds in flight by two special variants of the Boeing KC-135 Stratotanker designated at first KC-135Q and, after being retrofitted with new engines, KC-135T.

Developmental Highlights

Originally, what became the J58 was an outgrowth of the dual-cycle (turbojet/ramjet) P&W Model JTN9 (J91), which had been in competition with the more conventional axial-flow General Electric (GE) Model 7E (J93). The P&W J91 and the GE J93 engines, both of which delivered some 30,000lb (13,600kg) thrust, were being evaluated by Boeing and North American to power their respective Weapon System 110A/L entries. Weapon System 110A/L (WS-110A/L) was to be a high-speed, high-altitude, strategic bomber/reconnaissance bomber to at first supplement and then replace the subsonic Boeing B-52 Stratofortress. In the end, Boeing elected to propel its WS-110A/L entry with six P&W J91s while North American chose to power its contender with six GE J93s. North American eventually won the WS-110A/L competition and was awarded a contract to build what was soon designated B-70 and named Valkyrie. Another projected use of the P&W Model JTN9 was in hydrogen-fuelled form, to power the Lockheed Model

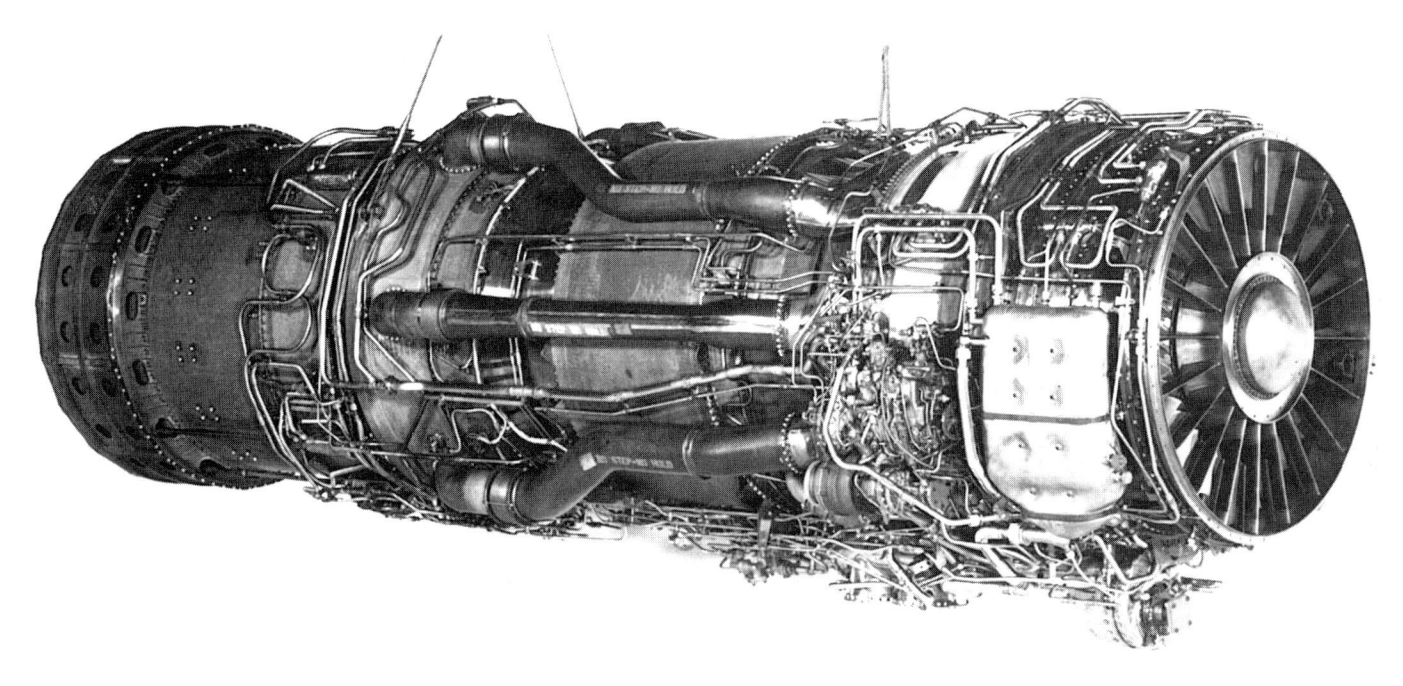

J58 bleed bypass turbojet engine details. Pratt & Whitney

THE J58 ENGINE

800°F 2000°F 1200°F

1400°F 3200°F

THIS PAGE:
TOP: **J58 phantom view showing relative temperature ranges.** Pratt & Whitney

ABOVE: **J58 on ground transport cart.** Paul R. Kucher IV Collection

OPPOSITE PAGE:
Engine air inlet spike positions and airflow patterns at Mach numbers 0.0 to 3.2. USAF

THE J58 ENGINE

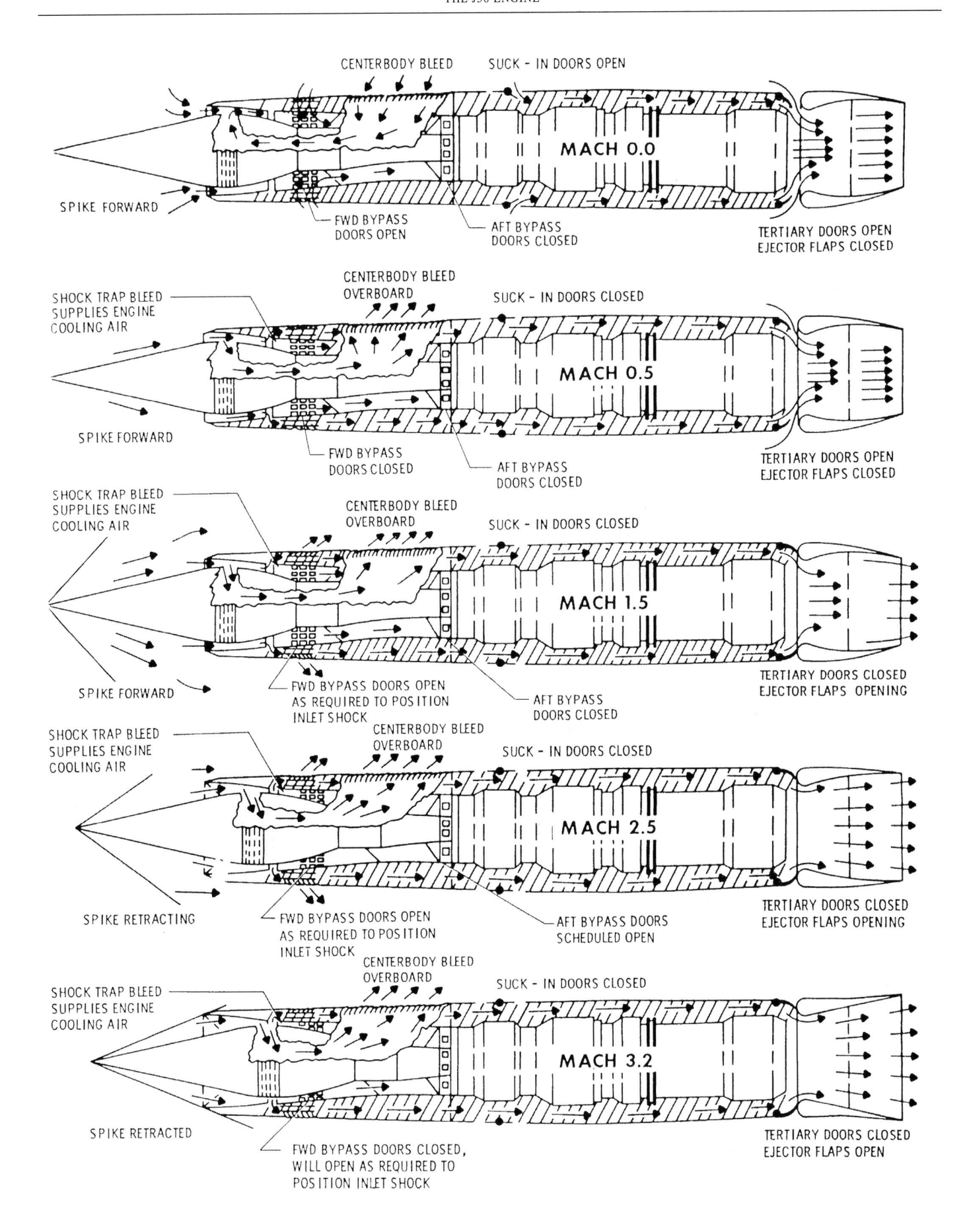

MACH 0.0
- CENTERBODY BLEED
- SUCK-IN DOORS OPEN
- SPIKE FORWARD
- FWD BYPASS DOORS OPEN
- AFT BYPASS DOORS CLOSED
- TERTIARY DOORS OPEN
- EJECTOR FLAPS CLOSED

MACH 0.5
- SHOCK TRAP BLEED SUPPLIES ENGINE COOLING AIR
- CENTERBODY BLEED OVERBOARD
- SUCK-IN DOORS CLOSED
- SPIKE FORWARD
- FWD BYPASS DOORS CLOSED
- AFT BYPASS DOORS CLOSED
- TERTIARY DOORS OPEN
- EJECTOR FLAPS CLOSED

MACH 1.5
- SHOCK TRAP BLEED SUPPLIES ENGINE COOLING AIR
- CENTERBODY BLEED OVERBOARD
- SUCK-IN DOORS CLOSED
- SPIKE FORWARD
- FWD BYPASS DOORS OPEN AS REQUIRED TO POSITION INLET SHOCK
- AFT BYPASS DOORS CLOSED
- TERTIARY DOORS CLOSED
- EJECTOR FLAPS OPENING

MACH 2.5
- SHOCK TRAP BLEED SUPPLIES ENGINE COOLING AIR
- CENTERBODY BLEED OVERBOARD
- SUCK-IN DOORS CLOSED
- SPIKE RETRACTING
- FWD BYPASS DOORS OPEN AS REQUIRED TO POSITION INLET SHOCK
- AFT BYPASS DOORS SCHEDULED OPEN
- TERTIARY DOORS CLOSED
- EJECTOR FLAPS OPENING

MACH 3.2
- SHOCK TRAP BLEED SUPPLIES ENGINE COOLING AIR
- CENTERBODY BLEED OVERBOARD
- SUCK-IN DOORS CLOSED
- SPIKE RETRACTED
- FWD BYPASS DOORS CLOSED, WILL OPEN AS REQUIRED TO POSITION INLET SHOCK
- TERTIARY DOORS CLOSED
- EJECTOR FLAPS OPEN

ABOVE: J58 with SR-71A at the Blackbird Air Park. Paul R. Kucher IV Collection

J58 engine start cart control details. Paul R. Kucher IV Collection

CL-400 under Project *Suntan*, as discussed in Chapter One.

Once these actions came about, P&W put further development of its JTN9/J91 onto the back burner. But some of the new technologies it had generated would soon be incorporated into the design of another advanced engine, the P&W Model JT11 or J58.

In the mid 1950s, the US Navy had contracted P&W to develop a Mach 3-rated engine for an advanced carrier-based light attack-bomber aircraft with a short-duration 2,000mph (3,200km/h) dash speed. Pratt & Whitney responded with the J58-P-2, which made its first test run in prototype form in mid-1958. The proposed US Navy attack bomber was cancelled, but the engine was also investigated for use in the Chance Vought Aircraft F8U-3 Crusader III all-missile-armed interceptor, if it beat] the McDonnell F4H-1 Phantom II. The US Navy, however, selected the two-seater, twin-engined Phantom II over the single-seater, single-engined Crusader III and development of the J58-P-2 went into limbo. (USAF turbojet engines have odd dash numbers while US Navy turbojets have even dash numbers.)

J58 Performance

So secretive was the *Gusto/Oxcart* programme that at first even the Pratt & Whitney Aircraft J58 propulsive system was given code names; the code-names used were *Cabbage Slicers* for the early-model J58 and *Tailfeathers* for the later ones. Moreover, since the J58 variants used by the Blackbirds were vastly different from earlier J58 designs, technically speaking they should have had a new designation, such as J95. But the programme was so secret that this was not desirable: since the early J58 had for the most part disappeared from public awareness by 1959, its designation did not generate any great interest any more, which suited the Blackbird programme perfectly.

On 13 May 1981 William H. 'Bill' Brown of Pratt & Whitney Aircraft presented a paper on J58 development to the American Institute of Aeronautics and Astronautics (AIAA) in Long Beach, California. Mr Brown's paper, in part, is reproduced on pages 104–105.

THE J58 ENGINE

J58 at the US Air Force Museum in Dayton, Ohio. Paul R. Kucher IV Collection

Another view of the J58 at the US Air Force Museum. Paul R. Kucher IV Collection

J58/SR-71 Propulsion Integration or the Great Adventure into the Technical Unknown

WILLIAM H. BROWN
Retired Engineering Manager, Government Product Division, Pratt & Whitney Aircraft Group, United Technologies Corporation

Successful integration of the J58 engine with the SR-71 aircraft was achieved by:

– Inherently compatible engine cycle, size and characteristics.
– Intensive and extensive design/development effort.

Propulsion integration involved aerodynamic compatibility, installation and structural technology advances, development of a unique mechanical power takeoff drive, and fuel system tailoring. All four areas plowed new ground and uncovered unknowns that were identified, addressed, and resolved. Interacting airframe systems, such as the variable mixed compression [air] inlet, exhaust nozzle, and fuel system were ground tested with the J58 engine prior to and coincident with flight-testing. Numerous iterative redesign-retest-resolution cycles were required to accommodate the extreme operating conditions.

Successful propulsion operation was primarily the result of

– Compatible conceptual designs.
– Diligent application of engineering fundamentals.
– Freedom to change the engine and/or aircraft with a minimum of contractual paperwork.
– A maximum of trust and team effort with engineer-to-engineer interchange.

The centreline of the basic J58 engine was laid down in late 1956. It was to be an afterburning turbojet rated at 26,000lb maximum takeoff thrust and was to power a US Navy attack aircraft which would have a dash capability of up to Mach 3 for several seconds. By the time Pratt & Whitney Aircraft, along with Lockheed and others, began to study the requirements several years later for what became the Blackbird series of aircraft, we had completed approximately 700 hours of full-scale engine testing on the J58.

In the Blackbird joint studies, the attitude of open cooperation between Lockheed and Pratt & Whitney Aircraft personnel seemed to produce better results than if a more 'arms-length' attitude were adopted. This open cooperation resulted in a more complete study which identified the enormous advances in the state-of-the-art and the significant amount of knowledge which had to be acquired to achieve successful engine/airframe integration. The completeness of this study was probably instrumental in Lockheed and Pratt & Whitney Aircraft winning the [*Gusto*-cum-*Oxcart*] competition. The government stated that the need for what became the Blackbird was so great that the program had to be conducted despite the risks and the technological challenge. Furthermore, the government expected the risks to be reduced by fallout from the [North American] X-15 and B-70 programs. Unfortunately, there was no meaningful fallout.

There were a number of increased requirements for the J58 compared to the requirements for the previous Pratt & Whitney Aircraft J75 engine [see table below]. As it turned out, even these requirements didn't hold throughout the Blackbird's actual mission. For example, the engine air inlet air temperature exceeded 800°F under certain conditions. The fuel inlet temperature increased to 350°F at times and the fuel temperature ranged from 600°F to 700°F at the main and afterburner fuel nozzles. Lubricant temperatures rose to 700°F and even to 1,000°F in some localized parts of the engine.

Because of these extremely hostile environmental conditions, the only design parameters that could be retained from the US Navy J58-P-2 engine were the basic size and the compressor and turbine aerodynamics. Even these were modified at a later date.

The extreme environment presented a severe cooling problem. It was vital to cool the pilot and aircraft electronics; but this left little or no heat sink in the fuel to cool the rest of the aircraft or the engine. Because of this, the only electronics on the engine was a fuel-cooled solenoid which was added later and a trim motor buried inside the engine fuel control. To keep cooling requirements to a minimum, we even had to provide a chemical ignition system using tetraethyl borane (TEB) for starting both the main engine and the afterburner. A new fuel and chemical lubricant had to be developed to meet the temperature requirements. Pratt & Whitney Aircraft together with the Ashland, Shell, and Monsanto Companies took on the task of developing these fluids.

Early in the development, we found that a straight turbojet cycle did not provide a good match for the [air] inlet nor the required thrust at high Mach number operating conditions. To overcome these problems, we invented the bleed bypass cycle with which we could match the inlet airflow requirements. Another advantage of this cycle was that above Mach 2, the corrected airflow could be held constant at a given Mach number regardless of the throttle position. The bleed bypass cycle also provided more than 20-percent additional thrust during high Mach number operation.

Fabrication and materials technology presented one of the greatest challenges. We had to learn how to form sheet metal from materials which previously had been used only for forging turbine blades. Once we had achieved this, we had to learn how to weld it successfully. Discs, shafts, and other components also had to be fabricated from high-strength, temperature-resistant turbine-blade-like materials to withstand temperatures and stresses encountered. I do not know of a single part, down to the last cotter key, that could be made from the same materials as used on previous engines. Even the lubrication pump was a major development. The newly developed special fuel was not only hot, but it had no lubricity. A small amount of fluorocarbon [a compound containing fluorine and carbon] finally had to be added to allow the airframe and engine pumps and servos to work.

Fuel was used as the engine hydraulic fluid to actuate the bleeds, afterburner nozzle, etc. Because there was nothing to cool the fuel, it just made one pass through the hydraulic system and then was burned.

Approximately three months before Pratt & Whitney finished the Pre Flight Rating Test which was 3 years and 4 months after go-ahead (the Model Qualification Test was completed 14 months later), the first [A-12] 'Blackbird' took to the air. It was powered by two afterburning [Pratt & Whitney] J75 turbojet engines to wring out the aircraft subsonically. As soon as Lockheed felt comfortable with the aircraft, a J58 was installed in one side. After several months of subsonic flight tests, J58 engines were installed in both sides, and we started flight testing for real.

Naturally there were problems. Here are a few notable ones and the solutions.

The first problem happened very early – the engine wouldn't start! The small inlet wind tunnel model did not show the inlet being so depressed at the starting J58 airflows. In fact, instead of airflowing out of the compressor 4th stage through the bleed ducts into the afterburner, it flowed the other way! As a temporary fix, Lockheed removed an inlet access panel for ground starts. They later added two suck-in doors and Pratt & Whitney added an engine bleed to the nacelle. These two changes eliminated the ground starting problem.

Originally, the blow-in door ejector or convergent-divergent nozzle was built as part of the engine. It was subsequently decided jointly by Lockheed and Pratt & Whitney Aircraft that it would save weight if it was built as part of the airframe structure. This was deemed appropriate, particularly as the main wing spar structure had to go around the throat of the ejector. Pratt & Whitney Aircraft, however, would still be responsible for nozzle performance in conjunction with the engine primary nozzle. In addition, we would perform all of the wind tunnel testing. In exchange, Pratt & Whitney Aircraft would build the remote gearbox because Lockheed's gearbox vendor had no experience with gear materials or bearings and seals that would withstand the temperatures required. As a matter of fact neither did we, but we were already committed to learn.

A problem partially related to the ejector was that the airplane burned too much fuel going transonic. To help solve the problem, thrust measurements were taken in flight, movies of ejector operation in flight were made, local Mach numbers were measured, etc. Two fundamental mistakes were uncovered. The back end of the nacelle [the ejector] went supersonic long before the airplane did, and the fairing of the transonic wind tunnel drag data was not accurate. While we were puzzling out the solution, some pilot decided to go transonic at a lower altitude and higher Keas [knots estimated air speed]. This for all intents and purposes solved the problem. From this we learned not to run nacelle wind tunnel tests unless the model contains at least a simulation of the adjacent aircraft surfaces. We also learned to take enough data points so that transonic drag wind tunnel data does not have to be faired.

As flight testing increased to the higher Mach numbers new problems arose.

The most sensational and the most confusing problem at the high Mach number condition was [air] inlet unstarts. These occurred without warning and were seemingly inconsistent. To add to the confusion, the pilots consistently reported the unstart occurring on the wrong side of the airplane. This anomaly was solved rather quickly when Lockheed found that the Stability Augmentation System (SAS) slightly overcompensated for the sudden one sided drag. This led the pilot to believe that the wrong side had unstarted, and consequently, his corrective action usually resulted in worsening the problem. Oddly enough, the engine did not blow-out. It just sat there and overheated because the inlet airflow was so reduced that the engine minimum fuel flow was

J58/SR-71 Propulsion Integration or the Great Adventure into the Technical Unknown

approximately twice that required. Worst of all, the inlet would not restart until the pilot came down to a much lower altitude and Mach number. A great many tests and investigations were conducted including the possibility of engine surge being the initiator. This was not the case. Three major causes were finally isolated:

1. Manual trimming of engine.
2. High, inconsistent nacelle leakage at the approximately 40:1 pressure ratio.
3. Alpha signal (angle of attack from nose boom) to inlet control subject to G-loading.

The following improvements were incorporated by Lockheed and Pratt & Whitney Aircraft essentially as a package:

1. Improved sealing of the inlet and bypass doors.
2. Auto-trimmer of engine installed.
3. Derichment valve with unstart signal installed on engine to protect turbine.
4. Increased area inlet bypass doors and addition of an aft inlet bypass door which bypassed inlet air direct to ejector.
5. Added a 'G' [forces] bias on inlet control.
6. Automated inlet restart procedure on both inlets regardless of which unstarted.

The foregoing six items essentially eliminated inlet unstarts as a problem. An additional benefit was also realized by the ability to use the aft inlet bypass door in normal flight instead of dumping all inlet bypass air overboard. As this air became heated as it passed over the engine to the ejector instead of going overboard, drag was substantially reduced. Also better sealing of the nacelle reduced drag further.

As you have probably noticed, I have had difficulty in differentiating between 'we' Pratt & Whitney Aircraft and 'we' Lockheed. But that is the kind of program it was.

In any complicated program of this magnitude we all do something dumb and we both did our share. Here is one from each of us: 'We', (Pratt & Whitney), became so obsessed with the problems of hot fuel and hot environment that we neglected the fact that sometimes the fuel was cold when the environment was hot and vice versa. When this occurred, the engine fuel control did not track well. To correct this, we had to insulate the main engine control body from the environment and make all the servos, etc., respond only to fuel temperature. Eventually, we had to make a major redesign of the control.

Lockheed and Pratt & Whitney Aircraft spent many hours coordinating the inlet and engine arrangement so that doors, bleeds, air conditioner drive turbine discharge, etc., would not affect any of the engine control sensors in the engine inlet. In fact, the air conditioner drive turbine discharge was located 45 degrees on one side of the vertical centreline and the engine temperature bulb was located 45 degrees on the opposite side. To save design time, Lockheed built one inlet as a mirror image of the other. It is now easy to conclude where the 1,200°F air conditioner turbine discharge turned out to be! For a while the fact that one engine always ran faster than the other was a big mystery!

Comparison of J58 Development Objectives with Then-Current Production P&W Engines

	J57 and J75	J58
Mach number	2.0 for 15min (J75 only)	3.2 (continuous)
Altitude	55,000ft	100,000ft
Compressor inlet temperature	250°F (J75 only)	800°F
Turbine inlet temperature	1,750°F (takeoff)	2,000°F
Maximum fuel inlet temperature	110–130°F	300°F
Maximum oil inlet temperature	250°F	550°F
Thrust/Weight ratio	4.0	5.2
Military operation	30min time limit	Continuous
Afterburner operation	Intermittent	Continuous

J58 Performance

(All thrust ratings are given for full afterburner operation at sea-level standard day conditions)

Aeroplane	Engine	Thrust
A-12	JT11D-20B	32,500lb (14,700kg)
YF-12A	JT11D-20B	32,500lb (14,700kg)
or	JT11D-20K	34,000lb (15,400kg)
M-21	JT11D-20K	34,000lb (15,400kg)
SR-71A	JT11D-20J	32,500lb (14,700kg)
or	JT11D-20K	34,000lb (15,400kg)

NOTE: The JT11D-20J or J58 J-engine of 32,500lb thrust incorporated fixed compressor-inlet guide-vanes, while the JT11D-20K or J58 K-engine of 34,000lb thrust incorporated two-position compressor-inlet guide-vanes. The vanes were automatically positioned axially below Mach 1.9 to provide increased airflow and increased thrust rating; above Mach 1.9, the vanes moved to a cambered position and the engine provided thrust equivalent to the J-engine. JP-7 had a flash point of 140°F (60°C).

KC-135Q and KC-135T Units

9th Air Refuelling Squadron (AREFS)	350th ARS
70th Air Refuelling Squadron (ARS)	376th Strategic Wing (SW)
100th Air Refuelling Wing (ARW)	380th AREFS
306th AREFS	903rd ARS
349th ARS	909th AREFS

KC-135Q and KC-135T Stratotanker Aircraft

A specially equipped fleet of tankers was needed to refuel the Blackbird aircraft while they were in flight. This unique fuel was called Jet Petroleum number 7 or JP-7 and it was used exclusively by the A-12, YF-12, M-21 and SR-71 aircraft. The Boeing KC-135Q had separate tanks for this fuel and was the first aerial refuelling aircraft with an integral boom intercom to allow aircraft-to-aircraft communication while still maintaining radio silence. The Qs were also among the first KC-135s to have the all-flying 'high-speed boom'. In all, fifty-four KC-135A aircraft were converted to 'Q' specification. When the KC-135Qs were re-engined with the 22,000–24,000lb thrust (10,000–11,000kg) CFM International F108-CF-100 (CFM-56-2) turbofan engine, their designation was changed to KC-135T. Following the retirement of the SR-71, the KC-135Q/KC-135T was likewise retired from pumping JP-7. Most, however, remain in service, pumping the less specialist JP-4 and JP-8.

CHAPTER NINE

Birds of a Feather

If an airframe and power plant combination works and works well it often leads to the creation of different versions. And so it was with the distinctive blending of the Lockheed A-12 airframe and the Pratt & Whitney J58 engine, which generated three successful follow-on derivatives – the YF-12, M-21 and SR-71.

During the *Oxcart* programme, especially early on, a number of A-12 derivatives were designed, engineered and offered but, in most cases because of military desires and politics, they were not proceeded with. For example, when the strategic bombing version of the A-12 – the B-12 – was offered to the USAF, the commander of the Strategic Air Command (SAC) at

The first A-12 dumps fuel during an early test flight near Groom Lake in July 1962. Lockheed Martin

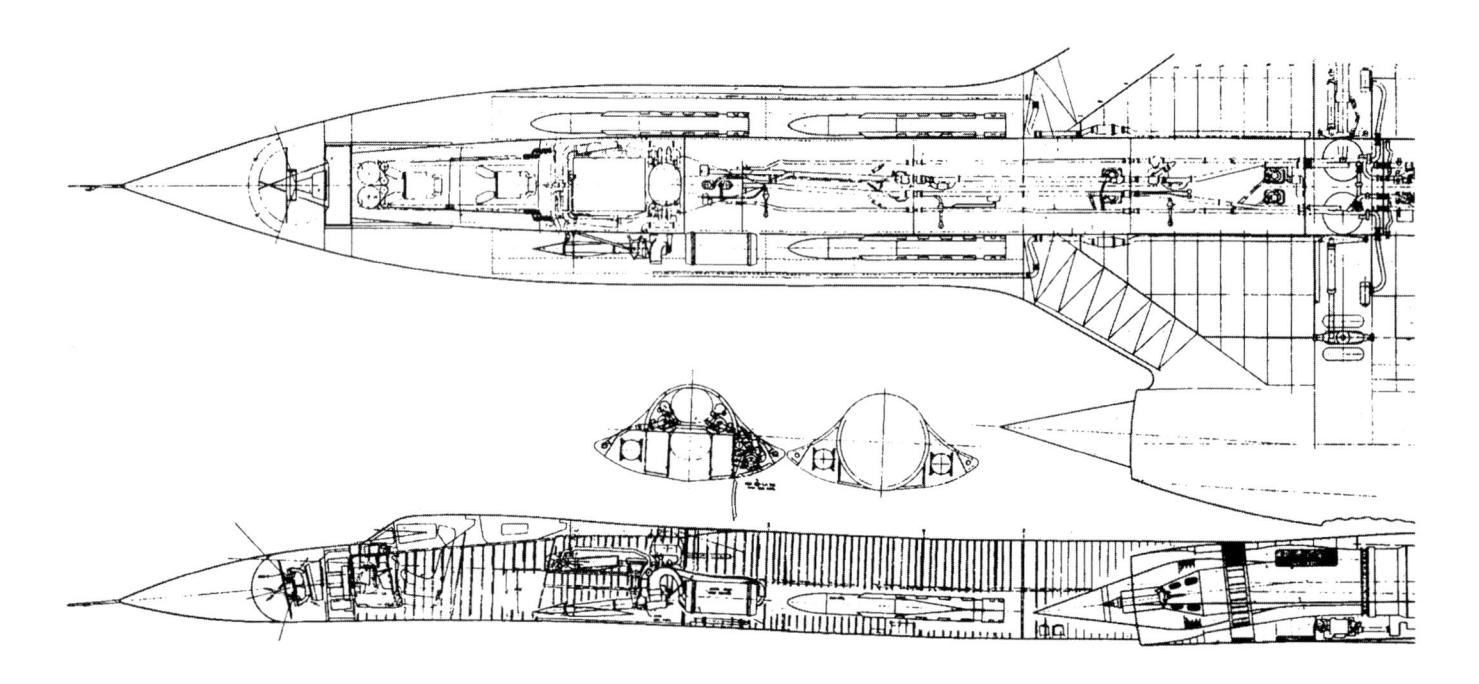

An early AF-12 proposal with three AIM-7 Sparrow AAMs and a Vulcan 20mm cannon. Lockheed Martin

the time, General Curtis E. LeMay, who wanted nothing to interfere with his 'baby', the North American B-70 Valkyrie, challenged both the USAF chain of command and Lockheed to get the B-12 out of the picture. And he was successful.

Nonetheless there were many interesting A-12 derivatives offered up. Finally, using Blackbird aircraft technology, there was the air-launched reconnaissance drone known as the D-21, as discussed in Chapter Four.

106

A-12 After eleven earlier *Archangel* designs were not proceeded with, twelve A-12s were built (60-6924/-6926, 60-6928/-6933 and 60-6937/-6939). The first A-12 made its official first flight on 30 April 1962 with Louis W. Schalk, Jr at the controls; it had made an unofficial first flight four days earlier on 26 April.

AF-12 AF-12 was the original Lockheed designation for what became the YF-12A. In one of its original forms the AF-12 was to be armed with three Hughes AIM-47B Falcon air-to-air missiles and a single General Electric M61 Vulcan six-barrel 20mm rotary cannon in the left-front weapons bay; provision was made for 1,000 rounds of ammunition.

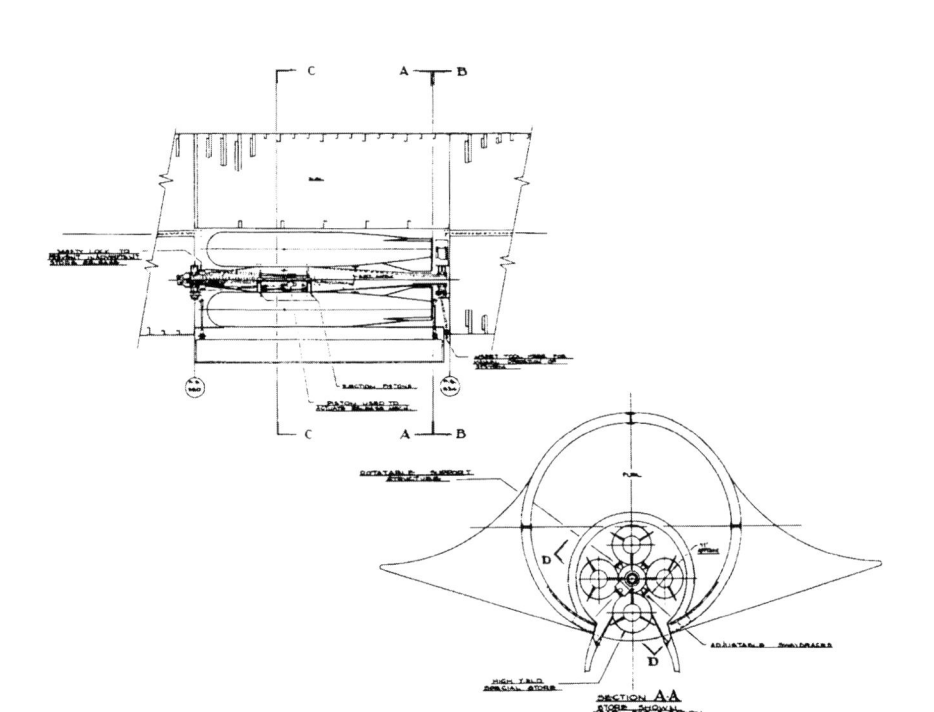

AQ-12 AQ-12 was a temporary designation preceding Q-12, which became D-21 (*see* Chapter Four).

B-12 The B-12 version of the A-12 was designed but never built. It was to be a dedicated strategic bomber and was referred to as the B-71 in some circles. It was offered to the USAF Strategic Air Command at a time when the proposed Mach 3 North American B-70 was extremely high on the agenda of SAC's then-commander, General Curtis E. LeMay. He staunchly supported the B-70 programme and ultimately received a promise from Kelly Johnson himself that he would no longer pursue USAF interest in a bomber version of the A-12, so as not to interfere with the B-70. Thus, the B-12/B-71 plan was dropped. However, these offerings were later revised by Lockheed when the USAF stated a requirement for an all-missile-armed reconnaissance strike aircraft, the RS-71, discussed below. The proposed B-12 featured a rotary bomb-dropping system complete with a rotary launcher for launching four nuclear stores.

LEFT: **The rotary bomb-launching system as proposed for the B-12.** Lockheed Martin

BELOW: **The FB-12 proposal with two AIM-7 Sparrow AAMs and two AGM-69 SRAMs.** Lockheed Martin

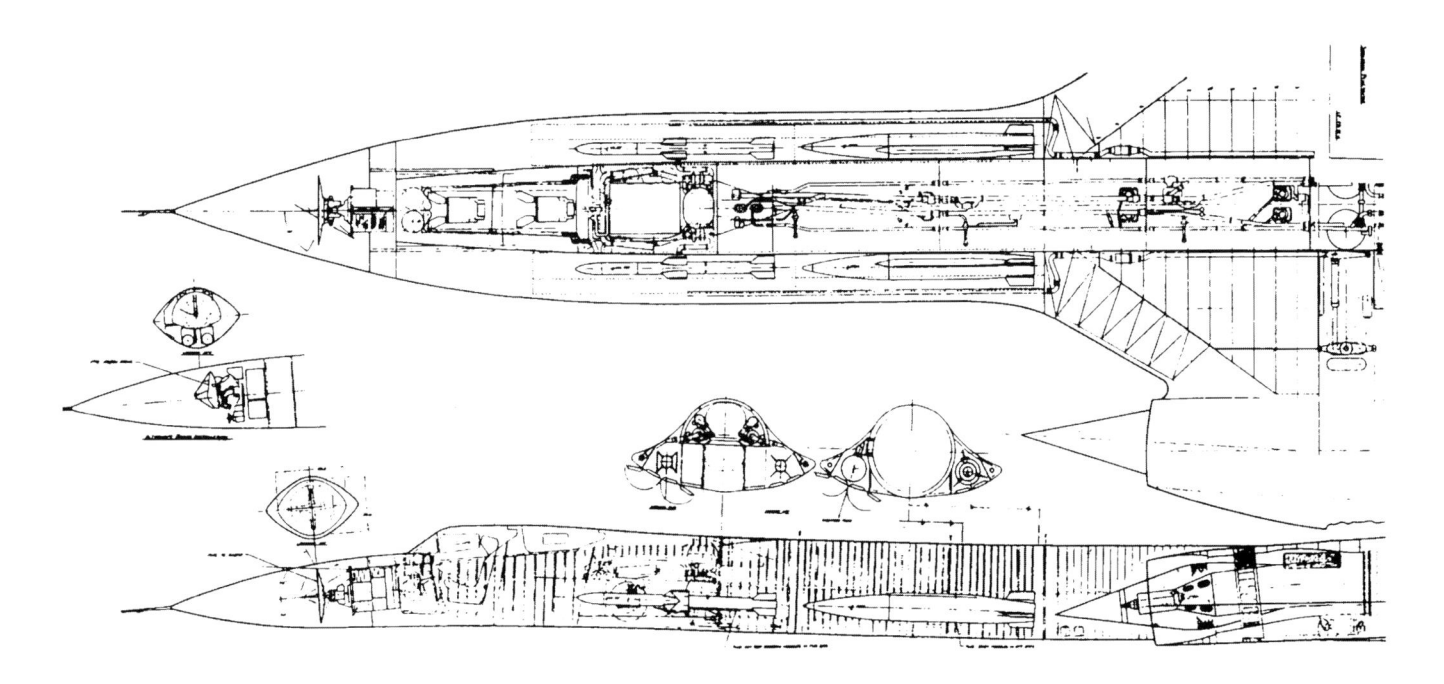

FB-12 The FB-12 fighter-bomber was to be similar to the almost-built F-12B air-defence fighter (discussed below), but would have carried two Hughes AIM-7E or AIM-7F Sparrow air-to-air missiles in its two forward weapons bays, and two Boeing AGM-69A Short-Range Attack Missiles (SRAMs) in its two aft weapons bays. Proposed radar systems for the FB-12 were the Westinghouse AN/AWG-10 Radar and Fire-Control System, the General Electric AN/APQ-114 Ku-Band Attack Radar (later used on the F-111A and FB-111A), and the Rockwell AN/APQ-130 Attack Radar (later used on the F-111D).

F-12B The proposed F-12B, if it had been produced, would have been the world's fastest and highest-flying interceptor. It also would have been the largest and heaviest one ever built. The F-12B would have been externally more or less identical to the three service-test YF-12As, but in its operational guise it was to be armed with four infra-red-guided Hughes AIM-47B Falcon air-intercept missiles. The USAF had wanted to buy ninety-three production F-12Bs, for which moneys were actually allocated, but in the end they were never built (*see* Chapter Three).

Q-12 Q-12 was the temporary Lockheed designation given to what became the D-21 reconnaissance drone (*see* Chapter Four).

TA-12 One two-seat A-12 pilot trainer and transition aeroplane was built in late 1962 and it made its first flight in January 1963. It featured a second, raised, cockpit

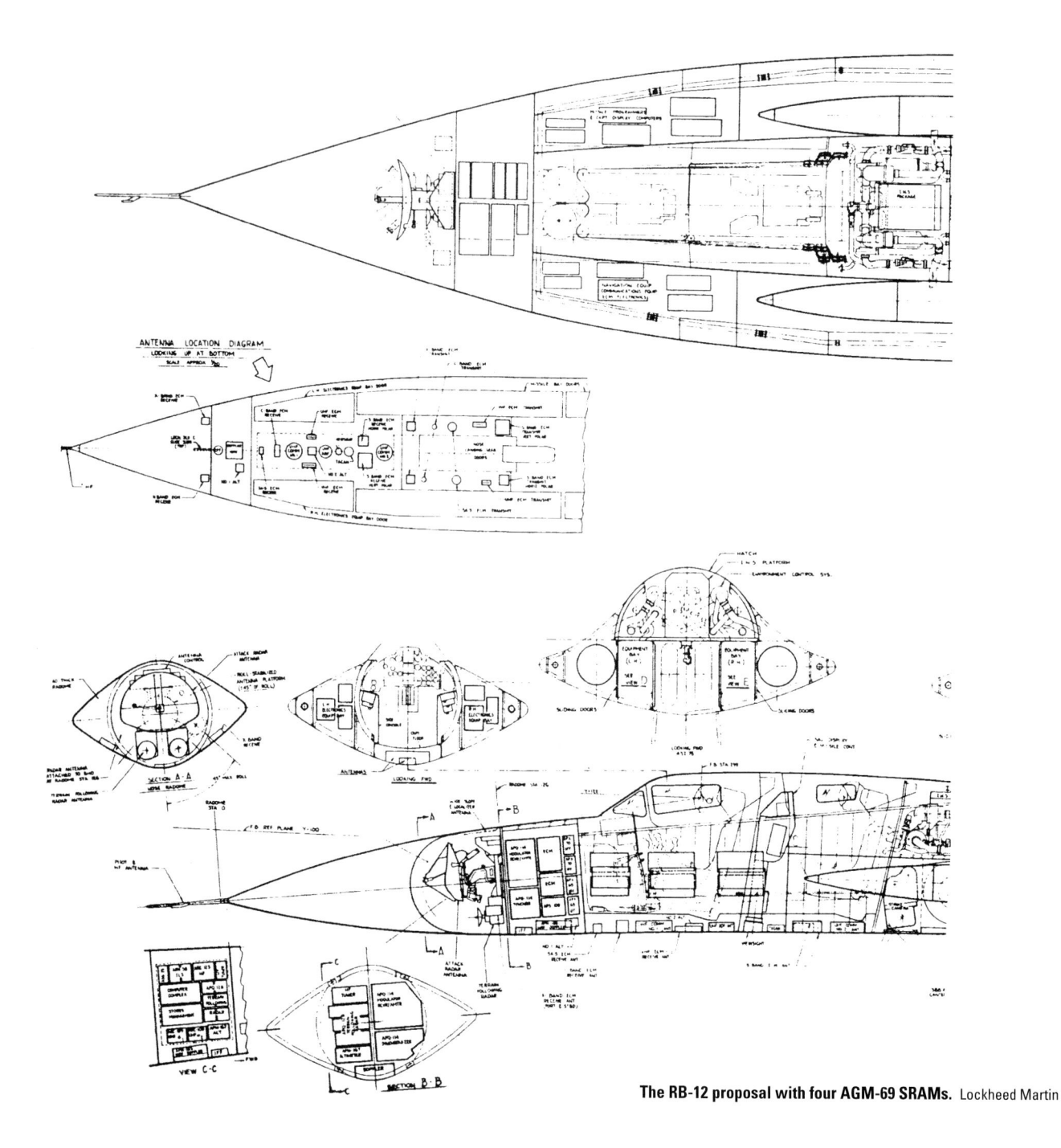

The RB-12 proposal with four AGM-69 SRAMs. Lockheed Martin

108

for the instructor pilot, aft of the primary cockpit. The TA-12 (60-6927) had two known nicknames, 'Tin Goose' and 'Titanium Goose', the latter being more common. It was powered by two afterburning Pratt & Whitney J75-P-19W turbojet engines throughout its career, never being retrofitted with J58s as was once planned.

YF-12A Three YF-12A service-test aeroplanes (60-6934/-6936) were built separate from the A-12 production line. The first made its maiden flight on 7 August 1963 with James D. 'Jim' Eastham at the controls (*see* Chapter Three).

YF-12C The sole, so-called 'YF-12C' (60-6937) was really SR-71A number two (61-7951). Since the USAF did not want NASA to have a 'full' SR-71 for its Blackbird programme (*see* Chapter Ten), the YF-12C came with metal engine air-inlet spikes rather than the composite spikes employed on the SR-71s; it may have had metal vertical tails as well, though this remains unclear. It was also powered by the 32,500lb thrust JT11D-20J engine rather than the improved 34,000lb thrust JT11D-20K engine used on other SR-71A aeroplanes.

D-21 The D-21 is the air-launched, ramjet-powered reconnaissance drone discussed below and in Chapter Four.

M-21 The two-place M-21 'Mother' was the original launch platform for the unmanned ramjet-powered D-21 'Daughter' reconnaissance drone. It featured a dorsal-mounted fuselage pylon on centreline to which the D-21 was attached and launched from. It also had a second cockpit for the Launch Control Officer (LCO) and was fitted with the 34,000lb thrust JT11D-20K engine. Two were built (60-6940 and 60-6941), but on 30 July 1966 M-21 number two (60-6940) was lost. M-21 number one currently resides at the Museum of Flight in Seattle, Washington (*see* Chapter Four).

R-12 R-12 was a short-lived designation for the dedicated photographic reconnaissance and electronic intelligence-gathering derivative of the A-12 for the USAF that eventually became the SR-71A.

RB-12 The RB-12 was to be a photographic-reconnaissance/bomber version of the A-12, with a rotary bomb launcher on the centreline carrying four nuclear stores. It eventually evolved into the RS-71 reconnaissance-strike version, carrying four SRAM missiles in four separate weapons bays, but it too was never built.

The SR-71

RS-71

In the late 1950s and early 1960s, in an attempt to resuscitate the cancelled North American B-70 Valkyrie strategic bomber, the USAF Strategic Air Command stated a requirement for a reconnaissance-strike version of the B-70 designated RS-70. The idea was that it could attack its targets, carry out a detailed bomb damage assessment and, if need be, return to re-strike the targets. To do this the proposed RS-70 was to carry twenty SRAM weapons with nuclear warheads in two rotary missile launchers – one in each one of its two weapons bays, which were placed in-line on the centreline and covered by flat-translating doors. The concept quickly gained favour and a number of RS-70s were ordered. But the Kennedy Administration and Secretary of Defense Robert S. McNamara saw to it that the RS-70 programme was cancelled as well. But there was a good reason for his action: an offering from Lockheed soon to be designated RS-71 which, as it turned out, was the final outgrowth of the A-12.

Since the proposed B/RB-12 version of the A-12 would not be built as had been planned early on, there remained a need for a reconnaissance strike aircraft. And since the A-12 was already flying at triplesonic speeds and very high altitudes (actually faster and higher than the two XB-70A prototypes ever flew), with two rather than six engines, McNamara pushed for production of the RS-71A as a weapon system for SAC with nothing to do with the CIA. This was done to the chagrin of General LeMay, the B/RS-70's biggest advocate. Nonetheless, the RS-70 was cancelled in May 1964 in favour of the Lockheed RS-71A, even though its armament would be four rather than twenty SRAM weapons.

In the event, the RS-71A was put into production without armament of any sort. It was planned that, with a different nose section attached to the airframe, the RS-71A could easily have been the reconnaissance-strike aircraft USAF SAC wanted. This was never done, however, and the RS-71A remained a dedicated photographic-reconnaissance platform.

Then on 25 July 1964, when President Lyndon B. Johnson announced the existence of the RS-71A, he erroneously called it the SR-71A as 'a long-range advanced strategic reconnaissance plane for military use'. Thus, the reconnaissance strike (RS) designation prefix was dropped and replaced by the strategic reconnaissance (SR) designation prefix. This caused Lockheed and the USAF a lot of grief. Rather than chastising President Johnson for his misspoken words, all paperwork (manuals, technical orders and the like) was altered to read 'SR-71A' instead of 'RS-71A'. And so the SR-71A was born.

SR-71A

Lockheed built twenty-eight SR-71A aeroplanes (61-7950/-7954, 61-7958/-7980). The first example (61-7950) made its first flight at Palmdale on 22 December 1964. It was piloted by Robert J. 'Bob' Gilliland (*see* Chapter Five).

SR-71B

Two SR-71B aeroplanes were built (61-7956 and 61-7957); they made their first flights at Palmdale on 18 November and 18 December 1965, respectively. The first flight crews were Bob Gilliland as pilot and Steve Belgau as RSO (SR-71B number one), and Bob Gilliland as pilot and Jim Eastham as RSO (SR-71B number two).

The SR-71B featured a raised second cockpit from where the instructor pilot could see past the trainee pilot's forward cockpit; this was more for seeing forward over the nose of the SR-71B than for watching the trainee pilot's actions.

The second SR-71B was lost on 11 January 1968 while it was on landing approach to Beale AFB. It had suffered fuel cavitation and both instructor pilot Lt Colonel Robert G. Sowers and student pilot Captain David E. Fruehauf ejected safely and survived the ordeal. The SR-71B, however, was a total loss. The other SR-71B served until the Blackbird fleet was retired in 1991, and it later became one of the three SR-71 Blackbirds assigned to and flown by NASA until 1999 (NASA number 831).

SR-71C

The unique SR-71C (61-7981) was the last Blackbird to come out of the factory, built to replace the lost SR-71B as a pilot trainer and transition aeroplane, with a raised second

A-12 and SR-71 Comparison		
	A-12	SR-71
Length	98.75ft (31m)	107.5ft (32.76m)
Maximum speed	Mach 3.35	Mach 3.32
Engine thrust	32,500lb (14,700kg)	34,000lb (15,400kg)
Maximum altitude	95,000ft (29,000m)	85,000ft (26,000m)
Maximum range (unrefuelled)	2,500 miles (4,000km)	3,250 miles (5,230km)
Empty weight	60,000lb (27,000kg)	67,500lb (30,600kg)
Gross weight	120,000lb (54,000kg)	152,000lb (69,000kg)
Payload	2,500lb (1,100kg)	3,500lb (1,600kg)

cockpit. It was not a new-build Blackbird, however, because it was created from the forward section of the SR-71A static structural test airframe (Lockheed factory serial number 2000) and the aft section and wings of the first YF-12A (60-6934) airframe. The latter had been written off and placed in storage on 14 August 1966 after being damaged in a landing mishap at Edwards AFB – instead of repairing it, it had proven easier to modify SR-71A 61-7951 as the YF-12A's replacement, and that particular aeroplane became the phoney YF-12C with the deceptive USAF serial number 60-6937, which was also used by the eleventh production A-12. Because of this rather odd joining of SR-71 and YF-12 airframes the SR-71C became known as 'The Bastard', and it made its first flight at Palmdale on 14 March 1969 with Bob Gilliland as pilot and Steve Belgau as RSO. In a little more than seven years the SR-71C eventually accumulated 556.4 flying hours, with its last flight coming on 11 April 1976.

The Different Configurations

While all the aircraft in the Blackbird series look superficially quite similar, there are numerous differences in their respective configurations.

The SR-71 of late 1964 owes its existence entirely to the A-12 of early 1962. The A-12 was even more capable as a photographic-reconnaissance platform than its SR-71 successor. How can this be? Because it was manned by a pilot only, the A-12 was able to carry a larger, heavier and much better camera in its aerial-reconnaissance suite. This camera was mounted in the Q-Bay of the A-12, directly aft of the cockpit. Since the SR-71 had a Reconnaissance Systems Operator as well as the pilot, requiring a second cockpit, it had less internal volume available and was heavier than the A-12. Thus, the A-12 could fly faster and higher than the SR-71. The A-12 was shorter in length than the SR-71 by some 5ft (1.5m) but their wingspans and wing areas are identical. Also, the SR-71's chines were wider at the nose apex than those of the A-12. But there were a number of other differences as shown in the table (*above*).

Differences: A-12 and TA-12, A-12 and M-21

The primary difference between the A-12 and TA-12 is that the latter has a second, raised cockpit for the instructor pilot in place of the Q-bay.

The differences between the A-12 and F-12 aircraft, on the other hand, are numerous. First and foremost the service-test YF-12 was the only armed version of the Blackbird to actually take wing. There were other armed versions on the drawing boards such as the B-12/B-71, but they never came to fruition. In the case of the YF-12, however, it was built and flight-tested as a dedicated weapon system. In its proposed F-12B production version, it was to be a triplesonic all-weather, all-missile-armed high-altitude interceptor armed with three radar-guided Hughes AIM-47 Falcon air-to-air missiles. To control the firing of these missiles the F-12B was to be equipped with the Hughes AN/ASG-18 radar and missile fire-control system. The F-12 had two cockpits, the aft one for the Fire Control Officer (FCO). Moreover, for missile-firing stability at very high speed, the F-12 came equipped with three ventral fins – one under either engine nacelle and one under the aft fuselage on the centreline, which folded sideways for runway clearance. But there are other differences as well, shown in the table (*below*).

From the foregoing it is easy to see how hard Kelly Johnson and his Skunk Works employees worked to make the A-12, YF-12, M-21 and SR-71 programmes as successful as they were, especially when one considers just how difficult it was to learn how to process and then manufacture fifty aeroplanes that were made entirely out of titanium alloy and high-temperature composite materials. Then one has to consider how difficult it was for Pratt & Whitney to create an engine capable of propelling aircraft to continuous Mach 3 cruise speeds at altitudes approaching 20 miles (30km). Moreover, new fuels and fluids, wiring and cooling techniques and a host of other difficulties had to be overcome before these aircraft could be built and flown. Suffice to say, as much as it cost to do this in 1962 to 1969 – when these aeroplanes were built and first flown – the moneys required to do the same today would be prohibitive. Finally, a question: just who on earth could now fill the shoes of Kelly Johnson, Ben Rich and the dedicated cadre of top-notch engineers and employees associated with the creation of these extraordinary aircraft?

A-12 and F-12 Comparison		
	A-12	F-12
Length	98.75ft (31m)	101ft 7in (32.80m)
Maximum speed	Mach 3.35	Mach 3.2
Engine thrust	32,500lb (14,700kg)	32,500lb (15,400kg)
Maximum altitude	95,000ft (29,000m)	85,000ft (26,000m)
Maximum range (unrefuelled)	2,500 miles (4,000km)	2,500 miles (4,000km)
Empty weight	60,000lb (27,000kg)	60,730lb (27,550kg)
Gross weight	120,000lb (54,000kg)	127,000lb (58,00kg)
Payload	2,500lb (1,100kg)	3,380lb (1,530kg)
Armament	None	Three AIM-47B Super Falcon

CHAPTER TEN

NASA Blackbirds

The National Aeronautics and Space Administration (NASA) began operations on 1 October 1958, absorbing its predecessor, the National Advisory Committee for Aeronautics (NACA). Both of these entities were established to investigate aeronautical sciences and the flying characteristics of manned and unmanned aircraft and, later, space vehicles and astronautics. Without these two extremely important aeronautical and astronautical arms of the US Government, flight sciences as we now know them could not and would not have advanced as rapidly as they have. And NASA helped us in a big way to understand the flight characteristics of high-speed, high-altitude aircraft such as the Blackbirds.

Only three organizations were fortunate enough to fly the Blackbird: the Central Intelligence Agency, with its cadre of former USAF pilots; USAF Strategic Air Command; and NASA.

NASA flew a total of seven different Blackbird aircraft from its Hugh L. Dryden Flight Research Centre (DFRC) located at Edwards AFB, California. These were YF-12A numbers two and three (60-6935 and 60-6936), the 'YF-12C' (60-6937 – actually SR-71A 61-7951), SR-71A numbers 16, 20 and 29 (61-7967, 61-7971 and 61-7980), and SR-71B number one (61-7956).

The two YF-12As, the YF-12C and SR-71C were flown beginning in the late 1960s, through the 1970s and into the early 1980s; they never received NASA tail numbers, but had the NASA logo in a bar running horizontally across their vertical tails.

The two SR-71As and the SR-71B carried NASA tail numbers 832, 844 and 831, respectively, and were loaned to NASA after the fleet of Blackbirds had been decommissioned at Beale AFB, California on 26 January 1990.

The NASA Blackbirds were used for many different test programmes, which are far too numerous to detail here. But suffice it to say that more than just a little aerodynamic data was gathered by them. A few of these programmes are discussed below.

NASA used YF-12A number two (60-6935) for a number of high-speed and high-altitude experiments during the late 1960s. NASA

111

ABOVE: **Another view of the second production YF-12A, still sporting its USAF Aerospace Defense Command logo.** NASA

The first of two SR-71B (61-7956) aeroplanes built served with NASA as tail number 831 after it retired from its USAF duties. NASA

Ultraviolet Experiment

One early research project flown on one of NASA's SR-71s consisted of a series of flights using the Blackbird as a science camera platform for the Jet Propulsion Laboratory (JPL) of the California Institute of Technology, which operates under contract to NASA. In March 1993, an upward-looking ultraviolet (UV) video camera placed in the SR-71's nose bay studied a variety of celestial objects in the ultraviolet-light spectrum.

The SR-71 was proposed as a test-bed for the experiment because it is capable of flying at altitudes above 80,000ft (24,000m) for an extended length of time. Observation of UV radiation is not possible from the Earth's surface because the atmosphere's ozone layer absorbs UV rays.

The flight programme was also designed to test the stability of the aircraft as a test-bed for UV observation. A joint flight programme was developed between the JPL and NASA's Ames-Dryden Flight Research Facility (which was re-designated the Dryden Flight Research Centre in 1994) in conjunction with South West Research Institute (SWRI) in Texas to test the hypothesis. NASA-DFRC modified the nose bay of the SR-71, creating an upward-observing window to carry SWRI's ultraviolet camera so it could make the required observations. The SR-71A used was NASA tail number 844, which was on loan from the USAF (USAF serial number 61-7980).

Cold Wall Experiment

The Cold Wall Experiment project, supported by NASA-Langley Research Center in Virginia, consisted of a stainless steel tube equipped with thermocouples and pressure-sensing equipment. A special insulation coating covered the tube, which was chilled with liquid nitrogen. At Mach 3, the insulation was pyrotechnically blown away from the tube, instantly exposing it to the thermal (high-heat) environment. The experiment caused numerous in-flight difficulties,

ABOVE: **NASA 832** was the twentieth production SR-71A (61-7971) and is now located at the Evergreen Aviation Museum in McMinnville, Oregon. NASA

BELOW: **NASA 844** was the twenty-ninth production SR-71A (61-7980) and it now appears in front of NASA Dryden Flight Research Center at Edwards AFB. NASA

such as engine unstarts, but researchers eventually got a successful flight.

The Dryden Flight Research Center's involvement with the YF-12A used in the Cold Wall programme began in 1967. Ames Research Center was interested in using wind-tunnel data that had been generated at Ames under extreme secrecy. Also, the Office of Advanced Research and Technology (OART) saw the YF-12A as a means to advance high-speed technology, which would help in designing the Supersonic Transport (SST) – then a high-priority US programme. At the time the USAF needed technical assistance to get the latest reconnaissance version of the A-12 family, the SR-71A, fully operational. Eventually, the USAF offered NASA the use of two YF-12A aircraft – number two (60-6935) and number three (60-6936). A joint NASA–USAF programme was mapped out in June 1969.

NASA and USAF technicians spent three months readying 60-6935 for flight.

On 11 December 1969, the flight programme got underway with a successful maiden flight piloted by Colonel Joe Rogers and Major Gary Heidelbaugh of the SR-71/F-12 Test Force. During the programme, the USAF concentrated on military applications while NASA pursued a loads-research programme. NASA studies included in-flight heating, skin-friction cooling, Cold Wall research (the aforementioned heat-transfer experiment), flow-field studies, shaker-vane research and tests in support of the Space Shuttle programme.

Ultimately, 60-6935 became the workhorse of the programme, with 146 flights between 11 December 1969 and 7 November 1979. The second YF-12A, 60-6936, made sixty-two flights but was lost in a non-fatal crash on 24 June 1971. It was replaced by the so-called 'YF-12C' (SR-71A 61-7951, modified with YF-12A inlets and engines and a bogus tail number 60-6937).

The NASA YF-12 research programme was ambitious; the aircraft flew an average of once a week unless 'down' for extended maintenance or modification. Programme expenses averaged $3.1 million per year just to run the flight tests. NASA crews for the YF-12 included pilots Fitzhugh Fulton and Donald Mallick, and flight-test engineers Victor Horton and Ray Young. Other NASA test pilots checked out in the YF-12A included John Manke, William Dana, Gary Krier, Einar Enevoldson, Tom McMurtry, Steve Ishmael and Michael Swann.

Linear Aerospike SR-71 Experiment

The Linear Aerospike SR-71 Experiment (LASRE) programme was performed between October 1997 and November 1998 to investigate the performance of a 20 per cent-scale, half-span model of the Lockheed Martin Single Stage to Orbit (SSTO) Reusable Launch Vehicle (RLV) – a lifting body shape (X-33, *see below*) without the fins. The test aerospike engine and its mount contained hydrogen fuel, water, helium and control computers, weighed in at 14,300lb (6,500kg) and was mounted atop SR-71A number 29, full-aft on the centreline between its two vertical tails. The mount measured 41ft (12.5m) in length. This particular SR-71A carried NASA tail number 844, formerly USAF serial number 61-7980.

The SSTO RLV concept was being developed in an effort to replace the NASA Space Shuttle fleet in the twenty-first century. An advanced technology demonstrator vehicle, the Lockheed Skunk Works designed X-33 – later named VentureStar – was to be built and flight tested in 1999. However, prohibitive problems with its fuel-tank system (liquid oxygen leaks) arose and the X-33 programme was cancelled in March 2001. In any event, after twelve test flights the in-flight part of the LASRE programme was deemed successful.

The last scheduled NASA research flight of a Blackbird was on 27 September 1999, with an evaluation of the LASRE flight-test fixture to gather baseline data for the possible use the LASRE flight-test fixture for future applications. But for the upcoming Edwards AFB Open House and Air Show on 9 October 1999, special permission for two demonstration flights was granted. So, oddly enough, it was not the USAF that made the last flight of a Blackbird – it was NASA, in a 1hr 14min flight during the show at Edwards. The aeroplane flown was NASA tail number 844 (SR-71A 61-7980) and Mach 3.21 and 80,100ft (24,400m) were attained. It was to make a second flight for the event the next day, but a fuel leak grounded it and no Blackbird ever flew again.

After the weekend of 9–10 October 1999, then, all three remaining NASA Blackbirds – two SR-71As and an SR-71B – were placed into flyable storage where they remained until 2002 when they were sent to museums. The information gathered by NASA through three decades of flying YF-12 and SR-71 aircraft was nothing less than priceless in the advancement of aeronautical and astronautical sciences.

The trio of NASA SR-71 Blackbirds at the NASA Hugh L. Dryden Flight Research Center. NASA

CHAPTER ELEVEN

Blackbird Survivors

Retired US military aircraft are almost always sent to various salvage yards throughout the USA to be scrapped out for their rare and sometimes semi-precious metals (such as titanium alloy) and salvaged systems (such as refurbished avionics) that can be re-used. However, in the case of the Blackbirds thirty survivors have been saved from the smelters; apparently these aircraft are far too important to aviation history to suffer such an ignominious fate. Thus, the aircraft that were not lost due to attrition and/or mishaps (twenty were lost out of the fifty built) are on display at numerous facilities as listed here. (In each case designation, Lockheed Build Number, USAF Serial Number and comments are given, in that order.)

Surviving A-12/YF-12s

A-12, 121, 60-6924 On display at Blackbird Air Park, Palmdale, California.

A-12, 122, 60-6925 To be moved from the flight deck of the aircraft carrier USS *Intrepid* at the USS *Intrepid* Sea–Air–Space Museum in New York, to be displayed at CIA Headquarters in Langley, Virginia.

TA-12, 124, 60-6927 On display at the California Museum of Science in Los Angeles, California.

A-12, 127, 60-6930 On display at the Space and Rocket Center Museum in Huntsville, Alabama.

A-12, 128, 60-6931 On display at the Minnesota Air National Guard Museum at the Minneapolis–St Paul International Airport, St Paul, Minnesota.

A-12, 130, 60-6933 On display at the San Diego Aerospace Museum in San Diego, California.

A-12, 131, 60-6937 On display at the Southern Museum of Flight in Birmingham, Alabama.

A-12, 132, 60-6938 On display at the USS *Alabama* Battleship Memorial Park in Mobile, Alabama.

The number two A-12 (60-6925) now resides on the deck of the USS *Intrepid* Sea–Air–Space Museum in New York City Harbour. Paul R. Kucher IV Collection

BLACKBIRD SURVIVORS

ABOVE: The number two YF-12A (60-6935) is displayed at the US Air Force Museum at Wright-Patterson AFB. AFFTC/HO

YF-12A, 1002, 60-6935 On display at the US Air Force Museum, Wright-Patterson AFB, Dayton, Ohio.

Surviving M-21s and D-21s

M-21, 134, 60-6940 On display at the Museum of Flight, Seattle, Washington.
D-21B, 502 (might be 510) Mounted atop M-21 (60-6940) at the Museum of Flight, Seattle, Washington.
D-21B, 510 Unknown location (not launched) – *see* above.
D-21B, 513 Stored at NASA-Dryden Flight Research Facility at Edwards AFB, California.

Canopy detail of YF-12A number two at the US Air Force Museum. Paul R. Kucher IV Collection

An excellent view of YF-12A number two at Area 51 in its original paint scheme. Lockheed Martin

116

D-21B, 522 Unknown location (not launched).
D-21B, 524 On display at the US Air Force Museum, Wright-Patterson AFB, Dayton, Ohio.
D-21B, 525 On display at the Blackbird Air Park, Palmdale, California.
D-21B, 528 Stored at Wright-Patterson AFB, Dayton, Ohio.
D-21B, 529 Stored at NASA-Dryden Flight Research Facility at Edwards AFB, California.
D-21B, 530 Stored at Aerospace Maintenance and Regeneration Center (AMARC) Davis-Monthan AFB, Tucson, Arizona.
D-21B, 531 Stored at AMARC Davis-Monthan AFB, Tucson, Arizona.
D-21B, 532 Stored at AMARC Davis-Monthan AFB, Tucson, Arizona.
D-21B, 533 At Pima Air Museum, Tucson, Arizona.
D-21B, 534 Stored at AMARC Davis-Monthan AFB, Tucson, Arizona.
D-21B, 535 Unknown location (not launched).
D-21B, 537 Stored at NASA-Dryden Flight Research Facility at Edwards AFB, California.
D-21B, 538 On display at the Museum of Aviation at Robins AFB, Georgia.

(NOTE: the twenty-two D-21s that were launched, lost and/or scrapped are not listed above.)

Surviving SR-71s

SR-71A, 2002, 61-7951 On display at the Pima Air Museum in Tucson, Arizona.
SR-71A, 2006, 61-7955 On display at the Air Force Flight Test Center Museum at Edwards AFB, California.

ABOVE: **The first of two M-21 'Mother' planes (60-6940) with its pylon-mounted D-21 (number 510) occupies a large area of the main gallery inside the Museum of Flight in Seattle, Washington.**
Lockheed Martin

The number two SR-71A (61-7951) when it was still known as the 'YF-12C' with NASA logo and borrowed A-12 serial number 60-6937 on vertical tails. NASA

TOP: **The sixth production SR-71A (61-7955) appears today at the Air Force Flight Test Center Museum at Edwards AFB, California.** AFFTC/HO

ABOVE: **The first of two SR-71B (61-7956) pilot trainer and transition aeroplanes is displayed at the Kalamazoo Air Zoo in Kalamazoo, Michigan.** AFFTC/HO

LEFT: **Canopy detail of the Kalamazoo Air Zoo SR-71B (61-7956).** Paul R. Kucher IV Collection

SR-71B, 2007, 61-7956 On display at the Kalamazoo Aviation History Museum in Kalamazoo, Michigan.
SR-71A, 2009, 61-7958 On display at the Museum of Aviation at Robins AFB, Georgia.
SR-71A, 2010, 61-7959 On display at the USAF Armament Museum at Eglin AFB, Florida.
SR-71A, 2011, 61-7960 On display at Castle AFB near Merced, California.
SR-71A, 2012, 61-7961 On display at the Kansas Cosmosphere and Space Center in Hutchinson, Kansas.
SR-71A, 2013, 61-7962 On display at the Imperial War Museum in Duxford, England.
SR-71A, 2014, 61-7963 On display at Beale AFB, California.
SR-71A, 2015, 61-7964 On display at the USAF Strategic Air Command Museum near Ashland, Nebraska.
SR-71A, 2018, 61-7967 To be displayed at the 8th Air Force Museum at Barksdale AFB, Louisiana.
SR-71A, 2019, 61-7968 On display at the Virginia Aviation Museum in Richmond, Virginia.
SR-71A, 2022, 61-7971 On display at the Evergreen Aviation Museum in McMinnville, Oregon.

ABOVE: In-flight view of the SR-71A (61-7959) known as 'Big Tail', which is now on display at the US Air Force Armament Museum, Eglin AFB, Florida. USAF via Peter W. Merlin

BELOW: This was the seventeenth SR-71A (61-7968) built and it is on display at the Virginia Aviation Museum in Richmond, Virginia. Lockheed Martin

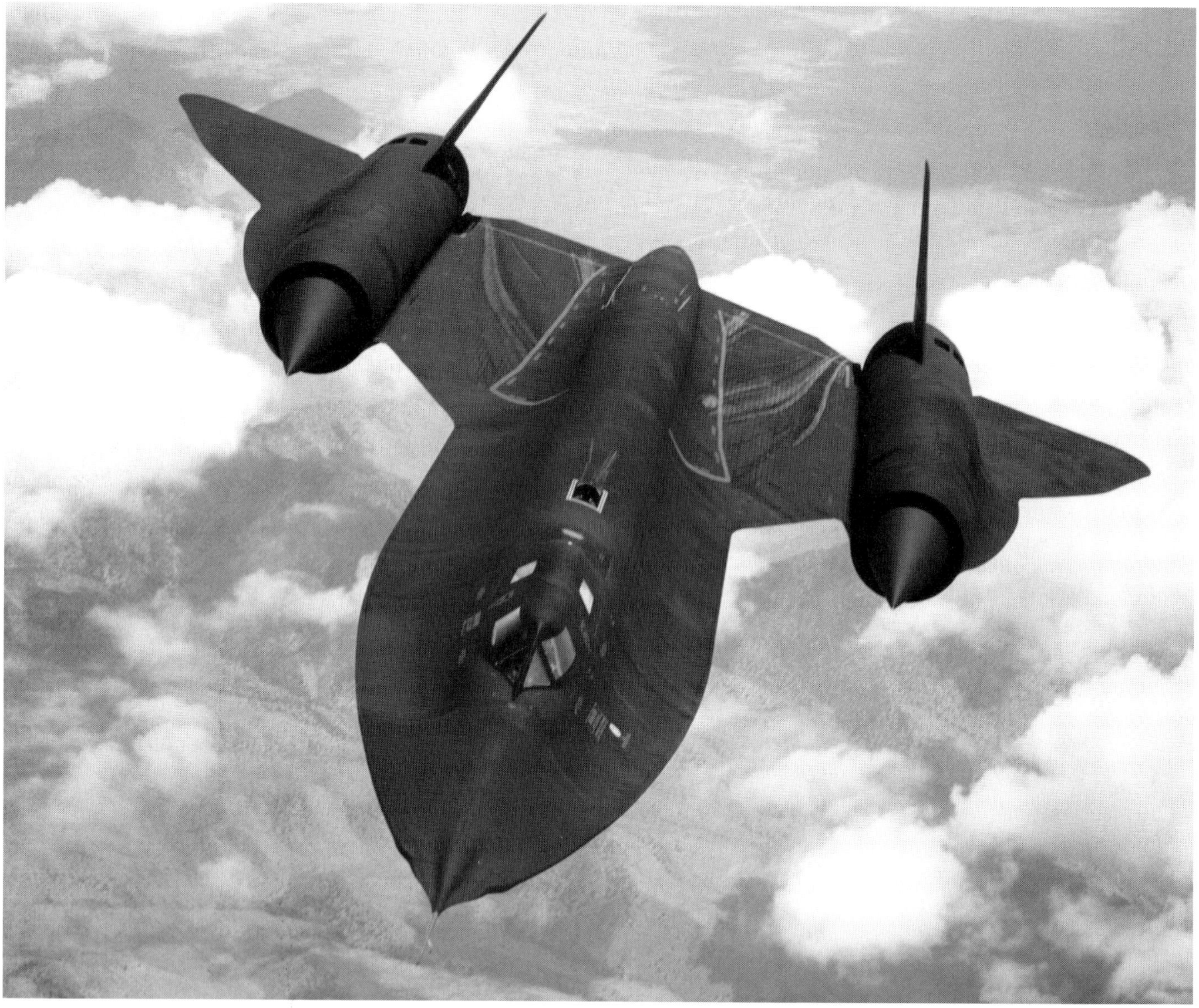

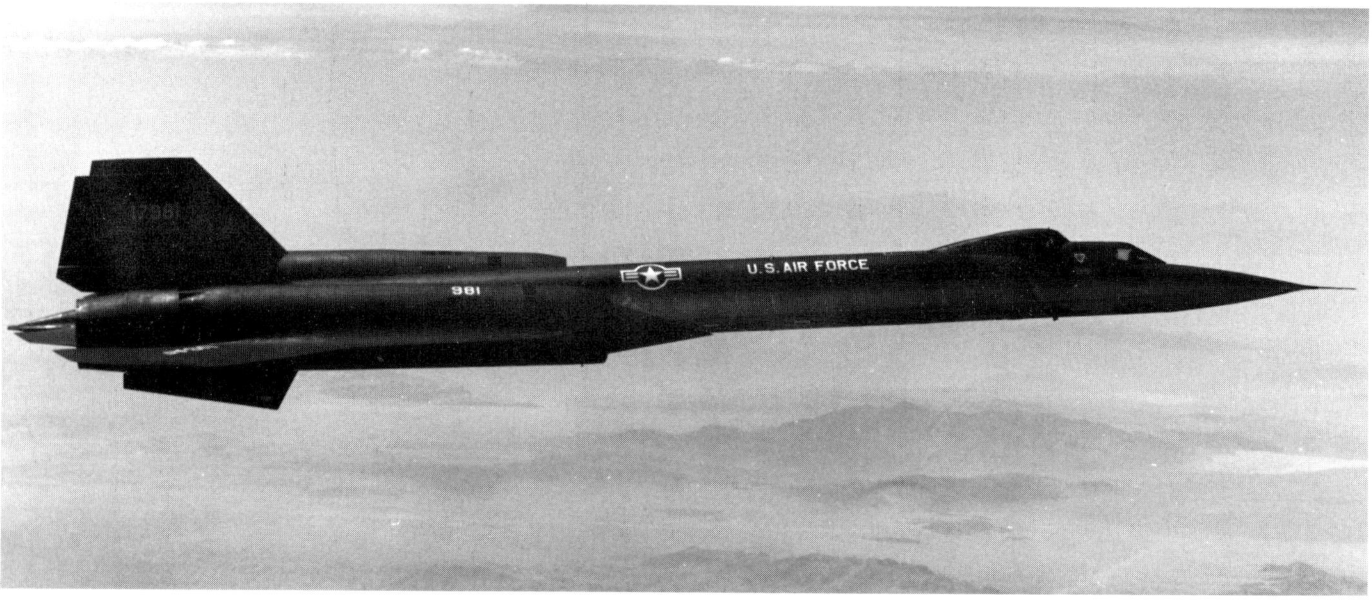
U.S. AIR FORCE
981

SR-71A, 2023, 61-7972 On display at the Steven F. Udvar-Hazy Center, a satellite of the Smithsonian Institution National Air and Space Museum located in Chantilly, Virginia.

SR-71A, 2024, 61-7973 On display at the Blackbird Air Park, Palmdale, California.

SR-71A, 2026, 61-7975 On display at the March Field Museum, March AFB, California.

SR-71A, 2027, 61-7976 On display at the US Air Force Museum, Wright-Patterson AFB, Dayton, Ohio.

SR-71A, 2030, 61-7979 On display at the USAF History and Traditions Museum at Lackland AFB, Texas.

SR-71A, 2031, 61-7980 On display at NASA-Dryden Flight Research Center, Edwards AFB, California (NASA tail number 844).

SR-71C, 2000, 61-7981 On display at the Hill Aerospace Museum, Hill AFB, Utah.

OPPOSITE PAGE:
TOP: This SR-71A (61-7979), the twenty-eighth built, is now on display at Lackland AFB, Texas. Lockheed Martin

BOTTOM: The sole SR-71C (61-7981) pilot trainer/transition aeroplane was the last Blackbird built and it survives at Hill AFB, Utah. AFFTC/HO

THIS PAGE:
RIGHT: A fine study of a sleek SR-71A Blackbird. Lockheed Martin

BELOW: Out of the black comes an SR-71A at Beale AFB in 1989. Lockheed Martin

BLACKBIRD SURVIVORS

It is highly unusual for an entire family of aircraft to find homes at special display areas or in aviation museums, but so it was with the Blackbirds and even a few of the surviving D-21 reconnaissance drones.

That this is not always the case, even for some very significant aircraft is clearly demonstrated by the case of the Boeing XB-52 and YB-52 Stratofortress prototypes. Both were scrapped in the mid-1960s before they could be saved for posterity – they had fallen prey to Lady Bird Johnson's 'National Highway Beautification Program' whereby, according to her, they were nothing more than eyesores and she ordered them removed. It is indeed splendid that thirty of the fifty Blackbird aeroplanes that were built are now on display for current and future generations to behold and marvel at. And all of those who were ever associated with them must be pleasantly pleased.

TOP: An SR-71 pilot with his Blackbird salutes the cameraman. Lockheed Martin

ABOVE: : Nine pilots with their nine RSOs are grouped together making eighteen crewmembers, with an SR-71A they all crewed at one time or another. Lockheed Martin

CHAPTER TWELVE

Summaries

Had we built the Blackbird in the year 2010, the world would still have been awed by such an achievement.
BEN RICH

Without a doubt the Lockheed SR-71 Blackbird strategic reconnaissance aircraft was the most sophisticated ever developed and put into operation within Earth's atmosphere. It was also one of the most expensive manned aircraft programmes that ever existed, and by the late 1980s the Blackbird's ultra-fast and expensive lifestyle in the upper reaches of the stratosphere was quickly coming to an end. Not because it wasn't doing its job properly, but because of the more advanced and sophisticated spy satellite systems, and the new, relatively inexpensive, unmanned aerial reconnaissance systems that were appearing and soon came on line as the Unmanned Aerial Vehicle (UAV). Moreover, the UAV not only supplies high-resolution photographic reconnaissance, but near- and real-time television coverage of the battlefield. So all good things must come to an end, and it was decided to phase out the 9th SRW's fleet of Blackbirds after nearly twenty-five years of operations: on 26 January 1990 the Lockheed SR-71 Blackbird was ceremoniously decommissioned at Beale AFB, California.

Benjamin R. 'Ben' Rich, most instrumental in the development of the Blackbird's engines and of its all-black paint scheme, gave a speech at the retirement ceremony. Its text is reproduced in the box (*see* p.124).

Bye, Bye Blackbird

During the next three months it was decided that an official retirement flight of the Blackbird should be made with an all-out effort to officially shatter the existing US coast-to-coast speed and time records. And on 16 March 1990 this was done in a big, big way. Manned by the two high-time Blackbird crewmembers, pilot Lt Colonel Ed Yeilding and RSO Lt Colonel Joseph T. 'JT' Vida, the twenty-first production SR-71A (61-7972) was used to smash the US West Coast to East Coast speed and time records on the Blackbird's official retirement flight to the National Air and Space Museum (NASM) in Washington, DC. The 1,998 mile (3,216km) distance was flown in a mere 67min 53.69sec at an average speed of 2,124.5mph (3,419km/h).

The previous and only existing supersonic coast-to-coast record flight had been established more than thirty-two years earlier, in July 1957, when US Marine Corps Major John H. Glenn Jr flew a Chance Vought F8U-1P Crusader from Los Angeles to New York in 3hr 23min. Thus, two hours and 15 minutes had been shaved off the old time record. (Later, of course, while piloting the Mercury space capsule 'Friendship 7' on 20 February 1962, Glenn crossed the USA in a matter of minutes rather than hours, at a speed of about 17,500mph or 28,000km/h.) In any event, the SR-71A crewed by Ed Yeilding and J.T. Vida on that historic day in March 1990 obliterated Glenn's transcontinental supersonic speed record.

The twenty-first production SR-71A Blackbird (61-7972) heads east on its record-setting retirement flight on the early morning of 6 March 1990. It flew coast-to-coast over the USA in just one hour and eight minutes at a speed of 2,124.5mph (3,418km/h) and a distance of 1,998 miles (3,215km). Lockheed Martin

Ben Rich's Speech at the Retirement of the SR-71

Congressman Herger, General Chain, honoured guests.

Tonight I salute the men and women of the 9th Strategic Reconnaissance Wing, the flying crew[s], the maintenance personnel, the planners, analysts and all those associated with the SR-71s – and let's not forget the support tankers and their crews and those from AFLC [Air Force Logistics Command] from Norton [AFB] and Palmdale, who gave us all the logistic and flight test support. On behalf of the Lockheed Corporation, and in particular the men and women of the Skunk Works, it is an honour to be here. I also have to thank the men and women of Pratt & Whitney who developed the marvellous J58 bleed bypass turbojet engine.

I cannot honestly say this is a happy day for me, seeing the retirement of the SR-71s – I can say I have seen them from cradle to grave.

I regret that two of my favourite people cannot be here. Kelly Johnson, father of the SR-71, seriously ill in the hospital, and the late Gen. Jerry O'Malley.

This amazing Blackbird is the fruit of the great military industrial complex, the US Air Force and the Lockheed Skunk Works.

I acknowledge and accept the need to retire the SR-71 because of the budget squeeze – but I don't agree with it.

I agree it is expensive – but so is the Fire Department, the Police Department and Life Insurance, but that doesn't mean you get rid of it.

Now let me give you some 'gee whiz' facts about this beautiful, exotic, one of a kind, amazing flying machine – the SR-71. I cannot give you precise numbers because the security folks will have a conniption!

1. This amazing machine had its first flight on 22 December 1964 with Bob Gilliland, over twenty-five years ago. Bob expresses his regrets that he couldn't be here today, as he had to be in Alaska and couldn't get out of it.
2. We delivered the aeroplane 12½ months later to Beale on 7 January 1966 – twenty-four years ago.
3. We will retire the aeroplane with all its speed and altitude records intact.
4. It is the only combat aeroplane in air force history to retire without the loss of a single crewmember – isn't that incredible for such a sophisticated aeroplane – not one air force person lost his life in war or peace with this aeroplane!
5. One of the few aircraft that flew in a combat environment and was never shot down.
6. This is the first time since 1968 – that all the aircraft and all the crews are in the US – twenty-two years of continuous overseas duty. It was an aircraft that was designed for peace not for war. It never carried any weapons.
7. This machine was flown almost 65 million miles, half of them over Mach 3 – that is equivalent to 2,600 trips around the Earth or 135 round trips to the Moon or two round trips to Venus.
8. I remember one flight from San Diego [California] to Savannah Beach, Georgia in 59 minutes!
9. On numerous occasions it flew half way around the world and returned – from the US to the Middle East and back; from England to Lebanon and back; from Okinawa to the Persian Gulf and back.
10. It is the first operational stealth aeroplane. Its radar cross section is what the B-1B is going to get this year. We had it twenty-five years ago!
11. It was the first aircraft with structural composite structure. A composite structure that was capable of 800°F – the temperature of a soldering iron.
12. The average surface temperature of the aeroplane is at 550°F. For the cooks in the audience – that is the temperature of the broiler in your oven. Can you imagine how shocked I was when the air force wanted the red, white and blue star and bar etc. put on this aeroplane! Someday paint a metal plate and put it under your broiler. It's hard enough to keep paint on, but keep white – white it turns to grey; blue turns to purple and red turns to maroon. We finally did it. It wasn't easy.
13. It is the only twenty-year-plus air force aeroplane that never had wing cracks or needed its wings replaced since it is mostly titanium.
14. When the air force wanted to simulate high-speed Russian fighters such as the MiG-23 for supersonic intercept manoeuvres, the SR-71 had to slow down.
15. Kelly [Johnson] offered $100 to anyone who could save ten pounds [4.5kg] on the aeroplane – no one collected. I suggested using helium in the tires instead of nitrogen or air. But helium would just leak through the rubber. I suggested to give every pilot an enema before every flight – that didn't go over very well!
16. It's the only aeroplane where the hydraulic oil cost more than Scotch whiskey!
17. The power plants have the thrust equivalent to that of the *Queen Mary*.

I could go on and on.

Let me tell you about its birth:

Kelly gathered about seventy-five people to develop this aeroplane – but the configuration was put together by five of us – four other engineers and myself, drawn on a spare door laid across two desks – that was the birth of this magnificent machine.

We corrugated the wing skin, so that as the skin expanded – any wrinkles would be stream wise and not cause drag.

The aeroplane gets 65 percent of its propulsive thrust from the [air] inlet; 25 per cent from the engine; and 15 percent from the ejector nozzle.

I remember calling the J58 engine the Macy [Department Store] engine – because they spent so much money. I told Bill Brown of Pratt & Whitney that if I gave that much to Macy's – they would have given me the engine.

That's enough pot-pourri for tonight. I want to thank each and every one of you here tonight who was associated with the Blackbird – this nation owes you all a great tribute. I'll close by saying – you dun good!

Hello..., Again

As the 1990s began the world went back to war. On 2 August 1990, President Saddam Hussein of Iraq sent seven divisions of the Iraqi Army (estimated to number 120,000 troops and 2,000 tanks) into Kuwait, which was quickly overwhelmed. Almost immediately thereafter, since oil-rich Saudi Arabia, which borders Kuwait to the south, would likely be next on Saddam's agenda, a coalition of the USA and her allies was formed to deal with the crisis. As the coalition moved its troops and equipment into the Middle East Operation *Desert Shield* was started. With the support of the United Nations, Iraq was given a deadline to withdraw from Kuwait. The deadline came and went, and on 17 January 1991 Operation *Desert Shield* became Operation *Desert Storm* and the Gulf War was on.

In the interim, as far as photographic reconnaissance went, the possibility was raised of returning at least some of the retired SR-71s to service for this action. The USAF wanted no part of this because, as it said in part, 'If we let them back in, we'll never get rid of them.' In fact, Air Force Chief of Staff, General Larry D. Welch, wanted the Blackbirds cut up and scrapped. Fortunately, the general never got his wish.

It was decided to place three SR-71s – 61-7962, 61-7967 and 61-7968 – in flyable storage at the Lockheed facility in Palmdale, California for possible USAF operations, while three more – 61-7956 (the surviving SR-71B), 61-7971 and 61-7980 – would be loaned to NASA for its ongoing high-speed research programmes. All of these aircraft arrived at their respective locations during 1991. So while the USAF's fastest birds sat out a lonely vigil on the Lockheed-Palmdale ramp, their NASA counterparts flew a number of scientific sorties out of Edwards.

Then, in September 1994, the US Congress voted that USAF SR-71 operations be reinstated while the 'spy satellite versus UAV' controversy would be further investigated. In doing so, Congress allocated $100 million to the reactivation effort. NASA tail number 832 (formerly 61-7971) had not yet been modified for dedicated flight research so it was taken out of storage to become one of the two reactivated USAF SR-71A aeroplanes. It was flown to Palmdale in January for refurbishment. Meanwhile at Palmdale, SR-71A 61-7967 was brought up to USAF operational standard. Thus, two SR-71As were now reinstated. And in early 1996 the two reactivated SR-71As (61-7967 and 61-7971) arrived at Edwards from Palmdale to begin operations with their new unit, Detachment 2 of the 9th Reconnaissance Wing.

The US Congress voted USAF SR-71 operational funding until Fiscal Year 1997 but the USAF never flew an operational mission. On 15 October 1997, the reactivated SR-71s having been ready for operational flights if needed, President Clinton signed a Line Item Veto and killed all further USAF operational SR-71 funding. The two SR-71As of the short-lived Det.2/9 RW, 61-7967 and 61-7971, were returned to their previous home at NASA Dryden.

Last flights, Final Goodbyes

From the first flight of the first A-12 (USAF serial number 60-6924) on 26 April 1962 to the last flight of SR-71A number twenty-nine (USAF 61-7980/NASA tail number 844) on 9 October 1999, more than thirty-seven years of Blackbird flight operations passed.

Without anyone knowing it the last USAF flight of an SR-71A came when Major Bert Garrison and RSO Captain Domingo Ochotorena flew a 4.1-hour training mission with 61-7967 on 10 October 1997, five days before President Clinton stopped further funding for USAF SR-71 operations. So without any fanfare whatsoever, operations by USAF Blackbirds came to an abrupt end.

Only the NASA Blackbirds would continue to fly. They did so for almost exactly two years to the day after the last USAF flight. On 9 October 1999 the last NASA flight of a Blackbird happened without a great deal of fanfare when an SR-71A (NASA tail number 844) flew at the Edwards AFB Air Show and Open House event. During that last flight, the last Blackbird to fly (61-7980) hit Mach 3.21 at 80,100ft (24,400m) during a 1hr 14min flight – the original design speed and altitude!

Sadly, on 22 December 1990, exactly twenty-six years after the first flights of both the SR-71A and the first-time mated M-21/D-21 aircraft, Clarence L. 'Kelly' Johnson had passed away at the age of eighty. On the following day, Ben Rich retired as head of the Skunk Works. During his retirement years, still working as a consultant to the Skunk Works, he teamed with noted writer Leo Janos and produced a bestselling book entitled *Skunk Works* (Little, Brown, New York, 1994). Shortly afterwards though, Benjamin R. 'Ben' Rich died at the age of sixty-nine, on 5 January 1995. These two legends – one an aeronautical engineering genius, the other an aerothermodynamicist of the highest calibre – were the most indispensable persons on the programmes that led to the successful developments of the Blackbird series of aircraft.

The Big 40

The fortieth anniversary of the official first flight of the A-12 came and went on 30 April 2002, while the Lockheed SR-71 Blackbird will mark its fortieth first flight anniversary more or less as this book goes to press, on 22 December 2004.

One has to go back in time to fully realize just how futuristic the A-12/SR-71 was forty-plus years ago. In looking that far back, to 30 April 1962, President John F. Kennedy was still in office, the Cuban Missile Crisis was months away, the Beatles had not yet had a No. 1 hit, colour television sets were only just beginning to appear, and the Vietnam War was in its infancy. But though the A-12 and SR-71 aeroplane designs are respectively forty-two and forty years old, in appearance, capability and performance they remain far ahead of their time.

Four crewmen pose with their respective Blackbirds at Beale AFB. Lockheed Martin

APPENDIX I

A-12, YF-12, M-21, SR-71 and D-21 Production

Designation	Article Number or Factory Serial Number	USAF Serial Number	Comment
A-12	121	60-6924	successfully completed official first flight on 30/4/62
A-12	122	60-6925	
A-12	123	60-6926	lost on 24/5/63
A-12	124 (also 124B)	60-6927	two-place pilot trainer and transition aeroplane; also TA-12 – nicknamed 'Titanium Goose' and/or 'Tin Goose'; never powered by Mach 3-rated J58 engines (used Mach 2-rated J75 engines throughout its career)
A-12	125	60-6928	lost on 5/1/67
A-12	126	60-6929	lost on 28/12/67
A-12	127	60-6930	
A-12	128	60-6931	
A-12	129	60-6932	lost on 5/6/68
A-12	130	60-6933	
YF-12A	1002	60-6934	first flight 7/8/63; pilot Jim Eastham; damaged 14/8/66 in landing accident, crew survived; aft section used to create SR-71C (61-7981)
YF-12A	1003	60-6935	on permanent display at USAF Museum at Wright-Patterson AFB, Dayton, Ohio
YF-12A	1004	60-6936	first flight 13/3/64; pilot Jim Eastham; crashed to destruction 24/6/71, crew survived
A-12	131	60-6937	
A-12	132	60-6938	
A-12	133	60-6939	lost 9/7/64
M-21	134	60-6940	first flight 4/64; first check flight with D-21 22/12/64
M-21	135	60-6941	crashed to destruction in Pacific Ocean 30/7/66; pilot Bill Park survived, launch control officer Ray Torick killed
SR-71A	2001	61-7950	lost at Edwards AFB on 10/1/67
SR-71A	2002	61-7951	
SR-71A	2003	61-7952	lost near Tucumcari, New Mexico on 25/1/66
SR-71A	2004	61-7953	lost near Shoshone, California on 18/12/69
SR-71A	2005	61-7954	lost at Edwards AFB on 11/4/69
SR-71A	2006	61-7955	

Designation	Article Number or Factory Serial Number	USAF Serial Number	Comment
SR-71B	2007	61-7956	
SR-71B	2008	61-7957	lost near Beale AFB on 11/1/68
SR-71A	2009	61-7958	
SR-71A	2010	61-7959	nicknamed 'Big Tail'; one-of-a-kind SR-71A with long, extended tail housing special ECM equipment
SR-71A	2011	61-7960	
SR-71A	2012	61-7961	
SR-71A	2013	61-7962	
SR-71A	2014	61-7963	
SR-71A	2015	61-7964	
SR-71A	2016	61-7965	lost near Lovelock, Nevada on 25/10/67
SR-71A	2017	61-7966	lost near Las Vegas, Nevada on 13/4/67
SR-71A	2018	61-7967	
SR-71A	2019	61-7968	
SR-71A	2020	61-7969	lost near Korat Royal Thai Air Force Base, Thailand on 10/5/70
SR-71A	2021	61-7970	lost near El Paso, Texas on 17/6/70
SR-71A	2022	61-7971	
SR-71A	2023	61-7972	
SR-71A	2024	61-7973	
SR-71A	2025	61-7974	lost in South China Sea near the Philippines on 21/4/89
SR-71A	2026	61-7975	
SR-71A	2027	61-7976	
SR-71A	2028	61-7977	lost at Beale AFB on 10/10/68
SR-71A	2029	61-7978	lost at Kadena AB on 20/7/72
SR-71A	2030	61-7979	
SR-71A	2031	61-7980	
SR-71C	2000	61-7981	nicknamed 'Bastard'; built as trainer with second raised cockpit to replace lost SR-71B; it was loaned to NASA with fictitious A-12 serial number 60-6937
D-21	501		accidentally dropped from B-52H on 28/9/67
D-21	502		
D-21	503		launched on 5/5/66 from M-21 (60-6941)
D-21	504		launched on 30/7/66 from M-21 (60-6941); collided with M21, both aircraft were destroyed
D-21	505		launched on 16/6/66 from M-21 (60-6941)
D-21	506		launched on 27/4/66 from M-21 (60-6941)
D-21B	507		launched on 6/11/67 from B-52H
D-21B	508		launched on 19/1/68 from B-52H
D-21B	509		launched on 2/12/67 from B-52H
D-21B	510		

Designation	Article Number or Factory Serial Number	USAF Serial Number	Comment
D-21B	511		launched on 30/4/68 from B-52H
D-21B	512		launched on 16/6/68 from B-52H
D-21B	513		
D-21B	514		launched on 1/7/68 from B-52H
D-21B	515		launched on 15/12/68 from B-52H
D-21B	516		launched on 28/8/68 from B-52H
D-21B	517		launched on 9/11/69 from B-52H; first operational mission
D-21B	518		launched on 11/2/69 from B-52H
D-21B	519		launched on 10/5/69 from B-52H
D-21B	520		launched on 10/7/69 from B-52H
D-21B	521		launched on 20/2/70 from B-52H
D-21B	522		
D-21B	523		launched on 16/12/70 from B-52H; second operational mission
D-21B	524		
D-21B	525		
D-21B	526		launched on 4/3/71 from B-52H; third operational mission
D-21B	527		launched 20/3/71 from B-52H; fourth operational mission (last known D-21B launch)
D-21B	528		
D-21B	529		
D-21B	530		
D-21B	531		
D-21B	532		
D-21B	533		
D-21B	534		
D-21B	535		
D-21B	536		
D-21B	537		
D-21B	538		

NOTES:
A-12, 139-145, 60-6942/-6948: these seven additional A-12s were cancelled, never built.
SR-71A, 2031-2034, 61-7982/-7985: these additional SR-71As were cancelled, never built.

The *Senior Bowl* B-52H aeroplanes were:
B-52H-BW 60-0036, nicknamed 'Tagboard Flyer'; currently assigned to 419th Flight Test Squadron (FLTS) at Edwards AFB, California.
B-52H-BW 61-0021, nicknamed 'Iron Eagle'; currently assigned to 93rd Bomb Squadron (BS) at Barksdale AFB, Louisiana.

APPENDIX II

Significant Facts and Figures

Operational sorties flown: 3,551

Total sorties flown: 17,300

Flight hours (operational): 11,008

Flight hours (total): 53,490

Mach 3 hours (operational): 2,752

Mach 3 hours (total): 11,675

Crewmembers to Mach 3 speed: 284

VIPs to Mach 3 speed: 105

Total persons to Mach 3 speed: 389

Cumulative Flight Hours by Crews
300 hours: 163

600 hours: 69

900 hours: 18

1,000 hours: 8

1,392.7 hours: 1 (RSO J.T. Vida, high-time crewmember)

Production Summary
A-12: 12

TA-12: 1

YF-12A: 3

YF-12C: 1 (actually SR-71A)

M-21: 2

SR-71A: 29 [1]

SR-71B: 2

SR-71C: 1 (built as replacement for lost SR-71B)

D-21: 6 [2]

D-21B: 32

NOTES:

[1] This figure does not include one SR-71C (61-7981) aeroplane created from salvaged YF-12A and SR-71A functional mock-up, and one YF-12C (61-7951) built as SR-71A but given 'YF-12C' designation and a phoney serial number (60-6937) for NASA test flights.

[2] The first six D-21s were later brought up to D-21B standard.

Significant Facts and Figures

Milestones at a Glance

26 April 1962: first A-12 flight (unofficial), flown by Lou Schalk

30 April 1962: first official A-12 first flight, flown by Lou Schalk

7 August 1963: first YF-12A flight, flown by Jim Eastham

29 February 1964: President Johnson announces A-11 (YF-12A) programme

25 July 1964: President Johnson announces RS-71 (SR-71) programme

22 December 1964: first SR-71 flight, flown by Bob Gilliland

22 December 1964: first captive carry flight of D-21 attached to M-1, flown by Bill Park

1 May 1965: YF-12A sets several world speed and altitude records

18 November 1965: first SR-71B flight

10 May 1966: USAF takes delivery of first SR-71A

21 March 1968: first USAF operational flight

14 March 1969: first SR-71C flight

11 December 1969: first YF-12A flight of combined NASA/USAF flight test programme

26 April 1971: SR-71A 15,000 mile non-stop flight in 10hr 30min

1 September 1974: SR-71A sets New York to London world speed record

13 September 1974: SR-71A sets London to Los Angeles world speed record

28 July 1976: SR-71s complete seven world speed and altitude records

31 October 1979: NASA YF-12 flight test programme ends

7 November 1979: final flight of YF-12 when 60-6935 is delivered to USAF Museum

1 October 1989: USAF SR-71 operations suspended (except for proficiency flights)

22 November 1989: all USAF SR-71 operations terminated

26 January 1990: SR-71 is decommissioned in ceremony at Beale AFB

6 March 1990: SR-71 61-7972 sets four world speed records while en route to Smithsonian Institute on last official USAF flight

25 July 1991: SR-71B 61-7956 (NASA tail number 831) officially delivered to NASA Dryden Flight Research Center, Edwards AFB, California

28 September 1994: US Congress votes to allocate $100 million for USAF reactivation of three SR-71s

28 June 1995: first reactivated SR-71 returns to USAF inventory

15 April 1996: Deputy Defense Secretary John White directed the Air Force to ground the Air Force's SR-71s due to conflicting language in Section 304 of the National Security Act of 1947

1 January 1997: SR-71 and crews are once more operational at Det 2, Edwards AFB, California

15 October 1997: President Clinton kills SR-71 funding with Line Item Veto

30 October 1998: Headquarters USAF directs termination of all SR-71 operations and subsequent disposal of the fleet

18 November 1998: NASA terminates SR-71 Linear Aerospike Research Experiment (LASRE) programme

APPENDIX III

Chronological Order of First Flights

Date	Designation	USAF Serial	Lockheed Serial	Comment
30/4/62	A-12	60-6924	121	official first flight; made unofficial fist flight 26/4/62
10/62	A-12	60-6925	122	
11/62	A-12	60-6926	123	lost 24/5/63
7/1/63	A-12	60-6927	124	two-seat trainer nicknamed 'Titanium Goose'
63	A-12	60-6928	125	lost 5/1/67
63	A-12	60-6929	126	lost 28/12/67
63	A-12	60-6930	127	
63	A-12	60-6931	128	
63	A-12	60-6932	129	
63	A-12	60-6937	131	
63	A-12	60-6938	132	
63	A-12	60-6939	133	lost 9/7/64
7/8/63	YF-12A	60-6934	1001	
26/11/63	YF-12A	60-6935	1002	
27/11/63	A-12	60-6933	130	
13/3/64	YF-12A	60-6936	1003	lost 24/6/71
64	M-21	60-6940	134	
64	M-21	60-6941	135	lost 30/7/66
22/12/64	SR-71A	61-7950	2001	lost 10/1/67
5/3/65	SR-71A	61-7951	2002	operated by NASA as YF-12C (60-6937)
	SR-71A	61-7952	2003	lost 25/1/66
4/6/65	SR-71A	61-7953	2004	lost 18/12/69
20/7/65	SR-71A	61-7954	2005	lost 11/4/69
17/8/65	SR-71A	61-7955	2006	
18/11/65	SR-71B	61-7956	2007	loaned NASA (NASA No. 831)
15/12/65	SR-71A	61-7958	2009	
18/12/65	SR-71B	61-7957	2008	lost 11/1/68
1/19/66	SR-71A	61-7959	2010	modified to 'Big Tail' configuration
9/2/66	SR-71A	61-7960	2011	
13/4/66	SR-71A	61-7961	2012	
29/4/66	SR-71A	61-7962	2013	
11/5/66	SR-71A	61-7964	2015	
9/6/66	SR-71A	61-7963	2014	

CHRONOLOGICAL ORDER OF FIRST FLIGHTS

Date	Designation	USAF Serial	Lockheed Serial	Comment
1/7/66	SR-71A	61-7966	2017	lost 13/4/67
10/6/66	SR-71A	61-7965	2016	lost 25/10/67
3/8/66	SR-71A	61-7968	2019	
18/10/66	SR-71A	61-7969	2020	lost 10/5/70
21/10/66	SR-71A	61-7970	2021	lost 17/6/70
17/11/66	SR-71A	61-7971	2022	loaned to NASA (NASA No. 832)
12/12/66	SR-71A	61-7972	2023	
8/2/67	SR-71A	61-7973	2024	
16/2/67	SR-71A	61-7974	2025	
13/4/67	SR-71A	61-7975	2026	
5/67	SR-71A	61-7976	2027	
6/6/67	SR-71A	61-7977	2028	
5/7/67	SR-71A	61-7978	2029	
10/8/67	SR-71A	61-7979	2030	
25/9/67	SR-71A	61-7980	2031	loaned to NASA (NASA No. 844)
14/3/69	SR-71C	61-7981	2000	created from forward half of SR-71A static test article and aft half of YF-12A No. 1 (60-6934), nicknamed 'The Bastard'; designated YF-12C early-on with fictitious A-12 serial number 60-6937

APPENDIX IV

The *Oxcart* Story

THOMAS P. McININCH

Unclassified security ratings are for historical interest only. This page and the document it comes from, entitled OXCART History (DON: SC-86-010115), has been UNCLASSIFIED according to Senior Crown Security Class Guide dated 1 November 1989, approved and dated 25 February 1991.

(S) – Secret; (C) – Classified; (U) – Unclassifed

(S) One spring day in 1962 a test pilot named Louis Schalk, employed by the Lockheed Aircraft Corporation, took off from the Nevada desert in an aircraft the like of which had never been seen before. A casual observer would have been startled by the appearance of this vehicle; he would perhaps have noticed especially its extremely long, slim, shape, its two enormous jet engines, its long sharp, projecting nose, and its swept-back wings, which appeared far too short to support the fuselage in flight. He might well have realized that this was a revolutionary airplane; he could not have known that it would be able to fly at three times the speed of sound for more than 3,000 miles without refuelling, or that toward the end of its flight, when fuel began to run low, it could cruise at over 90,000 feet. Still less would he have known of the equipment it was to carry, or of the formidable problems attending its design and construction.

(U) There was, of course, no casual observer present. The aircraft had been designed and built for reconnaissance; it was projected as a successor to the U-2. Its development had been carried out in profound secrecy. Despite the numerous designers, engineers, skilled and unskilled workers, administrators and others who had been involved in the affair, no authentic accounts, and indeed scarcely any accounts at all had leaked. Many aspects have not been revealed to this day, and many are likely to remain classified for some time to come. (S) The official designation of the aircraft was A-12. By a sort of inspired perversity, however, it came to be called OXCART, a code word also applied to the program under which it was developed. The secrecy in which it was so long shrouded has lifted a bit, and the purpose of this article is to give some account of the inception, development, operation, and untimely demise of this remarkable airplane. The OXCART no longer flies, but it left a legacy of technological achievement, which points the way to new projects. And it became the progenitor of a similar but somewhat less sophisticated reconnaissance vehicle called the SR-71, whose existence is well known to press and public.

(S) Sequel to the U-2

(S) The U-2 dated from 1954, when its development began under the direction of a group headed by Richard M. Bissell of CIA. In June 1956, the aircraft became operational, but officials predicted that its useful lifetime over the USSR could hardly be much more than 18 months or two years. Its first flight over Soviet territory revealed that the defense warning system not only detected but also tracked it quite accurately. Yet, it remained a unique and (S) invaluable source of intelligence information for almost four years, until on 1 May 1960, Francis Gary Powers was shot down near Sverdlovsk. (U) Meanwhile, even as the U-2 commenced its active career, efforts were under way to make it less vulnerable. The hope was to reduce the vehicle's radar cross-section, so that it would become less susceptible to detection. New developments in radar-absorbing materials were tried out and achieved considerable success, though not enough to solve the problem. Various far-out designs were explored, most of them seeking to create an aircraft capable of flying at extremely high altitudes, though still at relatively slow speed. None of them proved practicable.

(S) Eventually, in the fall of 1957, Bissell arranged with a contractor for a job of operations analysis to determine how far the probability of shooting down an airplane varied respectively with the plane's speed, altitude, and radar cross-section. This analysis demonstrated that supersonic speed greatly reduced the chances of detection by radar. The probability of being shot down was not of course reduced to zero, but it was evident that the supersonic line of approach was worth serious consideration. Therefore, from this time on, attention focused increasingly on the possibility of building a vehicle which could fly at extremely high speeds as well as great altitudes, and which would also incorporate the best that could be attained in radar-absorbing capabilities. Lockheed Aircraft Corporation and Convair Division of General Dynamics were informed of the general requirements, and their designers set to work on the problem without as yet receiving any contract or funds from the government. From the fall of 1957 to late 1958 these designers constantly refined and adapted their respective schemes.

(S) Bissell realized that development and production of such an aircraft would be exceedingly expensive, and that in the early stages at least it would be doubtful whether the project could succeed. To secure the necessary funds for such a program, high officials would have to receive the best and most authoritative presentation of whatever prospects might unfold. Accordingly, he got together a panel consisting of two distinguished authorities on aero-dynamics and one physicist, with E. M. Land of the Polaroid Corporation as chairman. Between 1957 and 1959 this panel met about six times, usually in Land's office in Cambridge. Lockheed and Convair designers attended during parts of the sessions. So also did the Assistant Secretaries of the Air Force and Navy concerned with research and development, together with one or two of their technical advisors. One useful consequence of the participation of service representatives was that bureaucratic and jurisdictional feuds were reduced virtually to nil. Throughout the program both Air Force and Navy gave valuable assistance and cooperation.

(S) As the months went by, the general outlines of what might be done took shape in the minds of those concerned. Late in November 1958, the members of the panel held a crucial meeting. They agreed that it now appeared feasible to build an aircraft of such speed and altitude as to be very difficult to track by radar. They recommended that the President be asked to approve in principle a further prosecution of the project, and to make funds available for further studies and tests. The President and his Scientific Advisor, Dr. James Killian was already aware of what was going on, and when CIA officials went to them with the recommendations of the panel they received a favorable hearing. The President gave his approval. Lockheed and Convair were then asked to submit definite proposals, funds were made available to them, and the project took on the code name GUSTO.

(C) Less than a year later the two proposals were essentially complete, and on 20 July 1959, the President was again briefed. This time he gave final approval, which signified that the program could get fully under way. (C) The next major step was to choose between the Lockheed and Convair designs. On 20 August 1959 specifications of the two proposals were submitted to a joint DOD/USAF/CIA selection panel:

	Lockheed	Convair
Maximum speed	3.2Mn	3.2Mn
Maximum range	4120nm	4000nm
Length	102ft	79.5ft
Wingspan	57ft	56ft
Gross weight	110,000lb	101,700lb

Operating Altitudes:
Start	84,000ft	85,000ft
Mid-range	91,000ft	88,000ft
End	97,600ft	94,000ft
Time to first flight	22 months	22 months

(S) The Lockheed design was selected, Project GUSTO terminated, and the program to develop a new U-2 follow-on aircraft was named OXCART. On 3 September 1959, CIA authorized Lockheed to proceed with antiradar studies, aerodynamic structural tests, and engineering designs, and on 30 January 1960 gave the green light to produce 12 aircraft.

(S) Pratt and Whitney Division of United Aircraft Corporation had been involved in discussions of the project, and undertook to develop the propulsion system. Their J-58 engine, which was to be used in the A-12, had been sponsored originally by the US Navy for its own purposes, and was to be capable of a speed of Mach 3.0. Navy interest in the development was diminishing, however, and the Secretary of Defense had decided to withdraw from the program at the end of 1959. CIA's requirement was that the engine and aircraft be further developed and optimized for a speed of Mach 3.2. The new contract called for initial assembly of three advanced experimental engines for durability and reliability testing, and provision of three engines for experimental flight-testing in early 1961.

(S) The primary camera manufacturer was Perkin-Elmer. Because of the extreme complexity of the design, however, a decision was soon made that a back-up system might be necessary in the event the Perkin-Elmer design ran into production problems, and Eastman Kodak was also asked to build a camera. Minneapolis-Honeywell Corporation was selected to provide both the inertial navigation and automatic flight control system. The Firewell Corporation and the David Clark Corporation became the prime sources of pilot equipment and associated life support hardware.

(U) Lockheed's designer was Clarence L. (Kelly) Johnson, creator of the U-2, and he called his new vehicle not A-12 but A-11. Its design exhibited many innovations. Supersonic airplanes, however, involve a multitude of extremely difficult design problems. Their payload-range performance is highly sensitive to engine weight, structural weight, fuel consumption, and aerodynamic efficiency. Small mistakes in predicting these values can lead to large errors in performance. Models of the A-11 were tested and retested, adjusted and readjusted, during thousands of hours in the wind tunnel. Johnson was confident of his design, but no one could say positively whether the bird would fly, still less whether it would fulfil the extremely demanding requirements laid down for it.

(U) To make the drawings and test the model was one thing; to build the aircraft was another. The most numerous problems arose from the simple fact that in flying through the atmosphere at its designed speed the skin of the aircraft would be subjected to a temperature of more than 550 degrees Fahrenheit. For one thing, no metal hitherto commonly used in aircraft production would stand this temperature, and those which would do, were for the most part too heavy to be suitable for the purpose in hand.

(S) During the design phase Lockheed evaluated many materials and finally chose an alloy of titanium, characterized by great strength, relatively light weight, and good resistance to high temperatures. Titanium was also scarce and very costly. Methods for milling it and controlling the quality of the product were not fully developed. Of the early deliveries from Titanium Metals Corporation some 80 percent had to be rejected, and it was not until 1961, when a delegation from headquarters visited the officials of that company, informed them of the objectives and high priority of the OXCART program, and gained their full cooperation, that the supply became consistently satisfactory. (S) But this only solved an initial problem. One of the virtues of titanium was its exceeding hardness, but this very virtue gave rise to immense difficulties in machining and shaping the material. Drills which worked well on aluminum soon broke to pieces; new ones had to be devised. Assembly-line production was impossible; each of the small OXCART fleet was, so to speak, turned out by hand. The cost of the program mounted well above original estimates, and it soon began to run behind schedule. One after another, however, the problems were solved, and their solution constituted the greatest single technological achievement of the entire enterprise. Henceforth it became practicable, if expensive, to build aircraft out of titanium.

(S) Since every additional pound of weight was critical, adequate insulation was out of the question. The inside of the aircraft would be like a moderately hot oven. The pilot would have to wear a kind of space suit, with its own cooling apparatus, pressure control, oxygen supply, and other necessities for survival. The fuel tanks, which constituted by far the greater part of the aircraft, would heat up to about 350 degrees, so that special fuel had to be supplied and the tanks themselves rendered inert with nitrogen. Lubricating oil was formulated for operation at 600 degrees F., and contained a diluent in order to remain fluid at operation below 40 degrees. Insulation on the plane's intricate wiring soon became brittle and useless. During the lifetime of the OXCART no better insulation was found; the wiring and related connectors had to be given special attention and handling at great cost in labor and time. (S) Then there was the unique problem of the camera window. The OXCART was to carry a delicate and highly sophisticated camera, which would look out through a quartz glass window. The effectiveness of the whole system depended upon achieving complete freedom from optical distortion despite the great heat to which the window would be subjected. Thus the question was not simply one of providing equipment with resistance to high temperature, but of assuring that there should be no unevenness of temperature throughout the area of the window. It took three years of time and two million dollars of money to arrive at a satisfactory solution. The program scored one of its most remarkable successes when the quartz glass was successfully fused to its metal frame by an unprecedented process involving the use of high frequency sound waves. (S) Another major problem of different nature was to achieve the low radar cross-section desired. The airframe areas giving the greatest radar return were the vertical stabilizers, the engine inlet, and the forward side of the engine nacelles. Research in ferrites, high temperature absorbing materials and high-temperature plastic structures was undertaken to find methods to reduce the return. Eventually the vertical tail section fins were constructed from a kind of laminated 'plastic' material–the first time that such a material had been used for an important part of an aircraft's structure. With such changes in structural materials, the A-11 was re-designated A-12, and as such has never been publicly disclosed.

(C) To test the effectiveness of antiradar devices a small-scale model is inadequate; only a full-size mock-up will do. Lockheed accordingly built one of these, and as early as November 1959, transported it in a specially designed trailer truck over hundreds of miles of highway from the Burbank plant to the test area. Here it was hoisted to the top of a pylon and looked at from various angles by radar. Tests and adjustments went on for a year and a half before the results were deemed satisfactory. In the course of the process it was found desirable to attach some sizable metallic constructions on each side of the fuselage, and Kelly Johnson worried a good deal about the effect of these protuberances on his design. In flight tests, however, it later developed that they imparted a useful aerodynamic lift to the vehicle, and years afterward Lockheed's design for a supersonic transport embodied similar structures. (S) Pilots for the OXCART would obviously have to be of quite extraordinary competence, not only because of the unprecedented performance of the aircraft itself, but also because of the particular qualities needed in men who were to fly intelligence missions. Brigadier General Don Flickinger, of the Air Force, was designated to draw up the criteria for selection, with advice from Kelly Johnson and from CIA Headquarters. Pilots had to be qualified in the latest high performance fighters, emotionally stable, and well motivated. They were to be between 25 and 40 years of age, and the size of the A-12 cockpit prescribed that they be under six feet tall and under 175 pounds in weight. (S) Air Force files were screened for possible candidates and a list of pilots obtained. Psychological assessments, physical examinations and refinement of criteria eliminated a good many. Pre-evaluation processing resulted in sixteen potential nominees. This group underwent a further intensive security and medical scrutiny by the Agency. Those who remained were then approached to take employment with the Agency on a highly classified project involving an extremely advanced aircraft. In November 1961, commitments were obtained from five of the group. The small number recruited at this stage required that a second search be undertaken.

(S) When the final screening was complete the pilots selected from the program were William L. Skliar, Kenneth S. Collins, Walter Ray, Lon Walter, Mele Vojvodich, Jr., Jack W. Weeks, Ronald 'Jack' Layton, Dennis B. Sullivan, David P. Young, Francis J. Murray, and Russell Scott. After the selection, arrangements were made with the Air Force to effect appropriate transfers and assignments to cover their training and to lay the basis for their transition from military to civilian status. Compensation and insurance arrangements were similar to those for the U-2 pilots.

(U) One thing to be decided in the earliest stages of the program was where to base and test the aircraft. Lockheed clearly could not do the business at Burbank, where the aircraft were being built, if for no other reason that its runway was too short. The ideal location ought to be remote from metropolitan areas; well away from civil and military airways to preclude observation; easily accessible by air; blessed with good weather the year round; capable of accommodating large numbers of personnel; equipped with fuel storage facilities; fairly close to an Air Force installation; and possessing at least an 8,000 foot runway. There was no such place to be found.

(S) Ten Air Force bases programmed for closure were considered, but none provided the necessary security, and annual operating costs at most of them would be unacceptable. Edwards Air Force Base in California seemed a more likely candidate, but in the end it also was passed over. Instead a secluded site in Nevada was finally picked. It was deficient in personnel accommodations and POL storage, and its long-unused runway was inadequate, but security was good, or could be made so, and a moderate construction program could provide sufficient facilities. Lockheed estimated what would be needed in such respects as monthly fuel consumption, hangars and shop space, housing for personnel, and runway specifications. Armed with the list of major requirements, Headquarters came up with a construction and engineering plan. And in case anyone became curious about what was going on at this remote spot, a cover story stated that the facilities were being prepared for certain radar studies, to be conducted by an engineering firm with support from the Air Force. The remote location was explained as necessary to reduce the effect of electronic interference from outside sources.

(S) Excellent as it may have been from the point of view of security, the site at first afforded few of the necessities and none of the amenities of life. It was far from any metropolitan center. Lockheed provided a C-47 shuttle service to its plant at Burbank, and a chartered D-18 (Lodestar) furnished transportation to Las Vegas. Daily commuting was out of the question, however, and the construction workers arriving during 1960 were billeted in surplus trailers. A new water well was dug, and a few recreational facilities provided, but it was some time before accommodations became agreeable.

(C) Construction began in earnest in September 1960, and continued on a double-shift schedule until mid-1964. One of the most urgent tasks was to build the runway, which according to initial estimates of A-12 requirements must be 8,500 feet long. The existing asphalt runway was 5,000 feet long and incapable of supporting the weight of the A-12. The new one was built between 7 September and 15 November and involved pouring over 25,000 yards of concrete. Another major problem was to provide some 500,000 gallons of PF-1 aircraft fuel per month. Neither storage facilities nor means of transporting fuel existed. After considering airlift, pipeline, and truck transport, it was decided that the last-named was the most economical, and could be made feasible by resurfacing no more than eighteen miles of highway leading into the base. (C) Three surplus Navy hangars were obtained, dismantled, and erected on the north side of the base. Over 100 surplus Navy housing buildings were transported to the base and made ready for occupancy. By early 1962 a fuel tank farm was ready, with a capacity of 1,320,000 gallons. Warehousing and shop space was begun and repairs made to older buildings. All this, together with the many other facilities that had to be provided, took a long time to complete. Meanwhile, however, the really essential facilities were ready in time for the forecast delivery date of Aircraft No. 1 in August 1961. (S) The facilities were ready, but the aircraft were not. Originally promised for delivery at the end of May 1961, the date first slipped to August, largely because of Lockheed's difficulties in procuring and fabricating titanium. Moreover, Pratt & Whitney found unexpectedly great trouble in bringing the J-58 engine up to OXCART requirements. In March 1961, Kelly Johnson notified Headquarters:

(U) 'Schedules are in jeopardy on two fronts. One is the assembly of the wing and the other is in satisfactory development of the engine. Our evaluation shows that each of these programs is from three to four months behind the current schedule.'

(S) To this Bissell replied: (U) 'I have learned of your expected additional delay in first flight from 30 August to 1 December 1961. This news is extremely shocking on top of our previous slippage from May to August and my understanding as of our meeting 19 December that the titanium extrusion problems were essentially overcome. I trust this is the last of such disappointments short of a severe earthquake in Burbank.'

(U) Realizing that delays were causing the cost of the program to soar, Headquarters decided to place a top-level aeronautical engineer in residence at Lockheed to monitor the program and submit progress reports. (C) Delays nevertheless persisted. On 11 September, Pratt and Whitney informed Lockheed of their continuing difficulties with the J-58 engine in terms of weight, delivery, and performance. Completion date for Aircraft No. 1 by now had slipped to 22 December 1961, and the first flight to 27 February 1962. Even on this last date the J58 would not be ready, and it was therefore decided that a Pratt and Whitney J75 engine, designed for the F-105 and flown in the U-2, should be used for early flights. The engine, along with other components, could be fitted to the A-12 airframe, and it could power the aircraft safely to altitudes up to 50,000 feet and at speeds up to Mach 1.6. (S) When this decision had been made, final preparations were begun for the testing phase. In late 1961 Colonel Robert J. Holbury, USAF, was named Commander of the base, with the Agency employee as his Deputy. Support aircraft began arriving in the spring of 1962. These included eight F-101s for training, two T-33s for proficiency flying, a C-130 for cargo transport, a U-3A for administration purposes, a helicopter for search and rescue, and a Cessna 180 for liaison use. In addition, Lockheed provided an F-104 to act as chase aircraft during the A-12 flight test period.

(S) Meanwhile in January 1962, an agreement was reached with the Federal Aviation Agency that expanded the restricted airspace in the vicinity of the test area. Certain FAA air traffic controllers were cleared for the OXCART Project; their function was to insure that aircraft did not violate the order. The North American Air Defense Command established procedures to prevent their radar stations from reporting the appearance of high performance aircraft on their radar scopes.

(S) Refuelling concepts required prepositioning of vast quantities of fuel at certain points outside the United States. Special tank farms were programmed in California, Eielson AFB Alaska, Thule AB Greenland, Kadena AB Okinawa, and Adana, Turkey. Since the A-12 use specially refined fuel, these tank farms were reserved exclusively for use by the OXCART Program. Very small detachments of technicians at these locations maintained the fuel storage facility and arranged for periodic quality control fuel tests.

(S) At the Lockheed Burbank plant, Aircraft No. 1 (serially numbered 121) received its final tests and checkout during January and February 1962, and was partially disassembled for shipment to the site. It became clear very early in OXCART planning that because of security problems and the inadequate runway, the A-12 could not fly from Burbank. Movement of the full-scale (S) radar test model had been successfully accomplished in November 1959, as described above. A thorough survey of the route in June 1961, ascertained the hazards and problems of moving the actual aircraft, and showed that a package measuring 35 feet wide and 105 feet long could be transported without major difficulty. Obstructing road signs had to be removed, trees trimmed, and some roadsides levelled. Appropriate arrangements were made with police authorities and local officials to accomplish the safe transport of the aircraft. The entire fuselage, minus wings, was crated, covered, and loaded on the special-design trailer, which cost about $100,000. On 26 February 1962, it departed Burbank, and arrived at the base according to plan.

(S) First Flights

(U) Upon arrival reassembly of the aircraft and installation of the J-75 engines began. Soon it was found that aircraft tank sealing compounds had failed to adhere to the metals, and when fuel was put into the tanks numerous leaks occurred. It was necessary to strip the tanks of the faulty sealing compounds and reline them with new materials. Thus occurred one more unexpected and exasperating delay in the program.

(U) Finally, on 26 April 1962, Aircraft 121 was ready. On that day in accordance with Kelly Johnson's custom, Louis Schalk took it for an unofficial, unannounced, maiden flight lasting some 40 minutes. As in all maiden flights minor problems were detected, but it took only four more days to ready the aircraft for its first official flight.

(U) On 30 April 1962, just under one year later than originally planned, the A-12 officially lifted her wheels from the runway. Piloted again by Louis Schalk, it took off at 170 knots, with a gross weight of 72,000 pounds, and climbed to 30,000 feet. Top speed was 340 knots and the flight lasted 59 minutes. The pilot reported that the aircraft responded well and was extremely stable. Kelly Johnson declared it to be the smoothest official first flight of any aircraft he had designed or tested. The aircraft broke the sound barrier on its second official flight, 4 May 1962, reaching Mach 1.1. Again only minor problems were reported.

(S) With these flights accomplished, jubilation was the order of the day. The new Director of Central Intelligence, Mr. John McCone, sent a telegram of congratulation to Kelly Johnson. A critical phase had been triumphantly passed, but there remained the long, difficult, and sometimes discouraging process of working the aircraft up to full operational performance. (C) Aircraft No. 122 arrived at base on 26 June, and spent three months in radar testing before engine installations and final assembly. Aircraft No. 123 arrived in August and flew in October. Aircraft No. 124, a two-seated version intended for use in training project pilots, was delivered in November. It was to be powered by the J-58 engines, but delivery delays and a desire to begin pilot training prompted a decision to install the smaller J-75s. The trainer flew initially in January 1963. The fifth aircraft, No. 125, arrived at the area on 17 December.

(S) Meanwhile the OXCART program received a shot in the arm from the Cuban missile crisis. U-2s had been maintaining a regular reconnaissance vigil over the island, and it was on one of these missions in October that the presence of offensive missiles was discovered. Overflights thereafter became more frequent, but on 27 October an Agency U-2, flown by a Strategic Air Force pilot on a SAC-directed mission, was shot down by a surface-to-air missile. This raised the dismaying possibility that continued manned, high-altitude surveillance of Cuba might become out of the question. The OXCART program suddenly assumed greater significance than ever, and its achievement of operational status became one of the highest national priorities.

(S) At the end of 1962 there were two A-12 aircraft engaged in flight tests. A speed of Mach 2.16 and altitude of 60,000 feet had been achieved. Progress was still slow, however, because of delays in the delivery of engines and shortcomings in the performance of those delivered. One of the two test aircraft was still flying with two J-75 engines, and the other with one J-75 and one J-58. It had long since become clear that Pratt & Whitney had been too optimistic in their forecast; the problem of developing the J-58 up to OXCART specifications had proved a good deal more recalcitrant than expected. Mr. McCone judged the situation to be truly serious, and on 3 December he wrote to the President of United Aircraft Corporation.

(U) 'I have been advised that J-58 engine deliveries have been delayed again due to engine control production problems....By the end of the year it appears we will have barely enough J-58 engines to support the flight test program adequately....Furthermore, due to various engine difficulties we have not yet reached design speed and altitude. Engine thrust and fuel consumption deficiencies at present prevent sustained flight at design conditions which is so necessary to complete developments'.

(U) By the end of January 1963, ten engines were available, and the first flight with two of them installed occurred on 15 January. Thenceforth all A-12 aircraft were fitted with their intended propulsion system. Flight testing accelerated and contractor personnel went to a three-shift work day. (U) With each succeeding step into a high Mach regime new problems presented themselves. The worst of all these difficulties – indeed one of the most formidable in the entire history of the program – was revealed when flight testing moved into speeds between Mach 2.4 and 2.8, and the aircraft experienced such severe roughness as to make its operation virtually out of the question. The trouble was diagnosed as being in the air inlet system, which with its controls admitted air to the engine. At the higher speeds the flow of air was uneven, and the engine therefore could not function properly. Only after a long period of experimentation, often highly frustrating and irritating, was a solution reached. This further postponed the day when the A-12 could be declared operationally ready.

(U) Among more mundane troubles was the discovery that various nuts, bolts, clamps, and other debris of the manufacturing process had not been cleared away, and upon engine run-up or take-off were sucked into the engine. The engine parts were machined to such close tolerances that they could be ruined in this fashion. Obviously the fault was due to sheer carelessness. Inspection procedures were revised, and it was also found prudent at Burbank to hoist the engine nacelles into the air, rock them back and forth, listen for loose objects, and then remove them by hand.

(U) All A-12 aircraft were grounded for a week during investigation of the accident. A plugged pitot static tube in icing conditions turned out to be responsible for the faulty cockpit instrument indications – it was not something which would hold things up for long.

(S) Loss of this aircraft nevertheless precipitated a policy problem, which had been troubling the Agency for some time. With the growing number of A-12s, how much longer could the project remain secret? The program had gone through development, construction, and a year of flight testing without attracting public attention. But the Department of Defense was having difficulty in concealing its participation because of the increasing rate of expenditures, otherwise unexplained. There was also a realization that the technological data would be extremely valuable in connection with feasibility studies for the SST. Finally, there was a growing awareness in the higher reaches of the aircraft industry that something new and remarkable was going on. Rumours spread, and gossip flew about. Commercial airline crews sighted the OXCART in flight. The editor of *Aviation Week* (as might be expected) indicated his knowledge of developments at Burbank. The secrecy was thinning out.

(S) The President's Announcement

(U) In spite of all this, 1963 went by without any public revelation. President Johnson was brought up to date on the project a week after taking office, and directed that a paper be prepared for an announcement in the spring of 1964. Then at his press conference on 24 February, he read a statement of which the first paragraph was as follows:

(U) 'The United States has successfully developed an advanced experimental jet aircraft, the A-11, which has been tested in sustained flight at more than 2,000 miles per hour and at altitudes in excess of 70,000 feet. The performance of the A-11 far exceeds that of any other aircraft in the world today. The development of this aircraft has been made possible by major advances in aircraft technology of great significance for both military and commercial applications. Several A-11 aircraft are now being flight tested at Edwards Air Force Base in California. The existence of this program is being disclosed today to permit the orderly exploitation of this advanced technology in our military and commercial program'.

(U) The President went on to mention the 'mastery of the metallurgy and fabrication of titanium metal', which has been achieved, gave credit to Lockheed and to Pratt & Whitney, remarked that appropriate members of the Senate and House had been kept fully informed, and prescribed that the detailed performance of the A-11 would be kept strictly classified.

(S) The President's reference to the 'A-11' was of course deliberate. 'A-11' had been the original design designation for the all-metal aircraft first proposed by Lockheed; subsequently it became the design designation for the Air Force YF-12A interceptor which differed from its parent mainly in that it carried a second man for launching air-to-air missiles. To preserve the distinction between the A-11 and the A-12 Security had briefed practically all witting personnel in government and industry on the impending announcement. OXCART secrecy continued in effect. There was considerable speculation about an Agency role in the A-11 development, but it was never acknowledged by the government. News headlines ranged from 'US has dozen A-11 jets already flying' to 'Secret of sizzling new plane probably histories best kept'. (U) The President also said that 'the A-11 aircraft now at Edwards Air Force Base are undergoing extensive tests to determine their capabilities as long-range interceptors'. It was true that the Air Force in October 1960, had contracted for three interceptor versions of the A-12, and they were by this time available. But at the moment when the President spoke, there were no A-11's at Edwards and there never had been. Project officials had known that the public announcement was about to be made, but they had not been told exactly when. Caught by surprise, they hastily flew two Air Force YF-12As to Edwards to support the President's statement. So rushed was this operation, so speedily were the aircraft put into hangars upon arrival, that heat from them activated the hangar sprinkler system, dousing the reception team which awaited them. (S) Thenceforth, while the OXCART continued its secret career at its own site, the A-11 performed at Edwards Air Force Base in a considerable glare of publicity. Pictures of the aircraft appeared in the press, correspondents could look at it and marvel, stories could be written. Virtually no details were made available, but the technical journals nevertheless had a field day. The unclassified *Air Force and Space Digest*, for example, published a long article in its issue of April 1964, commencing: 'The official pictures and statements tell very little about the A-11. But the technical literature from open sources, when carefully interpreted, tells a good deal about what it could and, more importantly, what it could not be. Here's the story ...'.

(S) Going Operational

(U) Three years and seven months after first flight in April 1962 the OXCART was declared ready for operational use at design specifications. The period thus devoted to flight tests was remarkably short, considering the new fields of aircraft performance, which were being explored. As each higher Mach number was reached exhaustive tests were carried out in accordance with standard procedures to ensure that the aircraft functioned properly and safely. Defects were corrected and improvements made. All concerned gained experience with the particular characteristics and idiosyncrasies of the vehicle. (S) The air inlet and related control continued for a long time to present the most troublesome and refractory problem. Numerous attempts failed to find a remedy, even though a special task force concentrated on the task. For a time there was something approaching despair and the solution when finally achieved was greeted with enormous relief. After all, not every experimental aircraft of advanced performance has survived its flight testing period. The possibility existed that OXCART also would fail, despite the great cost and effort expended upon it.

(S) A few dates and figures will serve to mark the progress of events. By the end of 1963 there had been 573 flights totalling 765 hours. Nine aircraft were in the inventory. On 20 July 1963 test aircraft flew for the first time at Mach 3; in November Mach 3.2 (the design speed) was reached at 78,000 feet altitude. The longest sustained flight at design conditions occurred on 3 February 1964; it lasted to ten minutes at Mach 3.2 and 83,000 feet. By the end of 1964 there had been 1,160 flights, totalling 1,616 hours. Eleven aircraft were then available, four of them reserved for testing and seven assigned to the detachment.

(C) The record may be put in another way. Mach 2 was reached after six months of flying; Mach 3 after 15 months. Two years after the first flight the aircraft had flown a total of 38 hours at Mach 2, three hours at Mach 2.6, and less than one hour at Mach 3. After three years, Mach 2 time had increased to 60 hours, Mach 2.6 time to 33 hours, and Mach 3 time to nine hours; all Mach 3 time, however, was by test aircraft, and detachment aircraft were still restricted to mach 2.9.

(S) As may be seen from the figures, most flights were of short duration, averaging little more than an hour each. Primarily this was because longer flights were unnecessary at this stage of testing. It was also true, however, that the less seen of OXCART the better, and short flights helped to preserve the secrecy of the proceedings. Yet it was virtually impossible for an aircraft of such dimensions and capabilities to remain inconspicuous. At its full speed OXCART had a turning radius of no less than 86 miles. There was no question of staying close to the airfield; its shortest possible flights took it over a very large expanse of territory.

(S) The first long-range, high-speed flight occurred on 27 January 1965, when one of the test aircraft flew for an hour and forty minutes, with an hour and fifteen minutes above Mach 3.1. Its total range was 2,580 nautical miles, with altitudes between 75,600 and 80,000 feet.

(U) Two more aircraft were lost during this phase of the program. On 9 July 1964 Aircraft No. 133 was making its final approach to the runway when at altitude of 500 feet and airspeed of 200 knots it began a smooth steady roll to the left. Lockheed test pilot Bill Park could not overcome the roll. At about a 45 degree bank angle and 200 foot altitude he ejected. As he swung down to the vertical in the parachute his feet touched the ground, for what must have been one of the narrower escapes in the perilous history of test piloting. The primary cause of the accident was that the servo for the right outboard roll and pitch control froze. No news of the accident filtered out.

(S) On 28 December 1965 Aircraft No. 126 crashed immediately after take-off and was totally destroyed. Detachment pilot Mele Vojvodich ejected safely at an altitude of 150 feet. The accident investigation board determined that a flight line electrician had improperly connected the yaw and pitch gyros – had in effect reversed the controls. This time Mr. McCone directed the Office of Security to conduct an investigation into the possibility of sabotage. While nothing of the sort was discovered, there were indications of negligence, as the manufacturer of the gyro had earlier warned of the possibility that the mechanism could be connected in reverse. No action had been taken, however, even by such an elementary precaution as painting the contacts different colours. Again there was no publicity connected with the accident.

(S) The year 1965 saw the test site reach the high point of activity. Completion of construction brought it to full physical size. All detachment pilots were Mach 3.0 qualified. Site population reached 1,835. Contractors were working three shifts a day. Lockheed Constellations made daily flights between the factory at Burbank and the site. Two C-47 flights a day were made between the site and Las Vegas. And officials were considering how and when and where to use OXCART in its appointed role.

(S) Targeting the OX

(S) After the unhappy end of U-2 flights over the Soviet Union, US political authorities were understandably cautious about committing themselves to further manned reconnaissance over unfriendly territory. There was no serious intention to use the OXCART over Russia; save in some unforeseeable emergency it was indeed no longer necessary to do so. What then, should be done with this vehicle?
(S) The first interest was in Cuba. By early 1964 Project Headquarters began planning for the contingency of flights over that island under a program designated SKYLARK. Bill Park's accident in early July held this program up for a time, but on 5 August Acting DCI Marshall S. Carter directed that SKYLARK achieve emergency operational readiness by 5 November. This involved preparing a small detachment, which should be able to do the job over Cuba, though at something less than the full design capability of the OXCART. The goal was to operate at Mach 2.8 and 80,000 feet altitude.

(C) In order to meet the deadline set by General Carter, camera performance would have to be validated, pilots qualified for Mach 2.8 flight, and coordination with supporting elements arranged. Only one of several equipments for electronic countermeasures (ECM) would be ready by November, and a senior intra-governmental group, including representation from the President's Scientific Advisory Committee, examined the problem of operating over Cuba without the full complement of defensive systems. This panel decided that the first few overflights could safely be conducted without them, but the ECM would be necessary thereafter. The delivery schedule of ECM equipment was compatible with this course of action.

(S) After considerable modifications to aircraft, the detachment simulated Cuban missions on training flights, and a limited emergency SKYLARK capability was announced on the date General Carter had set. With two weeks notice the OXCART detachment could accomplish a Cuban overflight, though with fewer ready aircraft and pilots than had been planned.

(S) During the following weeks the detachment concentrated on developing SKYLARK into a sustained capability, with five ready pilots and five operational aircraft. The main tasks were to determine aircraft range and fuel consumption, attain repeatable reliable operation, finish pilot training, prepare a family of SKYLARK missions, and coordinate routes with North American Air Defense, Continental Air Defense, and the Federal Aviation Authority. All this was accomplished without substantially hindering the main task of working up OXCART to full design capability. We may anticipate the story, however, by remarking that despite all this preparation the OXCART was never used over Cuba. U-2s proved adequate, and the A-12 was reserved for more critical situations. (S) In 1965 a more critical situation did indeed emerge in Asia, and interest in using the aircraft there began to be manifest. On 18 March 1965 Mr. McCone discussed with Secretaries McNamara and Vance the increasing hazards to U-2 and drone reconnaissance of Communist China. A memorandum of this conversation stated:

(S) 'It was further agreed that we should proceed immediately with all preparatory steps necessary to operate the OXCART over Communist China, flying out of Okinawa. It was agreed that we should proceed with all construction and related arrangements. However, this decision did not authorize the deployment of the OXCART to Okinawa nor the decision to fly the OXCART over Communist China. The decision would authorize all preparatory steps and the expenditure of such funds as might be involved. No decision has been taken to fly the OXCART operationally over Communist China. This decision can only be made by the President'.

(S) Four days later Brigadier General Jack C. Ledford, Director of the Office of Special Activities, DD/S&T, briefed Mr. Vance on the scheme, which had been drawn up for operations in the Far East. The project was called BLACK SHIELD, and it called for the OXCART to operate out of the Kadena Air Force Base in Okinawa. In the first phase, three aircraft would stage to Okinawa for 60-day periods, twice a year, with about 225 personnel involved.

(S) After this was in good order, BLACK SHIELD would advance to the point of maintaining a permanent detachment at Kadena. Secretary Vance made $3.7 million available to be spent in providing support facilities on the island, which were to be available by early fall of 1965.

(S) Meanwhile the Communists began to deploy surface-to-air missiles around Hanoi, thereby threatening our current military reconnaissance capabilities. Secretary McNamara called this to the attention of the Under Secretary of the Air Force on 3 June 1965, and inquired about the practicability of substituting OXCART aircraft for U-2s. He was told that BLACK SHIELD could operate over Vietnam as soon as adequate aircraft performance was achieved. (S) With deployment overseas thus apparently impending in the fall, the detachment went into the final stages of its program for validating the reliability of aircraft and aircraft systems. It set out to demonstrate complete systems reliability at Mach 3.05 and at 2,300 nautical miles range, with penetration altitude of 76,000 feet. A demonstrated capability for three aerial refuellings was also part of the validation process. (S) By this time the OXCART was well along in performance. The inlet, camera, hydraulic, navigation, and flight control systems all demonstrated acceptable reliability. Nevertheless, as longer flights were conducted at high speeds and high temperatures, new problems came to the surface, the most serious being with the electrical wiring system. Wiring connectors and components had to withstand temperatures of more than 800 degrees Fahrenheit, together with structural flexing, vibration, and shock. Continuing malfunctions in the inlet controls, communications equipment, ECM systems, and cockpit instruments were in many cases attributable to wiring failures. There was also disturbing evidence that careless handling was contributing to electrical connector failures. Difficulties persisted in the sealing of fuel tanks. What with one thing and another, officials soon began to fear that the scheduled date for BLACK SHIELD readiness would not be met. Prompt corrective action on the part of Lockheed was in order. The quality of maintenance needed drastic improvement. The responsibility for delivering an aircraft system with acceptable reliability to meet an operational commitment lay in Lockheed's hands. (S) In this uncomfortable situation, John Parangosky, Deputy for Technology, OSA, went to the Lockheed plant to see Kelly Johnson on 3 August 1965. A frank discussion ensued on the measures necessary to insure that BLACK SHIELD commitments would be met, and Johnson concluded that he should himself spend full time at the site in order to get the job done expeditiously. Lockheed President Daniel Haughton offered the full support of the corporation, and Johnson began duty at the site next day. His firm and effective management got Project BLACK SHIELD back on schedule.

(S) Four primary BLACK SHIELD aircraft were selected and final validation flights conducted. During these tests the OXCART achieved a maximum speed of Mach 3.29, altitude of 90,000 feet, and sustained flight time above Mach 3.2 of one hour and fourteen minutes. The maximum endurance flight lasted six hours and twenty minutes. The last stage was reached on 20 November 1965, and two days later Kelly Johnson wrote General Ledford:

(S) 'Over-all, my considered opinion is that the aircraft can be successfully deployed for the BLACK SHIELD mission with what I would consider to be at least as low a degree of risk as in the early U-2 deployment days. Actually, considering our performance level of more than four times the U-2 speed and three miles more operating altitude, it is probably much less risky than our first U-2 deployment. I think the time has come when the bird should leave its nest'.

(S) Ten days later the 303 Committee received a formal proposal that OXCART be deployed to the Far East. The Committee, after examining the matter, did not approve. It did agree, however, that short of actually moving aircraft to Kadena all steps should be taken to develop and maintain a quick reaction capability, ready to deploy within a 21-day period at any time after 1 January 1966. (S) There the matter remained, for more than a year. During 1966 there were frequent renewals of the request to the 303 Committee for authorization to deploy OXCART to Okinawa and conduct reconnaissance missions over North Vietnam, Communist China, or both. All were turned down. Among high officials there was difference of opinion; CIA, the Joint Chiefs of Staff, and the Presidents Foreign Intelligence Advisory Board favoured the move, while Alexis Johnson representing State, and Defense in the persons of Messrs. McNamara and Vance, opposed it. The proponents urged the necessity of better intelligence, especially on a possible Chinese Communist build-up preparatory to intervention in Vietnam. The opponents felt that better intelligence was not so urgently needed as to justify the political risks of basing the aircraft in Okinawa and thus almost certainly disclosing to Japanese and other propagandists. They also believed it undesirable to use OXCART and reveal something of its capability until a more pressing requirement appeared. At least once, on 12 August 1966, the divergent views were brought up to the President, who confirmed the 303 Committee's majority opinion against deployment. (S) Meanwhile, of course, flight testing and crew proficiency training continued. There was plenty of time to improve mission plans and flight tactics, as well as to prepare the forward area at Kadena. New plans shortened deployment time from the 21 days first specified. Personnel and cargo were to be airlifted to Kadena the day deployment was approved. On the fifth day the first OXCART would depart and travel the 6,673 miles in five hours and 34 minutes. The second would go on the seventh and the third on the ninth day. The first two would be ready for an emergency mission on the eleventh day and for a normal mission on the fifteenth day.

(S) An impressive demonstration of the OXCART's capability occurred on 21 December 1966 when Lockheed test pilot Bill Park flew 10,198 statute miles in six hours. The aircraft left the test area in Nevada and flew northward over Yellowstone National Park, thence eastward to Bismark, North Dakota, and on to Duluth, Minnesota. It then turned south and passed Atlanta en route to Tampa, Florida, then northwest to Portland, Oregon, then southwest to Nevada. Again the flight turned eastward, passing Denver and St. Louis. Turning around at Knoxville, Tennessee, it passed Memphis in the home stretch back to Nevada. This flight established a record unapproachable by any other aircraft; it began at about the same time a typical government employee starts his work day and ended two hours before his quitting time. (S) Shortly after this exploit, tragedy befell the program. During a routine training flight on 5 January 1967, the fourth aircraft was lost, together with its pilot. The accident occurred during descent about 70 miles from the base. A fuel gauge failed to function properly, and the aircraft ran out of fuel only minutes before landing. The pilot, Walter Ray, ejected but was killed when he failed to separate from the ejection seat before impact. The aircraft was totally destroyed. Its wreckage was found on 6 January and Ray's body recovered a day later. Through Air Force channels a story was released to the effect that an Air Force SR-71, on a routine test flight out of Edwards Air Force Base, was missing and presumed down in Nevada. The pilot was identified as a civilian test pilot, and the newspapers connected him with Lockheed. Flight activity at the base was again suspended during investigation of the causes both for the crash and for the failure of the seat separation device. (S) It is worth observing that none of the four accidents occurred in the high-Mach-number, high-temperature regime of flight. All involved traditional problems inherent in any aircraft. In fact, the OXCART was by this time performing at high speeds, with excellent reliability.

(S) BLACK SHIELD

(S) About May of 1967 prospects for deployment took a new turn. A good deal of apprehension was evident in Washington about the possibility that the Communists might introduce surface-to-surface missiles into North Vietnam, and concern was aggravated by doubts as to whether we could detect such a development if it occurred. The President asked for a proposal on the matter; CIA briefed the 303 Committee and once again suggested that the OXCART be used. Its camera was far superior to those on drones or on the U-2; its vulnerability was far less. The State and Defense members of the Committee decided to re-examine the requirements and the political risks involved. While they were engaged in their deliberations, Director of Central Intelligence, Richard Helms, submitted to the 303 Committee another formal proposal to deploy the OXCART. In addition, he raised the matter at President Johnson's 'Tuesday lunch' on 16 May, and received the Presidents approval to 'go'. Walt Rostow later in the day formally conveyed the President's decision, and the BLACK SHIELD deployment plan was forthwith put into effect.

(S) On 17 May airlift to Kadena began. On 22 May the first A-12 (Serial No. 131) flew nonstop to Kadena in six hours and six minutes. Aircraft No. 127 (S) Neither on this nor on other flights was there much trouble from sonic boom. To be sure, the inhabitants of a small village some 30 miles from the site were troubled as the aircraft broke through the sound barrier while gaining altitude. A change of course remedied this. At altitude OXCART produced no more than an ominous rumble on the ground and since the plane was invisible to the naked eye no one associated this sound with its actual source. (C) Departed on 24 May and arrived at Kadena five hours and 55 minutes later. The third, No. 129, left according to plan on 26 May 1967 and proceeded normally until in the vicinity of Wake Island where the pilot experienced difficulties with the inertial navigation and communications systems. In the circumstances, he decided to make a precautionary landing at Wake Island. The propositioned emergency recovery team secured the aircraft without incident and the flight to Kadena resumed next day.

(C) Arrangements were made to brief the Ambassadors and Chiefs of Station in the Philippines, Formosa, Thailand, South Vietnam, and Japan, and the High Commissioner and Chief of Station, Okinawa. The Prime Ministers of Japan and Thailand were advised, as were the President and Defence Minister of the Republic of China. The Chiefs of the Air Force of Thailand and the Republic of China were also briefed. Reactions were favorable. (S) On 29 May 1967, the unit at Kadena was ready to fly an operational mission. Under the command of Colonel Hugh C. Slater 260 personnel had deployed to the BLACK SHIELD facility. Except for hangars, which were a month short of completion, everything was in shape for sustained operations. Next day the detachment was alerted for a mission on 31 May, and the moment arrived which would see the culmination of ten years of effort, worry, and cost. As fate would have it, on the morning of the 31st heavy rain fell at Kadena. Since weather over the target area was clear, preparations continued in hopes that the local weather would clear. When the time for take-off approached, the OXCART, which had never operated in heavy rain, taxied to the runway, and took off while the rain continued.

(S) The first BLACK SHIELD mission followed one flight line over North Vietnam and one over the Demilitarized Zone. It lasted three hours and 39 minutes, and the cruise legs were flown at Mach 3.1 and 80,000 feet. Results were satisfactory. Seventy of the 190 known SAM sites in North Vietnam were photographed, as were nine other priority targets. There were no radar signals detected, indicating that the first mission had gone completely unnoticed by both Chinese and North Vietnamese.

(S) Fifteen BLACK SHIELD missions were alerted during the period from 31 May to 15 August 1967. Seven of the fifteen were flown and of these four detected radar tracking signals, but no hostile action was taken against any of them. By mid-July they had determined with a high degree of confidence that there were no surface-to-surface missiles in North Vietnam.

(C) All operational missions were planned, directed, and controlled by Project Headquarters in Washington. A constant watch was maintained on the weather in the target areas. Each day at a specified hour (1600 hours local) a mission alert briefing occurred. If the forecast weather appeared favourable, the Kadena base was alerted and provided a route to be flown. The alert preceded actual take-off by 28 to 30 hours. Twelve hours prior to take-off (H minus 12) a second review of target weather was made. If it continued favorable, the mission generation sequence continued. At H minus 2 hours, a 'go-no-go' decision was made and communicated to the field. The final decision, it should be noted, depended not solely on weather in the target area; conditions had to be propitious also in the refuelling areas and at the launch and recovery base. (S) Operations and maintenance at Kadena began with the receipt of alert notification. Both a primary aircraft and pilot and a back-up aircraft and pilot were selected. The aircraft were given thorough inspection and servicing, all systems were checked, and the cameras loaded into the aircraft. Pilots received a detailed route briefing in the early evening prior to the day of flight. On the morning of the flight a final briefing occurred, at which time the condition of the aircraft and its systems was reported, last-minute weather forecasts reviewed, and other relevant intelligence communicated together with any amendments or changes in the flight plan. Two hours prior to take-off the primary pilot had a medical examination, got into his suit, and was taken to the aircraft. If any malfunctions developed on the primary aircraft, the back-up could execute the mission one hour later.

(S) A typical route profile for a BLACK SHIELD mission over North Vietnam included a refuelling shortly after take-off, south of Okinawa, the planned photographic pass or passes, withdrawal to a second aerial refuelling in the Thailand area, and return to Kadena. So great was the OXCARTs speed that it spent only 12½ minutes over North Vietnam in a typical 'single pass' mission, or a total of 21½ minutes on two passes. Its turning radius of 86 miles was such, however, that on some mission profiles it might be forced during its turn to intrude into Chinese airspace.

(S) Once landed back at Kadena, the camera film was removed from the aircraft, boxed, and sent by special plane to the processing facilities. Film from earlier missions was developed at the Eastman Kodak plant in Rochester, New York. By late summer an Air Force Center in Japan carried out the processing in order to place the photo intelligence in the hands of American commanders in Vietnam within 24 hours of completion of a BLACK SHIELD mission. (S) Between 16 August and 31 December 1967, twenty-six missions were alerted. Fifteen were flown. On 17 December one SAM site tracked the vehicle with its acquisition radar but was unsuccessful with its Fan Song guidance radar. On 28 October a North Vietnamese SAM site for the first time launched a single, albeit unsuccessful, missile at the OXCART. Photography from this mission documented the event with photographs of missile smoke above the SAM firing site, and with pictures of the missile and of its contrail. Electronic countermeasures equipment appeared to perform well against the missile firing. (S) During the flight of 30 October 1967, pilot Dennis Sullivan detected radar tracking on his first pass over North Vietnam. Two sites prepared to launch missiles but neither did. During the second pass at least six missiles were fired at the OXCART, each confirmed by missile vapour trails on mission photography. Sullivan saw these vapour trails and witnessed three missile detonations. Post-flight inspection of the aircraft revealed that a piece of metal had penetrated the lower right wing fillet area and lodged against the support structure of the wing tank. The fragment was not a warhead pellet but may have been a part of the debris from one of the missile detonations observed by the pilot.

(S) Between 1 January and 31 March 1968 six missions were flown out of fifteen alerted. Four of these were over North Vietnam and two over North Korea. The first mission over North Korea on 26 January occurred during a very tense period following seizure of the *Pueblo* on the 23rd. The aim was to discover whether the North Koreans were preparing any large scale hostile move on the heels of this incident. Chinese tracking of the flight was apparent, but no missiles were fired at the plane.

(C) The Department of State was reluctant to endorse a second mission over North Korea for fear of the diplomatic repercussions, which could be expected if the aircraft came down in hostile territory. Brigadier General Paul Bacalis then briefed Secretary Rusk on the details and objectives of the mission, and assured him that the aircraft would transit North Korea in no more than seven minutes. He explained that even if some failure occurred during flight the aircraft would be highly unlikely to land either in North Korea or in China. Secretary Rusk made suggestions to alter the flight plan, thus becoming the project's highest ranking flight planner.

(S) Between 1 April and 9 June 1968 two missions were alerted for North Korea. Only the mission which flew on 8 May was granted approval.

(S) The SR-71

(S) All through the OXCART program the Air Force had been exceedingly helpful. It gave financial support, conducted the refuelling program, provided operational facilities at Kadena, and air-lifted OXCART personnel and supplies to Okinawa for the operations over Vietnam and North Korea. It also ordered from Lockheed a small fleet of A-11's, which upon being finished as two seated reconnaissance aircraft would be named SR-71. These would become operational about 1967. (S) The stated mission of the SR-71 was to conduct 'post-strike reconnaissance,' that is, to look the enemy situation over after a nuclear exchange. The likelihood of using the aircraft in the capacity hardly appeared great, but SR-71 was of course also capable of ordinary intelligence missions. For these purposes, however, the OXCART possessed certain clear advantages. It carried only one man, and largely for this reason it had room for a much bigger and better camera, as well as for various other collection devices which at the time could not be carried by the SR-71. It was certainly the most effective reconnaissance aircraft in existence, or likely to be in existence for years to come. Also it was operated by civilians, and could be employed covertly or at least without the number of personnel and amount of fanfare normally attending an Air Force operation.

(S) The fact the SR-71s were ordered eased the path of OXCART development, since it meant that the financial burden was shared with the Air Force, and the cost per aircraft was somewhat reduced by producing greater numbers. In the longer run, however, the existence of SR-71 spelled the doom of OXCART, for reasons which appear to have been chiefly financial and in a manner now to be related.

(S) Ending

(S) During November 1965, the very month when OXCART was finally declared operational, the moves toward its demise commenced. Within the Bureau of the Budget a memorandum was circulated expressing concern at the costs of the A-12 and SR-71 programs, both past and projected. It questioned the requirement for the total number of aircraft represented in the combined fleets, and doubted the necessity for a separate CIA (OXCART) fleet. Several alternatives were proposed to achieve a substantial reduction in the forecasted spending, but the recommended course was to phase out the A-12 program by September 1966 and stop any further procurement of SR-71 aircraft. Copies of this memorandum were sent to the Department of Defense and the CIA with the suggestion that those agencies explore the alternatives set out in the paper. But the Secretary of Defense declined to consider the proposal, presumably because the SR-71 would not be operational by September 1966.

(S) Things remained in this state until in July 1966 the Bureau of the Budget proposed that a study group be established to look into the possibility of reducing expenses on the OXCART and SR-71 programs. The group was requested to consider the following alternatives:

1. Retention of separate A-12 and SR-71 fleets, i.e., status quo.
2. Collocation of the two fleets.
3. Transfer of the OXCART mission and aircraft to SAC.
4. Transfer of the OXCART mission to SAC and storage of A-12 aircraft.
5. Transfer of the OXCART mission to SAC and disposal of A-12 aircraft.

(S) The study group included C.W. Fischer, Bureau of the Budget; Herbert Bennington, Department of Defense; and John Parangosky, Central Intelligence Agency.

(S) This group conducted its study through the fall of 1966, and identified three principal alternatives of its own. They were:

1. To maintain the status quo and continue both fleets at current approval levels.
2. To mothball all A-12 aircraft, but maintain the OXCART capability by sharing SR-71 aircraft between SAC and CIA.
3. To terminate the OXCART fleet in January 1968 (assuming an operational readiness date of September 1967 for the SR-71) and assign all missions to the SR-71 fleet.

(S) On 12 December 1966 there was a meeting at the Bureau of the Budget attended by Mr. Helms, Mr. Shultze, Mr. Vance, and Dr. Hornig, Scientific Advisor to the President. Those present voted on the alternatives proposed in the Fischer-Bennington-Parangosky report. Messrs. Vance, Schultze, and Hornig chose to terminate the OXCART fleet, and Mr. Helms stood out for eventual sharing of the SR-71 fleet between CIA and SAC. The Bureau of the Budget immediately prepared a letter to the President setting forth the course of action recommended by the majority. Mr. Helms, having dissented from the majority, requested his Deputy Director for Science and Technology to prepare a letter to the President stating CIA's reasons for remaining in the reconnaissance business.

(S) On 16 December Mr. Schultze handed Mr. Helms a draft memorandum to the President which requested a decision either to share the SR-71 fleet between CIA and SAC, or to terminate the CIA capability entirely. This time Mr. Helms replied that new information of considerable significance had been brought to his attention concerning SR-71 performance. He requested another meeting after 1 January to review pertinent facts, and also asked that the memorandum to the President be withheld pending that meeting's outcome. Specifically, he cited indications that the SR-71 program was having serious technical problems and that there was real doubt that it would achieve an operational capability by the time suggested for termination of the A-12 program. Mr. Helms therefore changed his position from sharing the SR-71 aircraft with SAC to a firm recommendation to retain the OXCART A-12 fleet under civilian sponsorship. The Budget Bureau's memorandum was nevertheless transmitted to the President, who on 28 December 1966 accepted the recommendations of Messrs. Vance, Hornig, and Schultze, and directed the termination of the OXCART Program by 1 January 1968. (S) This decision meant that a schedule had to be developed for orderly phase-out. After consultation with project Headquarters, the Deputy Secretary of Defense was advised on 10 January 1967 that four A-12's would be placed in storage in July 1967, two more by December, and the last four by the end of January 1968. In May Mr. Vance directed that the SR-71 assume contingency responsibility to conduct Cuban overflights as of 1 July 1967 and take over the dual capability over South-east Asia and Cuba by 1 December 1967. This provided for some overlap between OXCART withdrawal and SR-71 assumption of responsibility.

(S) Meanwhile until 1 July 1967 the OXCART Detachment was to maintain its capability to conduct operational missions both from a prepared location overseas and from the US. This included a 15 day quick reaction capability for deployment to the Far East and a seven-day quick reaction for deployment over Cuba. Between 1 July and 31 December 1967 the fleet would remain able to conduct operational missions either from a prepared overseas base or from home base, but not from both simultaneously. A quick reaction capability for either Cuban overflights or deployment to the Far East would also be maintained. (S) All these transactions and arrangements occurred before the OXCART had conducted a single operational mission or even deployed to Kadena for such a mission. As recounted above, the aircraft first performed its appointed role over North Vietnam on the last day of May 1967. In succeeding months it demonstrated both its exceptional technical capabilities and the competence with which its operations were managed. As word began to get around that OXCART was to be phased out, high officials commenced to feel some disquiet. Concern was shown by Walt Rostow, the President's Special Assistant; by key Congressional figures, members of the President's Foreign Intelligence Advisory Board, and the President's Scientific Advisory Committee. The phase-out lagged, and the question was reopened.

(S) A new study of the feasibility and cost of continuing the OXCART program was completed in the spring of 1968 and four new alternatives were proposed.

1. Transfer all OXCART aircraft to SAC by 31 October 1968; substitute Air Force for contractor support where possible; turn the test A-12 aircraft over to the SR-71 test facility.
2. Transfer OXCART as in alternative 1, above, and store eight SR-71s.
3. Close the OXCART home base and collocate the fleet with SR-71's at Beale Air Force Base in California, but with CIA retaining control and management.
4. Continue OXCART operations at its own base under CIA control and management.

(S) Mr. Helms expressed his reactions to these alternatives in a memorandum to Messrs. Nitze, Hornig, and Flax, dated 18 April 1968. In it he questioned why, if eight SR-71s could be stored in one option, they could not be stored in all the options, with the resultant savings applied in each case. He questioned the lower cost figures of combining the OXCART with the SR-71s and disagreed, for security reasons, with collocating the two fleets. Above all, however, he felt that the key point was the desirability of retaining a covert reconnaissance capability under civilian management. It was his judgement that such a requirement existed, and he recommended that OXCART continue at its own base under CIA management.

(S) In spite of all these belated efforts, the Secretary of Defense on 16 May 1968 reaffirmed the original decision to terminate the OXCART Program and store the aircraft. At his weekly luncheon with his principal advisors on 21 May 1968, the President confirmed Secretary Clifford's decision.

(S) Early in March 1968, USAF SR-71 aircraft began to arrive at Kadena to take over the BLACK SHIELD commitment, and by gradual stages the A-12 was placed on standby to back up the SR-71. The last operational mission flown by OXCART was on 8 May 1968 over North Korea, following which the Kadena Detachment was advised to prepare to go home. Project Headquarters selected 8 June 1968 as the earliest possible date to begin redeployment, and in the meantime flights of A-12 aircraft were to be limited to those essential for maintaining flying safety and pilot proficiency. After BLACK SHIELD aircraft arrived in the US they would proceed to storage. Those already at base were placed in storage by 7 June.

(S) During its final days overseas the OXCART enterprise suffered yet another blow, as inexplicable as it was tragic. On 4 June Aircraft No. 129, piloted by Jack Weeks, set out from Kadena on a check flight necessitated by a change of engine. Weeks was heard from when 520 miles east of Manila. Then he disappeared. Search and rescue operations found nothing. No cause for the accident was ever ascertained, and it remains a mystery to this day. Once again the official news release identified the lost aircraft as an SR-71 and security was maintained. (S) A few days afterwards the two remaining planes on Okinawa flew to the US and were stored with the remainder of the OXCART family.

(S) Postscript

(S) In summary; the OXCART Program lasted just over ten years, from its inception in 1957 through first flights in 1962 to termination in 1968. Lockheed produced 15 OXCARTs, three YF-12A's and 31 SR-71's. The 49 supersonic aircraft had completed more than 7,300 flights, with 17,000 hours in the air. Over 2,400 hours had been above Mach 3. Five OXCARTs were lost in accidents; two pilots were killed, and two had narrow escapes. In addition, two F-101 chase planes were lost with their Air Force pilots during OXCART's testing phase. (U) The main objective of the program – to create a reconnaissance aircraft of unprecedented speed, range, and altitude capability – was triumphantly achieved. It may well be, however, that the most important aspects of the effort lay in its by-products – the notable advances in aerodynamic design, engine performance, cameras, electronic countermeasures, pilot life support systems, anti-air devices, and above all in milling, machining, and shaping titanium. Altogether it was a pioneering accomplishment.

(S) In a ceremony at the Nevada base on 26 June 1968, Vice Admiral Rufus L. Taylor, Deputy Director of Central Intelligence, presented the CIA Intelligence Star for valor to pilots Kenneth S. Collins, Ronald L. Layton, Francis J. Murray, Dennis B. Sullivan, and Mele Vojvodich for participation in the BLACK SHIELD operation. The posthumous award to pilot Jack W. Weeks was accepted by his widow. The United States Air Force Legion of Merit was presented to Colonel Slater and his Deputy, Colonel Maynard N. Amundson. The Air Force Outstanding Unit Award was presented to the members of the OXCART Detachment (1129th Special Activities Squadron, Detachment 1) and the USAF supporting units. (U) Wives of the pilots were present and learned for the first time of the activities in which their husbands had been involved. Kelly Johnson was a guest speaker at the ceremony, and lamented in moving words the end of an enterprise which had marked his most outstanding achievement in aircraft design. His own awards had already been received: The Presidents Medal of Freedom in 1964 and on 10 February 1966, the National Medal of Science, from President Johnson, for his contributions to aerospace science and to the national security.

Successor to the U-2

NOTE: *This document was approved for release by the CIA in Oct 1994; it is an expanded version of the history of the A-12. Some parts are missing (censored) which I have indicated by a [ ], and inside roughly the number of spaces blacked out. In italics I have included who I or what I think was censored. There are also some footnotes which appear at the bottom of the page, I have included these at the location of the footnote in* Univers. – John Stone, blackbirds.net.

The U-2's Intended Successor: Project *Oxcart*, 1956–1968

Before the U-2 became operational in June 1956, CIA project officials had estimated that its life expectancy for flying safely over the Soviet Union would be between 18 months and two years. After overflights began and the Soviets demonstrated the capability of tracking and attempting to intercept the U-2, this estimate seemed too optimistic. By August 1956, Richard Bissell was so concerned about the U-2's vulnerability that he despaired of its ability to avoid destruction for six months, let alone two years.

To extend the U-2's useful operational life, project officials first attempted to reduce the aircraft's vulnerability to detection by Soviet radars. Project RAINBOW's efforts to mask the radar image of the U-2 not only proved ineffective, but actually made the aircraft more vulnerable by adding extra weight that reduced its maximum altitude. Because Soviet radar operators continued to find and track U-2s equipped with antiradar systems, the CIA cancelled Project RAINBOW in May 1958.

Long before the failure of Project RAINBOW, Richard Bissell and his Air Force Assistant [15 spaces] had begun to look for a more radical solution to the problem of Soviet radar detection – an entirely new aircraft. In the late summer of 1956, the two officials visited a number of airframe contractors in a search for new ideas. Among the more unusual was Northrop Aviation's proposal for a gigantic aircraft with a very-high-lift wing. Because it would not be made of metal, the wing would require a type of bridge truss on its upper side to give it rigidity. The proposed aircraft would achieve altitudes 80,000 to 90,000 feet but only at subsonic speeds, just enough to keep it airborne.
Donovan Interview

The slow-flying Northrop design did not solve the problem of radar detection, and in 1957 the emphasis switched to supersonic designs. In August 1957, [64 spaces] that had been working on ways to reduce the U-2's vulnerability to radar, began to investigate the possibility of designing an aircraft with a very small radar cross section. [5 spaces] soon discovered that supersonic speed greatly reduced the chances of detection by radar.

(Thomas McIninch.'The Oxcart Story', Studies in Intelligence 15 (Winter 1971): 2[1 space]).

From this point on, the CIA's attention focused increasingly on the possibility of building an aircraft that could fly at both extremely high speeds and high altitudes while incorporating the best ideas in radar-absorbing or radar-deflecting techniques.

The Evaluation of Designs for a Successor to the U-2

By the autumn of 1957, Bissell and [9 spaces] had collected so many ideas for a successor to the U-2 that Bissell asked DCI Dulles for permission to establish an advisory committee to assist in the selection process. Bissell also felt that the support of a committee of prominent scientists and engineers would prove useful when it came time to ask for funding for such an expensive project. Edwin Land becomes the chairman for the new committee, which included some of the scientists and engineers who had served on previous advisory bodies for overhead reconnaissance: Edward Purcell, Allen F. Donovan, H. Guyford Stever, and Eugene P. Kiefer. The Air Force's chief scientist, Courtland D. Perkins, was also a member. The committee first met in November 1957 and held six more meetings between July 1958 and the late summer of 1959. The meetings usually took place in Land's Boston office and almost always included the Air Force's Assistant Secretary for Research and Development, Dr. Joseph V. Charyk, and his Navy counterpart, Garrison Norton. Designers from several aircraft manufacturers also attended some of the meetings.

(Clarence L. Johnson, Report No. SP-1362, 'History of the OXCART Program', Lockheed Aircraft Corp., Burbank, CA, 1 July 1968. p. 1 (TS Codeword).)

The two most prominent firms involved in the search for a new aircraft were Lockheed, which had designed the successful U-2, and Convair which was building the supersonic B-58 'Hustler' bomber for the Air Force and also working on an even faster model known as the B-58B 'Super Hustler'. Early in 1958, Richard Bissell asked officials from both firms to submit designs for a high-speed reconnaissance aircraft. During the spring and summer of 1958, both firms worked on designs concepts without government contracts or funds.

Following extended discussions with Bissell on the subject of a supersonic successor to the U-2, Lockheed's Kelly Johnson began designing an aircraft that would cruise at Mach 3.0 at altitudes above 90,000 feet. On 23 July 1958, Johnson presented his new high-speed concept to Land's advisory committee, which expressed interested in the approach he was taking. At the same meeting, Navy representatives presented a concept for a high-altitude reconnaissance vehicle that examined the possibility of developing a ramjet-powered, inflatable, rubber vehicle that would be lifted to altitude by a balloon and then be propelled by a rocket to a speed where the ramjets could produce thrust. Richard Bissell asked Johnson to evaluate this concept, and three weeks later, after receiving more details from the Navy representatives, Kelly Johnson made some quick calculations that showed that the design was impractical because the balloon would have to be a mile in diameter to lift the vehicle, which in turn would need a wing surface greater than one-seventh of an acre to carry the payload.

(Clarence L. Johnson, 'Development of the Lockheed SR-71 Blackbird', Studies in Intelligence 26 (Summer 1982):4 (U): Johnson, 'Archangel Log' 23 July 1958, 14 August 1958.)

By September 1958, Lockheed had studied a number of possible configurations, some based on ramjet engines, others with both ramjets and turbojets. Personnel at Lockheed's Skunk Works referred to these aircraft concepts as 'Archangel-1', 'Archangel-2', and so forth, a carry over from the original nickname of the 'Angel' given to the U-2 during its development. These nicknames for the various designs soon became simply 'A-1', A-2', etc.

In September 1958, the Land committee met again to review all the concepts then under consideration and to winnow out the few that were most practicable. Among the concepts rejected were the Navy's proposal for an inflatable, ramjet-powered aircraft, a Boeing proposal for a 190-foot-long hydrogen-powered inflatable aircraft, and a Lockheed design for a hydrogen-powered aircraft (the CL-400). The committee examined two other Kelly Johnson designs at this meeting – a tailless subsonic aircraft with a very-low-radar cross section (the G2A) and a new supersonic design (the A-2) and did not accept either one, the former because of its slow speed and the latter because of it dependence on exotic fuels for its ramjets and its overall high cost. The committee approved the continuation of Convair's work on a ramjet-powered Mach 4.0 'parasite' aircraft that would be launched from a specially configured version of the B-58B bomber. The design was termed a parasite because it could not take off on its own but needed a larger aircraft to carry it aloft and accelerate it to the speed required to start the ramjet engine. The Convair design was called the FISH.

OSA History, chap. 20, p. 8 [15 spaces] Johnson, 'Archangel Log', 17–24 September 1958

Two months later, after reviewing the Convair proposal and yet another Lockheed design for a high-speed reconnaissance aircraft (the A-3), the Land committee concluded in late November 1958 that it would indeed be feasible to build an aircraft whose speed and altitude would make radar tracking difficult or impossible. The committee, therefore, recommended that DCI Dulles ask President Eisenhower to approve further pursuit of the project and to provide fund for additional studies and tests.

OSA Chronology, p. 21 [20 spaces]. 'Oxcart Story' p. 3 [2 spaces]): OSA History, chap. 20, p. 8 [15 spaces]): Johnson. 'Archangel Log', 12 November 1958.

On 17 December 1958, Allen Dulles and Richard Bissell briefed the President on the progress toward a successor to the U-2. Also present were Land and Purcell from the advisory committee, Presidential Service Advisor James Killian, and Air Force Secretary Donald Quarles. DCI Dulles reviewed the results to the U-2 missions to date and stated his belief that a successor to the U-2 could be used all over the world and 'would have a much greater invulnerability to detection'.

Bissell then described two competing projects by Lockheed and Convair, noting that the chief question at the moment was whether to use air launch or ground take-off. The next phase, he added, would be detailed engineering, at the end of which it was proposed that 12 aircraft be ordered at a cost of about $100 million.

Although President Eisenhower supported the purchase of this type of aircraft, he questioned the plan to procure any before they had been tested. Promising that more thought would be given to the matter before such an order was placed,

Secretary Quarles noted that CIA, the Defense Department, and the Bureau of the Budget were working on a funding plan for the project. The President suggested that the Air Force 'could support the project by transferring some reconnaissance money.' At the close of the meeting, Eisenhower asked the group to return after completing the next work phase to discuss further stages of the project with him.

Andrew J. Goodpaster, 'Memorandum of Conference with the President, 17 December 1958, 10:26am', 22 December 1958. WHOSS, Alpha, DDEL (TS).

Competition between Lockheed and Convair

With funding for the proposed new type of aircraft now available, Richard Bissell asked Lockheed and Convair to submit detailed proposals. During the first half of 1959, both Lockheed and Convair worked to reduce the radar cross section of their designs, with assistance from [60 spaces]. In pursuing his antiradar studies, [8 spaces] had discovered a phenomenon that he believed could be used to advantage by the new reconnaissance aircraft. Known as the Blip/Scan Ratio but also referred to as the [16 spaces], this phenomenon involved three elements: the strength of a radar return, the altitude of the object being illuminated by the radar, and the persistence of the radar return on the screen (Pulse-Position Indicator display).

Most tracking radars in the late 1950s swept a band of sky 30 degrees to 45 deg. wide and 360 deg. in circumference. Any object encountered in this area reflected the radar pulse in a manner directly proportional to its size – the larger the object, the stronger the returning radar signal. This return appeared on the cathode-ray tube of the radar screen as a spot or blip, and the persistence of this blip on the radar screen also depended on the strength of the radar return, with blips from larger objects remaining on the screen longer. During the late 1950s and early 1960s, a human radar operator watched the radar screen and kept track of the blips that indicated aircraft within the radar's field of view.

[9 spaces] determined that a high altitude object moving two to three times as fast as a normal aircraft would produce such a small blip with so little persistence that a radar operator would have great difficulty tracking it, if indeed he could even see it. [8 spaces] estimated that for an aircraft to take advantage of this Blip/Scan Ratio phenomenon it must fly at altitudes approaching 90,000 feet and have a radar cross section of less than 10 square meters, preferably not achieve such a small radar cross section, its designers would have to make many concessions in its structural design and aerodynamics.

Unnumbered Convair document on the Blip/Scan Ratio [19 spaces]

By the summer of 1959, both firms had completed their proposals. In early June, Lockheed submitted a design for the ground-launched aircraft known as the A-11. It would have a speed of Mach 3.2, a range of 3,200 miles, an altitude of 90,000 feet, and a completion date of January 1961. Kelly Johnson had refused to reduce the aerodynamics of his design in order to achieve a greater antiradar capability, and the A-11's radar cross section, although not great, was substantially larger than that of the much smaller parasite aircraft being designed by Convair.

Johnson, 'Archangel Log', December 1958–July 1959

The Convair proposal called for a small, manned, ramjet-powered, reconnaissance vehicle to be air launched from one of two specially configured B-58B Super Hustlers. The FISH vehicle, a radical lifting body with a very-small-radar cross section, would fly at Mach 4.2 at 90,000 feet and have a range of 3,900 miles. Two Marquardt ramjets would power its Mach 4.2 dash over the target area. Once the FISH decelerated, two Pratt & Whitney JT-12 turbojets would bring it back to base. The ramjet exit nozzles and wing edges would be constructed of Pyroceram, a ceramic material that could withstand the high temperatures of very high speeds and would absorb radio frequency energy from the radar pulses. Convair stated that the FISH could be ready by January 1961.

OSA History, chap 20 p. 12, [14 spaces] Convair Division, General Dynamics Corporation, 'Project FISH Status Review', 9 June 1959 (S)

Convair's proposal depended on two uncertain factors. First and foremost was the unproven technology of the ramjet engines. At the time, no aircraft in existence could carry a large, ramjet-powered aircraft into the sky and then accelerate to sufficient speed for the ramjet engines to be ignited. Since ramjet engines had only been tested in wind tunnels, there was no available data to prove that these engines would work in the application proposed by Convair. The second uncertain factor was the B-58B bomber that was supposed to achieve Mach 2.2 before launching the FISH above 35,000 feet. The version of the B-58 was still in the design stage.

Convair's proposal suffered a major setback in June 1959, when the Air Force cancelled the B-58B project. Conversion of the older, slower B-58A into the supersonic launching platform for the FISH was ruled out by the high cost and technical difficulties involved. Moreover, the Air Force was unwilling to part with two aircraft from the small inventory of its most advanced bomber. Even had the B-58B program not been cancelled, however, the FISH proposal would probably not have been feasible. Convair engineers had calculated that the added weight of the FISH would prevent the B-58B from achieving the speed required to ignite the parasite aircraft's ramjet engines.

The Convair proposal was therefore unusable, but the Lockheed design with its high radar cross section was also unacceptable to the Land committee. On 14 July 1959, the committee rejected both designs and continued the competition. Lockheed continued to work on developing a design that would be less vulnerable to detection, and Convair received a new CIA contract to design an air-breathing twin-engine aircraft that would meet the general specifications being followed by Lockheed.

OSA History, chap. 20, p. 15 [13 spaces]

Following recommendations by the Land committee, both Lockheed and Convair incorporated the Pratt & Whitney J58 power plant into their designs. This engine had originally been developed for the Navy's large, jet-powered flying boat, the Glenn L. Martin Company's P6M Seamaster, and was the most powerful engine available. In 1958 the Navy had cancelled the Seamaster program, which left Pratt & Whitney without a buyer for the powerful J58 engine.

OSA History, chap. 20, p. 15 [13 spaces]

Although the Land committee had not yet found an acceptable design, it informed President Eisenhower on 20 July 1959 that the search was making good process. Concerned about the U-2's vulnerability to detection and possible interception and aware that the photo satellite project was encountering significant problems, the President gave his final approval to the high-speed reconnaissance aircraft project.

[8 spaces] n interview, 4 October 1983 [13

spaces] Joseph V. Charyk, interview by [19 spaces] tape recording, Washington, DC. 5 December 1984 [12 spaces]

The Selection of the Lockheed Design

By the late summer of 1959, both Convair and Lockheed had completed new designs for a follow-on to the U-2. Convair's entry, known as the KINGFISH, used much of the technology developed for the F-102, F-106, and B-58, included stainless steel honeycomb skin, planiform wing design, and crew capsule system, which eliminated the need for the pilot to wear a pressurized suit. The KINGFISH had two side-by-side J58 engines inside the fuselage, which significantly reduced the radar cross section. Two additional important design features that contributed to a small radar return were fibreglass engine inlets and wings whose leading edges were made of Pyroceram. Convair Division, General Dynamics Corporation.

'KINGFISH Summery Report' 1959 (S).

Kelly Johnson was very sceptical of the Convair design, noting in the Archangel project log on 1-20 August 1959: 'Convair have promised reduced radar cross section on an airplane the size of A-12. They are doing this, in my view, with total disregard for aerodynamics, inlet and afterburner performance'.

Lockheed's new entry was much like its first, but with several modifications and a new designator, A-12. It too, would employ two of the powerful J58 engines. Lockheed's major innovation in reducing radar return was cesium additive in the fuel, which decreased the radar cross section of the afterburner plume. This improvement had been proposed by Edward Purcell of the Land committee. Desiring to save weight, Kelly Johnson had decided not to construct the A-12 out of steel. Traditional lightweight metals such as aluminum were out of the question because they could not stand the heat that would be generated as the A-12 flew at Mach 3.2, so Johnson chose a titanium alloy.

On 20 August 1959, Lockheed and Convair submitted their proposals to a joint Department of Defense, Air Force, and CIA selection panel. As the table shows, the two aircraft were similar in performance characteristics, although the Lockheed design's specifications were slightly better in each category. The Lockheed design was also preferable in terms of overall cost. In the vital area of vulnerability to radar detection, however, the Convair design was superior. Its smaller size and internally mounted engines gave it a smaller radar cross section than the Lockheed A-12.

OSA History: chap. 20. pp. 18–19 ([13 spaces]

Comparison of Lockheed and Convair Designs

	Lockheed A-12	Convair Kingfish
Speed	Mach 3.2	Mach 3.2
Range (total)	4,120nmi	3,400nmi
Range (at altitude)	3,800nmi	3,400nmi
Cruising Altitude:		
Start	84,500ft	85,000ft
Midrange	91,000ft	88,000ft
End	97,600ft	94,000ft
Cost of twelve aircraft, without engines	$96.6m	$121.6m

Some of the CIA representatives initially favoured the Convair KINGFISH design because of its smaller radar cross section, but they were eventually convinced to support the Lockheed design by the Air Force members of the panel, who believed that Convair's cost over-runs and production delays on the B-58 project might be repeated in this new project. In contrast, Lockheed had produced the U-2 under budget and on time. Another factor favouring the A-12 was security. Lockheed had experience in running a highly secure facility (the Skunk Works) in which all of the key employees was already cleared by the Agency.

Despite its vote in favour of the Lockheed proposal, the selection panel remained concerned about the A-12's vulnerability to radar detection and therefore required Lockheed to prove its concept for reducing the A-12's radar cross section by 1 January 1960. On 14 September 1959, the CIA awarded a four-month contract to Lockheed to proceed with antiradar studies, aerodynamic structural tests, and engineering designs. This research and all later work on the A-12 took place under a new codename, Project OXCART, established at the end of August 1959 to replace its more widely known predecessor, Project GUSTO. The CIA's project manager for the OXCART was [17 spaces] John Parangosky who had long been associated with the U-2 program.

Efforts to Reduce the A-12's Radar Cross Section

During the spring of 1959, Kelly Johnson's Skunk Works crew – which then numbered only 50, had begun building a full-scale mock-up of the proposed aircraft. The mock-up was to be tested for its radar cross section by Edgerton, Germeshausen & Grier (EG&G) in cooperation with the [80 spaces] McDonnell-Douglas RCS Facility at Gray Butte. Lockheed objected to this site because its pylon would not support the full-scale mock-up and because the facilities were in full view of a nearby highway. On 10 September 1959, EG&G agreed to move its radar test facility [99 spaces]. *(Ed. note: as best as I can make out there is a footnote in this deleted space.)*

[8 spaces] interview, [4 spaces], OSA History, chap. 20, pp 19-21, [13 spaces]

When the new radar test facility with it's larger pylon was ready, Johnson put the A-12 mock-up on a specially designed trailer truck [38 spaces] Groom Lake, Nevada.

OSA History, chap. 20, p. 22 ([14 spaces]

By 18 November 1959, the mock-up was in place atop the pylon, and radar testing could begin. These tests soon proved that Lockheed's concept of shape, fuel additive, and non-metallic parts was workable, but it would take more than 18 months of testing and adjustments before OXCART achieved a satisfactory radar cross section.

It was in course of this radar testing that the OXCART received its characteristic cobra-like appearance. Edward Purcell and [17 spaces] had come up with a theory that a continuously curving airframe would be difficult to track with a radar pulse because it would present few corner reflections or sharp angles from which pulses could bounce in the direction of the radar. To achieve the continuously curving airframe. Kelly Johnson added thin, curved extensions to the engine housings and leading edges of the wings and eventually to the fuselage itself, creating what is known as a chine on each side. At first Johnson was concerned that these additions might impair the airworthiness of the plane, but wind tunnel testing determined that the chines actually imparted a useful aerodynamic lift to the vehicle. Because titanium was very brittle and therefore difficult to bend, Johnson achieved the necessary curvature by combining triangular-shaped pieces of titanium called fillets. These fillets were glued to the framework of the chines with a special adhesive, epoxy resin.

On later OXCART models the fillets were made from electrically resistive honeycomb plastic with a glass-fiber surface that would not melt at high speed. When struck by a radar pulse, the composite chines tended to absorb the pulse rather than reflect it. A similar approach was used for the leading edge of the wings. Again electrically resistive honeycomb material was fabricated into triangular shapes, known as wing teeth, and fitted into the titanium wings. Both the metal and composite fillets and teeth were held in place with the newly developed epoxy cements.

The greatest remaining area of concern in the A-12's radar cross section was the two vertical stabilizers. To reduce radar reflections, Kelly Johnson canted the stabilizers inward 15 deg. and fabricated them out of resin-impregnated non-metallic materials. Once these changes were completed, the only metal in each vertical stabilizer was a stainless steel pivot. The Air Force, which later ordered several versions of the OXCART aircraft for its own use, never adopted the laminated vertical stabilizers.

Johnson, 'Development of Lockheed SR-71', pp. 6–7: OSA History, chap. 20, p. 35 [8 spaces]

The Oxcart Contract

By mid-January 1960, Lockheed had demonstrated that its concept of shape, fuel additive, and non-metallic parts would reduce the Oxcart's radar cross section substantially. Richard Bissell, however, was very upset to learn that the changes had led to a reduction in the aircraft's performance, which meant it would not be able to attain the penetration altitude he had promised to President Eisenhower. Kelly Johnson then proposed to reduce the aircraft's weight by 1,000 pounds and increase the fuel load by 2,000 pounds, making it possible to achieve the target altitude of 90,000 feet. Afterward, he noted in the project log: 'We have no performance margins left; so this project instead of being 10 times as hard as anything we have done, is 12 times as hard.

This matches the design number and is obviously right'.

Johnson, 'Archangel log', 21 January 1960

These changes satisfied Bissell, who notified Johnson on 26 January that the CIA was authorizing the construction of 12 of the new aircraft. The actual contract was signed on 11 February 1960. Lockheed's original quotation for the project was $96.6 million for 12 aircraft, but technological difficulties eventually made this price impossible to meet. Recognizing that fabricating an aircraft from titanium might involve unforeseen difficulties, the CIA included a clause in the contract that allowed costs to be revaluated. During the next five years, this clause had to be invoked on a number of occasions as the A-12's costs soared to more than double the original estimate.

OSA History, chap. 20, pp 27–29, 33–34, 36 [13 spaces]

New Technologies Necessitated by OXCART's High Speed

According to the specifications, the OXCART aircraft was to achieve a speed of Mach 3.2 (2,064 knots or 0.57 miles per second, which would make it as fast as a rifle bullet), have a range of 4,120 nautical miles, and reach altitudes of 84,500 to 97,500 feet. The new aircraft would thus be more than five times as fast as the U-2 and would go almost 3 miles higher.

One major disadvantage of the OXCART's great speed was high temperatures. Flying through the earth's atmosphere at Mach 3.2 heated portions of the aircraft's skin to almost 900 deg. F. An aircraft operating at these high speeds and high temperatures required fuels, lubricants, and hydraulic fluids that had not yet been invented. The OXCART's fuel requirement called for low-vapour-pressure fuel with a low volume at operating temperatures; the fuel would also be a heat sink to cool various parts of the aircraft. The J58 engine required lubricants that did not break down at very high operating temperatures of Mach 3.2 speeds. This requirements led to the invention of synthetic lubricants. Lockheed also had to search long and hard for hydraulic fluid that would not vaporize at high speed but would still be usable at low altitudes. Finding a suitable hydraulic pump was just as difficult. Kelly Johnson finally modified a

pump that was being developed for the North American B-70 bomber project.

Johnson, 'Development of the SR-71' pp.11–12

Some of the greatest problems related to the high speeds and high temperatures at which the OXCART operated resulted from working with the material chosen for the airframe – titanium. After evaluating many materials, Johnson had chosen an alloy of titanium (B-120) characterized by great strength, relatively light weight, and good resistance to high temperature, but high in cost. As strong as stainless steel, titanium weighed slightly more than half as much. Obtaining sufficient quantities of titanium of a quality suitable for fabricating aircraft components proved very difficult because methods for maintaining good quality control during the milling of titanium were not fully developed. Up to 80 percent of the early deliveries from Titanium Metals Corporation had to be rejected. It was not until 1961, when company officials were informed of the objectives and high priority of the OXCART program that problems with titanium supply ended. Even after sufficient high-quality titanium was received, Lockheed's difficulties were not over. Titanium was so hard that tools had to be devised. Assembly line production was not possible, and the cost of the program mounted well above original estimates. [7 spaces],

'OXCART Story'. p 5[2spaces]); OSA History, chap. 20, p.33 [9 spaces]

The high temperature that the OXCART would encounter also necessitated planning for the pilot's safety and comfort because the inside of the aircraft would be like a moderately hot oven. To save weight, Kelly Johnson did not attempt to insulate the inside of the aircraft. The pilot would therefore have to wear a type of space suit with it's own cooling, pressure control, oxygen supply, and other necessities for survival.

Designing the Oxcart's Cameras

Providing cameras for the A-12 posed a number of unique problems. In late 1959, OXCART managers asked Perkin-Elmer, [13 spaces] Eastman Kodak and Hycon to develop three different photographic systems for the new aircraft. These cameras would provide a range of photography from high-ground-resolution stereo to extremely-high-resolution spotting data.

The Perkin-Elmer (P-E) entry, known as the Type-1 camera, was a high-ground-resolution general stereo camera using an f/4.0 18-inch lens and 6.6-inch film. It produced pairs of photographs covering a swath 71 miles wide with an approximately 30-percent stereo overlap. The system had a 5,000-foot film supply and was able to resolve 140 lines per millimetre and provide a ground resolution of 12 inches.

To meet severe design constraints in the areas of size, weight, thermal environment, desired photographic resolution, and coverage, Perkins Elmer's Dr. Roderick M. Scott employed concepts never before used in camera systems. These included the use of a reflecting cube rather than a prism for the scanner, a concentric film supply and a take-up system to minimize weight shift, a constant-velocity film transport that provided for the contiguous placement of stereo images on one piece of film, and airbars for the film transport and take-up systems.

OSA History, chap. 20, p.26 [19 spaces] 'OXCART Story' p. 4 (S)

[13 spaces] Eastman Kodak entry, called the Type-II camera, was a high-convergent stereo device using a 21-inch lens and 8-inch film. It produced pairs of photographs covering a swath 60 miles wide with an approximately 30-percent stereo overlap. It had an 8,400-foot film supply and was able to resolve 105 lines per millimetre and provide a ground resolution of 17 inches.

The Hycon entry, designed by James Baker and known as the Type-IV camera, was a spotting camera with an extremely-high-ground resolution. In fact, it was an advanced version of the highly reliable B camera developed for the original U-2 program. It used a 48-inch Baker-designed f/5.6 lens to focus images onto 9.5 inch film. Like the B camera it could provide seven frames of photography covering a swath 41 miles wide with a stereo overlap on 19 miles of the swath. The Hycon camera carried the largest film supply of the three cameras, 12,000 feet. It was able to resolve 100 lines per millimetre and provide a ground resolution of 8 inches. A version of this 48-inch Hycon camera, known as the H camera, later saw service in U-2R aircraft.

Each of these three camera systems had unique capabilities and advantages, so all three were purchased for the OXCART. Before they could be effectively employed in the aircraft, however, new types of camera windows were needed. The OXCART's camera windows had to be completely free from optical distortion. Achieving this goal was difficult in a window whose exterior would be subjected to 550 deg F while the interior surface would be only 150 deg F. After three years and the expenditure of $2 million in research and development, the Corning Glass Works, which had joined this effort as a Perkin-Elmer subcontractor, solved the problem of producing a camera window that could withstand tremendous heat differentials. Its quartz glass window was fused to the metal frame by an unprecedented process involving high-frequency sound waves.

Baker interview [13 spaces] 'OXCART Story' pp. 5–6 (S)

Later in the program, the OXCART received yet another camera system. In 1964 the Texas Instruments Corporation developed an infra-red camera for the Project TACKLE U-2s that were being used to determine whether the [75 spaces]. This stereo device, known as the FFD-4, was adapted for use in OXCART. The camera had an effective focal length of 50 inches and a 150-foot supply of 3.5-inch film. The camera's resolution was 3 deg. C thermally, 1 milliradian spatially, and 60 feet on the ground. It could be used for both day and night imagery collection.

Choosing Pilots for OXCART

Just as in the U-2 program, the Air Force provided considerable support to Project OXCART, including training, fuel storage, and weather service. One of the most important areas of support was the provision of pilots: all of the OXCART pilots came from the Air Force. Prospective pilots had to be qualified in the most advanced fighters and be emotionally stable and well motivated. [296 spaces] (*Ed note: it appears that a footnote occurs in this area.*)

[7 spaces], 'OXCART Story', pp. 6–7 [1 space]; OSA History, chap 20. pp. 45–50 [12 spaces] Geary interview with Pedlow [3 spaces].

Because of the limited size of the A-12 cockpit, they had to be under six feet tall and weigh less than 175 pounds. Following extensive physical and psychological screening, 16 potential nominees were selected for intensive security and medical screening by the Agency. By the end of this screening in November 1961, only five individuals had been approved and had accepted the Agency's offer of employment on a highly classified project involving a very advanced aircraft. A second search and screening process produced an elite group of pilots; all but one of these 11 officers eventually became generals. [139 spaces].

Selection of a Testing Site for the OXCART

From the very beginning, it was clear that Lockheed could not test the OXCART aircraft at its Burbank facility, where the runway was too short and too exposed to the public. The ideal testing site would be far removed from metropolitan areas, away from civil and military airways, easily accessible by air, blessed with good weather, capable of accommodating large numbers of personnel, near an Air Force installation, and having a runway at least 8,000 feet long. But no such place was to be found.

After considering 10 Air Force bases programmed for closing, Richard Bissell decided to [65 spaces]. Although its personnel accommodations, fuel storage capacity, and runway length were insufficient for the OXCART program, the site's remote location would greatly ease the task of maintaining the program's security, and a moderate construction program could provide adequate facilities. Construction began in September 1960; a C-47 shuttle service ferried work crews from Burbank to Las Vegas and from Las Vegas to the site.

The new 8,500 foot runway was completed by 15 November 1960. Kelly Johnson had been reluctant to have a standard Air Force runway with expansion joints every 25 feet because he feared the joints would set up undesirable vibrations in the speedy aircraft. At his suggestion 150-foot wide longitudinal sections were laid out in a staggered format. This layout put most of the expansion joints parallel to the direction of aircraft roll and reduced the frequency of the joints.

Additional improvements included the resurfacing of 18 miles of highway leading to the base so that heavy fuel trucks could bring in the necessary fuel. The need for additional buildings on the base was met by the Navy. Three surplus Navy hangers were dismantled, moved, and reassembled on the north side of the base, and more than 100 surplus Navy housing buildings were also transported to [8 spaces] Groom Lake, Nevada. All essential facilities were ready in time for the forecast delivery date of the first A-12 on 1 August 1961.

OSA History, chap. 20, pp. 39–40, 43, 51 [20 spaces]. 'OXCART Story' pp. 7–9 (S)

149

Unfortunately, this delivery date began to slip further and further into the future. Delays in obtaining the titanium, and later the J58 engines, caused the postponement of the final assembly of the first plane. Eventually, Kelly Johnson and Agency project officials decided to begin testing without waiting for the J58 engines by using Pratt & Whitney J75/19W engines, designed for the Convair F-106, to test the A-12 at altitudes up to 50,000 feet and at speeds up to Mach 1.6. Such a change, however, meant that the engine compartment of the first A-12 had to be modified by 22 December 1961 for its initial test flight by 27 February 1962.

Lockheed ran into so many technological problems with the OXCART effort that by October 1961 its costs had swollen to $136 million and were still climbing. Something obviously had to be done to reduce expenditures. After much refiguring, project officials decided to decrease the number of deliverable aircraft. Amendment No. 11 to the contract reduced from 12 to 10 number of A-12s, for a total cost of $161.2 million.

OSA History, chap. 20, pp. 46–47, 51–55 ([19 spaces] 'OXCART Story' p. 10 [3 spaces]

The cancellation of these two A-12s was offset by the Air Force order for the development of a supersonic interceptor variant of the A-12 to serve as a replacement for the North American F-108A Rapier interceptor project, which had been cancelled in late 1960. With the assistance of the [37 spaces] the Air Force entered into an agreement with Lockheed to produce three AF-12 aircraft based on the A-12 design but modified to carry a second crewman and three air-to-air missiles. This effort was called Project KEDLOCK. The AF-12 (later re-designated YF-12A) was designed to intercept enemy bombers long before they reached the United States, and initial Air Force plans envisioned a force of up to 100 of these supersonic interceptors. In fact, only three of these planes were built and delivered during the 1963–64 time frame because Secretary of Defence McNamara cancelled the program as a cost-cutting measure. The Air Force bore all of the costs of the YF-12A project; CIA was only involved in helping to write 'black' contracts.

OSA History, chap. 20, pp. 46–47, [13 spaces]

Lockheed was not the only OXCART contractor having trouble containing costs; Pratt & Whitney was fighting an even bigger battle. In mid-1961, Pratt & Whitney overruns threatened to halt the entire OXCART project. At the suggestion of Cdr. William Holcomb in the office of the Chief of Naval Materiel, Richard Bissell asked the Navy to assist in funding the J58's development. After hearing Bissell and Holcomb's suggestion that the J58 might be used in future Navy aircraft, VAdm. William A. Schoech, Chief of the Navy Materiel Command that had originally financed the J58 engine, authorized the transfer of $38 million in end-of-year funds to the project, thus keeping the OXCART's head above water.

[7 spaces]y interview, [3 spaces] OSA History, chap. 20, p. 55, ([13 spaces]

During this period, Kelly Johnson was very disappointed with Pratt & Whitney's work on the J58, particularly when they shocked him in September 1961 with the news that the engine would be overweight, underpowered, and late.

Johnson, 'Archangel log', 11 September 1961.

As it turned out, the J58 was never used in a Navy aircraft.

Delivery of the First OXCART

The first A-12, known as article 121, was assembled and tested at Burbank during January and February 1962. Since it could not be flown to the [13 spaces] the aircraft had to be partially disassembled and put on a specially designed trailer that cost nearly $100,000. The entire fuselage, without wings, was crated and covered, creating a load 35 feet wide and 105 feet long. To transport this huge load safely over the hundreds of miles to the site, obstructing road signs were removed, trees were trimmed, and some roadblocks had to be levelled. The plane left Burbank on 26 February 1962 and arrived at [7 spaces] two days later.

After the fuselage arrived in [7 spaces], it's wings were attached and the J75 engines were installed, but the aircraft was still not ready to be tested. This new delay was caused by leaking fuel tanks, a problem that would never be solved completely. Because the A-12's high speeds heat the titanium airframe to more than 500 deg. F, Lockheed designers had to make allowances for expansion. When the metal was cold, the expansion joints were at their widest. In the fuel tanks, these gaps were filled by pliable sealants, but the fuel for the A-12's engines acted as a strong reducing agent that softened the sealants, causing leaks. Thus, when fuel was first poured into the aircraft, 68 leaks developed. Lockheed technicians then stripped and replaced all the sealant, a tedious and time consuming procedure because the sealant required four curing cycles, each at a different temperature over a period of 30 to 54 hours. The engineers were never able to discover a sealant compound that was completely impervious to the jet fuel while remaining elastic enough to expand and contract sufficiently. The A-12's tanks continued to leak, so when it was fuelled, it only received enough fuel to get airborne. The plane would then rendezvous with a tanker, top off its tanks, and immediately climb to operating, causing the metal to expand and the leaks to stop.

OSA History, chap. 20, p. 62 ([18 spaces] 'OXCART Story' p. 1 [3 spaces]

Changes in the Project Management

Richard Bissell, whose concern for the viability of the U-2 in 1956 had led to the establishment of Project OXCART and who had directed its growth all along, was no longer in charge when the first OXCART aircraft took to the air. He resigned from the Agency in February 1962, and his departure brought a major reorganization of the reconnaissance program. The Development Projects Division of the Directorate of Plans, with its two aircraft (OXCART and U-2) and its [15 spaces] were transferred to the new Directorate of Research headed by [25 spaces]. The following year [6 spaces] resigned and this Directorate of Science and Technology, with [25 spaces] as its first head. The overhead reconnaissance projects belonged to the Office of Special Activities. These project management changes in the CIA had no immediate impact on the OXCART project because the aircraft was still in the development stage, handled mainly by the contractors. Moreover, a good deal of continuity was provided by officers who had served for a number of years with the U-2 program and were now involved with OXCART: [21 spaces] the Deputy Assistant Director for Special Activities; [15 spaces] the Air Force's project officer for the two aircraft; and [16 spaces] who oversaw the day-to-day affairs of the OXCART project.

OXCART's First Flights

With new sealants in its fuel tanks, the prototype OXCART was ready to take to the air. On 25 April 1962, test pilot Louis Schalk took 'article 121' for an unofficial unannounced flight, which was an old Lockheed tradition. He flew the craft less than two miles at an altitude of about 20 feet and encountered considerable problems because of the improper hook-up of several controls. These were promptly repaired and on the next day, 26 April, Schalk made the official 40-minute maiden flight. After a beautiful takeoff, the aircraft began shedding the triangular fillets that covered the framework of the chines along the edge of the aircraft body. The lost fillets, which had been secured to the airframe with epoxy resin, had to be recovered and reaffixed, a process that took the next four days.

Once the fillets were in place, the OXCART's official first flight took place on 30 April 1962, witnessed by a number of Agency personnel including DDR [24 spaces] Dick Bissell was also present, and Kelly Johnson noted in the project log. 'I was very happy to have Dick see this flight, with all he has contributed to the program'.

Johnson, 'Archangel log' 30 April 1962.

This official first flight was also the first flight with the wheels up. Piloted again by Schalk, the OXCART took off at 170 knots and climbed to 30,000 feet. During the 59 minute flight, the A-12 achieved a top speed of 340 knots. Kelly Johnson declared it to be the smoothest first test flight of any aircraft he had designed or tested. On 2 May 1962, during the second test flight, the OXCART broke the sound barrier, achieving a speed of Mach 1.1.

OSA History, chap 20. p. 63 [19 spaces].
'OXCART Story' pp. 11–12 [3 spaces]

Four more aircraft, including a two-seat trainer, arrived at the testing site before the end of the year. During the second delivery on 26 June 1962, the extra-wide vehicle carrying the aircraft accidentally struck a Greyhound bus travelling in the opposite direction. Project managers quickly authorized payment of $4,890 for the damage done to the bus in order to avoid having to explain in court why the OXCART delivery vehicle was so wide.

One of the biggest problems connected with flight testing the A-12 was keeping its existence secret. Realizing that the nation's air traffic controllers would be among the first unwitting people to learn about the plane, the Deputy Assistant Director for the Special Activities, [21 spaces] had called on Federal Aviation Administrator [19 spaces] Najib Halaby in early 1962 to brief all FAA regional chiefs on how to handle reports of unusually fast, high-flying aircraft. Air controllers were warned not to mention the craft on the radio but to submit written reports of sightings or radar trackings. The Air Force gave similar briefings to NORAD, the North American Air Defence Command.

[6 spaces] 'OXCART Story' pp. 10–11 [2 spaces]); OSA History, chap. 20, p. 60 ([13 spaces]

Initial testing could not explore the A-12's maximum potential, since the J58 engine was still not ready. Developing this power plant to OXCART specifications was proving much more difficult than had been expected because the J58 had to reach performance levels never before achieved by a jet engine, while operating under extremely difficult environmental conditions. To simulate the stress that the J58 would undergo during maximum power output (Mach 3.2 at 97,000 feet), the power plant was tested in the exhaust stream of a J75 engine. In the course of this extremely severe testing, the J58's problems were gradually overcome. By January 1963, Pratt & Whitney had delivered 10 J58 engines to the [9 spaces] testing site. The first flight of an A-12 with two J58 engines took place on 15 January 1963.

[19 spaces], J58/SR-71 Propulsion Integration', Studies in Intelligence 26 (Summer 1982): pp. 17–18 (U); OSA History, chap. 20, p. 58 [23 spaces]

Speed Related Problems

As J58-equipped A-12s reached higher and higher speeds, more difficulties arose. Major problems developed at speeds between Mach 2.4 and 2.8 because the aircraft's shockwave interfered with the flow of air into the engine, greatly reducing its performance. Solving this problem required long and often highly frustrating experimentation that ultimately required a complete redesign of the air-inlet system that controlled the amount of air admitted to the engine. In the new adjustable inlet the cone-shaped projection at the front-known as a spike- was designed to move in or out as much as three feet in order to capture and contain the shockwave produced by the aircraft at high speeds, thus preventing the shockwave from blowing out the fire inside the engine.

OSA History, chap. 20, p. 67 [14 spaces]

Another J58 engine problem in early 1963 was foreign object damage. Small objects such as pens, pencils, screws, bolts, nuts, and metal shavings that feel into the engine nacelles during assembly at Burbank were sucked into the power plant during initial engine testing at [7 spaces] and damaged impeller and compressor vanes. To control the problem Lockheed instituted a program that included X-rays, shaking of the nacelles, installing screens over various inlets to the engine, and even having workers wear coveralls without breast pockets. Another source of foreign object damage was trash on the runways. The giant J58 engines acted like immense vacuum cleaners, sucking in anything lying loose on the paving as they propelled the A-12 down the runway for takeoff. To prevent engine damage, [7 spaces] personnel had to sweep and vacuum the runway before aircraft takeoff.

Johnson, 'Development of Lockheed SR-71', p. 12

New Versions of the OXCART

In 1962 the Agency and the Air Force ordered two more versions of the OXCART (in addition to the A-12 and the YF-12A). One was a modification of the A-12 to carry and launch ramjet-powered, 43-feet-long drones capable of reaching Mach 3.3. The two seater mothership received the designation M-12; the drone was called the D-21. This project was known as TAGBOARD. The original development of the drones and mothership was sponsored by the CIA, but in June 1963 the project was turned over to the Air Force, which had overall responsibility for the unmanned reconnaissance aircraft. Development of the M-12/D-21 combination continued until 1966, when an unsuccessful D-21 launch caused the loss of its mothership and the death of one of the crewmembers. Afterward the Air Force turned to B-52 bombers to carry the drones.

OSA History, chap. 20, p. 71; Jay Miller, Lockheed SR-71 (A-12/YF12/D-21), Aerofax Minigraph 1 (Arlington, Texas; Aerofax, Inc. 1985), p. 3.

The second new version of the OXCART was another reconnaissance aircraft. In December 1962 the Air Force ordered six 'reconnaissance/strike' aircraft, which were designated to conduct high-speed, high altitude reconnaissance of enemy territory after a nuclear strike. This new aircraft differed from other A-12 versions in that it was longer, had a full blown two-seat cockpit, and carried a large variety of photographic and electronic sensors. The additional weight of all this equipment gave the Air Force craft a slower maximum speed and a lower operating ceiling that the Agency's A-12. In August 1963, the Air Force added 25 more aircraft to this contract, for a total of 31.

OSA History, chap. 20, pp. 71–72 [14 spaces]

The Question of Surfacing a Version of the OXCART

As the funds being spent on Air Force versions of the OXCART increased dramatically, the Defense Department became concerned that it could not offer any public explanation for these expenditures. At the same time, Agency and Defense Department officials recognized the growing danger that a crash or sightings of test flights could compromise the program. This led the Defense Department in late 1962 and early 1963 to consider surfacing the Air Force's interceptor version of the A-12 to provide cover for OXCART sightings or crashes and an explanation for the rise in Air Force spending. Some journalists had also become aware of the aircraft's existence, raising concern that the secret would eventually come out in the press. Agency officials remained reluctant to reveal the existence of any version of the A-12, and the issue soon came to the attention of the PFIAB, James Killian and Edwin Land strongly opposed disclosing Oxcart's existence, and in January 1963 they presented their views to President Kennedy at a meeting attended by DCI McCone and Defense Secretary Robert McNamara, Killian, Land, and McCone succeeded in persuading the President and Secretary of Defense to keep the Oxcart's existence a secret for the time being.

Later that year supporters of the idea of surfacing the OXCART found a mere powerful argument for their proposal – the need to disseminate the supersonic technology that had been developed for the OXCART. This technology would be invaluable for Air Force projects such as the B-70 bomber and for the civilian supersonic transport (SST) then being discussed in Congress. In the fall of 1963, several Presidential advisors expressed their concern to DCI McCone that Lockheed had received $700 million head start in the development of supersonic technology, giving the firm a tremendous advantage over other aerospace companies working on a supersonic transport. McCone passed these concerns on to President Kennedy on 12 November 1963, just 10 days before the fateful trip to Dallas. The President instructed the CIA and the Defense Department to develop a plan for surfacing the OXCART but to await further discussions with him before taking any actions.

John A. McCone, 'Memoirs of Meeting in Cabinet Room for the Purpose of Discussing the Surfacing of the OX'. 21 January 1963, DCI records, [14 spaces]: idem, Memorandum for the Record, Discussion with the President – October 21st – 6:00pm, 22 October 1963, DCI records [3 spaces]; OSA History, chap. 20, pp. 73–74, ([14 spaces]

President Lyndon B. Johnson received a detailed briefing on the OXCART program from McCone, McNamara, Bundy, and Rusk on 29 November, after just one week in office. McNamara strongly advocated surfacing a version of the OXCART. McCone was more cautious, calling for the preparation of a statement that could be used when surfacing became necessary but arguing that such a step was not yet needed. Agreeing with McCone's position, President Johnson said the issue should be reviewed again in February.

John A. McCone, 'Memorandum for the Record, Meeting with the President, Secretary McNamara, Mr. Bundy and DCI', 29 November 1963, DCI records [4 spaces], OSA History, chap. 20, p. 73, ([12 spaces])

One additional argument in favour of surfacing the OXCART was the realization that the aircraft could not be used to fly undetected over the Soviet Union. By 1962 the United States had become aware of the effectiveness of a new Soviet radar system, codenamed TALL KING. The introduction of this computer-controlled radar undercut one of the basic premises of the OXCART program, the assumption that radar operators would not be able to track high-flying supersonic targets visually because of their small, no persistent radar returns. By coupling a computer to a radar, the Soviets could now weight the individual radar returns and identify those produced by high-flying, very fast objects.

OSA History, chap. 20, pp. 147–149, [13 spaces]

By February 1964 DCI McCone had become convinced that surfacing was necessary. Soviet development of the TALL KING radar system had eliminated his hope that OXCART would eventually be able to carry out its original intended purpose – overflights of the USSR. The final decision on the issue of surfacing the OXCART came at a National Security Council meeting on 29 February 1964, at which all of the participants supported the decision to surface. The same day President Johnson held a news conference at which he announced the successful development of an 'experimental jet aircraft, the A-11, which has been tested in sustained flight at more than 2,000 miles per hour and at altitudes in excess of 70,000 feet'.

John A. McCone, Memorandum for the Record, 'Discussion at the NSC Meeting Attended by the President, all members and the four members of the President's personal staff. 29 February 1964', 2 March 1964, DCI records ([11 spaces] 'OXCART Story', p. 14 – erroneously identifies the date as 24 February – [3 spaces]

President Johnson had spoken of the A-11 rather than the Agency's A-12, and the aircraft that was actually revealed to the public was the Air Force's YF-12A interceptor, a project that had already been cancelled. President Johnson's use of the designator A-11 at the press conference has sometimes been called an error, but Kelly Johnson wrote the President's press release and chose this designator for security reasons because it referred to an earlier version of the aircraft that lacked the radar-defeating modifications of the A-12.

Johnson, 'Archangel log' 25 February 1964.

Following the President's announcement, two of these hastily flown to Edwards Air Force Base. From this point on, the Air Force versions of the OXCART were based at Edwards and provided a diversion so that the faster and higher flying A-12s at the [10 spaces] could continue testing out of the public eye.

The President's announcement did not mention the CIA's involvement in the project, which remained classified, but keeping the Agency's extensive role in the OXCART a secret was not an easy task. The first step had been to separate the Air Force's versions of the A-12 from the Agency's by moving the Air Force aircraft to California. Next, those firms that were to be given the new technology had to be briefed on the program and agree to abide by the same secrecy agreement then in force with Lockheed. Moreover, everyone witting of OXCART (including those no longer with the program, such as Allen Dulles, Richard Bissell, and General Cabell) had been briefed about the impending Presidential announcement, so that they would not think the need for secrecy about OXCART had ended.

OSA History; chap. 20, p. 76 ([13 spaces]

The process of surfacing versions of the OXCART continued on 25 July 1964, when President Johnson revealed the existence of a new Air Force reconnaissance aircraft, which he called the SR-71. Actually, the President was supposed to say RS-71 (for 'reconnaissance-strike'). Deciding that renaming the aircraft was easier than correcting President Johnson, the Air Force invented a new category – 'strategic reconnaissance' – to explain the SR-71's designation.

Additional Problems during Final Testing

The first A-12 crash occurred on 24 May 1963, when a detachment pilot, realizing the airspeed indication was confusing and erroneous, decided to eject. The pilot was unhurt, but the plane was destroyed when it crashed near Wendover, Utah. A cover story for the press described the plane as an F-105. All A-12s were grounded for a week while the accident was investigated. The malfunction was found to be caused by ice that plugged up the pitot-static tube used to determine airspeed.

Ibid, pp. 69–70 [17 spaces]

Two more A-12s were lost in later testing. On 9 July 1964, article 133 crashed while landing when a pitch-control servo device froze, rolling the plane into a wingdown position. Ejecting from an altitude of 129 feet, the pilot was blown sideways out of the craft. Although he was not very high off the ground, his parachute did open and he landed during the parachute's first swing. Fortunately he was unhurt, and no news of the accident filtered out of the base. Eighteen months later, on 28 December 1965, article 126 crashed immediately after takeoff because of an improperly wired stability augmentation system. As in the previous crash, the pilot ejected safely, and there was no publicity connected with the crash. An investigation ordered by McCone determined that the wiring error had resulted from negligence, not sabotage.

Ibid, pp. 80–81 [19 spaces], 'OXCART Story', pp. 17–18 [3 spaces]

The A-12 made its first long-range, high speed flight on 27 January 1965. The flight lasted 100 minutes, with 75 minutes of which were flown at speeds greater than Mach 3.1, and the aircraft covered 2,850 miles at altitudes of between 75,600 and 80,000 feet. By this time, the OXCART was performing well. The engine inlet, camera, hydraulic, navigation, and flight-control systems all demonstrated acceptable reliability.

Nevertheless, as the OXCART began flying longer, faster, and higher, new problems arose. The most serious of these problems involved the aircraft's wiring. Continuing malfunctions of the inlet controls, communications equipment, ECM systems, and cockpit instruments were often attributable to wiring failures. Wiring connectors and components had to withstand temperatures above 800 deg. F, structural flexing, vibration, and shock. Such demands were more than the materials could stand. Not all of the OXCART's problems could be traced to material failures, however, and Agency officials believed that careless maintenance by Lockheed employees also contributed to malfunctions.

OSA History, chap. 20, p. 94 [13 spaces]

Concerned that Lockheed would not be able to meet the OXCART's schedule for operational readiness, the Office of Special Activities' Director of Technology [19 spaces] met with Kelly Johnson on 3 August 1965 to discuss the project's problems. Johnson not only assigned more top-level supervisors to the project but also decided to go to [7 spaces] and take charge of the Oxcart's development himself. His presence made a big difference, as can be seen in his notes in the project log:

> I uncovered many items of a managerial, materiel and design nature.... I had meetings with vendors to improve their operation.... Changed supervision and had daily talks with them, going over in detail all problems on the aircraft.... Increased the supervision in the electrical group by 500%.... We tightened up the inspection procedures a great deal and made inspection stick. It appears that the problems are one-third due to bum engineering.... The addition of so many systems to the A-12 has greatly complicated the problems, but we did solve the overall problem.

Johnson, 'Archangel log' 5 August–30 April 1965

These improvements in on-site management got the project back on schedule.

By 20 November 1965, the final validation flights for OXCART deployment were finished. During these tests, the OXCART achieved a maximum speed of Mach 3.29, an altitude of 90,000 feet, and sustained flight time above Mach 3.2 of 74 minutes. The maximum endurance test lasted six hours and 20 minutes. On 22 November, Kelly Johnson wrote to [29 spaces] head of the Office of Special Activities, stating, 'The time has come when the bird should leave its nest.'

[6 spaces] 'OXCART Story', p. 23 [3 spaces]

Three years and seven months after its first flight in April 1962, the OXCART was ready for operational use. It was now time to find work for the most advanced aircraft ever conceived and built.

Discussions on the OXCART's Future Deployment

Although the OXCART had been designed to replace the U-2 as a strategic reconnaissance aircraft to fly over the Soviet Union, this use had become doubtful long before the OXCART was ready for operational use. The U-2 Affair of 1960 made Presidents very reluctant to consider overflights of the Soviet Union. Indeed, Presidents Eisenhower and Kennedy had both stated publicly that the United States would not conduct such overflights. In July 1962, Secretary of Defense McNamara told DCI McCone that he doubted that the OXCART would ever be used and suggested that improvements in [24 spaces] would very likely eliminate the need for the expensive OXCART program. Strongly disagreeing, McCone told McNamara that he had every intention of using OXCART aircraft to fly over the Soviet Union.

McCone raised this issue with President Kennedy in April 1963, at a time when the nation's [14 spaces] were experiencing a great number of failures and the intelligence community was clamoring for better photography to confirm or disprove allegations of the existence of an antiballistic missile system at Leningrad. Unconvinced by McCone's arguments for OXCART overflights, President Kennedy expressed the hope that some means might be devised for improving [17 spaces] instead.

John A. McCone, Memorandum for the Record. 'Summary of meeting with Secretary

153

McNamara and Secretary Gillispie, General Carter, and Mr. McCone on 5 July 1962'. 6 July 1962. DCI records (S); McCone, Memorandum for the File. 'Meeting with the President – 5:30–15 April 1963 in Palm Beach, Florida' DCI records (S).

Although overflights of the Soviet Union appeared to be out of the question, the OXCART's eventual employment elsewhere in the world remained a strong possibility, particularly after the Cuban Missile Crisis of October 1962 demonstrated the continuing need for manned strategic reconnaissance aircraft. Since [8 spaces] had not been able to supply the kinds of coverage needed, U-2s had carried out numerous overflights of Cuba. Nevertheless, the U-2 remained vulnerable to surface-to-air missiles (as had once again been demonstrated by the downing of a SAC U-2 during the Missile Crisis), and project headquarters had even briefly considered sending the A-12 over Cuba in October 1962, even though the aircraft still lacked the required J58 engines and would have to use much less powerful ones. On 23 October 1962, Johnson noted in his 'Archangel log': that the performance of an A-12 with J75 engines (as suggested by project headquarters for the possible use over Cuba) would hardly be spectacular'. After the Missile Crisis ended, Air Force U-2s continued to photograph Cuba under tacit superpower understanding that such monitoring of the withdrawal of the missiles would proceed without interference. But the possibility remained, raising the dismaying prospect that the United States would not be able to tell if the Soviet Union was reintroducing ballistic missiles into Cuba.

Such fears became acute in the summer of 1964 after Soviet Premier Nikita Khrushchev told foreign visitors such as columnist Drew Pearson, former Senator William Benton, and Danish Prime Minister Jens Otto Krag that, once the US elections had been held in November, U-2s flying over Cuba would be shot down. Project headquarters therefore began preparing contingency plans (Project SKYLARK) for the possible employment of OXCART over Cuba, even though the new aircraft was not yet ready for operations. On 5 August 1964, the Acting DCI, Gen Marshall S. Carter, ordered the project staff to achieve emergency operational readiness of the OXCART by 5 November 1964, in case Premier Khrushchev actually carried out his threat to shoot down U-2s.

Johnson, 'Archangel log', 17 August 1964 –

[6 spaces], 'OXCART Story', p. 1[4 spaces], OSA History, chap. 20, p. 81 ([9 spaces] d)

To meet this deadline, the Office of Special Activities organized a detachment of five pilots and ground crews to conduct flights to validate camera performance and quality pilots for Mach 2.8 operations. Simulating Cuban missions during training flights, the detachment demonstrated its ability to conduct overflights of Cuba by the 5 November deadline, which passed without any hostile action by the Soviets or Cubans. The detachment then worked to develop the capability for sustained operation with its five aircraft. All these preparations were valuable training for the OXCART program, even though the SKYLARK contingency plan was never put into effect. Since U-2s continued to satisfy collection requirements for Cuba, the A-12s were reserved for more critical situations.

When the Agency declared that OXCART had achieved emergency operational status on 5 November 1964, the aircraft was still not prepared for electronic warfare, as only one of the several planned electronic countermeasure devices had been installed. Nevertheless, a senior government panel decided that the OXCART could conduct initial overflights of Cuba without a full complement of warning and jamming devices, should the need for such a mission arise.

One reason for the delay in completing OXCART's electronic warfare preparations was the Air Force's concern that OXCART use of existing ECM devices could, in the event of the loss of an OXCART over hostile territory, compromise the ECM equipment used by the Air Force bombers and fighters. Even if OXCART's ECM devices were merely similar to military ECM systems, the Air Force still worried that their use would give the Soviets an opportunity to work out countermeasures.

Such concerns led the Agency to an entirely different approach to antiradar efforts in Project KEMPSTER. This project attempted to develop electron guns that could be mounted on the OXCART to generate an ion cloud in front of the plane that would reduce it's radar cross section. Although this project proved unsuccessful, the CIA also developed a number of more conventional ECM devices for use in the OXCART.

OSA History, chap. 20, pp. 149–151 [13 spaces] Notes on the OXCART project by [14 spaces], OSA records, [13 spaces]

As the OXCART's performance and equipment continued to improve, there was renewed consideration of deploying the aircraft overseas, particularly in Asia, where US military activity was increasing. On 18 March 1965, DCI McCone, Secretary of Defense McNamara, and Deputy Secretary of Defense Vance discussed the growing hazards confronting aerial reconnaissance of the [29 spaces] in three years the [29 spaces], and the Air Force had lost numerous reconnaissance drones. The three men agreed to go ahead with all the prepatory steps needed for the OXCART to operate over [6 spaces], so it would be ready in case the President decided to authorize such missions.

Project BLACK SHIELD, the plan for Far East operations, called for OXCART aircraft to be based at Kadena airbase on Okinawa. In the first phase, three planes would be flown to Okinawa for 60-day periods, twice a year, an operation which would involve 225 personnel. Later there would be a permanent detachment at Kadena. In preparation for the possibility of such operations, the Department of Defense spent $3.7 million to provide support facilities and real-time secure communications on the island by early autumn 1965.

OSA History, chap. 20, pp. 90–91 [11 spaces]

In the summer of 1965, after the United States had began introducing large numbers of troops into South Vietnam, southeast Asia became another possible target for the OXCART. Because the continued use of U-2s for reconnaissance missions over North Vietnam was threatened by the deployment of Soviet-made surface-to-air missiles, McNamara asked the CIA on 3 June 1965 whether it would be possible to substitute OXCART aircraft for U-2s. The new DCI Adm. William F. Raborn replied that the OXCART could operate over Vietnam as soon as it passed its final operational readiness tests.

[8 spaces], 'OXCART Story', p. 21

Formal consideration of proposed OXCART missions involved the same approval process that was used for U-2 overflights. In late November 1965, after the OXCART had passed its final validation tests, the 303 Committee met to consider a proposal to deploy the OXCART to Okinawa to overfly South-east Asia and [7 spaces]. Although the committee did not approve deployment, it ordered the development and maintenance of a quick-reaction capability, ready to deploy to Okinawa within 21 days after notification.

154

There the matter remained for more than a year. During the first half of 1966, DCI Raborn raised the issue of deploying the OXCART to Okinawa at five separate 303 Committee meetings but failed to win sufficient support. The JCS and PFIAB supported the CIA's advocacy of OXCART deployment. Top State and Defense Department officials, however, thought that the political risks of basing the aircraft in Okinawa – which would almost certainly disclose it to the Japanese – outweighed any gains from the intelligence the OXCART might gather. On 12 August 1966, the divergent views were presented to President Johnson, who upheld the 303 Committee's majority opinion against deployment for the time being.

[9 spaces] 'OXCART Story', p. 23 [3 spaces]: OSA History, chap. 20, pp. 110–111 [11 spaces]

The CIA then proposed an OXCART overflight of Cuba in order to test the aircraft's ECM systems in a hostile environment. On 15 September the 303 Committee considered and rejected this idea on the grounds that sending OXCART over Cuba 'would disturb the existing calm prevailing in that area of affairs'.

OSA History, chap. 20, p. 112, ([14 spaces]

With operational missions still ruled out, proficiency training remained the main order of business. This led to improvements in mission plans and flight tactics that enabled the detachment to reduce the time required to deploy to Okinawa from 21 days to 15. Records continued to fall to the OXCART. On 21 December 1966, a Lockheed test pilot flew an A-12 for 16,408 kilometers over the continental United States in slightly more than six hours, for an average speed of 2,679 kilometers per hour (which included in-flight refuelling at low speeds as low as 970 kilometers per hour). This flight set a record for speeds and distance unapproachable by any other aircraft.

[7 spaces] 'OXCART Story', p. 24 [3 spaces]

Two weeks later, on 5 January 1967, an A-12 crashed after a fuel gauge malfunctioned and the aircraft ran out of fuel short of the runway. Pilot [14 spaces] ejected, but was killed, when he could not become separated from the ejection seat. To preserve the secrecy of the OXCART program, the Air Force informed the press that an SR-71 was missing and presumed lost in Nevada. This loss, like the three preceding crashes, did not result from difficulties caused by high-speed, high-temperature flight but from traditional problems inherent in any aircraft.

Proposals for OXCART operations continued to surface, and in May 1967 the CIA forwarded a detailed request to the 303 Committee to use the OXCART to collect strategic intelligence about a new Soviet missile system. As early as 1962, the intelligence community began to be concerned about the actual purpose of the new missile installations that first appeared near Tallinn, Estonia, and soon spread along the north-western quadrant of the Soviet Union. Attempts to photograph the sites using [26 spaces] had been frustrated by the prevailing cloud cover in the region. Because of the lack of accurate information about the missile sites, there was a wide divergence of views ranged from the CIA's belief that the installations contained long-range, surface-to-air missiles designed to counter strategic bombers, to the Air Force's contention that Tallinn sites represented a deployed antiballistic missile system.

Photo interpreters insisted that imagery with a resolution of 12 to 18 inches was necessary to determine missile size, antenna pattern, and configuration of the engagement radars associated with the system. Electronic intelligence (ELINT) analysts also needed data about the Tallinn radars, but there were no collection sites that could monitor the Tallinn emanations when the radars were being tested. Moreover, the Soviets never operated the radars in the tracking and lock-on modes, a fact that prevented analysts from knowing the frequencies or any other performance characteristics of the radar.

To settle the question of the purpose of the Tallinn installations, Office of Special Activities planned a mission that would use the high resolution of the OXCART's camera along with the U-2's sophisticated ELINT-collection equipment. This project's unclassified name was Project SCOPE LOGIC; its classified title was Operation UPWIND.

The proposal project involved launched an A-12 OXCART aircraft from [19 spaces] and flying it to a Baltic Sea rendezvous with a Project IDEALIST U-2 flying from a [28 spaces]. The OXCART would fly north of Norway and then south along the Soviet-Finnish border. Shortly before Leningrad, the A-12 would head west-southwest down the Baltic Sea, skirting the coasts of Estonia, Latvia, Lithuania, Poland, and East Germany before heading west to return to [8 spaces]. The entire flight would cover 11,000 nautical miles, take eight hours and 38 minutes, and require four aerial refuellings.

Although the A-12 would never violate Soviet airspace during this dash, it would appear to Soviet radar network operators to be headed for an overflight penetration in the vicinity of Leningrad. It was hoped that the A-12's passage would provoke Soviet air defence personnel to activate the Tallinn system radars in order to track the swift OXCART aircraft. As the A-12 made its dash down the Baltic, its Type-1 camera would be filming the entire south coast. If Agency analysts were correct in their assumption that the Tallinn system was designed to counter high-altitude aircraft at long ranges, then the OXCART would be in jeopardy during this dash down the Baltic. Nevertheless, Agency weapons experts believed that the A-12 aircraft's speed and suite of electronic countermeasures would keep it safe from the standard Soviet surface-to-air missile installations.

While the A-12 was conducting its high-speed dash along the Baltic coast of Eastern Europe, the U-2 would be flying farther out to sea, beyond the range of all Soviet SAMs. [68 spaces].

Agency and Defense Department officials supported the proposed mission, but Secretary of State Dean Rusk strongly opposed it and the 303 Committee never forwarded the proposal to President Johnson.

Memorandum for DDCI R. L. Taylor from [65 spaces], Utilizing the OXCART and the U-2' 4 May 1967, DS&T records, [15 spaces].

[284 spaces].

First A-12 Deployment: Operation BLACK SHIELD

Although the Tallinn mission was still being considered in May 1967, another possible employment for the OXCART came under discussion. This time the proposal was for OXCART to collect tactical rather than strategic intelligence. The cause was apprehension in Washington about the possible undetected introduction of surface-to-air missiles into North Vietnam. When President Johnson asked for a proposal on the matter, the CIA suggested that the OXCART be used. While the State and Defense Departments were still examining the proposal's political risks, DCI Richard Helms raised the issue at President Johnson's 'Tuesday lunch' on 16 May. Helms got the President's approval, and the CIA put the BLACK SHIELD plan to deploy the OXCART to the Far East into effect later that same day.

[7 spaces] 'OXCART Story', p. 25, [3 spaces]

The airlift of personnel and equipment to Kadena began on 17 May 1967, and on 22 May the first A-12 flew non-stop from [6 spaces] to Kadena in six hours and six minutes, A second aircraft arrived on 24 May. The third A-12 left on 26 May, but the pilot had trouble with the inertial navigation system and communications near Wake Island. He made a precautionary landing at Wake, where a pre-positioned emergency recovery team was located. The problem was corrected and the aircraft continued on its flight to Kadena on the following day.

Before the start of the operations, the CIA briefed a number of key US and Allied officials on the operation. Included were US Ambassadors and [433 spaces]

By 29 May 1967, 13 days after President Johnson's approval, BLACK SHIELD was ready to fly an operational mission. On 30 May, the detachment was alerted for a mission on the following day. As the takeoff time approached, Kadena was being deluged by rain, but, since weather over the target area was clear, flight preparations continued. The OXCART, which had never operated in heavy rain, taxied to the runway and took off.

The first BLACK SHIELD mission flew one flight path over North Vietnam and another over the demilitarized zone (DMZ). The mission was flown at Mach 3.1 and 80,000 feet and lasted three hours and 39 minutes. While over North Vietnam, the A-12 photographed 70 of the 190 known surface-to-air sites and nine other priority targets. The A-12's ECM equipment did not detect any radar signals during the mission, which indicated that the flight had gone completely unnoticed by both the Chinese and North Vietnamese.

During the next six weeks, there were more alerts for 15 BLACK SHIELD missions, seven of which were flown. Only four detected hostile radar signals. By mid-July 1967, the BLACK SHIELD missions had provided sufficient evidence for analysts to conclude that no surface-to-air missiles had been deployed in North Vietnam.

[8 spaces] 'OXCART Story', pp. 25–28 [3 spaces] OSA History, chap. 20, pp. 119–124, annex 152 [13 spaces]

Project Headquarters in Langley planned and directed all operational BLACK SHIELD missions. [193 spaces]

A typical mission over North Vietnam required refuelling south of Okinawa, shortly after takeoff. After the planned photographic passes, the aircraft withdrew for a second aerial refuelling in the Thailand area before returning to Kadena. So great was the plane's speed that it spent only 12.5 minutes during a 'single-pass' mission, and 21.5 minutes during a 'two-pass' mission. Because of its wide 86-mile turning radius, the plane occasionally crossed into [18 spaces] when getting into position for a second pass.

After the aircraft landed, the camera film was removed and sent by special plane to processing facilities in the United States. By late summer, however, an Air Force photo laboratory in Japan began doing the processing in order to place the photo intelligence in the hands of US commanders in Vietnam within 24 hours of a mission's completion.

BLACK SHIELD activity continued unabated during the second half of 1967. From 16 August to 31 December 1967, 26 missions were alerted and 15 were flown. On 17 September one SAM site tracked the vehicle with its acquisition radar but was unsuccessful with its FAN SONG guidance radar. It was not until 28 October that a North Vietnamese SAM site launched a missile at the OXCART. Mission photography documented the event with photographs of missile smoke and its contrail. Electronic countermeasures aboard the OXCART performed well, and the missile did not endanger the aircraft.

Possible Successors to the OXCART

The OXCART was the last high-altitude reconnaissance aircraft produced for the CIA, although the Office of Special Activities did briefly consider several possible successors to the OXCART during the mid-1960s. The first of these, known as Project ISINGLASS, was prepared by General Dynamics to utilize technology developed for its Convair Divisions earlier FISH proposal and its new F-111 fighter in order to create an aircraft capable of Mach 4–5 at 100,000 feet. General Dynamics completed its feasibility study in the fall of 1964, and OSA took no further action because the proposed aircraft would still be vulnerable to existing Soviet countermeasures. In 1965 a more ambitious design from McDonnell Aircraft came under consideration as Project RHEINBERRY (although some of the work seems to have come under the ISINGLASS designation as well). This proposal featured a rocket-powered aircraft that would be launched from a B-52 mother ship and ultimately reach speeds as high as Mach 20 and altitudes of up to 200,000 feet. Because building this aircraft would have involved tremendous technical challenges and correspondingly high costs, the Agency was not willing to embark on such a program at a time when the main emphasis in overhead reconnaissance had shifted from aircraft to satellites. As a result, when the OXCART program ended in the summer of 1968, no more advanced successor was waiting in the wings – only the veteran U-2.

Summary of the OXCART Program

Intended to replace the U-2 as a collector of strategic intelligence, the OXCART was never used for this purpose, its brief deployment was strictly for obtaining tactical intelligence and its photographic product contributed very little to the Agency's strategic intelligence mission. By the time OXCART became operational [22 spaces] had filled the role originally conceived for it. The most advanced aircraft of the 20th century had become an anachronism before it was ever used operationally. On 26 January 1967 Kelly Johnson noted in his 'Archangel log': I think back in 1959, before we started this airplane, in discussions with Dick Bissell where we seriously considered the problem of whether there would be one more round of aircraft before the satellites took over. We jointly agreed there would be just one round and not two. That seems to have been a very accurate evaluation, as it seems that 30 SR-71s gives us enough overflight reconnaissance capability and we don't need the additional 10 Oxcart aircraft.'

The OXCART did not even outlast the U-2, the aircraft it was supposed to replace. The OXCART lacked the quick-response capability of the smaller craft: a U-2 unit could be activated overnight, and within a week it could deploy abroad, fly sorties, and return home base. The OXCART planes required precise logistic planning for fuel and emergency landing fields, and their inertial guidance systems needed several days for programing and stabilization. Aerial tankers had to be deployed in advance along OXCART's flight route and be provisioned with the highly specialized fuel used by the J58 engines. All of this required a great deal of time and the effort of several hundred people. A U-2 mission could be planned and flown with a third fewer personnel.

Although the OXCART program created a strategic reconnaissance aircraft with unprecedented speed, range, and altitude, the program's most important contributions lay in other areas: aerodynamic design, high-impact plastics, engine performance, cameras, electronic countermeasures, pilot life-support systems, antiradar devices, use of non-metallic materials for the major aircraft assemblies, and improvements in milling, machining, and shaping titanium. In all of these areas, the OXCART pushed back the frontiers of aerospace technology and helped lay the foundation for future 'stealth' research.

The only time the enemy came close to downing an OXCART was on 30 October 1967. During his first pass over North Vietnam, pilot [16 spaces] detected radar tracking. Two SAM sites prepared to launch missiles but neither did. During [12 spaces] second pass the North Vietnamese fired at least six missiles at the OXCART, each confirmed by vapour trails on mission photography. The pilot saw these vapour trails and witnessed three missile detonations near but behind the A-12, which was travelling at Mach 3.1 at about 84,000 feet. Post flight inspection of the aircraft revealed that a piece of metal had penetrated the underside of the right wing, passed through three layers of titanium, and lodged against a support structure of the wing tank. The fragment was not a warhead pellet but probably debris from one of the missile detonations that the pilot observed.

[6 spaces] 'OXCART Story', p. 28 [3 spaces]

BLACK SHIELD missions continued during the first three months of 1968, with four missions flown over North Vietnam out of 14 alerts. The last OXCART overflight of Vietnam took place on 8 March 1968. During this same three-month period, the OXCART made its first overflight of North Korea after the USS *Pueblo* was seized on 23 January 1968. The goal of this mission was to discover whether the North Koreans were preparing any large-scale hostile move in the wake of this incident. [133 spaces]

Secretary of State Dean Rusk was reluctant to endorse a second mission over North Korea for fear of diplomatic repercussions should the aircraft come down in hostile territory. The Secretary was assured that the plane could transit North Korea in seven minutes and was unlikely to land in either North Korea or China. The 303 Committee then endorsed a second mission over North Korea, which was flown on 19 February. A third and final overflight of North Korea on 8 May 1968 proved to be the last operational deployment of the OXCART aircraft.

Ibid, pp. 28–29 [3 spaces]

The End of the OXCART Program

Almost a decade had elapsed between the time when the concept for the OXCART aircraft was first examined and the first A-12 operationally deployed. Now after only 29 operational missions, the most advanced aircraft ever built was to be put out to pasture. The abandonment of the OXCART did not result from any shortcomings of the aircraft; the causes lay in fiscal pressures and competition between the reconnaissance programs of the CIA and the Air Force. *[There was also a blanked out photo in this paragraph.]*

Throughout the OXCART program, the Air Force had been exceedingly helpful; it gave financial support, conducted the refuelling program, and provided operational facilities at Kadena, and airlifted OXCART personnel and supplies to Okinawa for the Vietnam and Korean operations. Air Force orders for variants of the CIA's A-12, the YF-12A interceptor and the SR-71 reconnaissance aircraft-had helped lower development and procurement costs for the OXCART. Nevertheless, once the Air Force had built up its own fleet of reconnaissance aircraft, budgetary experts began to criticize the existence of two expensive fleets of similar aircraft.

In November 1965, the very month that the A-12 had been declared operational, the Bureau of the Budget circulated a memorandum that expressed concern about the costs of the A-12 and SR-71 programs. It questioned both the total number of planes required for the combined fleets, and the necessity for a separate CIA fleet. The memorandum recommended phasing out the A-12 program by September 1966 and stopping any further procurement of the SR-71 models. The Secretary of Defense rejected this recommendation, presumably because the SR-71 would not be operational by September 1966.

OSA History, chap. 20, p. 130 [20 spaces], 'OXCART Story', p. 30 [3 spaces]

In July 1966, at the Bureau of the Budget's suggestion, a study group was established to look for ways to reduce the cost of the OXCART and SR-71 programs. The study group consisted of [12 spaces] from the Bureau of the Budget [21 spaces] from the Department of Defense, and [18 spaces] from CIA. The study group listed three possible courses of action: maintain both fleets, mothball the A-12s but share the SR-71s between CIA and the Air Force, or mothball the A-12s and assign all missions to the Air Force SR-71s. On 12 December 1966, four high-level officials met to consider these alternatives. Over the objections of DCI Helms, the other three officials – Deputy Secretary of Defense Cyrus Vance, Bureau of the Budget Director Charles L. Schultze, and Presidential Scientific Advisor Donald F. Hornig – decided to terminate the OXCART fleet. Concerned that this recommendation would strip the CIA of its supersonic reconnaissance capability, Helms then asked that the SR-71 fleet be shared between CIA and the Air Force.

OSA History, chap. 20, pp. 130–133 [20 spaces] 'OXCART Story', pp. 30–31 (S)

Four days later, Schultze handed Helms a draft memorandum for the President requesting a decision either to share the SR-71 fleet between CIA and the Air Force or to terminate the CIA entirely. Having just received new information indicating that the SR-71's performance was inferior to that of the A-12, Helms asked for another meeting to review this data. His concern was the SR-71 could not match the photographic coverage that the A-12 could provide. Only one of the SR-71's three camera systems was working anywhere near the original specifications, and that was its Operational Objective system which could only photograph a swath 28 miles wide with a resolution of 28 to 30 inches. The A-12's Type-I P-E camera could photograph a swath 72 miles wide with a nadir resolution of 12 to 18 inches and oblique resolution of 54 inches. Thus the A-12's camera covered three times as much territory as the SR-71's cameras and did so with better resolution. In addition, the A-12 could fly 2,000 to 5,000 feet higher than the SR-71 and was faster, with a maximum speed of Mach 3.1 compared to the SR-71's Mach 3.0.

[8 spaces] 'OXCART Story', p. 31 (S); OSA History, pp. 133–134 [14 spaces]

In spite of Helm's request and the strength of his arguments, Bureau of the Budget memorandum was submitted to President Johnson. On 28 December 1966, the President approved the termination of the OXCART Program by 1 January 1968.

This decision meant that the CIA had to develop a schedule for orderly phase-out of the A-12. This activity was known as Project SCOPE COTTON. Project headquarters informed Deputy Defense Secretary Vance on 10 January 1967 that the A-12s would be gradually be placed in storage, with the process to be completed by the end of January 1968. In May 1967, Vance directed that SR-71s would assume responsibility for Cuban overflights by 1 July 1967 and would add responsibility for overflights of South-east Asia by 1 December 1967. Until these capabilities were developed, OXCART was to remain able to conduct assignments on a 15-day notice for Southeast Asia and a seven-day notice for Cuba.

[8 spaces] 'OXCART Story', p. 31 [3 spaces] OSA History, p. 138 [13 spaces]

All these arrangements were made before the OXCART had conducted a single operational mission, which did not occur until 31 May 1967. In the months that followed the initiation of operations in Asia the OXCART demonstrated its exceptional technical capabilities. Soon some high-level Presidential advisors and Congressional leaders began to question the decision to phase out OXCART, and the issue was reopened.

The CIA contended that the A-12 was the better craft because it flew higher, faster, and had superior cameras. The Air Force maintained that its two-seat SR-71 had a better suite of sensors, with three different cameras (area search, spotting, and mapping), infra-red detectors, side-looking aerial radar, and ELINT-collection gear. In an effort to resolve this argument, the two aircraft were pitted against each other in a fly off codenamed NICE GIRL. On 3 November 1967, an A-12 and an SR-71 flew identical flight paths, separated in time by an hour, from north to south roughly above the Mississippi River. The data collected during these missions were evaluated by representatives of the CIA, DIA, and other Defense Department intelligence organizations.

The results proved inconclusive. Both photographic systems provided imagery of sufficient quality for analysis. The A-12 Type-I camera's 72-mile swath width and 5,000-foot film supply were superior to the SR-71 Operational Objective camera's 28-mile swath and 3,300-foot film supply. On the other hand, the SR-71's infra-red, side looking aerial radar, and ELINT/COMINT equipment provided some unique intelligence not available from the A-12. Air Force planners admitted, however, that some of this equipment would have to be sacrificed in order to provide the SR-71 with ECM gear. Information supplied by [38 spaces]

Although the fly off had not settled the question of which aircraft was superior, the OXCART did win a temporary reprieve in late November 1967. The Johnson administration decided to keep both fleets for the time being, particularly because the OXCART was actually flying missions over North Vietnam. With expenditures for the Vietnam War rising steadily, the question of reducing the costs of competing reconnaissance programs was bound to surface again. In the spring of 1968, there was yet another study of the OXCART and SR-71 programs. On 16 May 1968, the new Secretary of Defense, Clark Clifford, reaffirmed the original decision to terminate the OXCART program and store the aircraft. President Johnson confirmed this decision on 21 May.

[7 spaces] h; 'OXCART Story', pp. 32–38 [3 spaces], OSA History, chap 20. pp. 143–146 [7 spaces]

Project headquarters selected 8 June 1968 as the earliest possible date for phasing out all OXCART aircraft. Those A-12s already at the [13 spaces] were placed in storage, and the aircraft on Okinawa were scheduled to return by 8 June. Unfortunately, tragedy struck before this redeployment took place. On 4 June 1968 during a test flight from Kadena to check out a new engine, an A-12 disappeared 520 miles east of Manila. Search and rescue missions found no trace of the plane or its pilot, Jack W. Weeks. Several days later the remaining two A-12s left Okinawa to join the other eight OXCART aircraft in storage in Palmdale, California. Because the A-12s were smaller that either of the Air Force's versions, the only parts that could be used were the J58 engines. The Oxcart's outstanding Perkin-Elmer camera cannot be used in the SR-71 because the two-seater Air Force aircraft has a smaller camera compartment than that of the A-12. Constructed from one of the most durable metals known to man but unable to fly for want of engines, the OXCART aircraft are fated to remain inactive at Palmdale for many, many years.

APPENDIX V

World Records: SR-71 and YF-12

The Lockheed SR-71A and YF-12A aircraft established a number of speed and altitude world records during their tenure with the US Air Force Strategic Air Command and Aerospace Defense Command. None of their records have been broken, nor, most likely, will they ever be.

The Blackbird had an announced top speed of Mach 3.35. That is 2,484mph, or 3,997km/h, or 3,643.2ft/sec, or 1,110.45m/sec. Faster than the muzzle velocity of any bullet!

The Blackbird also had an announced maximum altitude of more than 85,000ft (26,000m) and it is rumoured to have flown as high as 95,000–100,000ft (27,000–30,000m).

SR-71A Altitude, Distance and Speed Records

1 – SR-71A (61-7972): 1 September 1974 – elapsed time over a recognized course, New York to London, of 3,490 miles (5,616.6km) in 1hr, 54min and 56.4sec. Major James V. Sullivan, pilot; Major Noel F. Widdifield, RSO.

2 – SR-71A (61-7972): 13 September 1974 – elapsed time over a recognized course, London to Los Angeles, of 5,645 miles (9,085km) in 3hr, 47min, 35.8sec. Captain Harold B. Adams, pilot; Captain William C. Machorek, RSO.

3 – SR-71A (?): 27/28 July 1976 – altitude in horizontal flight of 85,068.997ft (25,929.031m). Captain Robert C. Helt, pilot; Major Larry A. Elliot, RSO.

4 – SR-71A (?): 27/28 July 1976 – speed over a straight 15/25km (9.3/15.5-mile) course of 2,193.167mph (3,529.56km/h). Captain Eldon W. Joersz, pilot; Major George T. Morgan, RSO.

5 – SR-71A (?): 27/28 July 1976 – speed over a 1,000km (621.4-mile) closed course of 2,092.294mph (3,367.221km/h). Major Adolphus H. Bledsoe, Jr, pilot; Major John T. Fuller, RSO.

6 – SR-71A (61-7972): 6 March 1990 – distance, elapsed time and average speed over a recognized course, Los Angeles, California to the US East Coast, 2,086 miles (3,357km) in 1hr, 7min, 53.69sec at an average speed of 2,124.5mph (3,419km/h). Lt Colonel Ed Yeilding, pilot; Lt Colonel Joseph T. Vida, RSO.

6a – Los Angeles to Washington, DC, 1,998 miles (3,215.5km) in 1hr, 4min, 19.89sec at 2,144.83mph (3,451.7km/h).

6b – St Louis, Missouri to Cincinnati, Ohio, 311.44 miles (501.2km) in 8min, 31.97sec at 2,189.94mph (3,524km/h).

6c – Kansas City, Kansas/Missouri to Washington, DC, 942.08 miles (1,516km) in 25min, 58.53sec at 2,176.08mph (3,502km/h).

NOTE:
Records 6, 6a, 6b and 6c were all flown by the same crew and the same SR-71A.

YF-12A Altitude, Distance and Speed Records

1 – YF-12A (60-6936): 1 May 1965 – absolute altitude of 80,257.86ft (24,390m). Colonel Robert J. 'Fox' Stephens, pilot; Lt Colonel Daniel Andre, FCO.

2 – YF-12A (60-6936): 1 May 1965 – absolute speed over a straight course of 2,070.101mph (3331.5km/h). Colonel Stephens, pilot; Lt Colonel Andre, FCO.

3 – YF-12A (60-6936): 1 May 1965 – absolute speed over a 500km (310.7-mile) closed course of 1,688.889mph (2,718km/h). Lt Colonel Walter F. Daniel, pilot; Major James P. Cooney, FCO.

4 – YF-12A (60-6936): 1 May 1965 – absolute speed over a 1,000km (621.4-mile) closed course of 1,643.041mph (1,020.9km/h). Lt Colonel Daniel, pilot; Major Noel T. Warner, FCO.

A-12 Performance

Since the Lockheed A-12 programme was Top Secret it was never used to establish official speed and altitude world records. However, due to its lighter weight, it was even faster and higher flying than the YF-12 and SR-71 aircraft. Though this is undocumented, it is likely that the A-12 may have flown as fast as Mach 3.5 (2,595mph/4,175km/h) and as high as 105,000ft (32,000m). But these figures remain to be verified.

APPENDIX VI

Blackbird Flight Hours

Compiled by PAUL R. KUCHER IV
17 April 2002

After doing extensive research and obtaining information from Peter W. Merlin of the NASA-Dryden Flight Research Center at Edwards AFB, the following flight hours are 100 per cent accurate. As for the missing aircraft flight hours, I am still waiting for this information to surface. Even though none of these aircraft have flown for quite some time now, this compilation is accurate as of the date shown above.

A-12 and TA-12

A-12 60-6224 – 332 flights, 418.2 flight hours
A-12 60-2925 – 122 flights, 177.9 flight hours
A-12 60-6926 – 79 flights, 135.3 flight hours
TA-12 60-6927 – 614 flights, 1,076.4 flight hours
A-12 60-6928 – 202 flights, 334.9 flight hours
A-12 60-6929 – 105 flights, 169.2 flight hours
A-12 60-6930 – 258 flights, 499.2 flight hours
A-12 60-6931 – 232 flights, 453.0 flight hours
A-12 60-6932 – 268 flights, 410.49 flight hours
A-12 60-6933 – 217 flights, 406.3 flight hours
A-12 60-6937 – 177 flights, 345.8 flight hours
A-12 60-6938 – 197 flights, 369.9 flight hours
A-12 60-6939 – 10 flights, 8.3 flight hours

M-21

M-21 60-6940 – 80 flights, 123.9 flight hours
M-21 60-6941 – 95 flights, 152.7 flight hours

YF-12A

YF-12A 60-6934 – 80.9 flight hours
YF-12A 60-6935 – 534.7 flight hours
YF-12A 60-6936 – 439.8 flight hours

SR-71A and SR-71B

SR-71A 61-7950 – ?
SR-71A 61-7951 – 796.7 flight hours
SR-71A 61-7952 – 79.47 flight hours
SR-71A 61-7953 – 290.2 flight hours
SR-71A 61-7954 – ?
SR-71A 61-7955 – 1,993.7 flight hours
SR-71B 61-7956 – 3,967.5 flight hours
SR-71B 61-7957 – ?
SR-71A 61-7958 – 2,288.9 flight hours
SR-71A 61-7959 – 866.1 flight hours
SR-71A 61-7960 – 1,669.6 flight hours
SR-71A 61-7961 – 1,601 flight hours
SR-71A 61-7962 – 2,835.9 flight hours
SR-71A 61-7963 – 1,604.4 flight hours
SR-71A 61-7964 – 3,373.1 flight hours
SR-71A 61-7965 – 204.6 flight hours
SR-71A 61-7966 – 64.4 flight hours
SR-71A 61-7967 – 2,765.5 flight hours
SR-71A 61-7968 – 2,279.0 flight hours
SR-71A 61-7969 – ?
SR-71A 61-7970 – 545.30 flight hours
SR-71A 61-7971 – 3,512.5 flight hours
SR-71A 61-7972 – 2,801.1 flight hours
SR-71A 61-7973 – 1,729.9 flight hours
SR-71A 61-7974 – ?
SR-71A 61-7975 – 2,854 flight hours
SR-71A 61-7976 – 2,985.7 flight hours
SR-71A 61-7977 – ?
SR-71A 61-7978 – ?
SR-71A 61-7979 – 3,321.7 flight hours
SR-71A 61-7980 – 2,353.8 flight hours
SR-71C 61-7981 – 556.4 flight hours

APPENDIX VII

Blackbird Serial Numbers and Production Summaries

Compiled by PETER W. MERLIN

Lockheed SR-71 series (USAF serial number/ Lockheed ship number)

SR-71A (61-7950/2001) – Prototype aircraft, service test
SR-71A (61-7951/2002) – Service test, flown by NASA as 'YF-12C, tail number 60-6937'
SR-71A (61-7952/2003) – Service test
SR-71A (61-7953/2004) – Service test, used for CAT II tests
SR-71A (61-7954/2005) – Service test
SR-71A (61-7955/2006) – Service test
SR-71B (61-7956/2007) – Trainer
SR-71A (61-7957/2008) – Trainer
SR-71A (61-7958/2009)
SR-71A (61-7959/2010)
SR-71A (61-7960/2011)
SR-71A (61-7961/2012)
SR-71A (61-7962/2013)
SR-71A (61-7963/2014)
SR-71A (61-7964/2015)
SR-71A (61-7965/2016)
SR-71A (61-7966/2017)
SR-71A (61-7967/2018)
SR-71A (61-7968/2019)
SR-71A (61-7969/2020)
SR-71A (61-7970/2021)
SR-71A (61-7971/2022)
SR-71A (61-7972/2023)
SR-71A (61-7973/2024)
SR-71A (61-7974/2025)
SR-71A (61-7975/2026)
SR-71A (61-7976/2027)
SR-71A (61-7977/2028)
SR-71A (61-7978/2029)
SR-71A (61-7979/2030)
SR-71A (61-7980/2031)
SR-71C (61-7981/2000) – Trainer

Here are some examples of Blackbird serial numbers, and their sources:

USAF Accident/Incident Report (AF Form 711), 25 January 1966
'Vehicle Involved: SR-71, SN 61-7952 (#2003)'
'On 25 January 1966, SR-71, 61-7952, was airborne from Edwards...'

USAF Accident/Incident Report (AF Form 711), 25 October 1967
'Vehicle Involved: SR-71A, SN 61-7965'
'SR-71 serial number 61-7965, call sign ASPEN 28, departed Beale AFB at...'

Aircraft Flight Status and Maintenance Record (AF Form 781H), October 1967:
'ACFT SERIAL NO. 61-7965'

USAF Accident/Incident Report (AF Form 711), 18 December 1969
'Aircraft/Serial Number SR-71 61-7953'
'SR-71 Serial Number 61-7953, production number 4, was assigned...'

Maintenance Discrepancy/Work Record, December 1969:
'Serial No. 61-7953'

Special Order AB-147, 18 December 1969:
'...to investigate the SR-71, SN 61-7953, aircraft accident...'

Weight and Balance Clearance Form (DD Form 365F), 18 December 1969:
'Serial No. 61-7953'

SR-71A Category II Performance Tests, March 1970:
'These tests were conducted on SR-71A USAF S/N 61-7953 at the...'
'evaluation was conducted on SR-71B USAF S/N 61-7956 during the...'

USAF Accident/Incident Report (AF Form 711), 17 June 1970:
Vehicles Involved:
'SR-71A SN 61-7970, KC-135Q, SN 59-1474'
'SR-71A, Serial Number 61-7970, call sign ASPEN 33, was...'

Aircraft Flight Status and Maintenance Record (AF Form 781H), 25 May 1970:
'ACFT SERIAL NO. 61-7970'

Technical Manual: Power plant (SR-71-2-4), 15 November 1984:
'Applicable to AF S/N 61-7956 and subsequent.'

Technical Manual: Mission Recorder System (SR-71-2-12), 1 May 1985:
'Aeroplane Serial Number Wiring Diagram'
'AF SER NO 61-79( )( )'

Technical Manual: Airframe Group (SR-71-2-2), 15 September 1987:
'AF Serial No. 61-7950 until 61-7955'
'AF S/N 61-7956 and subsequent'

Operations Fact Sheet, 15 April 1997:
'SR-71B NASA Tail Number 831 (S/N 61-7956)'

Aerospace Vehicle Flight Report and Maintenance Document (AF Form 781F), 1997:
'Serial Number 61-7956'

Blackbird Production Summary

A-12
Total built: 12
Serial numbers:
60-6924
60-6925
60-6926
60-6928
60-6929
60-6930
60-6931
60-6932
60-6933
60-6937
60-6938
60-6939

TA-12
Total built: 1
Serial number:
60-6927

YF-12A
Total built: 3
Serial numbers:
60-6934
60-6935
60-6936

M-21
Total built: 2
Serial numbers:
60-6940
60-6941

SR-71A
Total built: 30
Serial numbers:
61-7950
61-7951
61-7952
61-7953
61-7954
61-7955
61-7956
61-7957
61-7958
61-7959
61-7960
61-7961
61-7962
61-7963
61-7964
61-7965
61-7967
61-7968
61-7969
61-7970
61-7971
61-7972
61-7973
61-7974
61-7975
61-7976
61-7977
61-7978
61-7979
61-7980

SR-71B
Total built: 2
Serial numbers:
61-7956
61-7957

SR-71C
Total built: 1
Serial number:
61-7981

APPENDIX VIII

Blackbird Timeline, 1950s to the Early 2000s

1950s

24 December 1957: First J-58 engine run (BB).
21 April 1958: First mention of the *Archangel* programme in Kelly Johnson's diary (LSW).
29 August 1959: CIA accepts A-12 design (LSW; BB).
3 September 1959: CIA approves project *Oxcart* studies (LSW).
November 1959: A-12 mock-up undergoes RCS testing at Groom Lake (SME; LSW).

1960s

30 January 1960: CIA approves funding for twelve A-12s (SME; LSW; BB).
February 1960: CIA proposes to Lockheed to begin search for twenty-four pilots for A-12.
September 1960: Work begins to enlarge and lengthen runway at Groom Lake.
January 1961: Kelly Johnson sends proposal to Dr Joseph Charyk (SAF), Colonel Leo Geary (YF-12 Project Officer), Lew Meyer (Finance Officer) for RB-12 Strategic Reconnaissance Bomber (LSB; SME).
26 February 1962: First A-12 leaves Burbank for Groom Lake by truck (SME; LSW).
28 February 1962: A-12 arrives by truck at Groom Lake (SME).
24 April 1962: A-12 high speed taxi tests; Lockheed ADP test pilot: Lou Schalk (AM1; LSB).
26 April 1962: First flight of A-12 article #121/#6924; Lockheed test pilot: Lou Schalk (BIA; AM1; LSB; BB).
30 April 1962: A-12 article #121/#6924, first official flight; Lockheed test pilot: Lou Schalk.
May 1962: Bill Park joins Lou Schalk as 2nd pilot for A-12 programme.
4 May 1962: A-12 goes supersonic (Mach 1.1) for first time (LSW).

4 June 1962: SR-71 mock-up reviewed by USAF (BB; LSW-14 May).
26 June 1962: Second A-12 article #122/#6925 arrives at Groom Lake (now on display at USS *Intrepid* Museum, NYC) (SME).
30 July 1962: J-58 completes pre-flight testing (BB).
August 1962: Third A-12 article #123/#6926 arrives at Groom Lake (SME; LSW).
August 1962: Jim Eastham becomes third pilot for Blackbird programme (LSW).
October 1962: Second A-12 flies at Groom Lake (SME).
October 1962: Letter of Intent for $1 million for AF-12 (YF-12) delivered to Lockheed (LSW).
5 October 1962: A-12 flies with J-75 (left nacelle) and J-58 (right nacelle) engines (LSW).
10 October 1962: Skunk Works receives authorization for drone (Q-12) study from CIA.
November 1962: Fourth A-12 (two-seat trainer) article #124/6027 arrives at Groom Lake (SME).
17 December 1962: Fifth A-12 article #125/#6928 arrives at Groom Lake (LSW).
28 December 1962: Lockheed signs contract to build six SR-71 aircraft (AM1; LSB; BB).
7 January 1963: A-12 trainer flies for first time (TL; SME; LSW).
5 January 1963: Bob Gilliland hired as fourth pilot for 'Program' (LSW).
15 January 1963: First fully J-58 engined A-12 flies (SME; LSW).
15 January 1963: Bob Gilliland arrives at Groom Lake (LSW).
February 1963: William Skliar joins *Oxcart* programme (LSB).
March 1963: Jim Eastham begins writing Flight Handbook for YF-12 (LSB).
24 May 1963: First loss – A-12 article #123/#6926 crashed near Wendover, Utah; Ken Collins survived after pitching up and becoming inverted during subsonic flight (AM1; LSB; SME; BB).

31 May 1963: Mock-up review of AF-12 (LSW).
June 1963: Q-12 drone fit check to A-12 (RK).
20 July 1963: First Mach 3 A-12 flight (LSW).
7 August 1963: First YF-12 flight; Lockheed test pilot: James Eastham (AM1; LSB; LSW; BB).
1 October 1963: Q-12 design finalized, and renamed D-21 (RK).
November 1963: A-12 design speed (Mach 3.2) and altitude (78,000ft).
3 February 1964: A-12 cruises at Mach 3.2 and 83,000ft for 10 minutes (LSW).
29 February 1964: President Johnson announces existence of A-11 (actually A-12, and showed YF-12 photographs) (LSW; BB).
13 March 1964: First flight of YF-12 #6936, Lockheed test pilot: James Eastham (RK).
April 1964: M-21 #6940 first flight.
16 April 1964: First AIM-47 ejected in flight from YF-12; Lockheed test pilot/FCO: Jim Eastham/Ray Scalise (RON; RS).
May 1964: Secretary of Defense Robert McNamara cancels RS-70 programme (Recon/Strike) in favour of SR-71 programme (Recon) (SME).
June 1964: Final A-12 #6939 delivered to Groom Lake (RK).
19 June 1964: Fit check of mating of M-21 #134 and D-21 #504 is successful (LSW).
9 July 1964: Bill Park forced to eject from A-12 article #133/#6939 on final at Groom Lake; stuck outboard aileron servo valve (LSW).
24 July 1964: President Johnson makes public announcement of RS-71 and reverses name to SR-71 (LSW).
5 August 1964: Cuban overflights *Skylark* planning starts (Emergency operational status by 5 Nov) (SME).
29 October 1964: SR-71 #950 prototype delivered to Palmdale, Site 2, Air Force Plant 42 in two large trailers (BB).

163

10 November 1964: First operational A-12 mission and penetration of denied airspace over Cuba (CIA denies this) (LSW).

7 December 1964: Beale AFB, CA announced as base for SR-71 (BB) (LSB says Oct 64).

18 December 1964: First engine run of SR-71 prototype (BB).

21 December 1964: SR-71 taxi tests (BB).

22 December 1964: First flight of SR-71 #950; Lockheed test pilot Bob Gilliland at Palmdale; flew for 1 hour and over 1,000mph (AM1; BB).

22 December 1964: First flight mated M-21/D-21 at Groom Lake; Lockheed test pilot Bill Park (piloted all M-21/D-21 flights) (BIA; SME; BB).

1 January 1965: 4200 SRW Activated at Beale AFB, CA, along with 4200 HQS, AEMS, FMS, OMS, Medical Group (BIA; LSB; SME).

9 January 1965: Jim Eastham flies YF-12A at Mach 3.2 for 5 minutes.

27 January 1965: A-12 flown for 1hr 40 min at Mach 3.1 or higher for a distance of 3,000 miles (SME).

5 March 1965: First flight of SR-71A #951, Lockheed test pilot/RSO: Bob Gilliland/ Jim Zwayer (now on display at Pima Air Museum, AZ) (LSW; BB).

18 March 1965: First firing of AIM-47 from YF-12A; Lockheed test pilot/FCO: Jim Eastham/John Archer (LSW; RON; RS).

22 March 1965: Deputy Secretary of Defense Cyrus Vance briefed on Project *Black Shield* plan to base A-12s at Kadena AB, Okinawa (SME).

April 1965: Acton delivers the first 3 Type H (60in focal length) cameras for A-12 (SME).

1 May 1965: Two YF-12As (#6934 & #6936) sets Speed and Altitude Records: Class C, Group III Sustained Altitude (absolute): 80,258ft USAF pilots/FCO: Colonel Robert Stevens/Lt Colonel Daniel Andre 15/25km closed circuit: 2,070.102mph, USAF pilot/FCO: Colonel Robert Stephens/Lt Colonel Daniel Andre 500km closed circuit: 1,643.042mph, USAF pilot/FCO: Major Walter Daniel/ Major Noel Warner 1,000km closed circuit: 1,688.891mph, USAF pilot/FCO: Major Walter Daniel/Captain James Cooney (BIA; LSW).

1 June 1965: Combined SR-71/YF-12 test force formed at Edwards AFB.

3 June 1965: Secretary of Defense Robert McNamara inquires of Under Secretary of USAF practicality of substituting A-12 for U-2 over Vietnam (LSW).

4 June 1965: First flight of SR-71A #953; Lockheed test pilots: Bill Weaver/George Andre (LSW; BB).

1 July 1965: Colonel J.A. Des Portes becomes 4200 SRW Commander until 17 July 1965 (9RW).

7 July 1965: First T-38 companion trainers arrive at Beale AFB, CA (LSB; SME; BB).

20 July 1965: First flight of SR-71A #954; Lockheed test pilot/RSO: Bill Weaver/ George Andre (LSW; BB).

17 August 1965: First flight of SR-71A #955; Lockheed test pilot/RSO: Bill Weaver/George Andre (Now on display at USAF Flight Test Museum, Edward AFB, CA) (LSW; BB).

18 September 1965: Colonel D.T. Nelson becomes (again) 4200 SRW Commander until 24 June 1966 (9RW; BB).

28 September 1965: AIM-47 fired from YF-12A at Mach 3.2 at 75,000ft, with target at a range of 36 miles; missed target by 6ft.

5 November 1965: Project *Skylark* (Cuban overflights) on emergency operational status (SME).

18 November 1965: First flight SR-71B #956; Lockheed test pilot/RSO: Bob Gilliland/Steven Belgau (BB; JS).

20 November 1965: A-12 flies for 6hr, 20min (longest flight to date) (LSW; SME).

2 December 1965: '303 Committee' asked to deploy *Oxcart* to Far East (*Black Shield*); they reject proposal, but want quick-reaction capability in twenty-one days (SME).

14 December 1965: Colonel W.R. Hayes becomes 9th SRW Commander until 26 June 1969 (9RW; BB).

15 December 1965: First flight of SR-71A #958; Lockheed test pilot/RSO: Bill Weaver/George Andre (LSW; BB).

18 December 1965: First flight of SR-71B #957; Lockheed test pilot/RSO: Bill Weaver/Jim Eastham (LSW; BB).

7 January 1966: First SR-71B #956 delivered to USAF flown to Beale AFB by Ray Haupt/Doug Nelson (AM! SME; LSW; LSB).

9 January 1966: First flight SR-71A #960; Lockheed test pilot/RSO: Bill Weaver/ George Andre (LSW; BB).

19 January 1966: First flight SR-71A #959; Lockheed test pilot/RSO: Bill Weaver/ George Andre (now on display Eglin AFB, FL) (BB).

25 January 1966: First SR-71A crash, #952 crashed near Tucumcary, New Mexico; Lockheed test pilot Bill Weaver ejected at over Mach 3; RSO Jim Zwayer was killed (LTR).

11 February 1966: Staff Crew #1 completes initial qualification in SR-71, USAF Crew: Doug Nelson/Russell Lewis (RLL).

5 March 1966: First D-21 #503 launched from M-21 #6941, and flew 150nm; Lockheed test pilot/FCO: Bill Park/Keith Beswick (LSW).

13 April 1966: First flight SR-71A #961; Lockheed test pilot/RSO: Bill Weaver/ George Andre (LSW; BB).

27 April 1966: Second D-21 #506 launched from M-21 #6941 and flew 1,120nm; Lockheed test pilot/LCO: Bill Park/Ray Torick (LSW).

29 April 1966: First flight SR-71A #962; Lockheed test pilot/RSO: Bill Weaver/ Steven Belgau (in flyable storage at Palmdale, CA) (LSW; BB).

29 April 1966: Second batch of fifteen D-21s ordered.

11 May 1966: First flight SR-71A #964, Lockheed test pilot/RSO: Bill Weaver/ Steven Belgau (LSW; BB).

24 May 1966: First SR-71A #958 delivered to Beale AFB. USAF pilots: Bill Campbell/Al Pennington (LSB says 10 May; LSW says 4 April 1966) (WC).

24 May 1966: Second SR-71A #962 delivered to Beale by USAF crew Douglas Nelson/Russell Lewis, from Palmdale (WC).

16 June 1966: Third D-21 #505 launch from M-21 #6941, it flew 1,600nm; Lockheed test pilot/LCO: Bill Park/Keith Beswick (LSW).

9 June 1966: First flight SR-71A #963, Lockheed test pilot/RSO: Bill Weaver/ Steven Belgau (LSW; BB).

10 June 1966: First flight SR-71A #965, Lockheed test pilot/RSO: Bill Weaver/ Kenneth Moeller (LSW; BB).

25 June 1966: 4200 SRW inactivated, 9th SRW formed (9RW; BIA; LSB; SME).

1 July 1966: First flight SR-71A #966, Lockheed test pilot/RSO: Bob Gilliland/ Steven Belgau (LSW; BB).

30 July 1966: Fourth D-21 #504 launch from a M-21 #6941, results in the D-21 colliding with the M-21, both crew eject; pilot Bill Park survives, but LCO Ray Torick drowns, ending M-21/D-21 programme (AM1; SME).

3 August 1966: First flight of SR-71A #967, Lockheed test pilot/RSO: Bill Weaver/George Andre (LSW; BB).

14 August 1966: YF-12A #6934 crashed (rear half mated to front half of SR-71 static model to make SR-71C #64-17981).

10 October 1966: First flight of SR-71A #968, Lockheed test pilot/RSO: Bill Weaver/George Andre (LSW; BB).

18 October 1966: First flight of SR-71A #969, Lockheed test pilot/RSO: Bill Weaver/Steven Belgau (LSW; BB).
21 October 1966: First flight of SR-71A #970, Lockheed test pilot/RSO: Bill Weaver/Steven Belgau (LSW; BB).
17 November 1966: First flight of SR-71A #971, Lockheed test pilot/RSO: Bill Weaver/Kenneth Moeller (now being flown by NASA as #832) (LSW; BB).
12 December 1966: First flight of SR-71A #972, Lockheed test pilot/RSO: Bill Weaver/Steven Belgau (LSW; BB).
21 December 1966: Bill Park flies A-12 10,200 miles (statute) in 6hr (LSW; SME; ADR).
23 December 1966: Decision is made to terminate A-12 Operation by 1 June 1968 (LSW).
5 January 1967: A-12 #6928 lost on training mission from Groom Lake having run out of fuel due to a faulty fuel gauge; CIA pilot Walt Ray killed when he failed to separate from ejection seat after ejecting from A-12 (AM1; SME).
10 January 1967: SR-71A #950 crashes at Edwards during maximum gross weight anti-skid brake test; Lockheed test pilot Art Peterson survived, no RSO on flight (LSW; PH).
10 January 1967: Secretary of Defense Cyrus Vance advised that four A-12s will be placed in storage by July, and two more in December, and four more in January 1968 (SME).
18 January 1967: First flight of SR-71A #973, Lockheed test pilot/RSO: Bill Weaver/Darrell Greenameyer (LSW).
16 February 1967: First flight of SR-71A #974, Lockheed test pilot/RSO: Bill Weaver/Steven Belgau (LSW; BB).
13 April 1967: First flight of SR-71A #975, Lockheed test pilot/RSO: Bill Weaver/Steven Belgau (LSW; BB).
13 April 1967: First SR-71 #966 lost by 9th SRW crew, crashes near Las Vegas, New Mexico, as a result of over-extended angle of attack and stalled aircraft; USAF pilot/RSO: Earle Boone/Richard Sheffield (crew E-12) (LSW; PH).
17 April 1967: R.L. 'Silverfox' Stevens flies SR-71 14,000 miles and is awarded FAI Gold Medal (BIA; BB).
May 1967: Deputy Secretary of Defense Cyrus Vance directs that SR-71 assume Cuban overflights in July 1967 and in Vietnam by December 1967 from CIA's A-12s (SME).

May 1967: First flight of SR-71A #976, Lockheed test pilot/RSO: Bob Gilliland/Steven Belgau (LSW; BB).
17 May 1967: First support components for operation *Black Shield* airlifted to Kadena AB, Okinawa (OL-8) (LSW).
22 May 1967: First A-12 article #131/#937, flown to Kadena AB; Civilian pilot: Mel Vojvodich (LSW).
24 May 1967: Second A-12 article #127/#933, flown to Kadena AB, Civilian pilot: Jack Layton, A-12 lost TDI after take-off but he proceeded anyway to Kadena (SME).
26 May 1967: A-12 article #129/#932, lands at Midway Island with INS problems on way to Kadena AB, Okinawa deployment; Civilian pilot: Jack Weeks (SME).
27 May 1967: Photo of initial SR-71 crews taken at Beale AFB, CA (LSB).
27 May 1967: Third A-12 art#129/#932 arrives at Kadena AB after stop-over at Midway Island (SME).
29 May 1967: *Black Shield* unit declared operational (SME; LSW).
31 May 1967: First A-12 (article #131/#937) mission, it was over North Vietnam and lasted 3hrs 39min; CIA pilot: Mel Vojvodich (SME; LSW; RON).
15 August 1967: Since 31 May 1967, fifteen A-12 missions alerted, but only seven flown (SME).
6 June 1967: First flight of SR-71A #977, Lockheed test pilot/RSO: Bob Gilliland/Darrell Greenameyer (LSW; BB).
2 July 1967: Jim Watkins and Dave Dempster flew first international sortie in SR-71A #972 when on a training mission the INS failed and they flew into Mexican airspace (SME).
5 July 1967: First flight SR-71A #978, Lockheed test pilot/RSO: Bill Weaver/Steven Belgau; aircraft became known as 'Rapid Rabbit' (LSW; BB).
10 August 1967: First flight SR-71A #979, Lockheed test pilot/RSO: Darrel Greenameyer/Steven Belgau (now on display at Lackland AFB, TX) (LSW; BB).
25 September 1967: First flight SR-71A #980, Lockheed test pilot/RSO: Bob Gilliland/Steven Belgau (LSW; BB).
28 September 1967: D-21 #501 accidentally dropped from B-52H (LSW).
25 October 1967: SR-71A #965 crashed near Lovelock, Nevada after ANS failure; USAF pilot/RSO: Roy St Martin/John Carnochan (crew E-18) survived (LSB; SME; LSW).
30 October 1967: Dennis Sullivan flying an A-12 mission over North Vietnam had

six missiles launched against him, three detonated; on post-flight inspection, they found a small piece of metal from missile imbedded in lower wing fillet area (LSW).
3 November 1967: A-12 and SR-71 pitted against each other in a reconnaissance fly-off, code named *Nice Girl* over the Mississippi Valley, 1 hour apart. Results were inconclusive (RK).
6 November 1967: D-21 #507 launched from B-52H and flew 134nm (LSW).
2 December 1967: D-21 #509 launched from B-52H and flew 1,430nm (LSW).
28 December 1967: A-12 article #126/#929 crashed at Groom Lake due to cross-wired SAS, CIA pilot Mel Vojvodich survived (LSB; SME; PH).
31 December 1967: Since 16 August 1967, twenty-six A-12 missions alerted, fifteen flown (LSW).
5 January 1968: Skunk Works receives official USAF notice closing down YF-12 operations (LSW).
11 January 1968: SR-71B #957 crashes near Beale AFB due to double generator failure; USAF pilots Robert Sowers/David Fruehauf survived (LSB; LSW; BB).
19 January 1968: D-21 #508 launched from B-52H and flew 280nm (LSW).
26 January 1968: First A-12 overflight of North Korea, this was during *Pueblo* incident, CIA pilot: Frank Murray (SME; LSW).
5 February 1968: Lockheed receives letter from USAF, instructing them to destroy A-12, YF-12 and SR-71 tooling (LSW).
8 March 1968: First SR-71A #978 arrives at Kadena AB, Okinawa (OL-8); USAF pilot/RSO Buddy Brown/David Jensen (LSB, SME, BB).
10 March 1968: Second SR-71A #976 deployed to Kadena AB, Okinawa (OL-8); USAF pilot/RSO: Jerry O'Malley/Edward Payne (SME).
13 March 1968: Third SR-71A #974 arrives at Kadena AB, Okinawa; USAF pilot/RSO: Robert Spencer/Keith Branham (SME).
15 March 1968: All three SR-71s operational at Kadena AB (SME).
16 March 1968: Fourth aircrew arrives at Kadena AB, Okinawa by KC-135Q (SME).
21 March 1968: First SAC/9th SRW SR-71 (SR-71A #976) operational mission flown from Kadena AB over Vietnam; USAF pilot/RSO: Jerry O'Malley/Edward Payne (Crew E-10) (LSB; SME) (BB says 30th).
30 March 1968: D-21 #511 launched from B-52H and flew 150nm (LSW).

31 March 1968: Since 1 January 1968, fifteen A-12 missions alerted, six flown (LSW).

8 May 1968: Last A-12 mission flown over North Korea, CIA pilot: Jack Layton (SME; LSW).

29 May 1968: CMSGT Bill Gormick starts tie-cutting tradition of HABU crew's neck-ties (SME).

4 June 1968: First overseas loss of A-12 article #129/#932, crashed for unknown reason (neither A-12 or pilot ever found) on post-maintenance test FCF, CIA pilot Jack Weeks was killed (LSW) (AM1; BB; SME says 5 June).

7 June 1968: A-12 article #131/#6937, had to divert to Wake Island on way from Kadena AB to Groom Lake due to fuel leak; CIA pilot: Ken Collins (SME).

9 June 1968: A-12 article #127/#930 deployed back to Groom Lake from Kadena AB in 5hr, 29min, CIA pilot: Denny Sullivan (SME).

16 June 1968: D-21 #512 launched from B-52H and flew 2,850nm, camera hatch recovered, but no camera was carried (LSW).

19 June 1968: Major Bill West writes poem for the too 'slow' A-12 flights from Kadena AB to Groom Lake (SME).

21 June 1968: Last A-12 article #131/#6937 flight, it was ferried from Groom Lake to Palmdale; CIA pilot: Frank Murray (SME; LSW; BB).

26 June 1968: Black Shield pilots Jack Layton, Frank Murray, Ken Collins, Denny Sullivan and Mel Vojvodich, and the widow of Jack Weeks receive CIA 'Intelligence Star for Valor' medal at Groom Lake from the Director of the CIA, Vice-Admiral Rufus Taylor (SME).

1 July 1968: D-21 #514 launched from B-52H and flew 80nm (LSW).

5 July 1968: High-time USAF SR-71 pilot Robert Powell, with 1,020.3hrs, first flies an SR-71.

26 July 1968: SR-71A #974 with USAF pilot/RSO Tony Bevacqua/?, fired on by SA-2 missile, which was photographed by the SR's cameras (SME).

28 August 1968: D-21 #516 launched from B-52H and flew 78nm (LSW).

September 1968: First in-air recall of SR-71 mission; USAF pilot/RSO: James Shelton/Lawrence Boggess (SME).

September 1968: Switched OL-8s SR-71s #974, #976, #978 with #962, #970, #980 (SME).

10 October 1968: SR-71A #977 crashes at Beale AFB (wheel hub fractured, sending shrapnel into fuel tanks starting fire on take-off); USAF pilot/RSO Gabriel Kardong/Jim Kogler survived (LSB).

2 November 1968: 9th SRW receives Air Force Outstanding Unit Award for 1 July 1967–30 June 1968 (LSB; BB).

December 1968: SR-71 Cat III operational testing ends.

15 December 1968: D-21 #515 launched from B-52H and flew 2,953nm, camera hatch recovered, photos are 'fair' (LSW).

11 February 1969: D-21 #518 launched from B-52H and flew 161nm (LSW).

5 March 1969: 9th SRW receives 15th Air Force Outstanding Recon Crew (Pat Halloran/Mort Jarvis) & Maintenance activity and Strategic Recon Wing Award for 1968 (9RW; PH).

14 March 1969: First flight of SR-71C #981, Lockheed test pilot/RSO: Bob Gilliland/Steven Belgau (now on display at Hill AFB, UT) (LSB; LSW; BB).

11 April 1969: SR-71A #954 crashes at Edwards during maximum-weight take-off test – left tyre blew out and set the aircraft on fire; Lockheed test pilot/RSO William Skliar/Noel Warner survived (LSB; SME; LSW; PH).

27 June 1969: Colonel C.F. Minter becomes 9th SRW Commander until 30 June 1970 (BB; 9RW).

10 July 1969: D-21 #520 launched from B-52H and flew 2,937nm, camera pallet recovered, photos good (LSW).

September 1969: SAC SR-71s had flown over 100 'hot missions' out of Kadena AB, Okinawa (LSW).

9 November 1969: First operational D-21 mission. D-21 #517 launched from B-52H, no camera pallet recovered (LSW).

11 December 1969: NASA's first YF-12 flight. YF-12A #6935, USAF pilot/FCO: Colonel Joseph Rogers/Major Garry Heilbaugh (BIA; LSB; LSW).

18 December 1969: SR-71A #953 crashes near Shosone, California; USAF pilot/RSO: Colonel Joe Rogers/Lt Colonel Garry Heidelbaugh ejected (after loud explosion and loss of power and control difficulties; accident caused by a plugged static line) (LSW; SME; LSW; PH; WC).

1970s

16 January 1970: YF-12/SR-71 Test Force re-designated 4786 Test Squadron (LSB; BB).

13 February 1970: 9th SRW, SR-71 crew receives 15th Air Force Aircrew of Year Award for 1969 (9RW).

20 February 1970: D-21 #521 launched from B-52H and flew 2,969nm, camera pallet recovered, photos good (LSW).

1 April 1970: First NASA-piloted YF-12 flight, NASA pilot: Donald L. Mallick (LSW).

10 May 1970: SR-71A #969 crashes near Korat RTAFB, Thailand; USAF pilot/RSO William Lawson/Gil Martinez ejected safely (LSW; PH).

1 June 1970: Colonel H.F. Confer, 9th SRW Commander until 30 May 1972 (9RW).

17 June 1970: SR-71A #970 crashes near El Paso, Texas, after striking KC-135Q during refuelling; USAF pilot/RSO Buddy Brown/Mort Jarvis (crew E-08) ejected and survived, along with the tanker and its crew (LSB; LSW; PH).

30 October 1970: OL-8 (Kadena AB, Okinawa) re-designated OL-RK (for Ryukyus, the chain of islands including Okinawa and Japan) (SME).

16 December 1970: Second operational D-21 mission. D-21 #523 launched from B-52H and flew 2,448nm, no camera pallet recovered (LSW).

31 December 1970: Air Force Logistics Command took over Functional Flight Check for SR-71 and Det 51 (Norton AFB) created; also Sacramento Air Logistics Center provides maintenance support for SR-71 (LSB; SME).

4 March 1971: Third operational D-21 mission. D-21 #526 launched from B-52H and flew 2,935nm; camera pallet jettisoned, but not recovered (LSW).

20 March 1971: Fourth and last operational D-21 mission. D-21 #527 launched from B-52H and flew 2,935nm; no camera pallet recovered (LSW).

23 March 1971: T-38 #91606 crashes on take-off with USAF SR-71 pilots on board; Jack Thornton survived, Jim Hudson killed (LSB).

1 April 1971: 99th SRS deactivated as an SR-71 unit (LSB; BB).

26 April 1971: USAF pilot/RSO Thomas Estes/Dewain Vick fly SR-71 #968 15,000 miles in 10hr 30min non-stop (BB; RK).

24 June 1971: NASA YF-12A #6936 crashed at Edwards AFB due to a fire in the right engine caused by a fatigued fuel line; NASA pilot/RSO Ronald Layton/Bill Curtis survived (AM1; LSW).

30 June 1971: 14 Strategic Aerospace Division takes command of 9th SRW.

15 July 1971: Lockheed receives word of D-21 programme cancellation (LSW).
16 July 1971: NASA receives YF-12C #937 (actually SR-71A #951).
26 October 1971: OL-RK re-designated OL-KA (Kadena AB, Okinawa) (SME).
6 January 1972: 9th SRW receives USAF Outstanding Unit Award for 1 July 1970–30 June 1971 (9RW).
12 January 1972: 4786th Test Sqn inactivated (LSB).
15 May 1972: SR-71A #978 loses both AC generators while over Hanoi and by the time pilot Tom Pugh got auxiliary power on had dropped to 41,000ft and Mach 1.1; Tom Pugh/Ron Rice landed safely at Udorn RTAFB, Thailand.
31 May 1972: Colonel J.F. O'Malley becomes 9th SRW Commander until 9 May 1973 (9RW).
6 July 1972: SR-71A #955 flew a refuelling flight envelope and 'dry boom' contact checks on a boom-equipped Boeing 747; USAF pilot/RSO: Merv Evanson/Cos Mallozzi (SME).
18 July 1972: Thomas Estes/Dewain Vick receive McKay Trophy for 15hr record SR-71 flight on 26 April 1971.
20 July 1972: SR-71A #978 'Rapid Rabbit' crashes at Kadena AB due to strong crosswinds; USAF pilot/RSO Denny Bush/Jimmy Fagg both survived (LSW; BB).
28 July 1972: SR-71A #975 flown for ECM cover for B-52 bombing missions (*Linebacker*) over Haipong & Hanoi; USAF pilot/RSO: Darrel Cobb/Reg Blackwell (SME).
23 January 1973: 9th SRW receives USAF Outstanding Unit Award for 1 July 1971–30 June 1972 (9RW).
10 May 1973: Colonel P.J. Halloran 9th SRW Commander until 29 January 1975 (9RW).
20 September 1973: President Richard M. Nixon awards Thomas Estes/Dewain Vick the Harmon International Aviator Award for their record flight on 26 April 1971.
11 October 1973: SR-71A #979 flown to Griffis AFB, New York, for *Giant Reach* operations; USAF pilot/RSO: James Shelton/Gary Coleman (BB).
12 October 1973: Middle East overflights from CONUS during Arab–Israeli Yom Kippur War from Griffis and Seymour-Johnson AFB, North Carolina; nine sorties were flown in Operation *Giant Reach* (BB).
13 October 1973: SR-71A #979 flown in *Giant Reach* operations; USAF pilot/RSO: James Shelton/Gary Coleman (BB).

25 October 1973: SR-71A #979 flown in *Giant Reach* operations; USAF pilot/RSO: Al Joersz/John Fuller (BB).
2 November 1973: SR-71A #979 flown in *Giant Reach* operations; USAF pilot/RSO: Bob Helt/Larry Elliott (left Griffis AFB and returned to Seymour-Johnson AFB) (BB).
11 November 1973: SR-71A #964 flown in *Giant Reach* operations; USAF pilot/RSO: Jim Wilson/Bruce Douglas (BB).
15 November 1973: Giant Reach operations moved to Seymour-Johnson AFB (OL-SB) (BB).
2 December 1973: SR-71A #964 flown in *Giant Reach* operations; USAF pilot/RSO: Jim Sullivan/Noel Widdifield (BB).
10 December 1973: SR-71A #979 flown in *Giant Reach* operations; USAF pilot/RSO: Pat Bledsoe/Reg Blackwell (BB).
21 January 1974: 9th SRW Aircrew won 15th Air Force Recon Crew of Year Award.
25 January 1974: SR-71A #971 flown in *Giant Reach* operations; USAF pilot/RSO: 'Buck' Adams/William Machorek (BB).
7 March 1974: SR-71A #979 flown in *Giant Reach* operations; USAF pilot/RSO: Ty Judkins/G.T. Morgan (BB).
6 April 1974: SR-71A #979 flown in *Giant Reach* operations; USAF pilot/RSO: Lee Ransom/Mark Gersten (BB).
30 April 1974: 9th SRW Maintenance Complex receives 15th Air Force Haskell Grey Award for outstanding aircraft maintenance in 1973 (9RW).
9 August 1974: Det 1, 9th SRW activated at Kadena AB, replacing OL-KA (SME; 9RW).
1 September 1974: First SR-71A visit to UK; setting World Record New York to London at 1,817mph: 3,490nm in 1hr 54min 56.4sec in SR-71A #972; USAF pilot/RSO: Jim Sullivan/Noel Widdifield (BB).
12 September 1974: First attempt to set London to Los Angeles record, returned due to oil warning.
13 September 1974: SR-71A #972 set World Record London to Los Angeles; 5,645 miles in 3hr 47min 35.8sec; USAF pilot/RSO: 'Buck' Adams/William Machorek (BB).
January 1975: Clarence L. 'Kelly' Johnson retires as head of the Skunk Works.
6 January 1975: 9th SRW selected Outstanding SAC Recon Organization for 1974 (9RW).
17 January 1975: Benjamin R. 'Ben' Rich becomes head of the Skunk Works.
18 January 1975: 9th SRW won 15 Air Force Recon unit and Aircrew of Year.

12 March 1975: OL-SB was inactivated at Seymour-Johnson AFB.
April 1975: TDY operations start at RAF Mildenhall, UK (Det 4) (BB).
15 May 1975: SR-71A #976 flew in support of Mayaquez incident; USAF pilot/RSO: B.C. Thomas/Jay Reid.
18 June 1975: Joseph T. Vida flies for the first time in a SR-71 as RSO; he would become the high-time crewmember with 1,392.7hr (BB).
30 June 1975: Colonel J.H. Storrie becomes 9th SRW Commander until 29 September 1977 (9RW).
20 November 1975: SR-71A #959 in 'Big Tail' configuration does high-speed taxi tests; Lockheed test pilot/RSO: Darrell Greenameyer/Steven Belgau (SME).
3 December 1975: First flight of SR-71A #959 in 'Big Tail' configuration; Lockheed test pilot/RSO: Darrell Greenameyer/Steven Belgau (LSW).
20 April 1976: TDY operations started at RAF Mildenhall in SR-71A #972; USAF pilot/RSO: Pat Bledsoe/John Fuller (SME).
April 1976: First operations sortie from Det 4 in SR-71A #972; USAF pilot/RSO: Maury Rosenberg/Don Bulloch (SME).
30 April 1976: SR-71A #972, returned to Beale AFB, CA after ten-day deployment to RAF Mildenhall, UK (SME).
5 May 1976: First flight of SR-71A #959 in 'Big Tail' configuration by USAF pilot/RSO: Tom Pugh/Jim Carnochan.
1 May 1976: USAF consolidates SR-71 and U-2 operations at Beale AFB, CA (9RW).
27 July 1976: SR-71A sets World Record for the Closed 100km Course at 2,092mph; USAF pilot/RSO: A. Bledsoe/John Fuller (LSB; LSW; BB).
28 July 1976: SR-71A #962 sets an Altitude World Record of 85,068.997ft; USAF pilot/RSO: Bob Helt/Larry Elliott (LSB; BB).
28 July 1976: SR-71A #958 sets a World Straight 15 & 25km Course Record with a speed of 2,193mph; USAF pilot/RSO: Eldon Joersz/George Morgan (LSB; BB).
4 July 1976: SR-71A #959 'Big Tail' flown to Mach 3 by USAF pilot Tom Pugh.
6 September 1976: SR-71A #962 arrives at RAF Mildenhall, UK for a twelve-day deployment (SME).
28 October 1976: Last flight of SR-71A #963 (now on display at Beale AFB, CA) (LSW).
29 October 1976: Last flight of SR-71A #959 'Big Tail'; USAF pilot/RSO: Tom Pugh/William Frazier (now on display at USAF Armament Museum, Eglin AFB,

FL to where it was transported by truck) (SME; LSW).

7 January 1977: SR-71A #958 arrives at RAF Mildenhall for ten-day deployment (SME).

2 February 1977: Last flight of SR-71A #961, later used as a parts aircraft (on display at Cosmosphere and Space Center, Hutchinson, KS) (LSW, JSS).

1 September 1977: Det 51 reorganized to Det 6, Norton AFB, California, reporting to 2762 Logistics Squadron (LSB).

30 September 1977: Colonel L.M. Kidder becomes 9th SRW Commander until 31 January 1979 (9RW).

24 February 1978: 9th SRW wins 15 Air Force Recon Unit of Year Award for 1977 (9RW).

31 March 1978: 9th SRW awarded USAF Outstanding Unit Award for 1 July 1975–30 June 1976 (9RW).

28 September 1978: Eighty-eighth and last flight of NASA YF-12C (SR-71A #951) (LSW).

28 October 1978: YF-12C (SR-71A #951) retired from NASA (LSW).

7 November 1978: Cuban overflights renewed until April 1983 (BB).

1 February 1979: Colonel F. Shelton 9th SRW Commander until 16 July 1980 (9RW).

12 March 1979: SR-71A #972 arrives at Det 4 for reconnaissance of Saudi Arabia and Yemen tensions; USAF pilot/RSO: Rich Graham/Don Emmons (SME).

28 March 1979: SR-71A #972 returns to Beale AFB after deployment to Det 4; USAF pilot/RSO: Rich Graham/Dom Emmons (SME).

31 March 1979: Det 4 (RAF Mildenhall) activated (LSB; BB).

17 April 1979: SR-71A #979 deployed to Det 4 until 2 May (SME).

18 October 1979: SR-71A #976 deployed to Det 4 until 13 November (SME).

31 October 1979: Last NASA flight of YF-12A (#935) ending YF-12A test flights (BB).

7 November 1979: The last remaining YF-12A (#935) flown to USAF Museum at Wright-Patterson AFB, Ohio; pilot/RSO: Jim Sullivan/Uppstrum (AM1; LSW; BB).

1980s

18 May 1980: Mount St Helens disaster relief flights (LSB; BB).

1 July 1980: SR-71A #962 flies from Kadena AB to Diego Garcia to test facility; USAF pilot/RSO: Bob Crowder/Don Emmons (SME; RG).

August 1980: Honeywell starts conversion of analogue flight & inlet control system (AFICS) to digital automatic flight & inlet control system (DAFICS) (SME).

October 1980: SR-71A #955 flies S-Band space transponder to evaluate C-Band tracking, communication and navigation system for Space Shuttle (LSB).

6 March 1981: SR-71A #972 deployed to Det 4 until 5 May 1981 (SME).

6 May 1981: Refuelling tests with KC-10 #N110KC and SR-71A #955; USAF pilot/RSO: Calvin Jewett/Bill Flanagan (SME).

1 August 1981: 4029 Strategic Recon Training Squadron formed to train SR-71 crews (BB).

12 August 1981: SR-71A #964 had to divert to Bodo, Norway, when a low engine oil problem arose; USAF pilot/RSO: B.C. Thomas/Jay Reid (SME).

16 August 1981: SR-71A #964 returned from being diverted to Bodo, Norway (it was then nicknamed the 'Bodonian Express'); USAF pilot/RSO: B.C. Thomas/Jay Reid (LSB; SME).

31 August 1981: 'Kelly' Johnson announces that the SR-71 has had over 1,000 missiles launched against it, but none successful (BB).

15 January 1982: SR-71B #956 flies its 1,000th sortie (LTR).

24 February 1982: 9th SRW wins the 15 Air Force Outstanding Recon Wing and Crew for 1981 (9RW).

June 1982: Internal Navigation System (INS) changed to Singer–Kearfott SKN-2417 from the gyro flight reference system (SME).

20 July 1982: Colonel T.S. Pugh becomes 9th SRW Commander until 22 July 1983 (9RW).

17 March 1983: SR-71A #955 conducted aerial refuelling tests with KC-10; USAF pilot/RSO: Thomas Tilden/J.T. Vida (SME).

18 April 1983: SAC awards the 9th SRW the Outstanding Unit Award for 1 July 1981 until 20 June 1982 (9RW).

1 July 1983: SR-71A #955 flies the first ASARS-1 familiarization flight; USAF pilot/RSO: B.C. Thomas/John Morgan (SME).

9 July 1983: SR-71A #955 arrives at Det 4, as #962, to test ASARS-1 (SME).

23 July 1983: Colonel D.H. Pinsky becomes 9th SRW Acting Commander until 3 August 1983 (9RW).

4 August 1983: Colonel G.V. Freese becomes 9th SRW Commander until 28 January 1985 (9RW).

10 November 1983: 9th SRW awarded Best Active Duty Tanker Unit and best unit in SAC Bombing and Navigation competition (9RW).

5 April 1984: British Government announces that they will permit two SR-71s to be based at RAF Mildenhall (Det 4) (SME).

1 November 1984: 9th SRW Tanker crew awarded the Navigation Trophy in the SAC Bombing and Navigation Competition (9RW).

7 November 1984: First Nicaraguan SR-71 overflights from Beale AFB; USAF pilot/RSO: Bob Behler/Ron Tabor (who flew thee of six sorties) (SME; BB).

24 January 1985: 722nd and last sortie of SR-71A #955; USAF pilot/RSO: Thomas Tilden/Bill Flanagan (SME).

28 January 1985: Colonel D.H. Pinsky becomes 9th SRW Commander until 17 July 1987 (9RW).

28 January 1985: SR-71A #955 did runway roughness evaluation then was parked at Palmdale, CA; USAF pilot/RSO: Thomas Tilden/Bill Flanagan (now on display at USAF Flight Test Center museum, Edwards AFB) (SME; LSW).

20 April 1985: General Jerry O'Malley, his wife Diane and the crew of T-39 were killed when landing in western Pennsylvania (SME).

8 August 1985: SR-71 hangars at RAF Mildenhall used for the first time by SR-71A #962 (LSB).

18 September 1985: USAF awards Jerome F. O'Malley Award for Best Recon Crew to USAF pilot/RSO Bob Behler/Ron Tabor (9RW; PH).

November 1985: Honeywell completes conversion of SR-71s from analogue to digital automatic flight and inlet controls systems (SME).

7 January 1986: Twentieth anniversary of the SR-71's arrival at Beale AFB.

8 February 1986: 9th SRW won 15th Air Force Outstanding Recon Wing for 1985 (9RW).

15 April 1986: SR-71A #980 performs post-bombing damage assessment flights over Libya in support of Operation *Eldorado Canyon*; USAF pilot/RSO: Jerry Glasser/Ron Tabor (SME; BB).

15 April 1986: First operational use of JP-7 equipped KC-10s (#30079; #30082; #30075) as refuelling aircraft for SR-71 (TU; LSB; SME).

16 April 1986: SR-71A #960 performs post-bombing damage assessment flights over Libya in support of Operation *Eldorado*

Canyon; USAF pilot/RSO: Brian Shul/Walter Watson (BB; TU).

17 April 1986: SR-71A #980 performs post-bombing damage assessment flights over Libya in support of Operation *Eldorado Canyon*; USAF pilot/RSO: Bernie Smith/Denny Whalen (BB; TU).

17 July 1987: Colonel Richard H. Graham becomes 9th SRW Commander until 28 November 1988 (9RW).

21 July 1987: Last flight of SR-71A #973 (now on display at Blackbird Airpark, Palmdale, CA) (LSW).

22 July 1987: Persian Gulf missions from Det 4; SR-71A #967; USAF pilot/RSO: Smith/Doug Soifer; 9 August 1987: SR-71A #975; 26 October 1987: SR-71A #967; and 30 April 1988: SR-71A #974 (BB).

20 October 1987: USAF pilot/RSO Warren MacKendree/Randy Shelhorse fly from Kadena AB to Iran on a *Giant Express* mission to look for Silkworm missile batteries in Iran during Iran–Iraq War (SME).

5 March 1988: 1 Strategic Reconnaissance Squadron celebrates seventy-fifth anniversary, it is the oldest unit in the USAF (AFM).

6 December 1988: Colonel J.S. Savarda becomes 9th SRW Commander until 12 June 1990 (9RW; BB).

21 April 1989: SR-71A #974 crashes off coast of Philippines, the last SR-71 lost by a USAF crew to date; USAF pilot/RSO: Dan House/Blair Bozek (SME; LSW).

1 October 1989: USAF SR-71 operations suspended except for minimum proficiency flights (LSW; BB).

22 November 1989: USAF SR-71 programme officially terminated by order of General Larry D. Welch (SME; LSW; BB).

1990s and into the early 2000s

21 January 1990: Last SR-71 #962 left Kadena AB (Det 1) for Beale AFB, at 0500 (tail art: a tombstone which read 'Det 1 RIP 1968–1990') (BM).

26 January 1990: SR-71 is decommissioned at Beale AFB (LSW).

26 January 1990: Last flight of SR-71A #960 (this was the high-mission SR) from Beale to Castle AFB, California; USAF pilot/RSO: Steven Grzebiniak/Jim Greenwood. (LSW).

12 February 1990: Last flight of SR-71A #968, Beale AFB to Palmdale (now on display at Virginia Aviation Museum, Richmond, Virginia) (LSW; DA).

14 February 1990: Last flight of SR-71As #962 & #967, Beale AFB to Palmdale; kept in flyable storage at AF Plant 2; #967 now being flown by USAF Det 2, Edwards AFB (LSW).

23 February 1990: Last flight of SR-71A #958 (holds World Speed Record set 27-28 July 1976), Beale AFB to Robins AFB, GA; USAF pilot/RSO: Don Watkins/Bob Fowlkes (LSW).

28 February 1990: Last flight of SR-71A #975, Beale AFB to March AFB, California; USAF pilot/RSO: Steven Grzebiniak/Jim Greenwood (LSW).

6 March 1990: SR-71A #972 makes last flight and sets four World Records, Palmdale to Dulles International Airport; USAF pilot/RSO: Ed Yeilding/J.T. Vida; US Coast to Coast (2,404 miles): 67min 54sec for 2,124.5mph; Los Angeles to Washington, DC (2,300 miles): 64min 20sec for 2,144.8 mph Kansas City to Washington, DC (942 miles): 25min 58.53sec for 2,176mph; St Louis to Cincinnati (311 miles): 8min 31.97sec for 2,189.94mph (EY).

6 March 1990: Last flight of SR-71A #979, Beale AFB to Lackland AFB, Texas; USAF pilot/RSO: Steven Grzebiniak/Stanley Gudmundson (LSW).

20 March 1990: Last flight of SR-71A #964, Beale AFB to Offutt AFB, New England; USAF pilot/RSO: Terry Pappas/Mike Finan (LSW; BB).

27 March 1990: Last flight of SR-71A #976, Beale AFB to USAF Museum at Wright-Patterson AFB; USAF pilot/RSO: Don Watkins/Bob Fowlkes (this SR-71 flew the first operational sortie 21 March 1968) (LSW; BB; PH).

22 December 1990: Clarence L. 'Kelly' Johnson dies at the age of eighty.

23 December 1990: Ben Rich retires as the Head of the Skunk Works.

1 July 1991: NASA pilot Steve Ishmael makes first flight in SR-71B #956 (BB).

25 July 1991: SR-71B #956(NASA #831) officially delivered to NASA Dryden Center, Edwards AFB (BB).

October 1991: Marta Bohn-Mayer becomes first female SR-71 crewmember (BB).

27 October 1991: A-12 article #128/#6931 delivered to Minnesota ANG Museum, by New York ANG C-5 (SME; JG).

19 September 1992: Joseph T. Vida (high-time SR-71 crewmember) dies (RG).

9 March 1993: NASA's first SR-71 flight test (LSW).

28 September 1994: Congress votes to allocate $100 million for reactivation of three SR-71s (RG).

5 January 1995: Benjamin R. 'Ben' Rich dies at the age of sixty-nine (AWST).

12 January 1995: SR-71A NASA #832 (USAF #971) flown from Edwards AFB to Palmdale for overhaul before USAF 'borrows' it; NASA pilot/RSO: Steve Ishmael/Marta Bohn-Mayer (AFNS; LS).

March 1995: ACC selected three crews for the reactivation of the SR-71: pilots Gil Luloff, Tom McCleary and Don Watkins; and RSOs Blair Bozek, Michael Finan and Jim Greenwood (RG).

26 April 1995: SR-71A #971 (ex-NASA #832) flown for the first time after reactivation and renovation at Air Force Plant 42, Palmdale; NASA crew: Ed Schneider/Marta Bohn-Mayer; Sortie #1054-1, low and slow (AS #1).

28 June 1995: First reactivated SR-71 returns to USAF inventory: Dennis E. Thompson (Lockheed) presented SR-71 #971 to General Bill Rutledge (9RW CO) in a ceremony at Air Force Plant 42 (AFNS; AWST).

30 June 1995: First USAF crew flies reactivated SR-71 #971.

25 July 1995: First solo USAF crew (Lt Colonels Gil Luloff and Mike Finan) flies reactivated SR-71 #971; 80,100ft at Mach 3.23 for 2.5 hours; sortie #1060-7 (AS #1).

28 August 1995: SR-71A #967 makes 'maiden' flight after being refurbished by Lockheed Martin Skunk Works; NASA crew: Ed Schneider/Bob Meyer; Sortie #854-1, low and slow (LS & AS #1).

29 August 1995: Crew #1 Mission Ready (MR): Lt Colonels Luloff and Finan (AS #1).

17 January 1996: Lt Colonels Don Watkins and Jim Greenwood make solo flight in SR-71A #971; 80,100 ft at Mach 3.25 for 2.5 hour, sortie #105-22, from Palmdale, CA (AS #1).

30 January 1996: SR-71 #967 leaves Palmdale and arrives at Edwards AFB, Det2/9RW after a 1.5-hour flight; USAF pilot/RSO: Tom McCleary/Michael Finan (TL).

1 February 1996: Second aircraft (SR-71A #971) delivered to Det. 2/9 RW from Palmdale; USAF pilot/RSO: Lt Colonels Tom McCleary/Mike Greenwood; 77,200ft at Mach 3.05 for 2.7 hours (AS #1).

15 February 1996: SR-71 #967 makes first flight test of real-time data transmission at Det 2; USAF pilot/RSO: Lt Colonels Tom McCleary/Mike Finan; 72,700ft at Mach 3.01 for 3.1 hours (AS #1 & AWST).

15 April 1996: Deputy Defense Secretary John White directs the Air Force to ground the Air Force's SR-71s due to conflicting language in Section 304 of the National Security Act of 1947 and Section 102 of the Intelligence Authorization Act for FY-96 (Inside the Air Force; RG; AWST).

21 September 1996: House and Senate Appropriation committees agree to fund the Air Force's two operational SR-71s for Fiscal Year 1997 (RG; RON).

1 January 1997: SR-71 and crews are operational at Det 2, Edwards AFB (RG; AFNS).

18 April 1997: Colonel Charles Simpson assumes command of 9th RW from Brigadier General Robert Behler (SS).

19 August 1997: The first new Air Force SR-71 crew in nine years solos at Edwards AFB: Major Bert Garrison (pilot) and Captain Domingo Ochotorena (RSO) (SS).

26 August 1997: NASA mated the LASRE engine with NASA SR-71 #844 (PM; RON).

September 1997: Second new crew was selected to fly the SR-71: Captains Greg Barber (pilot) and Dale Zimmerman (RSO) (RG, BG).

10 October 1997: Final USAF SR-71 flight; Major Bert Garrison (pilot) and Captain Domingo Ochotorena (RSO) flew SR-71A #967 on the Brandy route duration of 4.1 hours; Tom McLeary flew the chase aircraft and Ted Carlson photographed the flight (at the time no one knew that this would be the final USAF flight) (BG).

15 October 1997: President Clinton kills SR-71 funding with Line Item Veto (RG, AH, ABC News).

31 October 1997: NASA SR-71 #844 (AF #980/Lockheed #2031) flew for the first time with the Aerospike engine piggy-backed on it, the first in a series of flights in the LASRE (Linear Aerospike and SR-71 Experiment). It reached a speed of Mach 1.19 at an altitude of 27,000–33,000ft (NASA, AWST).

30 June 1999: Final shutdown of the SR-71 programme: Det 2 is shut down, officially ending the USAF SR-71 programme.

17 Dec 2002: NASA #831(956/2007) transferred to Kalamazoo Air Zoo Museum, Kalamazoo, Michigan (NASA)

Information for the foregoing timeline was researched by John Stone from the sources as follows:

ADR - A.D. Rossetti
AH - Art Hanley
AM1 - *Aerofax Minigraph 1* by Jay Miller
AFNS - USAF News Service
AS1 - Anonymous Source number 1
AWST - *Aviation Week & Space Technology*
BB - Buddy Brown
BIA - *SR-71 Blackbird in Action* by Lou Drendel
BM - Bob Miller
BG - Bert Garrison
CC - Dr Coy Cross
DA - David Allison
EY - Ed Yeilding
HF - *High Flyer* (new name for Beale AFB newspaper)

LB - *Lockheed Blackbirds* by Anthony M. Thornborough & Peter E. Davies
LS - Lockheed Skunk Works Star
LSB - *Lockheed SR-71 Blackbird* by Paul F. Crickmore
LSW - *Lockheed's Skunk Works - The First 50 Years* by Jay Miller
LTR - Lockheed Tech Rep
NASA - National Air and Space Administration Public Affairs
PH - Pat Halloran
PM - Peter Merlin
RG - Richard H. Graham
RK - Ron Kloetzli
RLL - Lt Colonel Russell L. Lewis
RON - Ron Girouard
RS - Ray Scalise

SD - *Sled Driver* by Brian Shul
SME - *Lockheed SR-71: The Secret Missions Exposed* by Paul F. Crickmore
SS - *Space Sentinel* (Beale AFB newspaper; *see also* 'HF')
SW - *Skunk Works* by Ben Rich & Leo Janos
TB - Tony Bevacqua
TL - Tony Landis
UN - *The Untouchables* by Brian Shul & Walter Watson
WC - William Campbell
9RW - 9th Reconnaissance Wing History

Compiled by John Stone
www.blackbirds.net

Abbreviations, Acronyms and Codenames

AB	afterburner
ADC	Air (also Aerospace) Defense Command
ADF	Automatic Direction Finder
ADP	Advanced Development Projects
ADS	Accessory Drive System
AFB	Air Force Base
AFCS	Automatic Flight Control System
AFFTC	Air Force Flight Test Center
AICS	Air Inlet Computer System
AIM	Air Intercept Missile
Angel	Code name for the U-2 Project
ANS	Astro-inertial Navigation System
AOA	Angle of Attack
Archangel	Lockheed ADP code name for Project *Gusto* A-1 through A-12
ARDC	Air Research and Development Command
Area 51	Groom Lake, Nellis AFB, Nevada
ASARS	Advanced Synthetic Aperture Radar System
BIT	Built-in Test
Black Shield	Codename for A-12 Operations
CG	Centre of Gravity
CP	Centre of Pressure
CIA	Central Intelligence Agency
CIP	Compressor Inlet Pressure
CIT	Compressor Inlet Temperature
COMINT	Communication Intelligence
DAFICS	Digital Automatic Flight and Inlet Control System
Det	Detachment
DFRC	Dryden Flight Research Center
DMZ	Demilitarized Zone
ECM	Electronic Counter Measures
ECCM	Electronic Counter-Counter Measures
EGT	Exhaust Gas Temperature
ELINT	Electronic Intelligence
EWS	Electronic Warfare System
FCF	Functional Check Flight
FCO	Fire Control Officer
FCS	Fire Control System
Fish	Codename for the Convair Parasite Aircraft
Gusto	Codename for U-2 replacement aircraft
Habu	Nickname for the Blackbird
IFF	Identification Friend or Foe
IGV	Inlet Guide Vanes
ILS	Instrument Landing System
INS	Inertial Navigation System
IP	Instructor Pilot
IR	Infra-red
JP	Jet Petroleum
KCAS	Knots Calibrated Air Speed
KEAS	Knots Equivalent Air Speed
Kedlock	F-12 Air Defense Fighter programme
KIAS	Knots Indicated Air Speed
Kingfish	Codename for Convair competitor in *Gusto* programme
KTAS	Knots True Air Speed
LCO	Launch Control Officer
NACA	National Advisory Committee for Aeronautics
NASA	National Aeronautics and Space Administration
nm	Nautical Mile
NRO	National Reconnaissance Office
OL	Operating Location
Oxcart	CIA codename for A-12
RAF	Royal Air Force
RAM	Radar Absorbing Material
RS	Reconnaissance Squadron
RSO	Reconnaissance Systems Officer
RW	Reconnaissance Wing
SAC	Strategic Air Command
SAM	Surface to Air Missile
SAS	Stability Augmentation System
Senior Bowl	D-21B/B-52H Programme
Senior Crown	SR-71 programme
SIGINT	Signals Intelligence
SLAR	Side Looking Airborne Radar
Sled	Nickname for SR-71
SLR	Side Looking Radar
SRS	Strategic Reconnaissance Squadron
SRW	Strategic Reconnaissance Wing
TACAN	Tactical Air Navigation
Tagboard	D-21/M-21 Programme
TAS	True Air Speed
TEB	Triethylborane
UHF	Ultra High Frequency

Bibliography

Brown, William H., 'J58/SR-71 Propulsion Integration or the Great Adventure into the Technical Unknown', *Lockheed Horizons*, winter 1981–82 (Lockheed Aircraft Corporation)

Crickmore, Paul F., *Lockheed SR-71: The Secret Missions Exposed* (Osprey Publishing, 2001)

Francillon, Rene J., *Lockheed Aircraft since 1913* (Naval Institute Press, 1987)

Jenkins, Dennis R., *Lockheed Secret Projects: Inside the Skunk Works* (Motorbooks International, 2001)

Johnson, Clarence L., 'Development of the Lockheed SR-71 Blackbird', *Lockheed Horizons*, winter 1981–82 (Lockheed Aircraft Corporation)

Johnson, Clarence L. with Smith, Maggie, *Kelly: More Than My Share of it All* (Smithsonian Institution Press, 1990)

Landis, Tony, 'Putting the Ox before the Cart', *Airpower*, May 2002 (Republic Press)

Landis, Tony, 'Blacksheep of the Blackbirds', *Airpower*, September 2002 (Republic Press)

Landis, Tony, 'Tagboard and Senior Bowl', *Airpower*, January 2003 (Republic Press)

Landis, Tony, 'Mach 3 Masterpiece', *Airpower*, May 2003 (Republic Press)

McInich, Thomas P., 'The Oxcart Story', *Studies in Intelligence 15*, 25 February 1991 (Central Intelligence Agency)

Merlin, Peter W., *Mach 3+: NASA/USAF YF-12 Flight Research, 1969–1979* (NASA History Division, 2002)

Miller, Jay., *Lockheed's Skunk Works: the First Fifty Years* (Aerofax, 1993)

Pace, Steve, *Lockheed Skunk Works* (Motorbooks International, 1992)

Rich, Ben R. and Janos, Leo, *Skunk Works* (Little, Brown, 1994)

Spivak, Walter A., letter to author, 24 July 1989.

'The U-2's Intended Successor: Project *Oxcart*, 1956–1968' Central Intelligence Agency, October 1994. (Expanded version of 'The Oxcart Story', author unknown.)

Index

Actron Type H camera 89, 98
Adams, Capt Harold B. 159
Advanced Development Projects 7
Advanced Tactical Fighter 21
Aerospace Defence Command 53
Air Combat Command 20
Air Defense Command 53
Air Defense Fighter 45–46
Air Materiel Command 10, 16
Air Research and Development Command 16
Ames-Dryden Research Facility 112
Andre, Lt Col Daniel 15
Area 51 17
Arnold, Gen Henry H. 'Hap' 10

Bacalis, Brig Gen Paul 142
Beale Air Force Base 75, 81, 111
Belgau, Steve 110
Bell aircraft:
    X-16 16-17
Bennington, Herbert 143
Bissell Jr., Richard M., 133, 144
Bledsoe Jr., Maj Adolphus H. 159
Bodo Air Base 82
Boeing aircraft:
    B-52H Stratofortress 62–64
    KC-135Q Stratotanker 105
    KC-135T Stratotanker 105
    X-32 23
Brown, William H. 99, 104

California Institute of Technology 112
Central Intelligence Agency 7, 16–17
Charyk, Joseph V. 146
Clark, Secretary of Defense Clifford 158
Cold Wall Experiment 112–114
Collins, Kenneth S. 135
Convair aircraft:
    B-58A Hustler 47, 146
    B-58B Super Hustler 146
    F-106 Delta Dart 49
    F-106C 54
    F-106X 53–54
Cooney, Maj James P. 159

Culver, Irving H. 'Irv' 10
Cygnus 44

Dana, William 114
Daniel, Lt Col Walter F. 159
David Clark Corporation 134
Defense Advanced Research Projects Agency 19
Department of Defense 19
Diego Garcia 82
Digital Automatic Flight and Inlet Control System 94
Dryden Flight Research Facility 111

Eastham, James D. 'Jim' 86–87
Eastman Kodak 134, 149
Edwards Air Force Base 81, 111
Eilson Air Force Base 81
Eisenhower, President Dwight D. 26
Elliot, Maj Larry A. 159
Enevoldson, Einar 114

Farley, Harold C. 'Hal' 20
Firewell Corporation 134
Fischer, C. W. 143
Flickinger, Brig Gen Don 135
Fuller, Maj John T. 159
Fulton, Fitzhugh 114

Garrison, Maj Bert 125
General Dynamics, Convair Division 133
General Electric J93-GE-3 engine 45
Gilliland, Robert J. 'Bob' 70, 73, 87–88
Glenn, Maj John H. 123
Griffiss Air Force Base 82
Groom Lake 17, 42
Gross, Robert E. 10

Habu 82
Helms, Richard 143
Hibbard, Hall L. 9
Holbury, Col Robert J. 136
Holloman Air Force Base 20–21
Horton, Victor 114
Hugh L. Dryden Flight Research Center 111

Hughes aircraft:
   AIM-47 Falcon 46–47
   AIM-47B 54
   AN/ASG-18 pulse-Doppler Radar and Missile Fire Control System 45–47
   GAR-9 47
   XAIM-47A 54
   YAIM-47A 54
Hycon H camera 149

Ishmael, Steve 114
Itek KA-102A camera 89, 98

Jet Propulsion Laboratory 112
Johnson, Clarence L. 'Kelly' 7, 9, 83–84, 125, 134
Johnson, President Lyndon B. 44–45, 65, 138
Joint Strike Fighter 23
Joersz, Capt Eldon W. 159
JP-4 42
JP-7 42, 98–99, 105

Kadena Air Base 44, 82
Kamerer, Dorsey 17
Kennedy, President John F. 125
Killian, James 152
Krier, Gary 114

Land, Edwin M. 134
Layton, Ronald 'Jack' 135
LeVier, Anthony W. 'Tony' 84–85
Linear Aerospike SR-71 Experiment 114
Lockheed aircraft:
   A-1 27–28
   A-2 28
   A-10 28
   A-11 28, 49, 134, 138
   A-12 28, 35, 46, 51, 106–107, 115, 133–134, 138
   AF-12 46–47, 106–107
   AQ-12 107
   Archangel I 27–28
   Archangel II 27–28
   B-12, 106
   C-5 Galaxy 8
   C-130 Hercules 8
   C-141 Starlifter 8
   CL-325 18
   CL-400 18–19
   Constellation 8
   Electra 8
   F-4 Lightning 8
   F-5 Lightning 8
   F-12B 108
   F-35 'Shadow' 8
   F-35A 23
   F-35B 23
   F-35C 23
   F-80 Shooting Star 8, 10
   F-94 Starfire 8, 12
   F-104 Starfighter 8, 14–15
   F-117A Nighthawk 8, 20
   F/A-22 Raptor 8, 22–23
   FB-12 108
   D-21 59–64, 109
   D-21 'Daughter' 35, 59
   D-21B 63–64, 116–117
   Harpoon 8
   Have Blue XST 19
   Hudson 8
   L-133 9
   Loadstar 8
   M-21 'Mother' 35, 59, 63, 109, 116
   P-2 Neptune 8
   P-3 Orion 8
   P-38 Lightning 8
   Q-12 55, 108
   R-12 55, 109
   RB-12 55, 109
   RS-71 59, 69–70, 107, 109
   RS-71A 109
   S-3 Viking 8
   SR-71 59, 133
   SR-71A Blackbird 109, 117, 119–120
   SR-71B Blackbird 109, 119
   SR-71C Blackbird 109, 120
   Super Electra 8
   TA-12 108, 115
   T-1 SeaStar 12
   TR-1A 74
   T-33 T-Bird 8, 12
   U-2 16, 133
   U-2A 18
   U-2R 18
   U-3 27
   Ventura 8
   X-35A 23
   X-35B 23–24
   X-35C 23–24
   XF-90 13–14
   XF-104 Starfighter
   XFO-1 15
   XFV-1 'Salmon' 15
   XP-49 9
   XP-58 Chain Lightning 9
   XP-80 *Lulu-Belle* 10–11
   XP-80A Shooting Star 12
   YF-12A 48–53, 109, 116

YF-12C 109
YF-22A 21
YF-94C Starfire
YF-97A Starfire
YF-104A Starfighter 15
YF-117A 20
Lockheed Advanced Development Projects group 10
Lockheed Aircraft Corporation 8, 133
Lockheed Martin Corporation 8
Lockheed Martin Aeronautics Company 8
Long Range Interceptor, Experimental 45
Loughead, Allan 8
Loughead brothers 8
Loughead, Malcolm 8

Machorek, Capt William C. 159
Mallick, Donald 114
Manke, John 114
Martin Marietta Corporation 8
Materiel, Experimental 10
McCone, John A. 137
McDonnell aircraft:
   XF-88A Voodoo 14
   F-101 Voodoo 14
McNamara, Secretary of Defense Robert S. 53–54
McIninch, Thomas P. 133
Minneapolis-Honeywell Corporation 134
Morgan, Maj George T. 159
Murray, Francis J. 135
MX numbers:
   MX-409 10, 16
   MX-1787 46
   MX-2147 16

National Advisory Committee for Aeronautics 111
National Aeronautics and Space Administration 111
NASA-Langley Research Centre 112
Nelson, Maj Gen Douglas 75
North American aircraft:
   B-70 107
   F-108 Rapier 7, 45–46
   RS-70 69–70, 109
   XB-70A Valkyrie 7
Norton Air Force Base 81

Ochotorena, Capt Domingo 125
Operations, programs and projects:
   Aquatone 17–18
   Arrow 26
   Archangel 25
   Bald Eagle 16
   Black Knight 82
   Black Shield 44, 55, 139–141, 156–157

   Desert Shield 124
   Desert Storm 124
   Fansong 156
   FISH 26, 145–146
   Giant Reach 82
   Glowing Heat 82
   'G' (*Gusto*) 25–26
   Gusto 25–27, 35, 134, 147
   Have Blue 19–20
   Isinglass 156
   Kedlock 150
   Kempster 154
   Kingfish 27, 147
   Nice Girl 158
   OXCART 25, 35, 77, 133–158
   RAINBOW 144
   Scope Cotton 158
   Scope Logic 155
   Senior Bowl 62
   Senior Crown 77
   Senior Trend 20
   SKYLARK 139, 154
   Suntan 18
   Tagboard 55, 59–61, 151
   Tall King 152
   Upwind 155

Palmer, Don 10
Paradise Ranch 17
Parangosky, John N. 140
Park, William M. 'Bill' 88, 140
Perkins, Courtland D. 145
Peterson, Art 80
Perkin-Elmer 134
PF-1 fuel 136
Polaroid Corporation 134
Powers, Francis Gary 133
Pratt & Whitney engines:
   F119-PW-100 22
   YF119-PW-100 22
   F135-PW-200 23
   F135-PW-400 23
   F135-PW-600 23
   J58 99–100, 102–105, 136–137, 146
   J75 136–137
   J75-P-19W 42
   Model JT11D-20 99

Q-bay 98, 110

Ralston, Bill 10
Ray, Walter 135
Raytheon AIM-9X Sidewinder 23

INDEX

Raytheon AIM-120C 23
Reconnaissance Strike 69
Republic Aviation aircraft:
   F-103 'Thunderwarrior' 7
R-4808 17
Rich, Benjamin R. 'Ben' 85–86, 123–125
Ritland, Col Ozzie 17
Road Runners 44
Roth, Col M.S. 10
Royal Air Force Mildenhall 82

Schalk, Jr., Louis W. 'Lou' 86, 133, 137
Scorpion 1–5 20
Scott, Dr Roderick M. 149
Scott, Russell 135
Seymour Johnson Air Force Base 82
Shul, Maj Brian 6, 81
Skliar, William L. 135
Skunk Works 24
Slater, Col Hugh C. 141
Sled Driver 6
Stability Augmentation System 94–95
Stephens, Col Robert L. 'Silverfox' 159
Strategic Air Command 111
Strategic Reconnaissance 69
Sullivan, Dennis B. 135
Sullivan, Maj James V. 159
Supersonic Transport 113
Swann, Michael 114

Tin Goose 126
Titanium Goose 126
Titanium Metals Corporation 134, 148
Tonopah Test Range Airfield 20
Torick, Ray 59–60, 126

Ultraviolet Experiment 112
United Aircraft Corporation, Pratt & Whitney Division 134
Units:
   1st Strategic Reconnaissance Squadron 6, 81–82
   9th Strategic Reconnaissance Wing 6, 75, 82
   9th Wing 81
   37th Tactical Fighter Wing 20
   49th Fighter Wing 20
   99th Strategic Reconnaissance Squadron 81
   1129th Special Activities Squadron 44
   2762nd Logistics Squadron 82
   4200th Strategic Reconnaissance Wing 62, 81
   4450th Tactical Group 20
   Detachment 1 (Det. 1) 44, 82
   Detachment 2 (Det. 2) 81
   Detachment 4 (Det. 4) 82
   Detachment 5 (Det. 5) 81
   Detachment 6 (Det. 6) 81–82
   Detachment 8 (Det. 8) 82
   Detachment 51 (Det. 51) 81–82
   OL-Bodo 82
   OL-8 44, 82
   OL-KB 82
   OL-SB 82
Unmanned Aerial Vehicle 7, 123
US Air Force 10
US Air Force Plant 42
US Army Air Corps 10
US Army Air Forces 10
US Office of Special Activities 44
USS *Pueblo* 44, 142

Vance, Secretary of Defence Cyrus 157
Vojvodich, Mele 135
Vida, Lt Col Joseph T. 123, 159

Warner, Maj Noel T. 159
Warner-Robins Air Force Base 82
Weapon System numbers:
   WS-201B 45
   WS-202A 45
   WS-204A 46
Weaver, Bill 77
Weeks, Jack W. 135
Welch, Gen Larry D. 124
Widdifield, Maj Noel F. 159
Wright J67-W-1 46
Wright RJ55-W-1 46

Yeilding, Lt Col Ed 123
Yeager, Charles E. 'Chuck' 77
Yom Kippur War 82
Young, David P. 135

Zwayer, Jim 77